Meredith Now

Meredith Now

Some Critical Essays

edited by

Ian Fletcher

Department of English
University of Reading

BARNES & NOBLE, PUBLISHERS
NEW YORK

Contents

Preface

The title indicates something of this book's modesty of scope. These essays are not offered as a total 'revaluation' of Meredith, though most of the contributors, I dare say, would urge the proposition that he is a major if flawed artist. They would also argue that he is now undervalued; that he is too little read and that the literature on him is relatively thin. Though modest, the note is not defensive. Had the intention been actively polemical, one might perhaps have slanted an account of Meredith's 'after-life' towards examining the insidious canon-formation that has somewhat affected his present status. Meredith, like Pater, Moore, Wilde and others, is still hidden in the trough created by those propagandizing flurries for the 'modern movement' that so affected Milton's reputation. He is also hidden by the contrivance of a 'great tradition' that could exclude Richardson, Dickens and Hardy and use *The Egoist* as a counter to exalt Henry James or, when tactics demanded, to deflate E. M. Forster. This can itself be placed in a context of the 'debunking' 1920s: Murry with his amusing comment that 'Love in the Valley' combines the ear of the organ-grinder with the eye of the chorus-fancier, or Virginia Woolf's remark of Meredith that 'now he twists himself into iron knots, now he lies flat as a pancake'.

However, in his examination of Meredith's reputation from the 1890s on, John Lucas, rightly I think, avoids polemics; or rather reserves those for the hysterical admirers who after all were most responsible for Meredith's dismal fortunes. Of the images that cohered, Lucas focuses on Meredith, dithyrambist of the Surrey bosks, Meredith, surrogate of Shakespeare, and Meredith, stylist of an elegant opacity.

These essays are critical rather than scholarly in their emphasis; apparatus, as a consequence, has in general been drastically reduced. An index in such a modest volume might appear somewhat pretentious; but one is furnished for the reader's convenience. And it has not been thought mandatory to adopt a patristic approach to our predecessors. There may well be a case for such baroque courtesies when writing of Shakespeare or of Milton, where the available secondary literature is of a strangling efflorescence. But if one excepts *Feverel* or the *Egoist*, what is available on particular Meredith novels can virtually be numbered on the toes of one foot. Most of the authors here have mentioned the work of predecessors only where there is sharp disagreement or where some relevant insight has been commandingly conveyed. In most cases it has been assumed that what has been well put has entered the general thinking on Meredith.

John Lucas's essay on Meredith the poet, in attempting to treat its subject with a reasonable toughness without hedging its bets, strikes what is, I hope, a note typical of the other contributions. The problem of Meredith begins with his being so acutely mannerist a writer that his work tends to polarize response: he is dismissed summarily as 'unreadable' while to *dévots* the more obfuscly Meredithian he is, the more to be admired. So strong indeed is the pull of Meredith's style if one once submits that it requires an effort of will to write of him in any other. But what allowances should be made? As Dr J. M. S. Tompkins puts it: 'the reader needs to sympathize with the writer as such, to be interested in his problems and procedures and this is not necessary for the enjoyment of Dickens, though it deepens it'. Much may depend on where one begins. Most readers, I suppose, start on Meredith young, and are likely to choose a novel that does not immediately appeal: in spite of Meredith's mannerism, the novels *do* offer variety: the variety of approaches to him in this volume is an indication of that. But Meredith's fictions have the disadvantage, never more felt than now, of harsh entries: the opening chapter of *Diana of the Crossways* is a notorious example. Yet, as David Howard observes, the novels improve as they lengthen, somewhat as though Meredith wished to sift up to that 'acute but honourable minority' which in a limited sense made up an ideal audience. And Meredith improves on re-reading, as Dr Tompkins's essay on

Evan Harrington demonstrates. Dr Tompkins is mainly concerned with the more traditional modes of the novel: with characterization, motivation, events; but what has been described as their 'poetic logic' often emerges to displace any immediate impression of arbitrary leaps and insolent gaps in narrative or inexplicable shifts of character. The unity of a Meredith novel may consist in its imagery or in subtle relationships between characters; or in the force exerted by Meredith's commentators or special machinery; the role, for example, of 'The Pilgrim's Scrip' in *Feverel* as 'the play within the play', as commentary and directive.

It remains possible that Meredith will emerge at this particular moment through a 'contemporary' quality in his work, accessible to sociological and psychological techniques. Juliet Mitchell discusses *Feverel* partly in terms of sexual roles (the importance of femininity in men, for example). She also seizes on the links between Bella-Lady Feverel-Lady Blandish, versions of the evil woman and the sexual mother, just as she glances at the codes of food used as semi-sexual seduction. But her main concern is with exposing the subtle unity of *Feverel*. Valuable too is her insight that Meredith's characters are 'in search of an author'.

Meredith's revolt against the form of the novel is not confined to structure; it extends to evading the taboos of high Victorianism: the novel as didactic and idealizing. It is not that he abstains from moral commentary, but that his comments are disconcerting in the historical context. His various images of the 'fallen' woman furnish a clear example, but his puns are peculiarly pungent. Willoughdy, for example, has the leg of Wycherley, no less than that of Rochester. *The Egoist*, conceived as comedy, actually takes place 'on stage' and the persons take their cues; but the degree to which it looks to *Restoration* comedy could be indicated by this:

> She was astonished by his readiness, and thankful for the succour. Her look was cold, wide, unfixed, with nothing of gratitude or of personal in it. The look however stood too long for Willoughby's endurance. Ejaculating, 'Porcelain!' he uncrossed his legs: a signal for the ladies Eleanor and Isabel to retire (xxiv).*

> 'A porcelain vase!' interrupted Sir Willoughby.
> 'China!' Mrs Mountstewart faintly shrieked.

* Bracketed numbers throughout refer to volumes (VII), chapters (vii) and pages (160).

The idiom is appropriately seventeenth century with Darwinism reinforcing the power drives of naturalism and Hobbesism.

A cardinal oddity in the structure of Meredith's novels is defined by David Howard, writing of *Rhoda Fleming*, where difficulty seems willed to a degree. We must remember, Howard remarks, that 'Meredith is the most irritating novelist of the nineteenth century and if we ignore that capacity to irritate we are inventing a safe Meredith to argue about'. And this main way of irritating? 'I don't know what's going on, I don't know who is who. . . . And this can combine with Meredith's habit of concentrating on trivial incident and character to the exclusion of and often in place of major event and character . . . of course the two irritations can combine into an overwhelming single irritation: first nothing happens and then everything happens at once, but usually somewhere else.' This is true of major as well as of minor novels. Meredith seems to dodge any description of Mrs Mountstuart Jenkinson's party, particularly after it has been so prepared for and when its resonances are quite prolonged. The manic pace at the end of *The Egoist* furnishes an example of dividends from 'everything happening at once', but almost everything has in this case been happening already. And James, after all, can afford to let us pass an evening at Tishy Grendon's.

Of all Meredith's novels, *The Egoist* has received most critical recognition, but even on that evaluation remains problematic. The essay here argues that it is not finally very helpful to demonstrate its internal efficiency; what is needed is a means of assessing the novel's terms of reference. In this perspective, most criticism has arrived at a somewhat negative judgment. John Goode's essay tries to counter this by affirming the saliency of *The Egoist*'s theme, and showing that its declared aesthetic is merely a point of departure which, as the theme develops, is radically revised.

Again, one feels inclined to stress that Meredith's equivocal status owes something to his relation to the reader: distanced, ambivalent, suspicious, almost from the beginning. Still, Meredith's impatiences do anticipate later developments in the form, and the 'novels' themselves constitute 'conversations' about form, language, communication. It is through the novels as 'dramas of language' that Gillian Beer approaches *One of Our Conquerors*. Like *The Awkward Age,* that novel seems strikingly concerned with communication, the splendours and miseries of interior monologue. While communication breaks down in *The Awkward Age* –

Mitchy's tears – in *One of Our Conquerors* language modulates into music, as indeed it had in *Vittoria*, but now in a manner almost *symboliste*, Wagner rather than Verdi, with attendant resources of myth and the numinous.

Margaret Tarratt, on the other hand, looks at *Harry Richmond* in terms of its formal inheritance, a contamination of 'kinds': *Bildungsroman* and the 'historical' novel in Lukács' definition. She attempts to show that some of its puzzling aspects can be resolved by relating it to *Wilhelm Meister* and other German *Bildungsromane* rather than to any contemporary English 'autobiographical' novel, but that *Harry Richmond* is in no sense the mere imitation of a genre, but an interpretation and comment on British society. Leonée Ormond's approach to *The Tragic Comedians* is in terms of imagery, and Bernard Richards adopts a similar approach to *One of Our Conquerors*. He suggests that we must develop, for the reading of Meredith, 'complex habits of interpretation'. The grounding of Meredith's characters is often as loose as James asserted in his notorious comment on this novel, so that the 'symbolism' of a Meredith novel becomes an essential part of a complete understanding of the work in a manner that is not true of James or George Eliot. 'When coming to an understanding of Meredith's work, it is sometimes the case that reading habits nurtured by the works of Spenser and Blake are of more use than reading habits acquired in studying Richardson or Jane Austen.' Emblem as orientation: Bernard Richards selects an 'emblem' which points to the heart of *One of Our Conquerors*. In a discursive way, I have tried my hand at treating *Shagpat* as a poem.

Meredith's imagery was first looked at consistently in this way by Barbara Hardy and what her examination of 'fire' and 'water' in *Harry Richmond* revealed was that the imagery was not schematized readily. Here, Professor Hardy (in an essay written in 1968) studies Meredith's two last novels, *Lord Ormont* and *The Amazing Marriage*, as instances of an imaginative trial and error in the working out of the feminist theme of authoritarian marriage. The institution of marriage, she argues, is both symptom and symbol of a disordered society; but the critic's concern is not only with Meredith's social criticism, but also with his successful rendering in narrative form. *The Amazing Marriage*, Professor Hardy appreciates as an unsentimental and individualized novel about tragic sexual affinity in an imprisoning relationship, and the man is seen as victim as well as the woman. Professor Hardy also discusses briefly the relationship between particularity and fable in fiction, and gives glancing consideration to the critical temptations to reject Meredith and to admire him too much. Arnold Kettle 'places' *Beauchamp's Career* with firmness and sympathy, raising the same issue as did Dorothy Van Ghent in her objections against the presentation of Willoughby in *The Egoist*. The final effect there, as in *Beauchamp*, seems undramatized distance to such a degree that the audience remains indifferent to the outcome. The variety of Meredith's fiction emerges from Ioan Williams's essay 'Emilia in England and Italy' and from Jan B. Gordon's study of *Diana*. Meredith's approach is partly in terms of myth; Artemis and Psyche appear in *One of Our Conquerors,* and it could be argued that *Diana* anticipates a good amount of detail in Farnell's *Cults of the Greek City States*: as Hecate she is associated with 'Crossways'; the hound is her familiar sacrificial animal; her virginity is not insisted on; she haunts the shores (swimming when Dacier appears), is predominantly the goddess of women; she is torch-bearer from the fifth century on and a watcher over graves and deathbeds and so comes with lamplight to watch over Dannisburgh's death-bed; she is moon subdued by Redworth's sun; but one role she emphatically never plays – that of married woman. Protectress of the child bed, where is she to be found with child? The ending of *Diana* cannot be rescued through irony; Meredith violated the myths and his art.

Jan B. Gordon's piece on *Diana* views the mythological huntress on the threshold of becoming the 'new woman' of twentieth-century fiction. Meredith's heroine inhabits one of those houses that stand at the crossroads of modern civilization and so joins a legacy that includes the prospect of *Mansfield Park, Wuthering Heights, Carbury Hall* and even *Howard's End*. In what is an essentially structuralist approach to Meredith's work, Professor Gordon sees this particular novel as emblemizing the development in general of nineteenth-century fiction: from the internalized diary and novel of manners, through gossip (which fills up the existential spaces of the mid-Victorian novel), and finally to the enactment of gossip as scandal in the literature of the *fin de siècle*. Diana, in her own career as an artist, duplicates an aesthetic evolution which abuts in self-consciousness. Not unlike Stephen Dedalus, in another 'Portrait of an Artist', Diana is at her most sincere when she is most fictional, when the internal history and the brainstuff of her fiction are identical; an authoress of two natures.

Of peculiar interest is Gordon's observation that gossip functions organically in *Diana of the Crossways* to hold disparate classes together. Gossip fills the spaces of the novel with a self-reflexive language which, having no locus in space and time, enables all the 'hummers and hawers' to engage in a participatory environment for which they assume no responsibility. In claiming that Meredith is largely responsible for recognizing this constitutive role for gossip (and by relating it to the *Essay on Comedy*), Gordon associates its ever-increasing volume with the gradual urbanization of the novel as a form. Concomitancy replaces communication as a cultural value and gossip becomes the agent for a peculiar form of cultural feed-back. As the spaces of the Victorian drawing-room close down with urbanization, the country manor house becomes a museum of overheard voices. Diana's future as a novelist re-capitulates the movement (structurally) from the private spaces of the diary to the public spaces of newspaper scandal columns. And with it, the country estate becomes a public place inhabited by the inheritors of the new England.

A collection of pieces by different hands, structuralist, phenom-enological or plain no-nonsense, often provokes the reader to question the symmetry of the volume in which they appear. It is Meredith himself, irritating, various, surprising, who is the unifier. It will certainly be seen that there has been no attempt at unity of tone or of critical approach. Each contributor was simply invited to select a novel that would act as focus for his interest. My special thanks are due to Ioan Williams and to John Goode, whom I asked to write on novels that were not their choice. I regret that it has not proved possible to furnish an essay on the short prose tales which (like most works in their kind) have aroused too sparse an attention. I regret also that the new edition of Meredith's letters appeared too late to be of help in the composition of these essays.

I. F.

Contributors

John Lucas	University of Nottingham
Ian Fletcher	University of Reading
Juliet Mitchell	Formerly University of Reading
Margaret Tarratt	
J. M. S. Tompkins	Formerly Royal Holloway College, University of London
David Howard	University of York
Ioan Williams	University of Warwick
Professor Arnold Kettle	The Open University
John Goode	University of Reading
Leonée Ormond	King's College, University of London
Professor Jan B. Gordon	State University of New York at Buffalo
Gillian Beer	Girton College, University of Cambridge
Bernard A. Richards	Corpus Christi College, University of Oxford
Professor Barbara Hardy	Birkbeck College, University of London

Meredith's Reputation

John Lucas

Anyone who so much as glances over the history of Meredith's reputation is bound to notice how very odd it is. It may even be unique, at least as far as English literature is concerned. Certainly it is not easy to think of a parallel. Meredith is not the object of a cult-worship, for example. There is no evidence that successive generations of admirers have for him the sort of smouldering affection that occasionally breaks out into flame, a flame that is always kept well-stoked and banked. He is not, let us say, like Kipling. But then neither is he like Philip James Bailey. His reputation came to him late, grew steadily until his death, and a few years later was gone. He never had the following of a Dickens or even a George Eliot. Yet amongst his admirers he was unswervingly regarded as a great artist. When they spoke of him, it tended to be in reverential whispers. 'Of course,' Richard Le Gallienne wrote, recalling a visit to Box Hill during the 1890s, 'the wonderful thing was that the novelist who wrote of Lucy and Richard by the river and the poet of "Love in the Valley" should actually be reading to me at all. It was almost like listening to Shakespeare read *Hamlet*.'[1] But a few years after his death the whispers turned into rude noises. In 1918 Ezra Pound wrote to tell John Quinn that Meredith is 'chiefly a stink'.[2] It seems a remark of terrible finality.

Not even Pound, however, can so easily dispose of a writer. And Meredith, after all, has had later critics. Since the Second World War there have been full-length studies by such critics as Sassoon, Jack Lindsay, Lionel Stevenson and Norman Kelvin; and there will no doubt be others.

Yet if the growing library of Meredith studies proves anything it is that Meredith is more or less a dead issue. He may help establish an academic reputation or boost a publications list, but he is not essentially a living force. Every so often a well-intentioned person spots him, dusty and neglected, takes him down from the shelf of forgotten writers and sticks the label 're-discovered' on him. But it comes off. Nobody notices. And back on the shelf he goes. To be sure, there is the *Egoist*, there is 'Modern Love'; there is even the *Comic Spirit*. But for the rest? Little is reprinted. Very little is read. Hardly anything is known. Meredith seems one with Revett, with Lever, with Dallas. Sixty years ago the books on him poured out, all intended to help establish or simply salute the deathless reputation. And such titles! *George Meredith, His Life, Genius and Teaching; George Meredith, a Primer to theNovels; George Meredith, His Life and Art in Anecdote and Criticism; George Meredith, Novelist, Poet, Reformer; The Philosophy and Poetry of George Meredith; George Meredith, a Study* (a sober enough title, but the authoress makes up for it by a breathless insistence that 'Shakespearian is the word to describe Meredith').[3] 'His words wing on as live words will', Hardy wrote at the time of Meredith's death.[4] In fact, they have plummeted out of sight – or almost. How did it happen?

The nature of the reputation itself must take most of the blame. It is a fact of literary history that Meredith became accepted as a great master in the 1890s. In 1898, for example, T. H. S. Escott wrote that Meredith is 'the foremost of English novelists now living', and he remarked that although, like Browning, Meredith had suffered from years of neglect and indifference the situation was now being corrected. In both cases the invincible indifference of the inappreciative has

> been coerced into a meek acquiescence in the beauties of a genius which it would require the same courage to deny to the one as to the other.[5]

Escott's praise is a form of canonization. This does not mean that Meredith was suddenly discovered in the 1890s, or that his election to the Presidency of the Society of Authors following Tennyson's death in 1892 was unpredictable. But the plain fact is that in the 1890s the audience which Meredith himself had called the 'acute but honourable minority' became both larger and more assertive. It is in the 1890s that comparisons between Meredith and Shakespeare become commonplace. Hannah Lynch and Richard Le Gallienne are not alone in coupling the names; most commentators on Meredith did. Perhaps the first was W. E. Henley. In an essay of 1879 he called Meredith Shakespearian, four years later Mark Pattison repeated the claim,[6] and R. L. Stevenson told an American reporter that *Rhoda Fleming* 'is the strongest thing in English letters since Shakespeare died, and if Shakespeare could have read it he would have jumped and cried, "Here's a fellow!"'[7] By the time Meredith died it seemed unthinkable not to make the comparison. Sturge Henderson noted that Meredith's novels 'include a horizon, they allow for the uncluttered part of our speech; and this is probably the truth that has been aimed at in the comparison of his works with Shakespeare's'.[8] J. A. Hammerton quotes Elton's essay in which Elton says that 'Meredith is sound like Shakespeare',[9] Photiadès simply asserts that 'Meredith bears a greater resemblance to Shakespeare than any other novelist', and Trevelyan claims that 'Modern Love' has the 'same kind of spiritual and intellectual beauty as saves *Othello* from being morbid, and *Hamlet* from being decadent'.[10]

The comparison with Shakespeare is not really a studied or suggestive one. It is merely a way of asserting Meredith's stature. And the very interesting feature of Meredith criticism in the 1890s is that most of his admirers insist that his greatness is more or less proved by the fact that he had been for so long ignored or treated with contempt. This brings us to the famous argument about Meredith's obscurity. The sceptical insisted that Meredith was difficult and rapidly getting worse. But for the admirers obscurity, so called, required commendation. Meredith, they argued, was obscure or difficult only for those who had neither the patience, intelligence nor sensitivity to understand him. He did not pander to his audience, he challenged his readers to follow him. '[Meredith] reaches his thought by means of ladders which he kicks away', James Barrie wrote. 'Too sluggish to climb, the public sit in the rear, flinging his jargon at his head, yet aware, if they have heads themselves, that one of the great intellects of the age is on in front.'[11] Amy Cruse, who lived through the period of Meredith's greatest fame, reaches to the heart of the matter:

For the true Meredithians . . . it was this intellectual brilliance that gave his works their greatest attraction. It attracted also a large number of painstaking readers who, admiring intellect above all things, and longing to be – and to be recognized as – its possessors, often succeeded in persuading themselves – and others – that they read with pleasure. Earnest young men and women belonging to Literary Societies wrote papers full of psychology and sociology, ethics and dialectics on the works of Meredith, but usually failed to convince the unregenerate majority among their fellow members.[12]

As the tone of that passage very clearly shows, Amy Cruse was herself one of the unregenerate; and altogether Meredith and the Meredithians had to put up with a good deal of mockery throughout the 1890s. Quite apart from Oscar Wilde's famous gibe about Meredith and Browning (a commonplace comparison that had been given an early airing in the *Tobacco Plant* for May 1879, where it was suggested that Meredith was the 'Robert Browning of our novelists' and that 'his day is bound to come, as Browning's at length has come')[13] there is Mrs Windsor of the *Green Carnation*, who remarks that

> Mr. Amarinth says that he is going to bring out a new edition of [Meredith's works], 'done into English' by himself. It is such a good idea and would help the readers so much. I believe he could make a lot of money by it, but it would be very difficult to do, I suppose. However, Mr. Amarinth is so clever that he might manage it.[14]

Still, gibes, jeers and jokes clearly mean that Meredith had become a force to be reckoned with. The interesting point is that not all could make up their minds as to what sort of a force he was. George Saintsbury, for example. In 1896 Saintsbury published a *History of Nineteenth Century Literature*, and in the chapters 'The Second Poetical Period' and 'The Novel since 1860' Meredith is conspicuous by his absence. Browning, Arnold, the Rossettis, Thomson, George Eliot, Kingsley, the Trollopes, Stevenson – yes, they and many more are there. But not Meredith. And yet he is listed as part of the achievement of English fiction in the nineteenth century. Not even France, Saintsbury says, can 'show such a "gallaxy-gallery" as the British novelists'.[15] And he mentions Dickens, Thackeray and Meredith. It is something of a facing-all-ways position.

But if Saintsbury and a few others hedged their bets, most commentators backed Meredith wholeheartedly. 'Meredith is one of the greatest artists of our time', James Oliphant declared in 1899, 'indeed [he is] the only living writer of English novels who can be ranked unhesitatingly among the giants.'[16] As for his obscurity – well, 'No one has ever tried to make words convey so much meaning as Meredith, and very few have had so much meaning to express.'[17] And most of Meredith's champions saw in his alleged obscurity an opportunity to attack the hostile, indifferent or plain ignorant public. The champions are not merely the young and earnest whom Amy Cruse indicates. There are also practising writers, Le Gallienne, Stevenson, Henley, and above all Gissing.

Gissing may not have been of substantial help in building Meredith's reputation, but he does provide substantial reasons for its immense authority. For what Gissing says about Meredith is clear proof of how Meredith's reputation belongs to the history of taste and was *bound* to rise at the end of the nineteenth century. 'He is great, there is no doubt of it', Gissing wrote to his brother in 1885, 'but too difficult for the British public. What good thing is not?'[18] A little later he is telling the same person that

> George Eliot never did such work, and Thackeray is shallow
> in comparison. . . . For the last thirty years he has been
> producing work unspeakably above the best of any living
> writer and yet no one reads him outside a small circle of
> highly cultured people. Perhaps that is better than being
> popular, a hateful word.[19]

There is no doubt that Gissing takes Meredith's cause very much to heart, since his own comparative failure to attract attention embittered him against popularity and the public. Meredith indeed could easily become the hero for all those writers who in the last years of the nineteenth century saw a wedge being driven between art and popularity and for whom the rise of the best-seller spelled the doom of the novel as a serious literary form. From now on to be good was to be unpopular. In an important essay on the art of fiction in the 1880s, John Goode has pointed out that it is during the penultimate decade of the nineteenth century that a really radical and apparently unbridgeable gap between good and popular novels begins to open up. Gissing's attitude to Meredith may well have been sharpened by the debate between Sir Walter Besant and Henry James on the art of fiction, which had taken place in 1884.[20] Certainly, he himself was deeply concerned with what he took to be the impossibility of his ever achieving much fame or due notice; and what he says of Edwin Reardon in the semi-autobiographical *New Grub Street* of 1891 comes very close to what he had said of Meredith in 1885: 'Strong characterization was within his scope, and an intellectual fervour, appetising to a small section of refined readers, marked all his best pages.'[21] Reardon is not Meredith, but Jasper Milvain's remark that Reardon is 'the old type of unpractical artist' who 'won't make concessions, or rather . . . can't make them; he can't supply the market'[22] – that might easily have been said of Meredith. The fact that he did not write the sort of novels which would assure him of a sizeable audience came to be seen as an essential part of his integrity. And, in all fairness, it has to be said that Meredith was a novelist of integrity. As far as his reputation is concerned, the result of this refusal to supply the market could be seen as proof of his unswerving dedication to his art, so that it was customary to admire – indeed venerate – him less for what he had accomplished than for what he stood for. Meredith, quite simply, became a cause to rally round. His obscurity was a useful pointer to his integrity, and where in the 1860s Justin McCarthy might regret that 'Meredith is too much the thinking man';[23] by the latter half of the 1880s he could not be too much of a thinking man for his admirers. 'Get hold of *Diana of the Crossways*,' Gissing told his brother. 'It needs to be read twice or even three times, but that is because there is more "brain stuff" in the book, than many I have read for long.'[24] No use for Conan Doyle to grumble that Meredith was 'clever, but neither interesting nor intelligible'.[25] Lafcadio Hearn put the case for the admirers when, in an essay of 1900, he declared Meredith to be

> the poet of scholars; the poet of men of culture. Only a man of culture can really like him – just as only a man long accustomed to good living can appreciate the best kinds of wine. Give wine to a poor man accustomed only to drink coarse spirits, and he will not care about it. So the common reader cannot care about Meredith. He is what we call a 'test-poet' – your culture, your capacity to think and feel, is tested by your ability to like such a poet. The question, 'Do you like Meredith?' is now in English and even in French literary circles, a test.[26]

Reading that now, you feel that with friends like Hearn Meredith hardly needs enemies. And there is no doubt that it was Hearn's sort of snobbish adulation that helped create such a sharp reaction against the reputation. Still, Hearn's remarks are justified to the extent that in poetry and prose alike Meredith's 'obscurity' sprang from his wanting to be taken seriously as a great thinker. Indeed, he wanted to be a philosophical writer. Perhaps his admirers found it easier to convert ambition into achievement just because of the neglect from which he suffered. There is a real sense in which the history of Meredith's career opens him up to a variety of clichés: a prophet without honour in his own country, the 'difficult' artist who is called obscure only by the philistines, the artist of integrity who can expect to win only scorn, etc.

This brings us to an important point. Much of Meredith's reputation is founded on his being a man of ideas. A glance at the books people wrote about him will establish that much. It is not necessary here to detail what the ideas were: enough to note that they were taken to stand for a radical reappraisal of lines of thought associated with Victorian England. Feminism, little England, paganism, advanced liberalism, scepticism, the Comic Spirit even: whatever marked a rejection of high-Victorianism could be attributed to Meredith. He became the figure who embodied modernity, a man for the times. One can go further, of course, and claim that Meredith at the end of the nineteenth century was seen as a truth-teller, a sage. And as soon as we put the matter that way, we see that he is very recognizably in the line that finds one dominant point in Arnold's claim that

> Without poetry, our science will appear incomplete; and most of what passes with us for religion and philosophy will be replaced by poetry.[27]

For while the matter of Meredith's ideas may be said to represent a denial of high-Victorianism, in manner he is entirely a product of Victorian ideas and assumptions about literature and the artist. Meredith took himself to be, and was accepted as, a spokesman, consoler and sage. 'He is essentially a psychological poet,' Hearn remarked, 'but he is also an evolutionary philosopher . . . he alone of all living Englishmen really expresses the whole philosophy of the modern scientific age.'[28] For Hannah Lynch

> Mr. Meredith is above and beyond all a thinker, less simple and direct, less wholly preoccupied with the mission of improving humanity and beautifying life, than either George

Eliot or Tolstoi. Perhaps he has a healthier conviction that the world is very well as it is, and that in the main it is all the better that we are neither so muddy nor so pink as realists and sentimentalists would have us believe, but are just comfortably spotted and well-meaning to escape excess of censure or admiration.[29]

Yet, she laments, the British public has been too stupid to recognize the presence of a 'prophet in its midst'.[30] It is not very easy to understand from Hannah Lynch just what Meredith is supposed to be a prophet of, but there is no doubting the fervency of her campaign for establishing him as a great modern thinker. Sturge Henderson's campaign has an even more exalted note:

Intermittently, Mr. Meredith is a great artist; primarily and consistently, he is a moralist – a teacher. He has pondered on man and his destiny till his insight has perceived whole regions and vistas of human possibility that as yet are untenanted, and he has made it the object of his existence to nerve his fellows to seize and enter on the fullness of their inheritance. It may appear paradoxical that pages which would not have been published by lesser writers, should have found favour with an artist towering head and shoulders above any but the masters, but the explanation is simple enough. It is to be found in Meredith's conviction that he has a message to deliver and in his willingness to sacrifice all other considerations to its delivery.[31]

We go in dread of what praise such as Henderson's implies, but Meredith himself would have welcomed it. As Kenneth Graham points out, Meredith saw his art as aiding a 'vague ethical idealism' (very Victorian, that):

As an enemy of the conventional prudery implied in the word 'morality', he uses instead such words as 'philosophy', 'thought', 'problems of life', 'the Spirit', and 'Idea' to describe his aims. The novel, he holds, must be an instrument of Civilization and the Comic Spirit, opposed to scientific materialism, and uncovering 'the laws of existence' and the 'destinies of the world'.[32]

Graham is almost certainly wrong to think Meredith opposed scientific materialism, though in his defence it can be suggested that he was probably misled by Meredith's rather murky desire to be on both sides of just about every fence. But he is quite right to see that Meredith makes the novel a vehicle for his messages (the fact that Meredith also said that the novel should be dramatic and free from the omniscient author does not alter the truth of what Graham and Henderson say; it merely provides another example of Meredith's wanting to have it both ways). Even contemporary admirers sometimes regretted his willingness to sacrifice the drama or organic unity of the novel to abstract theorizing or musing. 'In Meredith,' Katherine Bradley remarked, 'the living heat rarely kindles the overplus of intellect.'[33] And Graham quotes J. A. Noble on Meredith's lack of ' "organic integrity" ("The one thing needful in the novel is that it should be a whole")'.[34] On the other hand, if you wanted your artist to be a thinker you had to be prepared to accept an occasional blemish in the art. And all the evidence points to the fact that Meredith's champions saw him as exonerated just because he was a great thinker. Photiadès puts the case in its most strident form:

> As Meredith grew older he gained in wisdom what he lost in imagination, so that the didactic tendencies of his art and teaching became still more intensified. His reason waged a pitiless war against his fancy . . . the master's decision was irrevocable and high-minded; he knew that his works would give pleasure only to an *élite*.[35]

Oh, that's all right, then.

Meredith, of course, came to look the part of the great thinker and teacher. It is one more cliché. Crusty, deaf, increasingly lame, he is the image of what might seem to epitomize the remorselessly honest seeker after truth, willing to endure the world's slings and arrows in his pursuit of . . . of what exactly? At this point the admirers are apt to grow a little coy. After all, if you know, you don't need telling. If you don't know – well, that is what the 'test-case' is all about. Not that the admirers resist any analysis or explanation of Meredith's ideas. But the ideas are apt to look more than a little obvious when brutally exposed to plain statement. And one notices that even the most devoted give the impression of looking uneasily over their shoulders in case there should be any ignorant non-*elite* and test-case failure ready to announce that the Emperor isn't wearing any clothes.

I do not wish to be cynical about Meredith. If he became his admirers, it was not entirely his fault. He did suffer for his art, he was unjustly and even outrageously neglected for many years, he was treated with brutish stupidity by critics and readers, many of whom should have known better; and even after he had become the sage of Box Hill it is clear that he derived little enjoyment from his late fame. He cannot be blamed because in old age he becomes eminently one to be painted, photographed and peered-at, his head beautiful, gnarled, leonine – everyman's ideal philosopher. Nor can he be blamed because young people saw in him an image of the writer who embodied a rejection of what they took Victorianism to be (Meredith is the unofficial Laureate of the 1890s, inevitably opposed to Alfred Austin). But the unavoidable truth is that the sort of reputation which Meredith acquired has done him lasting damage. To praise him because he was an intellectual novelist whose style was properly opaque and to insist that he was a great intellectual and a fearless spokesman for modern ideas was to invite disaster. Sooner or later someone in full retreat from Victorianism or in pursuit of new gods would be bound to shout that the Emperor really wasn't wearing any clothes. And that, of course, is what happened.

There is no need to trace in detail the catastrophic collapse of Meredith's reputation. But one or two of the more important contributions may be noted. There is Pound's attack on the famous style, for example. Writing of *Tarr*, Pound remarked that on occasions Lewis's expression is 'as bad as that of Meredith's floppy sickliness'. But at least 'In place of Meredith's mincing we have something active'.[36] The phrases are disconcertingly memorable. They also typify much twentieth-century response to Meredith as a writer of prose and, for that matter, of poetry. To his admirers Meredith was the Glad Day of modernity and the dedicated artist. To later generations he was merely the false dawn.

After Pound, the deluge. In particular, Forster's demolition of Meredith the great thinker:

> His philosophy has not worn well. His heavy attacks on
> sentimentality – they bore the present generation, which
> pursues the same quarry but with neater instruments. . . . And
> his visions of Nature – they do not endure like Hardy's, there
> is too much Surrey about them, they are fluffy and lush. . . .
> What is really tragic and enduring in the scenery of nature
> was hidden from him, and so is what is really tragic in life.

When he gets serious and noble-minded there is a strident overtone, a bullying that becomes distressing. . . . And his novels: most of the social values are faked. The tailors are not tailors, the cricket matches are not cricket, the railway trains do not even seem to be trains, the county families give the air of having been only just that moment unpacked. . . .[37]

And, of course, Dr Leavis. Forster knocks Meredith down; Leavis counts him out. The poetry is 'the flashy product of unusual but vulgar cleverness working upon cheap emotion'.[38] And the novels?

As for Meredith, I needn't add anything to what is said about him by Mr. E. M. Forster, who, having belonged to the original *milieu* in which Meredith was erected into a great master, enjoys peculiar advantages for the demolition-work.[39]

There is no doubt that the destruction of Meredith's reputation had to come. For it was absurd. Meredith is not a great stylist, he is not a great intellectual, not for the reasons his admirers gave, anyway. Yet destroying the reputation should not have meant destroying Meredith. And at least some of the demolition workers clearly felt that by knocking down the Meredith created by erring admirers, Meredith himself would emerge plain. After the passage in which Forster breaks down the image of Meredith the thinker, he adds: 'And yet he is in one way a great novelist. He is the finest contriver that English fiction has ever produced.'[40] Clearly it was not *that* remark which Leavis had in mind when he suggested that Forster had said all that was needed about Meredith. Leavis also quotes James's famous letter to Gosse about *Lord Ormont and his Aminta*: 'It fills me with a critical rage, an artistic fury, utterly blighting in me the indispensable principle of *respect*.'[41] He does not, however, quote James's remark in an essay of 1905, in which Meredith is called 'that bright particular genius of our day'.[42] Virginia Woolf, echoing Forster in saying that Meredith's teaching 'seems now too strident and too optimistic and too shallow', adds, 'to read Meredith is to be conscious of a packed and muscular mind'.[43] And even in the 1890s it is possible to find critics like Lionel Johnson and Arthur Symons writing about Meredith with tactful good sense. Both see much to regret and also much to acclaim.

But it was not measured praise that won Meredith his reputation, and it does seem to be the case that in demolishing the nonsense later writers have, no matter what their intention, more or less buried Meredith in the rubble. He ought to survive the worst his reputation did for him and the worst that has been done to his reputation. But it is not certain that he has. If we are to try to recover Meredith, therefore, we have to begin by clearing the rubble away. He can never again be taken seriously as a great philosopher, and as for the style – we are properly less ready to turn its defects into virtues, even if improperly reluctant to recognize its virtues for what they are. The reluctance is understandable. Meredith is badly flawed, often infuriating, sometimes downright silly and vulgar. But he is also – or he ought to be – of permanent interest, and at his best he is probably a master.

Notes

1 Richard Le Gallienne, *The Romantic 90s*, 1926, 40.
2 *The Letters of Ezra Pound, 1907–1941*, 1950, 137.
3 Hannah Lynch, *George Meredith. A Study*, 1891, 39.
4 T. Hardy, 'George Meredith', *Collected Poems*, 1960, 280.
5 T. H. S. Escott, *Personal Forces of the Period*, 1898, 254, 256.
6 See *George Meredith, Some Early Appreciations*, ed. Forman, 1909, 193, 227.
7 L. Stevenson, *The Ordeal of George Meredith*, 1954, 277.
8 M. Sturge Henderson, *George Meredith, Novelist, Poet, Reformer*, 1907, 42.
9 J. A. Hammerton, *George Meredith, Life and Art in Anecdote and Criticism*, rev. ed., 1911, 310.
10 G. M. Trevelyan, *The Philosophy and Poetry of George Meredith*, 1906, 21.
11 Quoted in Amy Cruse, *After the Victorians*, 1935, 174.
12 Ibid., 175.
13 *George Meredith: Some Early Appreciations*, 194.
14 Robert Hichens, *The Green Carnation*, 1894, 44.
15 G. Saintsbury, *A History of Nineteenth Century Literature*, 1896, 444.
16 J. Oliphant, *Victorian Novelists*, 1899, 143.
17 Ibid., 146.
18 *Letters of George Gissing to Members of his Family*, 1927, 155.
19 Ibid., 170–2.
20 See 'The Art of Fiction: Walter Besant and Henry James', in *Tradition and Tolerance in Nineteenth Century Fiction*, Howard, Lucas and Goode, 1966.
21 *New Grub Street*, Penguin Books, 1968, 93.
22 Ibid., 38.
23 Quoted in L. Stevenson, *The Ordeal of George Meredith*, 135.
24 *Letters of George Gissing*, 156.

25 *After the Victorians,* 174.
26 Lafcadio Hearn, *Pre-Raphaelite and Other Poets,* ed. J. Erskine, 1923, 373.
27 M. Arnold, *Essays in Criticism,* 2nd Series, 1908, 2–3.
28 *Pre-Raphaelite and Other Poets,* 312.
29 H. Lynch, *George Meredith, A Study,* 7–8.
30 Ibid., 8.
31 M. Sturge Henderson, *George Meredith,* 2–3.
32 Kenneth Graham, *English Criticism of the Novel 1865–1900,* 1965, 74.
33 See *After the Victorians,* 175.
34 Kenneth Graham, op. cit., 115.
35 C. Photiadès, *George Meredith, His Life, His Genius, His Teaching,* 1913, 250–2.
36 *Literary Essays of Ezra Pound,* ed. T. S. Eliot, 1954, 425.
37 E. M. Forster, *Aspects of the Novel,* 1953, 85–6.
38 F. R. Leavis, *New Bearings in English Poetry,* Penguin Edn., 1963, 25 (he is talking specifically of 'Modern Love).
39 Ibid., *The Great Tradition,* 1948, 23.
40 *Aspects of the Novel,* 86.
41 *The Great Tradition,* 23.
42 'The Lesson of Balzac', in *The House of Fiction,* ed. Edel, 1957, 67.
43 'The Novels of George Meredith', *The Common Reader,* 1932, 235–6.

Meredith as Poet

John Lucas

When Oscar Wilde called Meredith a prose Browning he was no doubt thinking of the novels, but his remark can be applied with equal justice to the poetry. For there is an undeniably prosaic quality about much of Meredith's large output of verse; it seems to have no inner compulsion or buoyancy, and above all it is unnatural. Anybody who sets himself the task of reading the collected poems is bound to come away from them recognizing that Meredith too often forced himself into the role of poet, that only a very small amount of his poetry repays close attention, and that even his best poems are not entirely free from his characteristic vices. In an age of careful craftsmen Meredith stands out as extraordinarily slipshod, not so much by design as through indifference. It took considerable art to be as cavalier as Browning often chose to be; but where Browning is deliberately outrageous, Meredith is merely inept. Browning's experiments with metre have about them an air of swaggering abundance, but Meredith's are at best resolute (the galliambic measure he tries out in 'Phaeton' provides a good example of stiff determination). And his ear for rhythm is mostly dull and liable to be appalling. Indeed, more often than not he sticks doggedly to metre in a way that works well enough for the ballads, but which becomes obtrusively mechanical in the meditative poems. As for his handling of rhyme, he seems to have been deaf to or unaware of his customary badness. Characteristically he makes use of intricate stanzaic and rhyming schemes, with the result that he has to fracture syntax in order to manipulate the rhyme words into position (much of Meredith's reputation for being a 'difficult' poet comes from his inability to handle rhyme without overtaxing his hold on sense). The failure cannot be attributed to the impetuosity of youth or the fatigue of old age; at any point in his writing career, you can find verse made horridly turgid by his effort to manufacture such rhymes as cloud/endowed, burned/discerned, renewed/food, saith/death, fore/roar, hurled/world. And the inadequacy of these rhymes is made more marked by the distortions of syntax, intricacy of stanza-form in which they so frequently occur, and remorseless end-stopping of lines. In addition, Meredith's defective ear shows in cacophonous phrasing typified by the first line of 'Meditation under Stars': 'What links are ours with orbs that are.' Such flaws occur too often for us to disregard them. It is not that Meredith sometimes writes carelessly, but that he rarely writes well.

This extends to his handling of imagery. Much of it has a reach-me-down staleness, as where he speaks of stars giving 'radiance as from a shield' ('Meditation under Stars'). I think we can probably reconstruct how Meredith came to this phrase, and it reveals how derivative and literary his verse can be. I would guess that his first thought, of stars as flashing, led him to recall Wordsworth's great image of gleams like the flashings of a shield. But since he could not take over the whole phrase, he retained 'shield' and substituted 'radiance' for 'flashings'. The result is that all the surprise and precision of the original is lost and we are left with a phrase that is vague and dull. This is typical. Equally typical is the piling of one conventional or derivative image on another to the confusion of both – another reason for the 'difficult' reputation. For instance, Meredith addresses the Comic Spirit as one who

> darest probe
> Old institutions and establishments,
> Once fortresses against the floods of sin,
> For what their worth; and questioningly prod
> For why they stand upon a racing globe,
> Impeding blocks, less useful than the clod.
>
> (402)[1]

The imprecisions of thought and language (How do you prod a fortress? Do fortresses exist to turn back floods? What has happened to the floods? If the globe is racing, what do the blocks impede?) are not bolstered by the rhetorical grandiloquence with its too obvious Miltonic echoes. Indeed, almost throughout the 'Ode to the Comic Spirit' Meredith reveals enough incompetence in the handling of language to make even the most sympathetic of readers wonder whether his poetry merits serious attention at all. I think it does, which is why I want to anticipate the likely objections. For the admirer of Meredith cannot pretend that there are not serious charges to be brought against him. The only valid way of rescuing him from neglect is to maintain a proper critical severity, which means virtually dismissing a vast amount of his poetry. But to do this fairly means that I must provide some critical examination of it, no matter how tedious and embarrassing this may turn out to be – doubly embarrassing, really, because I am well aware that the first part of this essay reads as though it is intended as an unremitting hatchet job, and that this comes rather oddly from a professed admirer. But I can perhaps defend myself by saying that I think the task of clearing away dead growth is essential if we are to see the good poems plain, and that doing this will in the long run be better for Meredith's reputation – at least among readers who actually like poetry – than the sort of tactic employed by contributors to such magazines as *Victorian Poetry*, who assume that Meredith is unarguably a classic, that all of his poems are equally fine, and that the only relevant task for the critic-scholar is to unravel a poem's meanings, sources, variants. No: I think we have to be severe, and that we must resist the temptation to plead a special case. Remorseless explication is a fate worse than death for Meredith, because it encourages the pretence that he is always and justifiably a 'difficult' poet. Yet his failures do not stem from his being an intellectual writer. The 'Ode to the Comic Spirit' may be an ambitious performance, but there are any number of modest ones whose flaws are very disquieting. 'The Wisdom of Eld', for example, is a slight enough sonnet and on the whole it is competently written. Even so, Meredith manages to speak of an old man who with 'tottering shank/Sidled'. In one poem he images France as a Maenad 'Ravishing as red wine in woman's form' (are you supposed to drink it or take it to bed?), and in another image breeds image in an uncontrollable riot: 'Though past the age where midway men are skilled/To scan their senses wriggling under plough,/When yet to the charmed seed of speech distilled/Their hearts are fallow'. ('The Sage Enamoured and the Honest Lady'). This is nothing like Browning's apparently similar habit of letting one image disclose another so that meaning progressively unfolds as you are led from image to image (stanzas iv–v of 'By the Fire-side' provide a good point of comparison). Indeed, it must be said that if Meredith is a prose Browning, Browning is much more than a poetic Meredith. Of course, Meredith's lines make a sort of sense; you can see what he means. But for all their show of wit and intelligence they will not bear the weight of close scrutiny. Under it, the images collapse into muddle.

Much of Meredith's failure to control language arises from his mistaken belief that he had a real ability in the handling of epithet, that his gifts naturally tended towards the epigrammatic. In fact, he is at his worst when reflective or sententious, and that perhaps explains why his ballads emerge as so much better than most of his poetry. In 'Phantasy' (his Dream of Fair Women), in 'Archduchess Anne', 'Jump to Glory Jane' and a handful of others, Meredith tells a tale, and he does so with welcome pace and directness. Indeed, what are inadequacies elsewhere become advantages here, the obedience to metre speeding you over the poorer rhymes. With the exception of 'Archduchess Anne', which I shall have cause to mention again later, these ballads are sport poems and they demonstrate a measure of the necessary virtuosity that elsewhere Meredith struggled to achieve. It is also to be found in the ballad monologues of 'Juggling Jerry', 'The Old Chartist', 'A Stave of Roving Tim', and 'Martin's Puzzle'. Yet although this group of poems deserves to be praised, I would say that to indicate their comparative ease of movement, consistency of language and deft handling of narrative is to say all that is necessary. They lack both the psychological insight and social attentiveness we find in the verse of such minor figures as John Davidson and, taken as a whole, they feel curiously pointless. This is because Meredith seems to have written most of them to show off his powers as a virtuoso poet; and the fact is that he has demanded too little of himself in the poems for us to find the powers very remarkable.

This introduces an important point. Meredith, I am suggesting, wrote a great deal of poetry without really knowing what he wanted to do or say. In the last analysis it exists as an assertion of his right to be taken seriously as a poet, and no doubt for this reason it is so varied in genre, style and form. The poetry declares the poet. And yet for all the variety of this verse – and of all his contemporaries, only Browning and Hardy can match his wide choice and invention of forms – there is a very disturbing anonymity about much of Meredith's verse. No matter how various it may be, Browning's and Hardy's poetry is immediately recognizable as their own. But Meredith's is not; it does not seem to have been written by anyone in particular. To read Meredith in bulk is to become aware that he commonly lacked both a style and a subject. Take even one of his better-known and more successful sonnets and the awareness holds. 'Lucifer in Starlight' opens well enough. In describing Lucifer's flight from Hell the verse is surprisingly terse and direct. But then the poem quite simply fades out. Nothing happens, except that when Lucifer reaches 'the middle height'.

> at the stars,
> Which are the brain of heaven, he looked, and sank.
> Around the ancient track marched, rank on rank,
> The army of unalterable law (182).

The poem breeds inevitable questions: Why are the stars the brain of Heaven? (Do they hold intelligences, if so what sort, if not is the image meant to be visual?) What is the army of unalterable law? Who is Lucifer? (At the beginning of the sonnet he seems to be Satan, but if he is, why is he defeated by the sight of this un-Christian army?) I say this realizing that the poem has been favourably commented on by Brooks and Warren in *Understanding Poetry*. They say that 'the order of the stars demonstrates the reasonableness of the universe against which it is useless to rebel'.[2] But questions remain: Is the reasonableness God-ordained? If not, why are the stars the brain of Heaven? If so, what is the army of unalterable law? To these and other questions Brooks and Warren try to provide answers, but I think they get too far from the words on the page to be really convincing. It is not that I wish to deny the poem a certain skill, but I simply cannot see that it has a genuine subject.

Here, however, we come on a highly problematic issue. Allowing that the poems I have so far mentioned were written in order to assert Meredith's claim to serious attention, we have to explain the presence of others for which the same excuse seems hardly applicable. After all, the poems I have spoken of can be regarded as occasional verse. Yet Meredith is also, perhaps more importantly, a didactic poet. And although we may say that the faults of a large proportion of his verse are due to his lacking a subject, it is difficult to see how this can be true of 'The Woods of Westermain', 'A Faith on Trial', 'The Test of Manhood', and many others. Even so, I do not think that the didactic poems provide any more proof of Meredith's talent than the occasional verse does, and, as with that verse, they seem to me to owe their existence to his desire for serious attention. Admittedly, this may seem little more than speculation; but we have somehow to explain the existence of a large body of didactic poetry that is plainly forced and for the most part bad, and it is at least possible that Meredith shared or hoped to capitalize on the common Victorian assumption that the poet with a philosophy to offer his audience was the poet who best deserved serious consideration. At all events, when his novels finally brought him to general fame, it was the didactic element in his poetry that was most earnestly attended to . And it is no accident that what is still the best known book on Meredith's poetry should have been written by someone who shared the assumption that the best poets are sages, nor that he should have called it *The Philosophy and Poetry of George Meredith*. As photographs and portraits of the later years sufficiently attest, the sage of Box Hill was born in the late 1880s. Inevitably, his poems were prized for their 'message', and they tended to be revered as a body of received truths.

It is not difficult to see why at the end of the nineteenth century Meredith became so significant as a didactic poet nor why he meant so much to young men of the Edwardian era. For Meredith was a robustly anti-Victorian iconoclast. He was anti-religious, anti-Imperial (he hated war and the physical bullying of the Imperial ethos, and spoke out against them in two sonnets, 'Warning' and 'Outside the Crowd'), and he championed the private virtues of love and friendship, the emancipation of women and the cause of sexual equality. True, he also insisted on the supreme importance of duty and selflessness, but those positivistic watchwords can stand many interpretations. And whatever difficulties lay in the way of creating a consistent and understandable philosophy out of the poetry, there can be hardly any doubt that Meredith's appeal lay in what he said, not the way he said it. The point may be made by reference to a late poem, 'With the Persuader'. From our vantage-point it looks almost distressingly adolescent in its pagan sensuality:

> A single nymph it is, inclined to muse
> Before the leader foot shall dip in stream:
> One arm at curve along a rounded thigh;
> Her firm new breasts each pointing its own way;
> A knee half bent to shade its fellow shy,
> Where innocence, not nature, signals nay.

The bud of fresh virginity awaits
The wooer, and all roseate will she burst:
She touches on the hour of happy mates;
Still is she unaware she wakens thirst. (533).

This is altogether too much like Leigh Hunt versifying Sir Frederick Leighton. As for 'Love in a Valley', in its first version written as early as 1851, but which there is no reason to suppose well known before Meredith's sudden rise to popularity, Orwell was probably right when he said that it held the appeal for one generation of adolescents that the *Shropshire Lad* held for the next. Yet it is obvious that Meredith's poems could recommend themselves to a generation in studious revolt from high-toned Victorianism. The attitudes of 'Love in a Valley' and 'With the Persuader' become ethical norms in *Where Angels Fear to Tread, A Room with a View* and *The Longest Journey*; and Forster also copies from Meredith the tactic of translating figures from Greek mythology into a contemporary English setting. The spirit of classicism defies the conquering spirit of the pale Galilean.

Verses on the delights of earthly love do not exhaust Meredith's stock of didactic poetry. He also writes about Nature and man's relationships with it; history and progress, and social morality. None of the didactic verse strikes me as any good, and the worst of it is appalling.

Meredith's didactic poems about social morality seem understandable in terms of his allegiance to altruistic thought in the latter half of the nineteenth century. In particular, we may feel that his 'placing' of sexuality is recognizably akin to the attitudes of George Eliot, Frederic Harrison, and John Morley. Yet there is also reason to feel that his readiness to urge that the pleasures must not on the passions browse has a more personal, or at least obsessive, meaning for Meredith than can be accounted for in terms of positivistic ideas. And I would guess that he turned with relief to a dogma which stressed the need for transcendence of the flesh. The guess hardens towards a certainty when we consider a remarkable group of poems to be found in *Ballads and Poems of Tragic Life*, from which I would select 'Archduchess Anne', 'King Harald's Trance', 'The Young Princess', 'A Preaching from a Spanish Ballad', and 'The Nuptials of Attila'. And here we approach the core of Meredith's achievement as a poet. For his best work, I would submit, ranges itself round a single subject, the incommunicabilities, deceptions and violent treacheries of love. Given this subject, and with fewer natural endowments than any of his important contemporaries, he was still able to produce a handful of remarkable and perhaps unique poems. The tragedy is that they should be nearly hidden under the dead wood of his didactic and occasional verse. The great poem is, of course, 'Modern Love'. But before I turn to that I want to say a little about the others I have mentioned.

With the exception of 'The Nuptials of Attila', they are all ballads. All of them dramatize relationships through a series of acutely perceived moments, and in their different ways all are concerned with the violent and uncontrollable emotions of outraged love. There are local failures, but what chiefly draws the attention is Meredith's ability to find the language he needs, itself proof of an unusual degree of engagement. The language of these poems is customarily bare, terse, rapid. It is intensely dramatic and it makes striking use of similes: I think, for example, of Kraken's eyes like 'spikes of spar' ('Archduchess Anne'), of Archduchess Anne's 'heart swung like a storm-bell tolled/Above a town ablaze',of this description of King Harald:

> Smell of brine his nostrils filled with might:
> Nostrils quickened eyelids, eyelids hand:
> > Hand for sword at right
> > Groped, the great haft spanned.
>
> Wonder struck to ice his people's eyes:
> Him they saw, the prone upon the bier,
> > Sheer from backbone rise,
> > Sword uplifting peer.
>
> Sitting did he breathe against the blade,
> Standing kiss it for that proof of life:
> > Strode, as netters wade,
> > Straightway to his wife.
>
> (284)

In each of these poems death is the outcome of love; it is the price people pay for deep personal involvement. And if the involvement is occasionally made to serve a social theme (as in 'A Preaching from a Spanish Ballad', which is about male tyranny) it is more frequently regarded with fear, almost horror. This is particularly evident in 'The Nuptials of Attila'. The horror here is intensified, and is perhaps betraying, because we are never allowed to know *why* Attila died. We are told of his army's prescient fear for him, since a woman 'holds him fast'. When soldiers break into his room the morning after his nuptials they find him dead and his wife mad, 'Humped and grinning like a cat,/Teeth for lips'. And she destroys not only him but the army's male comradeship, its unity: some want to kill her, others defend her. 'Death, who dares deny her guilt!/Death, who says his blood she spilt. . . . She, the wild contention's cause,/Combed her hair with quiet paws.' 'The Nuptials of Attila' is a poem which centres on a fearful unknowableness about love and in particular sexual passion. At its heart is the mystery of Attila's death, and although this can be fitted to the theme of social duty – Attila shouldn't have slipped back into a private life – it will not explain the poem's urgency, its obsessive feeling for the horror of personal involvement. It is a strange and compelling poem, and a deeply disturbing one. Partly this is because it seems to have come from something deep inside the poet that he hardly knew how to handle or control. A good deal of the detail is gratuitous and hints at Meredith's own uncertainty, his uneasiness as to what he was trying to write about. But the poem is also disturbing because it fends off all explanation; we simply do not know what went on inside that room. 'The Nuptials of Attila' is a statement, not an exploration; it turns its back on the mystery. For that reason its achievement is limited, though still real enough. But on a previous occasion Meredith had dared exploration, in the poem that is his one undoubted major triumph.

'Modern Love' comprises fifty sixteen-line sonnets (Meredith's own term), of which the first five and last two are spoken by a narrator, and the remainder by the husband with the narrator's occasional interpolations. The husband's sonnets are not all spoken in the first person; on one or two occasions he becomes a narrator himself, seeing himself from the outside, and the tactic, which is not overworked, allows for some brilliantly exploited ironies. Meredith's choice of form is extremely tactful. The sonnet is a definite enough structure to curb his impulse to sprawl as he does when he invents his own irregular metres; yet it is not so demanding as to force him into the weaknesses I have already pointed out. But the sonnet form is also a crucial and positive achievement. For Meredith has invented in the husband a person who has to be consistently realized and yet has to be shown in the process of the fluctuations, reversals, and modifications of his relationship with his wife and with the Lady whom he takes up as a part retort to his wife's lover. The invented form is ideal for this. Each sonnet in 'Modern Love' presents a considered point of view which the firm rhyme-scheme reinforces and each is surprised and upset by subsequent sonnets. And by dispensing with a concluding couplet Meredith remains in control of his material while avoiding the sort of pat or epigrammatic finality which would make his characters mere puppets for his comic spirit. I make this point in order to note that we do 'Modern Love' a serious injustice if we try to see it as a thesis poem. In spite of its title, which feels better if we assume it to be the narrator's choice, 'Modern Love' is not trying to argue a case about the collapse of moral values in the post-Darwinian world. Nor is it a study of that egoism which later engaged Meredith's attention in his *Essay on Comedy*. There, Meredith envisaged comic art as presenting a moral pattern of retributive justice; sooner or later the egoist will come unstuck, and his sins of self-deception and ignorance will rebound upon his head. But there is no point in looking for a moral pattern in 'Modern Love'. Only the narrator comes near to finding one, and it is clear that his Manoa-like, pious inanities are not meant to provide the definitive judgment on what is a beautifully sane study of the flow and recoil in a personal relationship.

Yet although we are not to identify the narrator with Meredith, I realize that the opening sonnets may encourage us to do so. In them 'poetry' wins, and with predictable consequences. It would be only too easy to show that the first four sonnets are badly flawed. They are challengingly complex in image and phrase, they puzzle and perplex; but if we take up the challenge the sonnets seem to offer, we find ourselves unravelling cliché and inconsistency. There is not much point in trying to blame the narrator rather than Meredith for all these faults, not only because they are so characteristically Meredithian, but because they are irrelevant to the narrator's function. On the other hand, they should not obscure the fact that there are intended badnesses which do belong to the narrator. Of course, this only makes Meredith's lapses more irritating. But having said that, I would add that it is not worth making too much of these flaws, because after sonnet IV they more or less disappear, and although we can find failures later on their effect is minimal; pointing to the flaws of 'Modern Love' becomes an increasingly trivial exercise.

The opening sonnet introduces us to the man and woman, 'Upon

their marriage tomb', 'Each wishing for the sword that severs all'.[3]
We are later to find that the narrator has, as is typical with him,
put the matter far too bluntly; the couple also desire each other.
But for the moment we stay with the narrator as he goes on to
speak of the husband's jealousy and sympathetically identifies
himself with what he assumes to be the husband's point of view.
Indeed, we may note that the narrator is much more sympathetic
to the husband than our own viewpoint allows us to be. And his
feeling for the husband goes with a simplistic moralizing on the
wife: 'But, oh, the bitter taste her beauty had!/He sickened as at
breath of poison flowers' (II). If this is true it is only partially so,
and the husband sees as the narrator does only when he is acting a
part of outraged innocence, as in VII: 'Yea! filthiness of body is
most vile,/But faithlessness of heart I do hold worse./The former,
it were not so great a curse/To read on the steel-mirror of her
smile.' Not the least of the successes of 'Modern Love' is its ability
to catch the note of the literary moralism of Victorian England,
with its grandiose and unearned echoes of the Bible. 'Modern Love'
exposes the cant which the husband tries out in these lines, and
from which the narrator never wavers. 'There is nothing personal
in morality', Mr. Pecksniff told his daughters. A good deal of the
narrator's moral ardour depends on that impersonal language which
the husband occasionally shares. And at the heart of 'Modern
Love's' achievement is a near reversal of Pecksniff's remark. Its
scrutiny of personalities leaves little time for moralizing. It is just
this scrutiny that the narrator avoids, as sonnet IV makes evident.
Here we are taken as far as possible from what may be called the
human situation Meredith treats of.

> Cold as a mountain in its star-pitched tent,
> Stood high Philosophy, less friend than foe:
> Whom self-caged Passion, from its prison bars,
> Is always watching with a wondering hate.
> Not till the fire is dying in the grate,
> Look we for any kinship with the stars.
>
> (135)

These lines provide one of the few instances in the opening sonnets
where we can be certain that the badness is the narrator's alone.
For it is not merely that the rhetoric is inept, but that what follows
makes the didacticism absurdly beside the point. Sonnet VI helps
to show how. Here, the husband tries out various roles, of horror,

grief, magnanimity, and in doing so he takes on the narrator's tone of voice. The sonnet rehearses most of the attitudes, bar love, that we are to find in the poem; and it introduces the dramatizing dialectic of the husband/wife relationship:

> It chanced his lips did meet her forehead cool.
> She had no blush, but slanted down her eye.
> Shamed nature, then, confesses love can die:
> And most she punishes the tender fool
> Who will believe what honours her the most!
> Dead! is it dead? She has a pulse, and flow
> Of tears, the price of blood-drops, as I know,
> For whom the midnight sobs around Love's ghost,
> Since then I heard her, and so will sob on.
> The love is here; it has but changed its aim.
> O bitter barren woman! what's the name?
> The name, the name, the new name thou hast won?
> Behold me striking the world's coward stroke!
> That will I not do, though the sting is dire.
> —Beneath the surface this, while by the fire
> They sat, she laughing at a quiet joke.
>
> (135–6)

Reading this, it is easy to see why Harley Granville-Barker thought Meredith would have made a great comic dramatist. The sonnet is about the husband's inner posturings, comically contained, as the structure shows, by casual domesticity. There can be no doubt of the debt to Browning; but it is justified. What we have in this sonnet is a variety of dramatis personae, as the husband seeks to discover a likely role for himself. Olympian detachment (ll. 3–5) yields to racked and forlorn love (ll. 6–9) and this gives way first to anger (ll. 11–12) and finally to magnanimity (ll. 13–14). As for the last two lines, they neatly place the impressive absurdity of that invitation to 'Behold me'. It is the husband who beholds himself, as sonnet IX cleverly shows:

> He felt the wild beast in him betweenwhiles
> So masterfully rude, that he would grieve
> To see the helpless delicate thing receive
> His guardianship through certain dark defiles.
> Had he not teeth to rend, and hunger too?

> But still he spared her. Once: 'Have you no fear?'
> He said: 'twas dusk; she in his grasp; none near.
> She laughed: 'No, surely; am I not with you?'
>
> (137)

The effect of this transition to the third person is to make clear the husband's inability to acknowledge his own frustration. If only she *would* fear him. But what is he threatening: 'Had he not teeth to rend, and hunger too?' Judging by her laugh, 'No and yes' is the answer to that two-pronged question. It would be too crude to say that this line is about thwarted sexuality alone; it is also about the impotence of the husband's own desires, which he partly, and perhaps unconsciously, conceals from himself by rhetorically violent language and the indirections of the third-person narrative. It is as though he sees himself as another person.

In sonnet IX incommunicability reaches towards a final point. It shows something of that psychological acuteness that helps make 'Modern Love' so remarkable. It also testifies to the entire poem's integrity, since the sonnet cannot be lifted from context without losing most of its force. If we do not see it in its relationship to the sequence as a whole we shall miss the point of the switch from first to third person, we shall settle for a simplistic reading; and in addition we may well take the sonnet as a 'key' to the poem. Indeed, most commentators make just this mistake: of pointing to one sonnet or group of sonnets as the centre of the poem's meaning. They do not realize that 'Modern Love' can have no centre; it is a ceaseless discovery of fluctuations; change is its only constant.[4] Yet although Meredith is fully alive to the comedy of this, the husband and wife are not formulated, sprawling on a pin. He has a compassion for them which is very different from the narrator's and only open to him because he knows so much. In his case, compassion depends on knowledge, whereas the narrator has merely the ignorant and complacent pity that goes with his dismissive attitude towards the woman and her lover: ('If he comes beneath a heel,/He shall be crushed until he cannot feel,/ Or, being callous, haply till he can', III.) For this reason, Meredith's attentive rendering of the way the husband dramatizes his roles has a justification that goes well beyond the comic – in the reductive sense in which he himself came to define the word. The shift of feeling and attitude between sonnets XV and XVI show how. Sonnet XV presents the husband as Othello, 'The Poet's black stage-lion of wronged love', entering his wife's bedroom with proof of her guilt:

'Sweet dove,
Your sleep is pure. Nay, pardon: I disturb.
I do not? good!' Her waking infant-stare
Grows woman to the burden my hands bear:
Her own handwriting to me when no curb
Was left on Passion's tongue. She trembles through;
A woman's tremble – the whole instrument:—
I show another letter lately sent.
The words are very like: the name is new.
(139–40)

So obvious an involvement with his melodramatic role reflects oddly upon the husband's earlier vow of magnanimity; it also implies not only a desire to push sympathy to the limits – he dares the response of disgust – but a compulsive need to be hateful, as self-protection against other feelings. And these exist right enough, as we discover in the next sonnet. It opens with a sentimental memory of happiness:

In our old shipwrecked days there was an hour,
When in the firelight steadily aglow,
Joined slackly, we beheld the red chasm grow
Among the clicking coals. Our library-bower
That eve was left to us: and hushed we sat
As lovers to whom Time is whispering.
(140)

I would say that such sentimentality is the husband's tacit admission of his inexcusable behaviour. It anticipates the reader's contempt. 'Don't blame me. I used to be happy, she's made me what I am'; this is the feeling that prods the lines into being. But we recognize it only by seeing the two sonnets in their connection with each other. The self-pitying sentimentality of sonnet XVI is a transparent attempt to ward off the self-disgust that sonnet XV caused, and the shift from one sonnet to the next enacts something of the complexities and uncertainties of a relationship from which love is not absent. I also think that the sonnets typify an effect that 'Modern Love' has, of disallowing a simple analysis or definition of any one moment, or line; seen in the context of other phrases, lines, sonnets, self-pity masks self-disgust which hints at love and its opposite. In this poem nothing is certain, nothing simply true; it is not more or less valid to suggest that the husband hates himself for pretending that his wife has killed their love than it is to say that he loves her. Sonnet XV, for example, says that it's her fault; sonnet XX says it's his:

> I am not of those miserable males
> Who sniff at vice and, daring not to snap,
> Do therefore hope for heaven . . .
> I have just found a wanton-scented tress
> In an old desk, dusty for lack of use.
> Of days and nights it is demonstrative,
> That, like some aged star, gleam luridly.
> If for those times I must ask charity,
> Have I not any charity to give?
>
> (142)

The sonnets contradict each other and in doing so testify to the poem's recognition that absolute terms of love and hate fail to make contact with what necessarily changes minute by minute, and is never clearly one thing. The recognition is psychological and observational. And the constant modulation of stand-point, together with subtle modifications of echo and prolepsis from sonnet to sonnet, makes 'Modern Love' one of the few Victorian poems to show a formal advantage over the achievements of the great nineteenth-century novel.

Indeed, Meredith deliberately challenges comparison with the novel. Sonnet XX introduced the Lady, and the next nineteen sonnets are mostly taken up with the husband's relationship with her. In sonnet XXV this is seen in terms of a French novel: 'These things are life.' But they are also predictable, and one of Meredith's most brilliant strokes is to introduce so 'shocking' an idea as the foursome of husband-Lady, wife-lover, and then play off its predictable complications against the deeper and unpredictable muddle of the husband-and-wife relationship. To a large extent, the husband's affair with the Lady is a response to his wife's affair. On the one hand it is an attempt to forget, 'Distraction is the panacea' (XXVII), and on the other to salve wounded pride, 'I must be flattered, the imperious/Desire speaks out' (XXVIII). But, *pace* Trevelyan and others, the affair is fully consummated. It moves from 'the game of Sentiment' (XXVIII) to sexual involvement, a transition marked by the truly astonishing sonnet XXXIII:

'In Paris, at the Louvre, there have I seen
The sumptuously-feathered angel pierce
Prone Lucifer, descending. Looked he fierce,
Showing the fight a fair one? Too serene!
The young Pharsalians did not disarray
Less willingly their locks of floating silk:
That suckling mouth of his upon the milk
Of heaven might still be feasting through the fray.
Oh, Raphael! when men the Fiend do fight,
They conquer not upon such easy terms.
Half serpent in the struggle grow these worms.
And does he grow half human, all is right.'
This to my Lady in a distant spot,
Upon the theme: *While mind is mastering clay*
Gross clay invades it. If the spy you play,
My wife, read this! Strange love talk, is it not?

(147–8)

We are drawn to notice the husband's apparent struggle with
conscience (ll. 9–10) over those hungers of gross clay which have so
disturbingly invaded the language of the first eight lines. Yet the
sexual language is directed as much at the wife as at the Lady; the
trap in the last lines is so self-consciously aware of its taunt. It is
also an attempt to deny the dramatized guilt of Sonnet XXIII ('I
know not how, but shuddering as I slept,/I dreamed a banished
angel to me crept'), and the torturings of lust in sonnet XXIV:

> that nun-like look waylays
> My fancy. Oh! I do but wait a sign!
> Pluck out the eyes of pride! thy mouth to mine!
> Never, though I die thirsting. Go thy ways!

(144)

The lust is more easily identified than its object, however; she
could be Lady or wife. The idea may seem ridiculous or horrible,
but then this study of a human relationship acknowledges the
existence of both, as sonnets XXXIV and XXXV make clear. In
sonnet XXXIV we are led to understand that the wife has indeed
played the spy, and that the husband will brazen it out: 'Madam
would speak with me. So, now it comes:/The Deluge or else Fire!
She's well; she thanks/My husbandship.' But neither deluge nor
fire occurs, with the result that the husband is cheated out of his

planned performance. Instead, he is forced to recognize that 'It is no vulgar nature I have wived' (XXXV). Sonnet XXXV is one of genuine compassion, but it invites the simplification to which the husband retreats at the end, where he speaks of 'this wedded lie!' Sympathy shades into self-justification. Once he has spoken of the lie, he can return to the Lady. This is a characteristic perception of the poem.

So is the language of sonnet XXXIX, where the husband tries to convince himself he is happy with what he's got. In sonnet XXXVIII he speaks of his relationship with the Lady in Platonic terms, but the next sonnet makes plain what has actually happened:

> She yields: my Lady in her noblest mood
> Has yielded; she, my golden-crownëd rose!
> The bride of every sense! more sweet than those
> Who breathe the violet breath of maidenhood.
>
> (150)

But the emphatic language we find here quickly gives way to the doubts of sonnet XL: 'Helplessly afloat,/I know not what I do, whereto I strive.'

In the next sonnet he returns to his wife, and pretends that for decency's sake he will forgo his deep love for the Lady: 'We two have taken up a lifeless vow/To rob a living passion.' It is a typical piece of dramatization and self-deception. Sonnet XLII destroys the act. It opens with the husband following his wife to their bedroom. 'I am to follow her.' But nobody is making him go; it is merely that putting it that way allows him to pretend he cannot help it. The sonnet ends: 'Her wrists/I catch: she faltering, as she half resists,/"You love. . . . ? love. . . . ? love. . . . ?" all on an indrawn breath.' As the wife's half-resistance shows, it is in fact the husband who is the pursuer; and her question applies equally to herself and the Lady. She wants reassurance before she yields. From a lifeless vow we have passed to a renewed sexual relationship. And in sonnet XLIII we move part-way back again, as we are told of 'the unblest kisses which upbraid/The full-waked sense'. *Post coitum, omne animal triste est.* In sonnet XLV the regression is complete: 'Here's Madam, stepping hastily.' This sonnet is less successful than most because it is too predictable; the point about the impossibility of emotional stasis is a bit crude in its irony. But the next two sonnets more than make up for the lapse.

These sonnets establish a rare moment of rest, of quietness, though it cannot be sustained. Sonnet XLVI is about failures and mistakes of love. The husband's 'disordered brain' leads him to suspect his wife of continuing her liaison with the Lover, but he triumphs over the moment of jealousy and in taking her arm becomes assured of her trustworthiness. He even finds it possible to tell her this, although he notes at the beginning of the sonnet that they are 'so strangely dumb/In such a close communion'. Speech destroys communication.

> I moved
> Toward her, and made proffer of my arm.
> She took it simply, with no rude alarm;
> And that disturbing shadow passed reproved.
> I felt the pained speech coming, and declared
> My firm belief in her, ere she could speak.
> A ghastly morning came into her cheek,
> While with a widening soul on me she stared.
> (153)

This discovery of incommunicability through communication is not merely ingenious; it is persuasive in its psychological attentiveness. The 'dumb' linking of arms creates that moment of trust in which the husband is able to speak the words of love that the wife mistakes for pity. All the same, there is a weakness to do with the last two lines, since if the husband has registered his wife's look, it is difficult to understand his unobservant complacency in the next sonnet. This, the most frequently anthologized of all the sonnets of 'Modern Love', is about a presumed companionableness: 'We saw the swallows gather in the sky . . ./Our spirits grew as we went side by side.' The sonnet catches well enough the note of quietness, but it loses its full force unless it is seen in context. As a Nature poem or love-lyric it is unremarkable, but it becomes remarkable as soon as we recognize that the moment of communication is also the moment of betrayal, which is what sonnet XLVIII reveals: 'We drank the pure daylight of honest speech./Alas! that was the fatal draught, I fear . . .': for though the husband thinks he is offering love, (and why should we trust him?) the wife sees only pity, rejects it, and flees the house. 'For when of my lost Lady came the word,/This woman, O this agony of flesh!/Jealous devotion bade her break the mesh,/That I might seek the other like a bird.'

And then we return to the narrator. Sonnet XLIX tells us that the husband brings the wife home, that she believes his love, and that she commits suicide out of terror 'lest her heart should sigh,/ And tell her loudly she no longer dreamed'/–dreamed, that is, that her husband now loves her. The last sonnet is predictably pious.

I am not sure that the wife's suicide is the best way of ending 'Modern Love'. For one thing it is misleadingly liable to hint at a progressiveness of her relationship with the husband. I also think it perhaps over-readily falls into the mode of reversal and unpredictability which Meredith handles with so much human awareness elsewhere in the poem. The suicide comes perilously near to lending itself to the narrator's tone: 'Thus piteously Love closed what he begat.' On the other hand, I recognize that 'Modern Love' can only really end by being cut short, for once Meredith has created this incessantly shifting dialectic of the relationship he needs the intervention of the arbitrary to halt the poem. And I suppose the suicide makes a further point: that such a relationship cannot be resolved; it can only stop. But however successful we think it, the ending of the poem must be discussed in this way; we can only regard it as a triumph of comic art if we take a Popeian view of the comic, which is not the view Meredith officially took. For this reason, I think it an unforgivable mistake to try fitting 'Modern Love' to theories Meredith was later to elaborate. If we do, we merely lay the poem open to F. R. Leavis's charge that it is 'the flashy product of unusual but vulgar cleverness working upon cheap emotion'. As I have tried to show, that charge can be met. But we need to take it seriously. Not to do so is a disservice to Meredith, whose reputation as a poet will not be restored in any way that matters while admirers find themselves so little capable of tackling the problematic issues his poetry as a whole presents. In particular, we must be able to account for the nature and level of the achievement of 'Modern Love', recognizing that it is not equalled elsewhere in his work and that only very occasionally is it approached.

Notes

1 My text is taken from *The Poetical Works of George Meredith*, with some notes by G. M. Trevelyan, 1912.
2 *Understanding Poetry*, New York, 1937, 370.

3 All future references will be to the number of the sonnet quoted.

4 I have not wanted to burden the text of my essay with references to the critics who have discussed 'Modern Love' because although the poem customarily receives high praise I do not think its complexities have been properly appreciated. The comments by Swinburne and Arthur Symons are generous and just, but they do not pretend to be more than general remarks (Swinburne praised the poem in his famous letter to the *Spectator*, 1862, protesting at the vulgar review of the poem that had appeared in its pages; Arthur Symons's essay was collected in his *Figures of Several Centuries*, 1916); Trevelyan, Jack Lindsay and Siegfried Sassoon stick far too closely to the biographical aspects, and as a result fail to notice how distanced Meredith is from the husband's point of view (Trevelyan's remarks are made in his notes to the *Collected Poems of George Meredith*, 1912, Sassoon's are in his *Meredith*, 1948, especially 64–7, and Lindsay's are in his *George Meredith, His Life and Work*, 1956, especially 83–7.) Norman Kelvin, it is true, half-sees his way to how the poem dislodges any effort at a simplistic reading, but he tries to find a moral core to it. Predictably it turns out to be the one offered by the narrator and involves Kelvin not only in a highly unlikely interpretation of some lines from the closing sonnet, but in the disastrous course of trying to identify the narrator's voice with Meredith's. Kelvin claims that the marriage is a failure because husband and wife 'have approached each other as barbarian aggressors. They are not individuals transformed by reason and capable of passion without destruction' (*A Troubled Eden; Nature and Society in the Works of George Meredith*, 1961, 26, and see 25–35). Such a view is woefully moral. Probably the best account of the poem is C. Day Lewis's. He recognizes that the movement of the poem is best seen as a 'series of impulses and revulsions proceeding from the conflict within the husband's mind, which swings wildly from jealousy to generosity, from pity to indignation, from hysterical egotism to civilised sympathy, from regret to cynicism, from cursing to blessing' (Introduction to his edition of 'Modern Love', 1948). My main quarrel with Day Lewis's argument is that he separates out the series of impulses too schematically and ignores the role of the narrator, whom he seems to feel speaks for Meredith; at least, verse which I find appalling (and deliberately) bad he thinks is good and that it offers a valid point of view

The Shaving of Shagpat:
Meredith's Comic Apocalypse

Ian Fletcher

I

The tyranny of categories is presumed to have died with the eighteenth century. A 'sport', though, still tends to be written down, partly because the tools of criticism elect their own vile bodies. It took a Frenchman to insist on the excellence of Hogg's *Confessions of a Justified Sinner*, while some of Shakespeare's middle works, evading a tidy neo-Aristoteleanism, had to be given identity by suggesting that the Bard had mulled over Ibsen. Even in the visionary area of Romanticism, however, it is difficult to find a work that more taxes the response than *The Shaving of Shagpat*. What kind of work is it? Or, more appropriately, what is its drift?

Drift, however, is misleading. The confidence of the book's surface vivacity, what Photiadès amiably calls its 'liquid' narrative – more thrusting than most of Meredith's insolent modulations of line – impresses a sense of the author's control over tone and direction. Even so, the reader is still discomfited. Two inset narratives that superficially have little to do with the main narrative account for about a quarter of the length, and the longer of the two occurs at a point where the main narrative has barely got under way. Moreover, the main narrative involves a plunge *in medias res* and some of the key events are presented obliquely through the heroine's recapitulation two-thirds of the way through. About a third of the book recounts the hero's complex ordeals in the underworld of Aklis. And granted that the mode is one of comic determinism: 'It was ordained that Shibli Bagarag ... should shave Shagpat, the Son of Shimpoor, the son of Shoolpi, the son of Shullum', Meredith defeats the purpose of a complicated plot structure: suspense. The book abounds in echoes and anticipations that become hypnotically repetitive and might suggest under the surface dazzle a tired imagination. Such repetitiveness extends to the woman characters who predominate: Shibli's helper and finally consort, Noorna bin Noorka; Goorelka, the witch Princess, and Rubesqurat, the drolly sensual but also sinister Mistress of Illusions, though their roles are vivid, tend to melt into one another. And *Shagpat* is not quite a book whose life is likely to be prolonged through redaction for the nursery. The whole point seems to be a baffling equilibrium between the surface and the deep prose.

We have even to deny ourselves the symmetrical pleasure of spotting Shibli as the first sentimental knight errant whose egoism is purged by self-directed laughter. This expectation is oddly foiled by what happens when Shibli looks behind the veil of Rubesqurat; his laughter makes an idiot noise. And Shagpat's smile in sleep represents the last satisfactions of an inane inwardness. Shagpat the tailor represents the old order which will not pass and the climax of the book is the 'apocalypse', literally 'uncovering', of the man beneath the patriarchal beard. The beard becomes arbitrarily the 'sign' to which both kings and people orient themselves. But Meredith treats the violence that Shagpat's inertness breeds with an irony and detachment the more remarkable for the book itself being a purgation of self-pity; masking an autobiographical crux. Meredith is hero and villain in his own dramatic poem.

Self-criticism begins with a probing of the social romanticism that both promoted and betrayed 1830 and 1848. It is both with his public role as writer and private role as lover and husband that Meredith is concerned. The surface of *Shagpat* is Oriental fantasy, the structure that of neo-classical mock-epic: the most signal instance being the use of the heroic sword of Aklis as a giant razor. But 'inverted' rather than simply scale-distorting better describes the means: the *Dunciad* rather than the *Rape of the Lock*. Of course, the sword represents luminous common sense so that it can shrink to a pocket razor or expand to a cosmic ray; but can common sense really have such a desolating effect as the sword does when it pierces Rubesqurat's veil? Its association with Aklis gives it more the quality of *ratio recta*, a junction of imagination and common sense sufficient to suggest the nihilistic underside of comedy. The *Dunciad* misleads as an analogy. The villains do indeed tend to non-being; even Karaz, who is incessantly active, is always foiled and has a cave by the Putrid Sea, but the end of *Shagpat* reverses the last book of the *Dunciad*, where human history dies in laudanum, though the episode I've just mentioned shows Meredith recognizing the pleasures of nihilism. The inversions in *Shagpat* are peculiarly concerned with the self and illusion and must wait for later discussion. However, the book does combine a number of elements from the comic-sublime: heroic single combat in the final struggle between Shibli and Rubesqrat and her allies, recalling Homer and Book VI of *Paradise Lost*; the vision of the future dispersed through the book, granted to Noorna and absurdly assumed by Shibli; opening *in medias res*; descent into an underworld and a use for technology that matches Achilles' Shield, Pandemonium, or Sin and Death's discovery of construction engineering. There is a significant change, however: the theme of noble friendship between men disappears and is replaced by love and comradeship between man and woman. Patroclus and Raphael are replaced by Noorna and Gulravez. Woman is still the prize, but not the toy, whether of men or gods. Noorna is not Briseis or Dido or Eve, though *Shagpat*, or more precisely Shibli, has his Helen in Bhanavar and his false Helens in Goorelka and Rubesqrat.

The tradition of epic as encyclopaedia of the tribe appears as conversations with literature, remote and contemporary. A critique of the failure of the social revolution and of the poet's role in that would naturally begin from criticism of the social romanticism which had been its inspiration, since it was the claim of the romantic artist that he was not merely anticipating, but enacting the future. That romanticism had attempted to compensate for its failure. (In English terms, a movement through Shelley, Carlyle, and the Spasmodic poets.) Meredith's critique is not particularly linguistic, though there is some verbal parody; of Shelley, of the formulaic syntax of Lane's version of the *Arabian Nights*, of the Authorized Version, for example. The critique focuses on the role of woman, or rather her roles. Noorna stands for the energies of woman who must be liberated before the Revolution within and without can begin (a criticism perhaps of Carlyle's betrayal of Enfantin?). Woman can be liberated only with and through man. And what she must be liberated from are the roles which man has imposed on her. It was the romantics no less than the conservatives, literature no less than economics, the Enlightenment no less than Christianity which had been responsible for such impositions. She has been seen as vessel of death, fatal woman, shrine, slave, servant, victim of vanity, mediator of vanity, witch, biologically unsound and so forth. The means of exploitation through image might differ and be complicated by class attitudes, but Shelley and a mine-owning Capitalist expected too much of women. In this light the women of *Shagpat* must be seen, as woman, and specifically as woman released to assist the agent of change: Noorna as old woman and Shibli as vain youth. Shibli gets everything wrong, but it is the women who focus his failure to orient himself to reality. Of the images he makes of woman, only Noorna, who runs the gamut from ugliness to animal disguise to companion to victim to consort and fellow-worker, along with the muse-figure Gulravez, survive. Noorna is Gulravez's surrogate to the point where Shibli can accept her as she is, and definer of himself.

One area where Meredith found a competing image of woman was in romance epic, among the Britomarts and Marfisas. Mock-epic modulates readily into romance epic, but that image, though astringent, is not altogether adequate, though it does assert noble friendship between man and woman. But Bradamante's role supports rather than subverts existing order. A question remains: what social and cultural norm does Meredith's mock-epic suppose, if it reacts against both revolution and tradition? This, of course, ranges beyond *Shagpat*. There I cannot see that it goes far beyond insistence that one must have small beginnings; a broken Eden and a social art that allows for mobility between classes, but in Meredith's post-lapsarian world, the woman is no longer subject to the man. To veil the theme under Oriental fable was to allow for the maximum ironic distortion.

The English drawing-room was *actually* an equivalent of the harem, though the exotic vehicle veers as far as possible both from the present and from the cultural past of Europe. The veil recalls Byron and *Lallah Rookh*, tales of love and egoism, but actually read and imaginatively enacted in drawing-rooms.

My tenor is that the emphasis on social change can be overdone; there is more stoicism than clearing the air in *Shagpat*. Common sense and earthy imagination may purge the self and literature, but won't have more than a marginal effect on the way things are; it is an unstable world and must be closely watched; but the pace of change is faster than one might think. (Meredith, of course, takes a more serene view of 1848–9 in *Vittoria*, which is his version of the straight epic. Woman there is released to be the 'voice' of change.) The axis of concern shifts from sanity to a sense of the sacredness of the self, through which one reorders the world, a self which must be profaned before it can be accommodated. Dr J. M. S. Tompkins seems to me profoundly right when she says that Shibli's vanity may constantly trip him up, but without that vanity he would be incapable of the ordeals that precede wielding the sword.

II

The Shaving of Shagpat at once poses a difficulty which loses Meredith a good many readers in each generation – what David Howard aptly terms 'manic accumulation of plot'. It has to be dogged through at least three times before one can grasp on a surface level what it is all about. People have been told that it is worth doing this with George Eliot and Henry James and will duly persist. But few people think there is much to miss in Meredith. At the risk of boring the reader, I must treat him to an elongated summary.

The heroine Noorna is discovered lying beside her dead mother in the wilderness and brought up by Raveloke, leader of the King of Oolb's armies. At twelve she is glimpsed by Goorelka, Princess of Oolb, who has received a warning from her lover, Karaz the Genie, that the 'little castaway' will be her ruin. Raveloke reveals to Noorna that he is only her foster-parent and warns her against Goorelka. To celebrate Noorna's birthday, Raveloke gives her a gold coin. Noorna proceeds to the Bazaar, accompanied by Kadrab, a black slave, and is accosted by a feeble, grimy beggar. Moved by his plight, she gives him her coin and he asks her what she wants in return. Noorna opts first for a blue dress with golden adornments, then for a book of magic. The beggar asks Kadrab the same question; the slave ironically replies: 'a plaster for sores as broad as my back and a camel's hump'. The beggar hobbles off and Noorna comes to a confectionery shop. She begs Kadrab for a small coin; he gives it her on condition that she stops encouraging beggars. A still more abject beggar appears and Noorna gives him the coin. Kadrab angrily kicks the beggar, who takes off over the roof-tops. When she returns to her room Noorna discovers a blue dress with gold adornments and a grimoire. Kadrab's wish has been less propitiously granted and Noorna's first essay in magic is to relieve him of hump and plaster.

Enjoined to secrecy, Kadrab blabs about his cure and alarms Goorelka, who tests Noorna's knowledge of magic, finding it already too deep for summary attack. Next to Goorelka's salon is an aviary, each bird with a ringed mark of gold round its throat and 'stamps of divers gems' similar in colour to a ring on Goorelka's right forefinger. Plied with exotic fluids, Noorna becomes drowsy, unwary, but is woken up by a bird with a wry topknot, black heavy bill and gorgeously ragged plumage, who begins hoarsely laughing and is echoed by the other birds. The Princess throws a furious slipper at this *chef d'orchestre* and shakes him into silence. She proposes a treaty with Noorna, asking some questions of proleptic importance: 'Can she fix the eyes of the world on one head and make the nations bow to it? Can she change men to birds?' and so on. Noorna returns that she has never misused her powers. Goorelka tells Noorna that she is the most fitting guardian for the Lily of the Sea.

Goorelka and Noorna travel enchanted waters in a cockleshell to the basin where the Lily springs. Noorna tends it devoutly, commuting from Oolb. She is warned by a portent mentioned in her magic books to accompany Raveloke when he leads an expedition against some rebels. One day she encounters the old beggar, who warns that 'the key to the mystery' will be given 'this night'. A vigilant Noorna surprises a young man, Raveloke's favourite and destined to marry Noorna, in an attempt to assassinate his patron. He admits to having been swayed by Goorelka's promise to marry him and appoint him to Raveloke's place. He knows 'his doom in loving her': to be her subject and to be denied the gift of laughter. He reveals that the birds in Goorelka's aviary are men transformed by her arts. Noorna revokes Goorelka's spell over the young man and he warns her to be wary of the genie Karaz, who has fallen in love with Noorna and is determined to possess her.

Returning to Oolb, Noorna decides to take a short-cut through a forest accompanied only by Kadrab. Kadrab attempts to make love to her; she strikes him; he seizes her and journeys through the air to a cave by the Putrid Sea: Kadrab turns out to be Karaz. Noorna bargains with Karaz and elicits the information that her true father, Feshnavat, is one of Goorelka's birds. When asked how Feshnavat can be freed, the genie makes Noorna swear an unconditional oath, using his own formula 'by the Identical', a powerful hair in the genie's head. She swears to give herself to the possessor of the Identical. Karaz, convinced that he has won Noorna, admits that though one of the mightiest of genies, he is the servant of Goorelka's ring, and 'could I get that ring from her and be slave to nothing mortal for an hour, I could light creation as a torch, and broil the inhabitants of earth at one fire'. Karaz also discloses that the way to exorcize Goorelka's victims is to keep them laughing at their condition and their own folly for one uninterrupted hour. Karaz then returns Noorna to Oolb.

Soon after, one of Goorelka's birds escapes from the aviary with the ring in its beak. Goorelka kills it, but Noorna takes the ring. As her books of magic inform her, it is 'mistress of the marvellous hair which is a magnet to the homage of men, so that they crowd and crush and hunger to adore it, even the Identical!' A necromantic *agon* follows between Noorna and Goorelka, with the Princess assuming shapes of snake, scorpion and lioness and Noorna leaping into ring after ring of charged water until Goorelka, exhausted, falls. Noorna sets the birds free through laughter; they assume their proper human appearance, though 'they laugh little in their lives from that time' and their faces reflect 'their dark experience'. Feshnavat and Noorna are reunited and Noorna orders the genie to restore all Goorelka's victims to their previous possessions and powers. The genie returns for his reward. He lays his head in Noorna's lap and lets slip that the Identical in another head than the genie's counteracts the power of the ring and the ring is powerless over it. Noorna decides to risk that, lulls Karaz to sleep and identifies the Identical by means of Goorelka's ring. She sees 'one of the thin lengths begin to twist and writhe, and shift lustres as a creature in anguish'. She wrenches out the Identical, the genie awakes roaring and soars into the air holding Noorna, who in turn holds the Identical, though somewhat insecurely, 'for it twisted and stung'. Noorna then 'sows' the Identical in the head of the inert, bearded Shagpat the Clothier, who at once becomes an object of adoration in his own city and then in others, so that the craft of the barber is despised and proscribed. Meanwhile, Goorelka sprinkles a dew which blights the Lily of the Sea and Noorna's beauty withers also: she assumes Goorelka's true appearance, while Goorelka wears, though less convincingly, Noorna's beauty. Using the ring, Noorna assists Feshnavat to become Vizier to the King of Shagpat's city and commands Karaz as her rebellious slave. Humbled by loss of beauty, she patiently waits the fulfilment of a magical text: 'a barber alone shall be the shearer of the Identical', and shall plant it in the underworld Kingdom of Aklis, 'where it groweth as a pillar, bringing due reverence to Aklis'.

After some time, Shibli Bagarag, a young barber, makes his way through the desert to Shagpat's city. The text begins here, *in medias res*. Shibli is weary, starving, puzzled at finding barbercraft execrated in most of the cities he has visited. An old woman (Noorna) encounters him and proclaims him 'Master of the Event', the shaving of Shagpat, though prophecy is far from fulfilment. Shibli is taken before the King and exalts his craft. The King's response is discouraging. He is appalled at Shibli's impudence, for now all cities, excepting Shiraz, honour Shagpat and reject barbercraft. The Vizier Feshnavat suggests whipping might bring Shibli to his senses. Shibli is whipped and hustled out of the palace. He wanders miserably until the sight of Shagpat, 'that tangle of glory', restores pride in his craft, but Shagpat is so enraged by the suggestion of a good shave that he calls on his wife to beat the barber. As he slinks out of Shagpat's shop, Shibli is followed, and again beaten by a mob, who hurl him through the city gate 'into the wilderness once more'.

Once more he encounters the hag, who assures him that his 'thwackings' will bring 'strength of mind' and 'sternness in pursuit of an object'. She assures Shibli that she is the 'head' of his fortune, but his present ambitions extend merely to food and drink. The old woman seems to fancy the youth. With an arch smile, she 'wriggled in her seat like a dusty worm', asks if he finds her attractive and will he pay her a compliment. Shibli obliges with a song, hinting that he will be ready to praise her beauty when he has eaten and drunk. The old woman smiles and again speaks of him mastering the Event, when he marries her. Shibli broods over this and agrees: after all, he will be a widower before too long, while the old woman 'wheedlingly looked at him and shaped her mouth like a bird's bill to soften it, and she drew together her dress, to give herself the look of slimness'.

The old woman then leads him to the Vizier's palace and tells him to proclaim his art. He does so and is again thwacked, this time by the Vizier's slaves. Alone with Shibli, however, the Vizier reveals that he has been acting a part and asks for further information about barbercraft. Shibli, in improvised verse, replies that instruction is hard on an empty stomach. While Shibli eats and drinks the Vizier reveals that Shagpat is his enemy and he wants him shaved. The Vizier leads Shibli into a further room where he finds the old woman, sumptuously clothed and somewhat younger-seeming, so that Shibli is reminded of the tale of Bhanavar the Beautiful, whose beauty was preserved by the sacrifice of her lovers. He recounts this at great length. Shibli and Noorna are betrothed, the Vizier having revealed that she is his daughter. After the betrothal kiss it is 'as if a splendid jewel were struggling to cast its beams through the sides of a crystal vase smeared with dust and old dirt and spinnings of the damp spider'. Noorna now discloses that she is 'a sorceress ensorcelled' and has escaped from Shagpat, who desired her in marriage, but was refused by the Vizier. Shibli begins boasting of how he will shave Shagpat and the Vizier tells his cautionary tale of Khipil, the talkative builder who completed nothing. Noorna then tells them that the only weapon with power to shear the Identical is the sword of Aklis. Whoever succeeds in entering that underworld and enduring its ordeals will be capable of wielding the sword. To achieve the sword three charms are needed: a phial full of the truth waters of Paravid, three hairs from the great horse Garaveen, and possession of the Lily of Light, of which Noorna had been the guardian.

Placing Shibli and Feshnavat in a runic circle, Noorna invokes Karaz, who passes through many illusory shapes before he is exposed as a 'genie of terrible aspect, black as a solitary tree seared by lightning'. Noorna changes him into an ass and jeers at him as he carries her and Shibli at high speed at Paravid, where Shibli gathers the drops in his phial. They travel on to Melistan, where Garaveen wanders. Following Noorna's instructions, Shibli attracts Garaveen with a battle call, flings a musk ball at his fetlock and traces a crescent figure on his forehead, enabling Shibli to mount him in order to pluck the three hairs. Shibli refuses to dismount and Garaveen gallops off with him towards a pit. Noorna is forced to use Karaz to unseat Shibli. Karaz mounts Garaveen himself and rushes out of the circuit of Noorna's magic. Fortunately, she has herself managed to take the three hairs while Shibli is playing the fool, and now ties these round Shibli's right wrist, telling the young man that they must part. When he wakes the following morning he finds himself alone.

As Noorna has directed, he set out for Oolb. Arriving at a port, a sea captain accosts him, saying that he expects Shibli: ''tis certain a trumpet was blown before thy steps . . . thou art chosen to bring about imminent changes'. This disarms Shibli: he agrees to travel to Oolb in the captain's boat. In his cabin he finds a hawk which screams out 'Karaz' when the captain enters. Karaz sinks through the bottom of the boat, which bursts into flames which pursue and envelop the hawk. Shibli plunges overboard and almost drowns, but is rescued by the hawk, which takes him by his 'Identical' hair and drags him by degrees to shore. The hawk urges him by signs to travel on to nearby Oolb and have audience with the King. At the hawk's direction, he tells the King the story of Roomdroom the Barber. Suspecting that Shibli belongs to the forbidden craft, the King orders in barber's tackle. Shibli betrays himself, and the hawk advises him to 'proclaim speech in the tackle'. The tackle speaks, the King is convinced and he and his subjects are shaved. The King asks the price of the hawk and, on the bird's advice once more, Shibli asks for the Princess's cockleshell. The King refuses and Shibli, still tutored by the hawk, accepts a china jar which brims inexhaustibly with wine, along with a dress conferring invisibility on its wearer. That night Shibli uses the jar to make the guards drunk and invisibly glides into Goorelka's bedroom. But he delays taking the cockleshell, so stunning is Goorelka's beauty, though the hawk attempts to distract him. Sensing that she is under a man's eye, the Princess wakes, realizes the guards are drunk, runs down to the sea and launches the cockleshell. Shibli clings to the back of the shell and Goorelka confirms his presence by the foam that sweeps after him.

Crossing the Enchanted Sea, they come to the Lily of Light. Goorelka tricks Shibli into disclosing himself and tempts him to drink the lily's dew. The dew is scattered by the hawk, which warns Shibli that it is poison, telling him to gather the lily by the root before it is too late. He does so. The lily streams with blood and the root palpitates like a living heart. The Princess begins to age and the hawk calls out 'Karaz'. The genie appears and looks at the Princess with loathing as she mutates into frog colour, camelback, pelican-throat and peacock-leg. Karaz gathers up the Princess 'in a bunch' and disappears in air. Shibli notes that the ugliness of the Princess resembles that of Noorna. The hawk too has disappeared. In its place, stands a girl, resembling but far more beautiful than the Princess had been: Noorna restored now to her true shape.

Noorna and Shibli plunge into the Enchanted Sea on their journey to Aklis, borne along at first by a stray current, then by a pearly shell, gift of Rubesqurat, Mistress of Illusions. In the shell, Noorna tells Shibli her story. Then the Mount of Aklis looms before them, blazing, a sign that visitors are nearing it. The lovers and the shell are swallowed by Karaz in form of a giant fish and pass through its body to the Court of Rubesqurat, who is enraged because they were planning to press on to Aklis without stopping by at her palace. Noorna is captured in a net by Abarak, a powerful dwarf, who emerges from a pillar and bundles Noorna away into it. Shibli faints and when he wakes has lost his identity, believing himself to be Rubesqurat's fiancé, but is preserved by the charms and the thwackings which bring a memory of Noorna. The lily reveals herself as Gulravez, daughter of Aklis, more beautiful even than Noorna. She instructs Shibli to take the heart out of her side and tie it to her feet. Shibli reluctantly obeys her and once more faints.

When he wakes, he takes the lily, whose light blasts the attendants and enchantments of the palace, and hacks his way by the force of Garaveen's hairs through the rock into the subterranean land of Aklis. There he finds Rubesqurat folded temptingly up in a hammock. He falls under her spell once more, but this time Rubesqurat concedes that he is not her fiancé, only her guest. While she is tempting him, he retains sufficient coolness to slip a drop of Paravid into her drink. She becomes unwary and reveals both her plans and her contempt for Abarak. Abarak appears and asks for the truth about his appearance. Shibli gives the gallant answer that Oscar Wilde is reported to have given Yvette Guilbert when she asked if she were not the ugliest woman in Paris: '*du monde, Madame, du monde*'. Abarak puts Rubesqurat to the test of the lily and she appears in a true, horrifying shape.

Abarak and Shibli then travel on through the freak, reddened landscape of Aklis. Shibli remembers Noorna and is granted a painful vision of her on a pillar in the midst of a stormy sea, but he cannot go to her rescue, for 'a step backward in Aklis is death'. The two stop at a stream; a veiled figure ferries them silently across to where an elephant, which kneels in the reeds, takes them on its back to the Palace of Aklis. Shibli triumphs through Paravid over another of Karaz's temptations, but falls into vanity. He accepts a crown of triumph before securing the sword. The crown is fixed immovably to his head; he is clamped to a throne, but released from that when he sees in a mirror that the crown is composed of 'bejewelled asses' ears stiffened upright and skulls of monkeys grinning with gems', and, like Goorelka's birds, laughs at himself and his own folly. He then traverses an abyss by a delicate passage of roc's eggs and just reaches the other side as the eggs break; so the roc is foiled. He meets the seven sons of Aklis, relieved from sharpening the sword now that one has come to claim it. Shibli sees that the subjects who had crowned him were asses and monkeys – presumably human beings transformed by Rubesqrat. Gulravez meanwhile has been transformed into an antelope. The brothers hunt the antelope in play and ask her to speak to their father, whom they have displeased by taking time off on earth. The antelope goes behind a curtain at the edge of the roc's pit and asks for approval of Shibli's quest and its purpose. A voice approves.

Shibli is still perturbed by Noorna's situation, but is told that he cannot rescue her till he possesses the sword. He unknots one hair of Garaveen to subdue a lion, endures an ordeal of thrusting his right hand into a furnace, surrenders the Lily of Light to the brothers and grasps the sword, which has two live serpents on its hilt and expands or contracts at will. The brothers take the hairs and place them round the antelope's neck, pour the contents of the phial from Paravid down her throat, she eats the lily with the bulb-heart and is transformed into her true shape. Shibli is stunned, but she recalls him to Noorna. Gulravez summons the great bird Koorookh, and she, Shibli and her brothers mount its back. Shibli sees Noorna still on her pillar with Karaz in the form of a giant fish swimming round it. Shibli severs Noorna's chains with the sword, chops the fishy monster in two and Noorna runs up the blade towards him. She is attacked by various evil forces and these are in turn countered by Koorookh, Gulravez and the brothers. The scene vanishes as Koorookh flies away with Noorna and the others, leaving Shibli alone. He has a vision of Feshnavat being led to execution and of kings coming to adore Shagpat. Through self-mockery again, Shibli loses his crown.

Returning to the world with Abarak, he imprudently uses the sword to penetrate the secret of the veiled figure, Rubesqrat herself, losing his identity. Abarak restores him to Noorna, who heals him by dropping him from a height and nursing him on her breast. Signs and wonders accompany the movement of the sword across the earth. Subtler now, Shibli plans a mock attack on Shagpat through his uncle, Baba Mustapha. This is foiled by Karaz, disguised as a flea. Analogously, Noorna pretends consent to marriage with Shagpat. While Shagpat sleeps like a child and kings adore him, an epic fight in the sky ensues between Shibli and Karaz, Rubesqrat and Goorelka, in which Shibli is almost defeated, despite his possession of the sword. Rubesqurat multiplies Shagpat into many and Shibli's arm grows tired as he strikes at an army of phantoms. Then he realizes that the sword can divide thoughts no less than matter. Subtle again, he divides the first and second thoughts in Rubesqurat's mind so that she loses control of her own illusions and begins multiplying Shibli, losing for ever her power over the double-thoughted. Shibli identifies the true Shagpat and severs the Identical. Feshnavat is released; but Shibli, crowned king of the city, must wait for Noorna, who has been wounded in the battle. She returns and the dynasty of Bagarags endures for centuries, till after a cycle of years a new illusion enters history.

I have tried not to slant this summary too radically towards my own interpretation, though the reader may have suspicions about current jargon like 'identity'; but it is difficult to avoid its use in describing the veil of Rubesqurat episode. It will be apparent that Meredith calls on folk myth and literary archetypes; Goorelka's ring, for example, is Solomon's ring, which the hero normally takes from the daughter of Hell. Here Noorna acts the hero's part, though she doesn't take the ring directly. What is also suggested is the romantic use of public myth as a vehicle for the deeper self.

III

Shagpat as literary satire, I suggested, mocks Romantic and Christian transcendence; ultimately mocks its own pretensions as sacred book of the self. I think that the reader is also mocked and by Meredith's not unusual means of foiling expectation and off-hand technique. The reader worries over the 'tub' of the apparently antonomous narrative and the apparent 'digressions' of Bhanavar aud Khipil. It is even possible to take Meredith's later evasive and contradictory statements about *Shagpat* as loose analogue to the Author's Apology, Bookseller's Dedication and other Swiftian stratagems, though the more relevant comparison would be with the outsider, prophet, editor and literary artist who qualify one another in *Sartor*. Meredith's prefatory note to the 1855 edition insists on 'originality' in a sense that might invite a look beyond the obvious sense of 'not translated'. Subsequent attempts to make simple allegorical equations, he evaded; still later he pretended that he had 'forgotten' the meaning of Shagpat, Noorna and Shibli, and finally admitted that the book was symbolical rather than allegorical. Allegory would have presumed a world of stable values which could be re-expressed (as critics later did) in such equations as 'Noorna *is* duty' or 'Noorna *is* the just reason'. *Shagpat* works at the reader through the instability of words and the uneasy polarity of images. But if Meredith's tone when commenting on *Shagpat* remains teasing – one should take his restatements in *The Ode to the Comic Spirit* cautiously – it was also defensive. For the 'single-thoughted' Meredith's speaker in *Shagpat* appears in impersonal motley; for the 'double-thoughted' allegory is teasingly confused by his waverings about the book's nature. The book became predictably popular in the 1890s through the Stevenson cult,[1] and some could be content with the garment's mere exuberance. Edmund Gosse, at one stage of his career a Parnassian art-for-art's-sake critic, found *Shagpat* merely exotic and fantastic, all that Gautier might desire, coiling 'directly from some bottle of a genie', radiantly meaningless. *Shagpat* had itself some influence on the mock-Oriental genre. Its own tone can be defined by quick comparison backwards with *Vathek*, which modulates from dry light into the romantic Eblis episodes, while *Vathek* and Peacock are reflected in Richard Garnett's *Twilight of the Gods*, short stories published as an ensemble in 1888 with a subdued unity suggested by the title. We catch some rays of dry light in *Shagpat*, but Garnett's *en plein* Voltaire is absent. Meredith wishes to do more than set up a simple argument between romance and common sense.

His treatment of Shelley, however, is fairly discreet. The veering and iridescent prose recalls the Shelley of the sea, vehicle for apocalyptic paper boats, pantheistic death and the quest for love-in-death:

So they . . . came upon a purple sea, dark-blue overhead, with large stars leaning to the waves. There was a soft whisperingness in the breath of the breezes that swung there, and many sails of charmed ships were seen in momentary gleams, flapping the mast idly far away. Warm as new milk from the full udders were the waters of that sea, and figures of fair women stretched lengthwise with the current, and lifted a head as they rushed rolling by. Truly it was enchanted even to the very bed (124).[2]

The Shelleyan marine landscape is transformed by the raw pastoral of 'warm as new milk from the full udders' and a disturbing physicality brims through the final pun. Shibli is accompanying Goorelka on a quest which could destroy him.

Demonic sexuality loads the world of *Alastor*, proleptic of Goorelka's attempted seduction of Shibli:

> the shore was one of sand and shells, their wet cheeks sparkling in the moonlight; over it hung a promontory, a huge jut of black rock . . . the reflection of the moon opposite was as a wide nuptial sheet of silver in the waters (125).

Play with imagery, comic overlushness rebuked by the disconcertingly concrete, are common to both extracts. Another passage alludes to the dangerous amount of free boating available on Shelley's visionary seas:

> And while they swam sweetly, behold, there was seen a pearly shell of flashing crimson, amethyst, and emerald, that came scudding over the waves towards them, raised to the wind, fan-shaped, and in its front two silver seats (130).

A sea-shell made for two. But that particular ride was arranged by Rubesqurat for her own nasty motives.

When one comes to think of it, *Shagpat* was an odd book to emerge from the years 1853–5. Meredith's work had not prospered; his literary identity had been challenged by his wife and his father-in-law, T. L. Peacock. His social identity, linked with his literary identity, remained uncertain. What kind of writer was he to be? Was he to be a writer at all? *Shagpat* capitalizes on the pressures acting on his sense of role as artist and the limited possibilities, financial and historical, that offered themselves. In 1851 Meredith had published an unsuccessful volume of verse, Shelleyan in some of its naïve political gesturings and its personal dislocation of Greek mythos. The young poet's view of Nature was sentimental and subjective. The volume contains also the first version of 'Love in the Valley' which celebrates the Eden-world of Meredith's courtship of Mary Nichols.

If *Poems* (1851) was unsuccessful, the popularity of those followers of Keats and Shelley known as the 'Spasmodics' was most marked between 1851 and 1854. The Spasmodics represented supreme egoism in the poet and were constantly taking (like Shibli) the word for the act. Philip James Bailey's *Festus* (1839) was the first of these uneasy, ambitious poems and provides the model. The hero in the revise of 1845 is poet in quest of an active role in history. The favoured Spasmodic device is that of 'a poet talking about himself and the very poem in which he has his being'. The tactic had been anticipated in *Sartor Resartus*. Through the interplay of various 'masks' a new self is defined, though where Carlyle's definition involved the distancing of grotesque and humorous, the Spasmodics mostly managed the involuntary grotesque and never the intentionally humorous. The aim is unification of the self through myth-making.

Like its successors, the medium of Bailey's poem is blank verse, interspersed with songs that have little organic relevance. Meredith's pertinent, sententious doggerel in *Shagpat* looks back at Lane's translation of the *Arabian Nights*, but may well comment on Spasmodic lyricism. The first edition of *Festus* (a modern Faust pushing beyond good and evil imaginatively to comprehend the present) comprised something over 8,000 lines, while the second edition of 1845 was extended to near on 13,000, and all his life Bailey went on expanding and flattening, the victim of his own verbal Frankenstein. *Festus* indeed devoured most of his later poems. Like *Shagpat*, the scene-shifts are ambitious: Earth, Heaven, Hell, Another and a Better World. Festus has pallidly libertine dealings with various undifferentiated ladies: Angela, Clara, Marian, Helen and Elissa, Lucifer's mistress, who is seduced by Festus. In spite of this, the hero remains fundamentally alone, unable to communicate except (hopefully) with the audience. The creed in the first edition of *Festus* involves a vague universalism: a speaking part for the Third Person of the Trinity, but also for gods from other pantheons and everybody except Lucifer is saved (even Lucifer gets by in later editions). By refusing to use Ockham's razor on his myths, Bailey's myth-making becomes confused and the unifactory purpose is negatived.

Alexander Smith's *Life Drama* (1852) and Sydney Dobell's *Balder* (1853) are later examples of the Spasmodic genre (Meredith wrote a laudatory sonnet to Smith in 1851). Smith's hero, Walter, is a poet and Coleridgean comparisons are made between his creative activities and those of God. Once more there are digressions, a 'fitful' structure and a number of isolated, impressive lines and florid metaphors. A recent study of the Spasmodics isolates the contradiction in all their poems: the Spasmodics insist on the social function of their work, but their heroes withdraw from the post-1848 world into an extreme of subjectivity. Dobell's *Balder*, to be sure, was intended as the first part of a trilogy, but only that first part which presented 'an egotistic hero of isolation and doubt' was completed: Dobell's health and the Spasmodic vogue both collapsed. Like Smith's *Life Drama*, the setting of *Balder* was contemporary, though without any tang of the actual Victorian scene. To the years in which *Shagpat* was being composed belong the attacks on the Spasmodics, culminating in Arnold's withdrawal of *Empedocles on Etna* (the grounds suggest that it was too 'spasmodic' for comfort) and Aytoun's incisive parody, *Firmilian*, of 1854. Arnold had emphasized the concentration on isolated images at the expense of structural values as characteristic of this decayed Romanticism. Meredith's 'single-thoughted' and 'double-thoughted' may well refer to failure to control tenor and vehicle as well as to double-thoughtedness as a means of controlling the flux of experience.

Meredith's friend, Richard Henry Horne, had remarked of one of the Spasmodic heroes, 'Gerald leaves his home feeling a strong impulse to do *something* great in the world. Here at once we see the old sad error – a vague aspiration of ambition mistaken for an object and a power.' Horne's 'farthing epic', *Orion*, seems designed to rectify that error, but by a return to the romantic dislocation of Greek mythos. In his prefatory note to the Australian edition of *Orion* (1854), Horne claims that the three-part structure of his poem owes something to his friend, Dr Leonard Schmitz, an admirer of Hegel. The poem's purpose, Horne asserted, was:

> to present a type of the struggle of man with himself, i.e. the contest between the intellect and the senses, when powerful energies are equally balanced. Orion is man standing naked before Heaven and Destiny, resolved to work as a really free agent to the utmost pitch of his powers for the good of his race . . . innocently wise . . . a dreamer of noble dreams, and a hunter of grand shadows (in accordance with the ancient symbolic mythos), all tending to healthy thought, or to practical action and structure. He is the type of a Worker and a Builder for his fellow-men. He presents the picture . . . of a great and simple nature, struggling to develope all its loftiest energies – determined to be, and to do, to obtain knowledge, and to use it . . . seeking its own reward and happiness in the consciousness of a well-worked life, and the possession of a perfect sympathy enshrined in some lovely object.[3]

The three parts of the poem are dominated by three goddesses who, unlike the 'spasmodic' ladies, play dynamic roles: Artemis, Merope and Eos, Eos in function corresponding to Keats's Luna. Artemis, who appears earlier in Horne's narrative than in traditional myth, also offers a vision of the ideal, but union with her is impossible. Merope acts as *femme fatale*, while spiritual and physical are synthesized in Eos. Orion's history is an ordeal. Blinded by Artemis, his sight is restored by Eos and he is killed by Artemis's arrow. Finally, he is granted apotheosis by the King of Gods. Horne's structure may indeed reflect his friend Schmitz's Hegelian interests. In his first phase Orion is an amiable, unthinking giant, creature of innocent physicality. The vision of Artemis brings about alienation and self-contradiction: Artemis's beauty can only be contemplated, not enjoyed (her counterpart is Gulravez); Orion becomes a poet, but the beauty of mortal woman, the pure carnality of Merope, leads him to the poetry of action.

Orion is counterpointed by several fellow-giants, who act without the vision of ideal beauty and whose tyrannous giants' strength brings about their own destruction. Enoclyon represents Conservatism; while Akinetos, presented with mildly ironic humour as 'The Great Unmoved', is also contrasted with Orion. His fellow-giants acknowledge Akinetos's wisdom, but consistently ignore his advice. The Great Unmoved ends comically. His time is given to brooding in his womb-cave: living is *his* inner contradiction. The droppings from the cave finally resolve him into a stalagmite and he regresses beyond cellular life into mere geology. Fully aware of his crystalline metamorphosis, he consents to it and, finally, by the irony of historical development, subserves action, progress and Victorian engineering:

> Reclining lonely in his fixed repose,
> The Great Unmoved unconsciously became
> Attached to that he pressed – and gradually –
> While his thoughts drifted to no shore – a part
> Of the rock. There clung the dead excrescence, till
> Strong hands, descended from Orion, made
> Large roads, built markets, granaries and steep walls, –
> Squaring down rocks for use, and common good.[4]

And so – Carlyle. *Orion* concludes with a reconciliation between Artemis the ideal and Eos the practical future and, consequent on their joint pleas to Zeus, Orion is translated, like Adonais, into a stellar mnemonic.

Yet though *Orion* possesses a structure firmer than that of Spasmodic epics, it suffers from defects similar to those. Horne shares the neo-Shelleyan image of the poet as a higher being whose mere incarnation transforms actuality. And although Horne rejects quietism, *Orion* does not act so much as provide some vague stimulus to action. The ladies may be dynamic, but the only one who is earthly is the *femme fatale*: *Orion* involves a more adequate image of the woman-helper, but only as goddess. The relationship of *Shagpat* to *Orion*, if affectionate, remains parody.

The precise connections of *Orion* with German Idealism and of both with *Shagpat* is hard to determine. Fortunately, by the 1840s and 1850s Kant and his followers had been vulgarized (Morrell's account of German philosophy in 1846 included Hegel). *Orion*'s structure, certainly, seems to involve a rough blue-print of Hegelian dialectic: opposition, alienation, reconciliation and further opposition is perhaps implied. Myth is used to cover the temporary truths of mental structure, while *Orion*'s 'sameness' in Heaven seems to involve the notion that those temporary structures remain part of 'new truth', the extension of mental models to Nature and society being indicated by Orion's lines:

> a soul
> That to an absolute unadulterate truth
> Aspires, and would make active through the world.[5]

Horne's amateur Hegelianism is reflected in, for example, Noorna's inability to project a model of her world through Raveloke as parent or through Karaz, though as surrogate on the natural and magical levels of Gulravez, she represents the imagination that can redeem Nature, and lastly the social world through her initial transformation of Shibli. The same process is, as we shall see, at work in Shibli. The sword of Aklis, however, can only be wielded when its possession has been secured through self-knowledge, of one's necessary dependence on a model; through a comic sense of self-limitation it unites action and intelligence. One of the Identical's areas of meaning in *Shagpat* appears to be the Hegelian identity of subject-object knowing itself: '*Das Absolute ist das mit sich Identische*' (*Encyclopaedia of Philosophy*, para. 109). But Shibli as possessor of the Identical offers it up in Aklis, the deeper self: the identity of subject-object consists in love experienced through limitation. Karaz, as we shall see, represents project-making or 'work' as an end in itself; the Identical passes from his head to that of his opposite, Shagpat. There may be other glances at the Hegelian system (Meredith's German education might have ensured some encounter with the master's work). The inevitability of the 'Event' reflects some pressure from the 'Time-Prince' and when the sheep-like inhabitants of Shagpat's city misinterpret the flaming of the Identical there may be some allusion to the unconscious workings of the *Volksgeist*. They worship themselves in the Identical, not perceived as contradiction. Shibli's progress appears to involve the dialectical development of Reason in history 'with attendant self-consciousness, so that true unity is achieved. But does essence become existence at the moment of self-consciousness? Given the volatility of Shibli's world, essence of its very nature seems evanescent, so that Meredith leans towards Yeats's grand theme of aesthetic failure; romantic imagination's failure to restore a first unity, though Meredith's version comes to comic and ironic solution.

Meredith's idiom of fantasy allows him complete freedom for myth-making. Horne had been tied to Greek mythos to the degree that Zeus has to reject Artemis's and Eos's joint plea that Orion be restored to earth: the myth insists on apotheosis; the narrative cannot end with a concrete universal. Use of prose allows Meredith a medium more flexible than blank verse and formal lyric to suggest a more restless dialectic, a more sceptical attitude to commitment. It was from Carlyle that Meredith caught the model of a prose lyrical, capricious, preferred from an elaborately mystifying stance. In *Sartor*, Carlyle uses distancing as a double-edged weapon: as a buffer, assuming the role of alienated pseudo-realist as determined by his more blatant efforts towards commitment as a means of indicating breadth of commitment, a style of elaborative possibilities, which can provide the basis of a truly convincing expression for assessing the problem of selfhood. Style as buffer can encompass style as mimetic fullness, can include the possibility of its own failure, absorbing doubt just as the device of distancing absorbs the commitment problem. This is of the first importance in approaching the problem of tenor and vehicle in *Shagpat*. The two works are so closely related on every level that one can only select what seems important to Meredith's reading of *Sartor*. I would say that the broad but serious parody is of Carlyle's ambition to redeem the social world through the insight that worker no less than poet can create his private world through the symbol-making faculty, however he may be deceived by the symbolic functions of others. Carlyle's Teufelsdröckh – his name, 'devils-dung' indicating his doubleness, but never translated it becomes tetragrammatic – like Meredith's Shibli, passes through phases of negation, indifference and rebirth. Like Sartor, Shibli asserts self as the first source of value; like Sartor, Shibli discovers that analogical thinking is inadequate; nothing is symmetrically as it seems or should be: there is no mirroring relationship between man and Nature. Symbols, the geography of signs, are worshipped when their value has become extrinsic merely. The mind has come to rest in its own patterns, which have become obsessive, forgetting that philosophy is 'an ever-renewed attempt to *transcend* the sphere of blind Custom' (*Sartor*, viii). Men have forgotten the reality which Shagpat's beard was intended to stifle. The Identical is the symbol-making faculty itself, but 'incautious beards will get singed' – read Nelson for Drake – (*Sartor*, iii, v) as the Phoenix death-rebirth ritual is played out until Shagpat is shaved (Noorna, Shibli, Feshnavat all 'die' and are 'reborn'). But for Carlyle the symbols may die, but what symbols themselves symbolize persists: man cannot live by immanence alone. The empirical world may be debris, but every phenomenon has its noumenon – one that is more than a deeper self. As Albert Levally puts it, 'change is affirmed as the basic principle behind social forms, but any of the possibilities of meaningless flux, any of the dissolutions of self-identity, that such a philosophy might imply are quickly covered by an assertion of the transcendence of eternity upon which change must rest. . . . Carlyle begins by polarizing the two forces and ends up by fusing them.'[6] Transcendence in *Shagpat* is associated with Rubesqurat, illusion, gulf, refuge of the single-thoughted. The double-thoughted must learn creative doubt.

With Carlyle's equation of artist and worker, with Carlyle's relativism, the sacredness and final decay of symbols, and with Carlyle's sympathy for the worker as the slave of illusion (Abarak in *Shagpat*) Meredith could sympathize, but as soon as man loses his mercifully segmented vision he can no longer order and orient himself within an order. By the 1840s, Carlyle's transformation of the literary tradition of nature as symbol for the divine into a psychological tradition in which matter was 'the reflex of our own inward force' was distinctly less creditable. The action of *Shagpat* obviously parallels that of *Sartor* through Shibli's attempt to re-move an extrinsic symbol. The repetitive demon-empire into which

Shibli strays comments on Carlyle's remark that 'innumerable are the illusions and legerdemain of custom . . . cleverest is her knack of persuading us that the miraculous by simple repetition ceases to be miraculous' (*Sartor*, iii, viii). Meredith's fantasy acts out Carlyle's insight that each man creates his universe of signs, but that signs condition roles (the automatically locking throne and the grafted crown in Aklis.) For Carlyle prophecy remains the great requirement: the romantic historian's attempt to enact the history he prophesies, so Shibli's exalted rehearsals of what he will do and what he will become.

In *Sartor* Carlyle explores alienation in the self and loss of social and religious tradition. Alienation appears to be actually brought about by the failure of erotic transcendence: the Blumine episode, in which the relationship between Nature and man defines itself as asymmetrical. With that part of Carlyle's analysis Meredith might agree, but the Blumine episode is 'corrected' in *Shagpat*. Awareness of alienation involves awareness of division and multiplicity, and through the various roles of self and their critical reaction a new self is gradually defined. Levally observes that in *Sartor* a novel type of self-questioning literature emerges as a consequence of Carlyle's conquest of alienation and of the constant pressure to unity through myth-making. The apocalyptic war with the procession of Shagpat's which immediately precedes 'the Event' is followed by a faltering Rubesqrat's multiplication of Shibli's, but this renders him invulnerable, accentuating his awareness of self until there is total definition through completion of 'the Event'; Shibli had himself rehearsed Rubesqrat's trick when he shook twenty drops from the well of Paravid which became twenty rocky voices. The multiplication of selves glances at the romantic topos of self-definition or destruction through the 'dark brother', the *Doppelgänger* (related to the imagery of mirrors in *Shagpat*). By projecting a procession of phantom selves, as by setting up the feint of Baba Mustapha's attempt on Shagpat, Shibli possesses and controls a plural world. It is the opposite of *Sartor's* world of 'natural supernaturalism', where spirit continuously eliminates matter.

The recurrence of such terms as 'Identical', 'Event', 'Single-thoughted' and 'Double-thoughted' applies Carlyle's notion that words dislocate old perceptions by absorbing and refracting new meanings. The 'Event' corresponds to Carlyle's 'Open Secret', finding true identity through role – an active role, since Shibli shears rather than receives the Identical. Before its separation from Shagpat, the 'Identical' accretes several meanings. The Hegelian has been glanced at. Criticism has also suggested that it alludes to the single hair by which the Muslim believer is at death lifted into Paradise or that it represents the soul-object with roots in the totemic tribe. When Noorna as talking hawk rescues Shibli from drowning, we are told that she takes the Identical in her beak. *The Golden Bough* provides an anthology of hair taboo, the notion of hair as representing the external soul of a sacred person being peculiarly relevant, (The tale that runs closest to *Shagpat* is that of King Nisus. His city was sacked and his life ended when his daughter Scylla, for love of his enemy, Minos, cut the single purple or golden hair in the middle of her father's head. In one version, Scylla is drowned. While she clings to the stern of Minos' boat, Nisus' soul in the form of a sea-eagle terrifies her into losing her hold.) Another relevant source has been found in the fifteenth canto of the *Orlando Furioso,* where a single hair makes Orillo, fruit of a hobgoblin and a fay, indissolvable. His head is finally shaved in the Gordian mode by Astolpho. The *Orlando* is the last of the texts with which *Shagpat* significantly confers.

English admiration for Italian poetry, particularly romance and mock-epic, was at its most acute in the first thirty years of the nineteenth century, and resulted in a number of admirable imitations, Frere's *Monks and Giants*, Tennant's *Anster Fair*, *Beppo*. After 1830 the vogue declined, but Meredith, with his mildly eccentric education, confirms the rough law for dating buildings: 'add thirty years for the provinces'. In a letter of 1850 he alludes to the *Orlando* and uses Ariosto's Hippogriff in *Sandra Belloni* as emblem of the sentimentalist, Wilfred Pole, who 'goes on accumulating images and living sensations till such time (if the stuff be in him) they assume a form of vitality and hurry him head-long. This is not passion, though it amazes men, and does the madder thing.' Koorookh is clearly a version of Ariosto's Hippo-griff, but his comically positive role is established by further association with Carlyle's Phoenix.

The distinct parallels between *Orlando* and *Shagpat* move beyond the shared idiom of romance. In Ariosto[7] as in Meredith, it is the women who are superior in energy and sacrifice; male heroism remains external; women play both male and female roles. The heroes, excepting a victim such as Zerbino or the savage Rodomante, are void of will. Orlando even leads a charmed life, which diminishes his moral intensity and renders personal bravery irrelevant. Ruggiero actually realizes the absurdity of infallible arms and deliberately hides away an enchanted shield. Of Ariosto's women, Angelica, the image of obsession who distracts both Christian and Pagan knights from the serious acts of war, changes her role from Mother Goddess to timid girl to flirt to Fatal Woman as she is constantly pursued through the woods of error. Isabella and Drusilla meet death with a courage that has tragic force. Marfisa, a fine example of the 'virago *intacta*', and Bradamante are the equal of the male paladins in battle and Bradamente unites female self-sacrifice with male energy and seems aware that the object of her love is light-minded. As Noorna saves Shibli, so Bradamante saves Ruggiero by her constancy. Rose, in the notes to his 1830 translation of the *Orlando*, had related that to the *Arabian Nights*, associating Labe with Circe and those sumptuous Circes of the Renaissance: Trissino's Acratia, Tasso's Armida and Ariosto's Alcina. The female enchantresses dominate in the *Orlando* as in *Shagpat*: Melissa's subtlety in white magic is superior to the male Atlante's, just as Karaz is continuously outwitted by Noorna till he is reinforced by Rubesqurat.

It is, however, the *Orlando*'s world of painful metamorphosis, of peripety and the obsessive quest to reduce the intense pointless play of plural life to unity that remains most relevant. The 'openness' of the first twenty-nine odd cantos, so severely qualifying the closed end, realizes a means of responding to life rarely attained, beyond either double- or single-thoughted. Ariosto's world is presented through modal discords that do not destroy the validity of the comic, pathetic and heroic elements he juxtaposes, while the veering between several narrative lines aids in establishing the fragmentariness of human perception. That of the *Orlando*, as those of *Shagpat* and *Sartor*, is a restless world. In *Shagpat* this disconcerting instability of words and objects represents itself in terms of incessant flickers of jewels and fountains; of light and fire (as in *Sartor*), whether the light half-stifled by Noorna's ensorcelment, the beam that strikes from the eye of Aklis or that fiery circuit of serpents that environs Bhanavar in her dancing. Criticism has also observed the continuous use in *Shagpat* of words expressing the revolt of objects, as in a child's world, the shift from human to animal and vice versa. Light or hills 'slant'; there is the 'branching wind of a way round a mountain slant', eyes are 'acid' or 'rapid'; there is 'a dust of Arabs', 'the beginning slope of

Bhanavar's bosom', a room that 'swam like an undulating sea of shifting sapphire', snake-eyes are 'discoloured blisters of venom', spears 'gloomed like locusts', a shell closes, 'writing darkness on their very eyeballs'. Things are disposed asymmetrically and frequent present participles insist on volatility.

IV

Shagpat is also autobiographical fantasia, but with none of the raw touches of *Feverel* and 'Modern Love'. And it is escapist only as a revenge of style. *The Arabian Nights* were among Meredith's favoured early reading and we gather that he composed 'Arabic' romances in his head as a means of abolishing the church services he was forced in his youth to attend, though romance and lessons fuse in *Shagpat's* style. 'Bhanavar the Beautiful', conceived as autonomous, was probably the first part written of *Shagpat*, and in its limited tragic mode (just at the story of Khipil suggests a limited comic mode), comments on a naïver Meredith no less than on romantic commonplaces in general, as well as provoking the modal discords.

But the composition of *Shagpat* can barely be viewed as reversion to a simpler idyllic world of pure romance, for what had Meredith to return to? His mother he had lost early, and he was to see little of his father after the age of eleven. Virtually, like his own Shibli, he was an orphan, and the marriage to Mary owes something at least to the wish for orientation within a family (they had met through Meredith's friend, Mary's brother). Mary and George published together in a manuscript magazine, antiphonally if not in competition. From Meredith's poem 'Marian', it seems that Mary offered many roles: comrade, intellectual equal and rival, mother, even the male. The fling with Wallis was to represent the desperate attempt of an ageing woman to find a new self. And just as Mary appeared several-faced, so the several women of *Shagpat* are one woman, responding to the male image of them. In her epiphany as woman, Gulravez, sharing a sacrificial role with Noorna (associated through her sea-role with the Uranian Venus) remains asexual, a beauty like that of Yeats's first and fifteenth phase that resists the imagination's hunger, since it is the Image itself. Noorna, 'sorceress ensorcelled' as she herself terms it, is not what she is – old and ugly – but 'as she will be', passing through phases of wise woman, maiden and nymph in proportion to Gulravez's epiphanizing. This is polarized with Shagpat's unspoken 'I am what I am'. Fictions of self-esteem are necessary to preserve identity: the perfect egoist lives in a world of absolute: 'Great I am, I worship me.' Shibli Bagarag is the imperfect egoist in his prefiguration of Meredith's numerous knight-errants tested by ordeals: the low-born alien who achieves the high-born lady and becomes a king.

Noorna herself has suffered a loss of identity and must be redefined to herself through the act of faith in Shibli's kiss and by his future acts. The paradox is that by restoration to her true shape she becomes more vulnerable (expectantly dependent now on Shibli's fitful will where the will of Goorelka had been firm.) Only by that vulnerability can Shibli be presumed to grow stronger, though his illusions about himself persist almost to the end. At the entrance to the book, he has left the ease and gossip of Shiraz and wanders, honoured sometimes, sometimes reviled, from city to city. By the time he arrives at the city of Shagpat he has earned the second part of his name, 'Bagarag'. Barbercraft is no longer art; it is now economic necessity (ironically, Carlyle's 'mechanism'). Shibli is an orphan, at the point of entire alienation when he is first promised honour in the city, but subsequently rejected with thwackings, so that his meaning for himself *qua* barber is denied. His quest is for another identity which still includes the old: barber, rhetor, redefined through and with Noorna. Noorna's acts up to a point parallel those of Mary: emblematically an old woman, her roles involve those of wise woman and mother, and she gives Shibli a family when she introduces him to her father, Feshnavat the Vizier, as prospective son-in-law.

The mean between Noorna, Rubesqurat and Goorelka is represented by that Bhanavar the Beautiful of Shibli's digression. Unsuspectingly, Shibli confirms the parallelism and divergence between Bhanavar and Noorna when he observes that 'the aspect of this old woman would realize the story of Bhanavar the Beautiful', the ironic reservation being that Shibli's kiss seems unlikely to restore the old woman's youth and beauty as the sacrifice of her lovers to the serpent guardians of the jewel restored Bhanavar's.

The Bhanavar story begins with her sharing an Eden world of innocent sensuality with her first lover. She compels him to steal the jewel of the Serpent Queen. He does so, but dies of the Queen's venom. Bhanavar mourns, but falls in love with her own magnified

c*

beauty when she wears the jewel, a beauty of surface, corresponding with the Identical in the main narrative. Accentuating that beauty, the jewel makes it dependent on the snake-spirits who inhabit the stone and periodically demand a sacrifice if Bhanavar is not to revert to an ugliness brought about precisely by the magnification of her beauty. Bhanavar falls in love with a young man, Almeryl, and sells the jewel to support both of them, but without the jewel both she and her lover become vulnerable. After a period of private happiness, her lover is captured and killed by a treacherous Vizier. Bhanavar agrees to become the King's concubine, though she refuses the King's rights, and plots revenge on the Vizier. She now falls in love with one of the warriors who had briefly captured her before, but whose mother had used stratagems to save him from the force of Bhanavar's beauty. Love again makes Bhanavar vulnerable; the serpents demand her new beloved as sacrifice instead of the King, who had derided her for her temporary loss of beauty. She refuses the sacrifice; both she and her lover are executed, but her original beauty, untainted by magic, is restored to her by death (the severed head, another romantic commonplace, announced already by that of Almeryl).

The minor relation to the main plot is borne by imagery of jewels, mirrors, pillars and serpents: Rubesqrat's wooing of Shibli, for example, is comically described in terms of touches 'as little snakes twisting and darting up, biting poison bites of irritating blissfulness'. For a moment we seem to wander in the world of 'Faustine' and 'Dolores'. Imagery is duplicated, but reversed in the retractable live snakes on the hilt of the Sword of Aklis, emblems there of proper wisdom, and in the Salomonic serpentine volutes of the Identical. Noorna explicitly dissociates her own quest for the return of her beauty, her true identity, from Bhanavar's pursuit of a false beauty, which more resembles that of Goorelka and Rubesqrat. But the larger relation is thematic: the struggle of women against identity being forced on them by men, particularly by so constricting a role as that of Fatal Woman.

The Bhanavar story acts as hinge of the diffused satire on romanticism. Bhanavar's initial acceptance of the Fatal Woman role, of her lover's subjection to her, leads to imprisonment in that role and hatred of her own body because its beauty is imposed, yet without that imposed beauty she turns to a despised, wrinkled old woman, 'her living youth and beauty' having been sacrificed to the serpents, demands vicarious sacrifice to be restored. She attempts to escape pursuit and the subjection of men by humbling herself to Almeryl in a quiet domestic life, but to secure that needs to sell the jewel, and ironically this makes her beauty public and brings about Almeryl's death, so confirming her Fatal Woman role. Even in her relationship with Almeryl, she is constricted by his worship of her beauty. The danger of that beauty is proclaimed by the imagery that accompanies it and Almeryl particularly voices that. She is 'a martial queen', 'a danger and dolour is thy wending', Swinburnian alliteration, rhythms of mania; she 'levels' her eyelids at one of her victims and 'her lustrous black eyelashes [are] as arrows'. Ruark, one of her lovers, 'would have veiled his sight from her'. It is the language of a love religion, Petrarchanism (associated in *Sartor* with Wertherism) which deifies woman as visible emblem of the divine. The connection is confirmed by Almeryl's recourse to the *Song of Songs*. Bhanavar is 'terrible as an army with banners' masochism confirming narcissism; the man and the woman have changed roles; Bhanavar's jewels confirm that she has become a work of art, she is not 'available to the living'. Almeryl recognizes this immediately before he is betrayed and huddled away to his death. The culminating imagery associated with Bhanavar is catachrestical: she is 'lustrous and dark', 'dark lightning', 'a fountain of fire', resuming the paradox of the Fatal Woman, the attempt to reconcile antinomies: beauty-terror, orgasm-death, knowledge-mystery.[8] It is one of the most familiar of romantic clichés: Shelley's 'tempestuous loveliness of terror', platonized again by Rossetti and making a splendidly apt curtain call in Yeats's 'terrible beauty' of a sacrificial Easter. That the Pre-Raphaelites should specially admire the Bhanavar story was predictable: Frederic Sandys did a popular illustration of her serpent dance. Besides connecting obviously with the romantic emblem of the artist's alienation (Keats's Lamia) the tale glances also at Mary, whose first husband had drowned tragically and whose second struggled against her to define a new self. (Shibli's near infidelities may also glance at Meredith's flirtations, which Sencourt tells us gave his wife cause for her jealousy; but some accounts lean towards Mary's continuing interest in other men.) Shibli in fantasizing to sustain identity is continuously mis-seeing Noorna, as Goorelka, as Rubesqurat, even as Gulravez. The scenes with the Circe figures anticipate Richard's engagement with Bella Mount in *Feverel*: Richard successively sees Bella as 'fallen' and then as 'fatal' woman before the reader grasps her as banal (her rather dainty butch role as Sir Julius still substantiates the 'fatal' woman image). The narrator empathizes with Richard in the account of his seduction, which could have taken place in Goorelka's cave or Rubesqrat's palace, with its allusions to 'sorcery in her breath, sorcery in her hair: the ends of it stung him like little snakes . . . Those witch underlids were working brightly.'

Shibli recounts his lugubrious parable to Noorna and her father, the Vizier (we recall that the Vizier in the Bhanavar story was a villain). The Vizier (Peacock) responds with his derisive parable of Khipil the builder, who tells tall stories and neglects the completion of the King's palace. The King punishes Khipil by pretending that the palace *has* been built and forces the idle builder into a set of indignities, which include the anal joke of squatting for some hours on an imaginary chair. Perhaps Peacock thought Meredith had better leave off high talk and take a stool at the East India Office, as he had himself done, to provide for wife, son and stepdaughter. Just now Peacock was doing the providing. The physical sufferings of Khipil look back at Shibli's thwackings, partly instigated by Noorna's father to protect himself. The juxtaposition of the Bhanavar and Khipil episodes also reflects the satiric method of Peacock: the confrontation of extremes. Shibli's tale of Roomdroom the Barber and Feshnavat's account of events in the city of Shagpat while Noorna and Shibli have been absent on their quest were both omitted in later editions. The omissions tend to economy; but also accentuate the two 'digressions' as modal discords. Feshnavat's later sufferings to the point almost of being executed are an amusing example of Freud's definition of art as the imaginary justification of unconscious wishes.

That the enchantresses melt into one another may be illustrated by Noorna's attempt to evade her promise to marry the genie Karaz, possessor of the Identical. Noorna's seduction of Karaz is reminiscent of Goorelka's and Rubesqrat's wiles and of the Danite harlot from whom Samson rather less energetically rose than does Karaz. The parallelism in *Shagpat* is incessant; Rubesqrat, for example, assumes the role of high-born maiden, doubling that of Noorna, though the memory of Shibli's thwackings finally preserves him.

If *Shagpat* moves between the topics of meaning in plurality and identity, illusion and awareness of illusion, we might expect this to be reflected in Meredith's use of names. He describes *Shagpat* as an 'Arabian' tale, one of free fantasy, but its action appears to be set broadly in Persia, while the principal names are both Persian and Arabic. It would be difficult to show that Meredith had access to a polyglot dictionary comprising Arabic and Persian with transliterations and translations into English. However, the names seem significant. If we bear in mind that English has literal resources not available to the Oriental tongues, with a little twisting and turning of letters and change of vowel positions the principal names will cede significant meanings. The normal bother about interpreting words in Arabic, that each one has two opposite meanings, a third meaning that is obscene and a fourth that has something to do with a camel, need be no embarrassment here. Shibli is a name without meaning in Persian, but in Arabic as *Shibli* it signifies 'young lion' and Shibli's journey is between the ass of folly and the lion of true kingship. Bagarag can (somewhat arbitrarily) be transliterated from *begirad*, the subjunctive of the verb to 'seize' or 'take'. 'Noorna' splits into *noor* both in Arabic and Persian, 'light' 'ray' or 'beam', though *nabin* in Persian is the imperative of 'do not see', which makes a nonsense unless it suggests that Noorna should exercise some suspension of judgment about Shibli, or alludes to her disguise of age. Karaz in the Persian bifurcates into *kar*, 'work' or 'business dealings', while *az* means 'from' while *raz* represents 'secret' or 'cherished desire'. His name becomes his restlessness and glances at Carlyle and the Victorian gospel of action. Karaz is the opposite of Khipil, which, if pronounced 'Khepel', would mean 'short', somewhat derogatory slang for a short person. 'Aklis' might conceivably be derived from *aghl*, Persian for 'brain' or 'intelligence', while 'Koorookh' breaks down into *kooruk*, Turkish for 'established' or 'settled', *koo*, Persian for 'where', and *rokh*, which in both Persian and Turkish means a 'face' or 'cheek'. If we ignore the possibility that the second syllable may be related to the roc, the name would seem to mean 'without face' 'faceless' or 'where is the face?', as sinister as the suffix for Goorelka, 'grave' or 'tomb', the pursuit of the Fatal Woman is the pursuit of death (Swinburne's *Laus Veneris* puts that explicitly). The game can be prolonged with the other names.

Shibli's progress is a comic version of the anguish between a first and second identity, between the claiming and acquisition of a name. He reverts to childhood when he refuses to dismount from the wild horse Garaveen, and his attempts at rebirth are associated with water, which in a traditional manner dissolves and recreates.

On the journey to Oolb Shibli plunges into the water from the burning ship:

> the great walls of water crumbled over him; strength failed him, and his memory ceased to picture images of the old time . . . (117).

Shibli dives to the bottom of the well of truth, Paravid, and discovers that what appears in a world of illusion to be the bottom is in fact the surface. It is presented as a journey of self-discovery:

> I . . . plunged, and the depth of that well seemed to me the very depth of the earth itself, so went I ever downward; and when I was near the bottom of the well I had forgotten life above, and lo! no sooner had I touched the bottom of the well when my head emerged from the surface . . . . But for a sign that I touched the bottom of the well, see, O Noorna bin Noorka, the Jewel, the one of myriads that glitter at the bottom, and I plucked it for a gift to thee.
>
> So Noorna took the Jewel from his hand that was torn and crimson, and she cried, 'Thou fair youth, thou bleedest with the plucking of it, and it was written, no hand shall pluck a jewel at the bottom of that well without letting of blood (107–8).

This episode glances back to the beginning of the Bhanavar story: Bhanavar persuades her first lover to steal the jewel, and when he returns with it, dying, she sees 'a small bite on the arm . . . spotted with seven spots of blood in a crescent'. Jewel and water are associated through an image of a 'melted' jewel; the serpent's jewel is reflected in lake water and the death of Bhanavar's first lover is associated with water imagery. It is by water that Shibli leaves Aklis, after having foolishly pierced the veil of the Ferrying Figure, who represents meaninglessness. Once again he plunges in to find that the bottom is in fact the surface, but this time his case is different:

> He, whose wits were in past occurrences, imagined that his enemy and the foe of Noorna split in two, crying 'How? Is Karaz a couple? and do I multiply him with strokes of the Sword' (192).

This looks forward to the final multiplication, not of Karaz by Shibli, but first of Shagpat and then of Shibli by Rubesqrat.

Name and identity recur in the scene where Noorna, awaiting Shibli's return from Aklis, attempts to teach the great bird Koorookh 'words of our language':

> and the bird fashioned its bill to the pronouncing of names, such as 'Noorna', and 'Feshnavat', and 'Goorelka'; and it said 'Karaz', and stuck not at the name 'Shagpat', and it learnt to say even 'Shagpat shall be shaved! Shagpat shall be shaved!' but no effort of Noorna could teach it to say, 'Shibli Bagarag', the bird calling instead, 'Shiparack, Shiplabrack, Shibolisharack'. And Noorna chid with her fore-finger, crying, 'O Koorookh! wilt thou speak all names but that one of my betrothed?' (193).

The bird's attempts wander from disaster 'shipwreck' to gibberish, and the word finally lengthens itself still more remotely from Shibli's true name:

> And the bird answered, imitating its best 'Shibberacaverack' (193).

The bird's inability to identify Shibli warns Noorna that Shibli 'bore now a name that might be uttered by none', a kind of Tetragrammaton that if uttered would undo creation. She recalls the mock-hero to rebirth and project-making, partly through the healing nearness of woman's flesh, but primarily through making Shibli undergo mock-deaths by being thrown from Koorookh's back in mid-air and then caught by the bird close to the ground. Finally, Shibli is doused not in any absolute, but in cold water; the allusion here is to the Dark Night of the Soul and forms part of the parody of Christian dogma that intensifies as the book arrives at its climax.[9] Throughout *Shagpat* examples of parallelism, anticipation and echo have been noted. In one sense they suggest a forward movement towards the great event, the disincarnation of the Identical. In another, they lend a final shape to the Biblical parody. *The Shaving of Shagpat* becomes a sacred book, interpretable in an indefinite number of ways forwards and backwards. As the book crowds to its climax, the Biblical allusions multiply. Noorna has assumed the Madonna role, cradling her betrothed when she sights Shibli and Abarak appearing in the water-cave after their escape from Aklis:

> that burden on her bosom; and it was Shibli Bagarag, her

betrothed, his eyes closed, his whole countenance colourless . . . (196).

This image is repeated when Rubesqrat cradles Shagpat to protect him from the strokes of the Sword of Aklis.[10] We move through a parody of Epiphany – like a sleeping child Shagpat is presented to the four foolish Kings – to allusions to the Book of Revelation, with Shibli riding Koorookh as though he were mounted on the white Horse of the Second Coming while Rubesqrat sours the sky like the star Wormwood, combining now her *pietà* role with that of Fatal Woman:

> But now was the hour struck when Rubesqrat could be held no longer serving the ferry in Aklis; and the terrible Queen streamed in the sky, like a red disastrous comet, and dived, eagle-like, into the depths, re-ascending with Shagpat in her arms cherishing him; and lo, there were suddenly a thousand Shagpats multiplied about, and the hand of Shibli Bagarag became exhausted with hewing at them. The scornful laugh of the Queen was heard throughout earth as she triumphed over Shibli Bagarag with hundreds of Shagpats, Illusions . . . (241).

And when this hazard is overcome, metamorphosis continues:

> the Genie Karaz re-ascended in the shape of a vulture with a fire-beak, pecking at the eyes of him that wielded the Sword, so that he was bewildered and shook this way and that over the neck of Koorookh, striking wildly, languidly cleaving towers and palaces, and monuments of earth underneath him. Now, Shibli Bagarag discerned his danger, and considered 'The power of the Sword is to sever brains and thoughts' . . . So he whirled Koorookh thrice in the crimson smoke of the atmosphere, and put the blade between the first and second thought in the head of Rubesqrat whereby . . . she used her powers as the fool does, equally against all, for the sake of mischief solely – no longer Mistress of her own illusions; and she began doubling and trebling Shibli Bagarag on the neck of monstrous birds, speeding in draggled flightiness from one point of the sky to another. Even in the terror of the combat, Shibli Bagarag was fain to burst into a fit of violent laughter at the sight of the Queen wagging her neck loosely, perking it like a mad raven . . . (241–2).

The mode is one of anti-climax, already associated with Rubesqurat. Fertile in illusion, she readily falls victim to her own capacities, as when she makes herself drunk while attempting to seduce Shibli. (Overplus as anticlimax is used in imagery, in the description, for example, of the nubiles whose serpentine dances dazzle the hero in Hell.) Rubesqrat, like the Devil, cannot create; she can only mar. The issue after Noorna and Goorelka have joined in the cosmic combat is one final, anticlimactic sentence: 'Day was on the baldness of Shagpat.' Mirrors, lamps, jewels, pillars, moon, caves, have decayed. Shagpat is seen face to face: the Apocalypse is ended.

The imagery of Shagpat is schematic, polar. Bhanavar's first lover at the point of his death turns into a pillar of memory while Noorna is dragged by Abarak into the 'seventh' pillar, crying out to Shibli, 'Remember'. The reversals of the jewel imagery have been noticed. There is probably a similar reversal as we pass from Garaveen to Koorookh. Man on the Great Horse is a familiar Renaissance icon of control (Castiglione, Sidney, Lord Herbert of Cherbury): man controls the beasts by reason and by art, a claim prematurely made by Shibli (though his promised fate in terms of art recalls Bellerophon on Perseus). Because of this premature assumption of the male role, Noorna is forced to part from Shibli, she can only protect him now in the disguise of the double-thoughted. Bhanavar's mirror, which confirms illusion, contrasts with Shibli's, which dissolves it. Karaz' futile busyness is polarized by Shibli's listless kingly role while he waits for Noorna's return from Aklis (a glance too at Carlyle's view of work as narcotic). The images are held together within the distanced narrative – so distanced that it absorbs its own absurdity of fullness, absorbs both selfhood and commitment. The mirrors reflect, distort, shiver, elide, reverse. Who can tell image from actuality? The reader, like Shibli, dives for the bottom of the well of truth and finds that the bottom is the surface.

Notes

1 Stevenson uses the Oriental Chinese-box technique with a mathematical frivolity. With Arthur Machen's *Three Imposters* of 1895, we enter a sickly demonic world which illustrates the popularity of

Shagpat with the writers of the 'decadence' – a further illustration would be Lafcadio Hearn's essay. Machen's tales of that period generally suggest a Manichaean horror, a far from cheery reading of Rubesqurat.

2 My edition is that of 1898.

3 *Orion, an Epic Poem*, Melbourne, 1854. I take this text from the 9th ed., 1872, iv-vi, which faintly elaborates that of 1854. Horne mentions that the young Meredith sent him an interpretation of the design and character of *Orion*: 'I am ashamed to say that I cannot recollect [his] words, or they would have stood in the place of mine', *Orion*, 1872, vi, i.

4 Ibid., 145.

5 Ibid., 157.

6 *Carlyle and the Idea of the Modern*, New Haven and London, 1968, 62. Morse Peckham's remarks on Carlyle in *Beyond the Tragic Vision*, New York, 1962, 177–86, have proved suggestive.

7 I have found T. Greene, *The Descent from Heaven, a Study in Epic Continuity*, New Haven and London, 1963, and D. S. Carne-Ross, 'The One and the Many', *Arion*, v, 2, Summer, 1966, 195–234, helpful in clarifying my notions about the *Orlando Furioso*.

8 That the *topos* of the Fatal Woman precedes Romanticism is shown in Merritt Hughes, 'Spenser's Acrasia and the Renaissance Circe', *Journal of the History of Ideas*, 1943, 382–94.

9 In this parody, Meredith could be drawing on dim awareness of the theme of sacred rapture, *mors osculi*, associated with birds of the air, Ganymede's eagle or Leda's swan. The iconography is discussed in E. Wind, *Pagan Mysteries of the Renaissance*, 2nd rev. ed., 1967, 152–70.

10 Eos figures in a *pietà* scene:

> Haggard and chill as a lost ghost, the Morn,
> With hair unbraided and unsandalled feet, –
> Her colourless robe like a poor wandering smoke, –
> Moved feebly up the heavens, and in her arms
> A shadowy burden heavily bore. . . .
>
> *Orion*, 1872, 138.

Abarak appears in this sequence as the Baptist figure, heralding revolution or Armageddon.

The Ordeal of Richard Feverel: A Sentimental Education

Juliet Mitchell

I

> ... It is so crystalline and brilliant in its principal passages, there is such purity mingled with its laxness, such sound and firm truth in the midst of its fantastic subtleties, that we hesitate whether to approve or condemn; and we have a difficulty even in forming a judgment on such strange contrarieties.
>
> *The Times*, 14.10.59.

The Times finally affirmed the purity of *Richard Feverel*; Mudie's Library banned it on account of its immorality. Bewilderment and misunderstanding were yet more rampant than prudery. The novel is a medley of romantic interludes, prosaic detail, burlesque, melodrama, pathos, fantasy, realism – everything except the naturalism which Meredith deplored. With hindsight, it has now been heralded as the first modern novel and earned for Meredith a reputation as the first highbrow novelist. Despite ingenious critical rationalization, the novel in its original, unedited form[1] remains intrinsically perplexing.

Sir Austin Feverel, of Raynham Abbey in the Thames Valley, is author of a book of aphorisms, 'The Pilgrim's Scrip', and of a system for educating boys into unsullied manhood. Both book and system are mainly directed against the corrupting influence of women. A realistic appraisal of the rotten state of society and in particular of women within it, if applied and rejected scientifically in education, could produce an ideal man and therefore an ideal society. Basing his Utopianism on this misanthropic premise, Sir

Austin brings up his son Richard accordingly. The novel is the story of Richard's life. But Sir Austin's apparently objective theory is the result of a traumatic experience. His wife ran off with his best friend and dependant, the poet Diaper Sandoe, leaving him nothing but the baby Richard.

Richard grows up at the Abbey surrounded by the Feverel family of dependants: his Uncle Hippias, dyspeptic glutton; his aunt, Mrs Doria Forey, and her daughter, Clare; his cousin and tutor, the epicurean Adrian Harley ('The Wise Youth'), a man as hard and cynical as Sir Austin claims to be (in an early draft he edited Sir Austin's 'Pilgrim's Scrip' – without this detail the relationship between the two is still retained in the novel). Also in residence is Richard's Great Aunt Grantly, nicknamed 'The Eighteenth Century', wealthy and a gourmet. Frequent visitors are his Uncle Algernon, who in the course of the story loses a leg and takes to drink to help his balance; and his cousin, Austin Wentworth, who was seduced by, married and is separated from his mother's housemaid, a man of kindness and integrity, a Republican, a philanthropist. For a period of his boyhood (and later in adult life) Richard has a companion in Ripton Thompson, son of his father's solicitor, and he finds a competitor in the Etonian youth, Ralph Norton of the neighbouring Poer Hall. He has an 'adoptive' mother in his father's friend and admirer, their widow neighbour, Lady Blandish. The custodian of the whole system is the butler, 'Heavy' Benson, a vengeful misogynist deserted by his wife.

The Feverel family are supposed to be pursued by a malign fate ('Mrs. Malediction'), the enduring of which constitutes their 'Ordeal'. Sir Austin only came to believe this superstition when his wife deserted him and he suffered an 'Ordeal'. On his seventh birthday Richard, in a hypnagogic state, sees a lady at his bedside. This 'Mrs. Malediction' turns out to be his mother, but that it is a bad omen is confirmed by the fact that Uncle Algernon loses his leg in a game of cricket that day.

After his wife's desertion, Sir Austin retreated from his noble prodigality into austerity, the only festive occasions at the Abbey being Richard's birthdays. On his fourteenth birthday, when his healthy flesh is beginning to feel the chains of the 'system', Richard, refusing to submit to medical examination, goes pheasant-shooting with Ripton Thompson. They are whipped by Farmer Blaize for poaching on his land; and in vengeance Richard bribes an unemployed labourer, Tom Bakewell, to set fire, with his aid, to the farmer's ricks. Bakewell is caught and imprisoned. After much manœuvring, bribery and confessions, Bakewell is released and employed as Richard's attendant. Richard has confessed all, and father and son are reconciled; the system triumphs.

In adolescence Richard takes to poetry, but his father manages to make him burn his poems. This repressive act ends the true confidence between them. This is the 'Magnetic Age' and all notion of love must be kept from Richard. His cousin Clare, intended by her mother as Richard's wife, is, unbeknownst to all, deeply in love with him. She is removed from Raynham. Benson controls the flirtatious activities of the housemaids. Sir Austin, however, is seen by Richard kissing Lady Blandish's hand. This opens his eyes. Perturbed, his father leaves Raynham in search of a young uncorrupted Eve, future bride for Richard. Meanwhile, Ralph Norton reveals to Richard that he is in love with Clare; immediately after this Richard sees Lucy Desborough, orphan niece of Farmer Blaize. It is love at first sight. Their love is spied on by Heavy Benson, who writes warning Sir Austin. Sir Austin summons Richard to him in London, retains him there while it is arranged that Lucy be sent back to the convent where she was educated. Sir Austin and Richard return to Raynham. Richard finds Lucy gone, and on the night of his birthday sets out to pursue her, but is taken desperately ill.

On recovery Richard seems to have forgotten his love. Once more the system triumphs. But in spring, on arriving with his Uncle Hippias in London, Richard discovers Lucy is temporarily there. His love revived, he meets her, installs her in lodgings with a Mrs Berry and marries her. At the church he finds he has lost the wedding-ring and has to take that of Mrs Berry. Lucy and Richard leave to honeymoon in the Isle of Wight. The Feverel family discover the marriage and Mrs Berry turns out to be a housemaid whom Sir Austin dismissed for witnessing him in tears over his deserted infant son.

Sir Austin's reaction to the forbidden marriage is to blame the inadequacies of humanity rather than his system. He remains formally charitable, but, despite Lady Blandish's interventions, will not see Richard. Adrian Harley arrives in the Isle of Wight and persuades Lucy to persuade Richard to return to London without her and await his father alone.

In London, despite Richard's efforts to prevent it, Clare is

married to an old man. Richard tries to reform the prostitutes and
courtesans of London, and he takes his mother away from Diaper
Sandoe and places her in lodgings with Mrs Berry. Richard is
seduced by one of the women he was reforming, Mrs Mount, and
comes to feel so ashamed that he cannot return to Lucy, who,
though pregnant, is herself pursued by a Lord Mountfalcon –
husband to Mrs Mount. Sir Austin comes to London to be reconciled to Richard, but Richard is out of town. Mrs Berry fearing
the worst, goes to fetch the ignorant Lucy and installs her in her
house. Richard will not see her, but asks his father to receive her
alone at Raynham Abbey. Sir Austin prevaricates.

At this point Clare commits suicide, leaving a diary confessing
her love for Richard. Richard, feeling himself a virtual murderer,
goes abroad 'to cleanse' himself. Lucy has a son. Austin Wentworth returns from the tropics and, on hearing the whole story
from Adrian, goes to Lucy and takes her and the child and Mrs
Berry to Raynham, where Sir Austin welcomes them. (Mrs Berry
discovers that her husband, who deserted her, has become Sir
Austin's valet.)

In Germany with a philanthropic acquaintance of Isle of Wight
days, Lady Judith Velle, Richard dreams of liberating Italy. He
opens no letters from England and only at last hears of his son's
birth from Austin Wentworth, who joins him in Germany. At
the news, Richard rushes alone into the forest, and there, in a
thunderstorm, 'the Spirit of Life' illumines him and he has a 'sense
of purification'. He starts out immediately for England. Stopping
in London *en route* to Raynham, he receives an old letter from
Bella Mount explaining that she was offered bribes to seduce him
so that Lord Mountfalcon might be able to seduce Lucy in his
absence. Outraged Richard rushes to insult Mountfalcon and
thereby provoke a duel. Mountfalcon tries to cool the whole affair,
but his message to this effect is never given, as Ripton Thompson
(its recipient) delays too long. At Raynham a wretched Richard is
sanctimoniously welcomed by his father and formally reconciled.
After a brief and passionate encounter with Lucy in which he
acknowledges and she forgives his infidelity, and an intensely
emotional glimpse of his son, Richard rushes out without explanation to fight his duel in Northern France.

The final scenes are described by Lady Blandish in a disillusioned letter to Austin Wentworth. Richard, seriously wounded,
is visited by the whole family. Because they are fearful that her

emotionality will disturb him, Lucy is not allowed to sit with Richard. He recovers, but she from her superhuman efforts at self-control has contracted brain-fever and dies. Mrs Forey is reminded of Clare's death and becomes distracted. The novel ends with Richard pictured as 'dead-in-life'.

The story starts in gladness to end in sadness; from gay childhood to disillusioned maturity. The style apparently reflects this shift: the novel opens with wit, even burlesque, passes through lyricism and ends with the brevity of tragedy. Contemporary reviewers deplored the gratuitous cruelty of Lucy's death,[2] and critics have continued to see the novel as a comedy in which the pathos of his story overtakes the author: Meredith, despite himself, goes deeper than the frivolity of his comic intentions and creates a tragedy.[3] It is inadequate to answer these charges of inconsistency with citations from Meredith's later developed theories of comedy, or offer the trite rejoinder of the seriousness of real comedy; though these statements would be true. The point is rather that the novel is not inconsistent, but heterogeneous; not chaotic, but strangely inclusive. Furthermore, it is this simultaneously and diversely in terms of the relationship of its content and its style. For example, Meredith is not only an 'intellectual' novelist in the sense that he overtly discusses 'ideas', but also in that, through echoes and allusions to other literature (most obviously Greek legends, the Bible, Shakespeare and Goethe), he verbally reiterates or questions others' concepts. At times it seems that Meredith is discussing the form of his novel while in the process of writing it; in this way following on from Sterne, preceding Joyce and being atypical of his own period. One of the most interesting features of the *Ordeal of Richard Feverel* is the relationship of 'The Pilgrim's Scrip' to the whole novel. The novel opens:

> Some years ago was printed, and published anonymously, dedicated to the author's enemies, a small book of original Aphorisms, under the heading, THE PILGRIM'S SCRIP. . . .
> Modern Aphorists are accustomed to make their phrases a play of wit, flashing antithetical brilliancies, rather than condensing profound truths. This one, if he did not always say things new, evidently spoke from reflection, feeling, and experience. . . . His thoughts were sad enough; occasionally dark; here and there comical in their oddness; nevertheless

there ran through the volume a fire of Hope; and they did
him injustice who said he lacked Charity. . . .
On the subject of Women, certainly, the Aphorist seemed
to lose his main virtue. He was not splenetic: nay, he proved
in the offending volume he could be civil, courteous, chivalrous
towards them: yet, by reason of a twist in his mental
perceptions, it was clear he looked on them as domesticated
Wild Cats. . . .
He gravely declared . . . 'I expect that Woman will be the
last thing civilized by Man.'
Singular to say, the one dangerous and objectionable feature
in this little volume, preserved it from limbo. Men read, and
tossed it aside, amused, or weary. They set the author down
as a Sentimentalist jilted . . . They, let us suppose, were
Sentimentalists not yet jilted' (1–3).

Autobiographical critics, rightly connecting Meredith's and his
baby son Arthur's desertion by his wife, Mary Peacock, with the
theme of the novel, have seen Sir Austin and his system as Meredith's cautionary tale of himself. This is too simple. So is the notion
that Meredith was completely condemning Sir Austin's system
and 'The Pilgrim's Scrip', when what is striking in the novel is
precisely that he sometimes approves and sometimes rejects it.
He thereby offers an apparently realistic appraisal of it. The main
and most fallacious claim that Sir Austin makes for his own
aphorisms is their realism: 'He conceived that the Wild Cats
[Women] would some day be actually tamed. *At present it was best
to know what they were*' (3, my italics). By ironizing the realism of
Sir Austin, Meredith wittily calls in question his own. Sir Austin
then is not just 'a caution' to himself but a take-off of himself for
setting up that caution. 'The Pilgrim's Scrip' is the work of 'a
sentimentalist jilted', so in a way is the novel, but a sentimentalist
who knows he is jilted and therefore is no longer a sentimentalist.
Hence the Edenic passages of Lucy and Richard's first meeting
and of Richard's resurrection in the German forest are not, as is
often thought, the poet Meredith bursting through his cynic's
shell, but the very contained romanticism of an author who can
contextualize these lyric strophes in a fallen world. The author/
narrator and Sir Austin are never one and the same, but their
opinions coincide as well as diverge.
'The Pilgrim's Scrip' illustrates Meredith's preoccupation with

form in another way. *The Times* reviewer regarded it as an obtrusive chorus in Greek fashion; rather it is a 'play-within-a-play' serving not only as a commentary, but as a directive. Yet it is more interesting than this. The characters within the novel created by Meredith are yet in search of an author who will describe their salient features in abstract. Meredith creates his flesh-and-blood characters, but the pre-novel blueprint of them is the work of 'The Pilgrim's Scrip', except that it is, of course, a post-novel abstract of them:

> 'Your Aunt Helen, I was going to say, my dear boy, is an extraordinary woman. It was from her originally that the Pilgrim first learned to call the female the practical animal. He studies us all, you know. THE PILGRIM'S SCRIP is the abstract portraiture of his surrounding relatives.' (Adrian Harley, 407.)

A further twist of the joke is that Meredith's flesh-and-blood characters are often just sketches, caricatures. Or a further twist, that 'the female' is conventionally called a 'practical animal' and Adrian is mocking Sir Austin for sensitive observation that only produces a commonplace. Meredith maintains a constant interrelationship between the scrip and the novel, so that the scrip is even used to comment on its own author: Sir Austin is with Lady Blandish after Richard has recovered from his first illness and with this his first love flush:

> Lady Blandish had been sentimentalizing for ten years. She would have preferred to pursue the game. The dark-eyed dame was pleased with her smooth life and the soft excitement that did not ruffle it. Not willingly did she let herself be won.
> 'Sentimentalists,' says THE PILGRIM'S SCRIP, 'are they who seek to enjoy Reality, without incurring the Immense Debtorship for a thing done.'. . .
> However, one who could set down, Dying for Love, as a Sentimentalism, can hardly be accepted as a clear authority. Assuredly he was not one to avoid the incurring of the immense Debtorship in any way: . . .
> [Sir Austin] expounded to her the distinctive character of the divers ages of Love. . . . And while they sat and talked, 'My wound has healed,' he said. 'How?' she asked. 'At the fountain of your eyes,' he replied and drew the joy of new life from her blushes, without incurring further debtorship for a thing done (266–7).[4]

Meredith, then, is writing a novel about a man writing a book of aphorisms conceived from the characters in his novel.

This game that Meredith plays with the art of novel-writing is less intricately, but still interestingly, worked out also in his treatment of the hero, Richard. At many junctures he stands back and calls him 'Hero'. This denomination looks two ways – it obviously describes the role Richard has in the novel, but it also depicts Richard's own role-playing:

> He [Richard] is foolish, God knows; but for my part I will not laugh at the Hero, because he has not got his occasion. Meet him when he is, as it were, anointed by his occasion, and he is no laughing matter (552).

Or:

> Richard was too full of blame of himself to blame his father: too British to expose his emotions. Ripton divined how deep and changed they were by his manner. He had cast aside the Hero, and however Ripton had obeyed him and looked up to him in the heroic time, he loved him tenfold now (562).

Meredith treats Lucy, less frequently, in the same way: 'The Heroine, in common with the Hero, has her ambition to be of use in the world – to do some good: and the task of reclaiming a bad man is extremely seductive to good women' (499). This meeting of the language of the art of fiction with that of the role of the character within it parallels at a linguistic level that, which is at a formalist level, between 'The Pilgrim's Scrip' and the novel structure. It also ensures a constant distancing of the author and reader from the characters, helped also, of course, by the wit and irony. It is maintained even at the end: the death of the heroine and spiritual annihilation of the hero are summarily described in a letter from Lady Blandish – hardly a device to encourage tragic participation. This 'distancing', an eighteenth-century or pre-Brechtian 'alienation', is highly atypical of the mid-Victorian novel: Meredith looked 'before and after' for his method.

II

> Ordeal: Judicial trial in use in the Middle Ages under the name of 'judgement of God': trial by water, trial by fire. . . .
> *Larousse.*

Anything . . . which . . . severely tests character or endurance, a trying experience.

N.E.D.

The Feverels have always considered themselves subject to a divine trial, their response to which is misinterpreted by the world as severe eccentricity or mild insanity:

> [Sir Austin] had regarded his father, Sir Caradoc, as scarce better than a madman when he spoke of a special Ordeal for their race; and when, in his last hour . . . the old Baronet caught his elder son's hand, and desired him to be forewarned, Austin had, while bowing respectfully, wondered that Reason was not vouchsafed to his parent at that supreme instant. From the morning hills of existence he beheld a clear horizon. He was no sooner struck hard than Sir Caradoc's words smote him like a revelation. He believed that a curse was in his blood; a poison of Retribution, which no life of purity could expel; and grew, perhaps, more morbidly credulous on the point than his predecessor: speaking of the Ordeal of the Feverels, with sonorous solemnity as a thing incontrovertibly foredecreed to them. . . . Sir Austin, strong in the peculiar sharpness of the sting darted into him, held that there was an entire distinction in their lot: that other men were tried by puny ailments; were not searched and shaken by one tremendous shock, as of a stroke of Heaven's lightning. He indicated that the Fates and Furies were quite as partial as Fortune (16–17).

This Fate is nicknamed 'Mrs. Malediction': 'Often had she all but cut them off from their old friend, Time, and they revived again. Whether it was the Apple-Disease, or any other, strong constitutions seemed struggling in them with some peculiar malady' (14). Having undergone his Ordeal in his wife's desertion, Sir Austin is convinced that it is the 'Apple-Disease': 'What he exactly meant by the Apple-Disease, he did not explain: nor did the ladies ask for an explanation. Intuitively they felt hot when it was mentioned' (12). Whether the 'Apple-Disease' is sexuality in general or, more specifically, venereal disease is unprovable and largely irrelevant to the larger themes, though interesting for an evaluation of the type of novel.[5] To Sir Austin it is as though God put woman in the garden to tempt Adam (as did in a minor way, but in a major literary tradition, the Satan of *Paradise Regained* to tempt Christ). The Feverels as Adam's heirs in each generation undergo a repetition of this original 'Ordeal'. Meredith thus makes Sir Austin use the term 'Ordeal' in its limited ancient sense. One of the brilliances of the book is that Meredith takes up the term and redeploys it in its more generalized and psychological sense; the 'Ordeal' that primarily Richard, and secondarily Sir Austin, undergo is the trial of enduring their inherited notion of the family's divine Ordeal; the 'ordeal' of an Ordeal.

This transition takes place as the novel develops. But Meredith is never content with simple progression: Austin Wentworth, the really 'good' man of the book, experiences and uses the term and its allied concept 'fate' in the modern sense throughout. Austin Wentworth's life is paralleled with that of his namesake, Sir Austin, and Richard's life repeats that of both of them. Austin Wentworth, prior to the story, seduced by his mother's maid, marries her, but lives separately:

> . . . he had gone and ruined himself: married that creature! The world of women turned from him as from a blighted rose.
>
> 'The compensation for Injustice,' says THE PILGRIM'S SCRIP, 'is, that in that dark Ordeal we gather the worthiest around us.'
>
> And Lady Blandish, and some few true men and women held Austin Wentworth high (30).

When Sir Austin considers that he is fighting a preordained Fate in Richard, Austin Wentworth realizes that the boy's real 'fate' is determined by his choice of truth and generosity; so when he feels Richard will not confess to arson and thus save Tom Bakewell by truth instead of heroics, he tells Adrian: 'The boy's fate is being decided now' (82). Where Austin Wentworth treats his and, later, Richard's experiences as earthly trials, Sir Austin Feverel retreats into supramundane abstraction and theory. Their two diverse reactions to their comparable experience structure Richard's trial. Richard's Ordeal becomes his 'ordeal', but Austin Wentworth was alway there as, so to speak, a diachronic pointer to this interpretation.

Sir Austin, believing in a perfected paradise that can be regained, educates his only son Richard to be a new Adam: 'by advancing him to a certain moral fortitude ere the Apple-Disease was spontaneously developed, there would be something approaching to a perfect Man' (12). He is not preparing Richard to avoid the fight, but bracing him for the struggle. The boy's childhood is marked by a number of crises which always fall on his birthdays. On the boy's seventh birthday, 'Mrs. Malediction' (in fact, his exiled mother), having visited Richard's bedside, Sir Austin is relieved to find the Ordeal deflected on to his brother Algernon, who loses a leg that day. On his seventh birthday a protesting Ricky is declared morally and physically fit. On his fourteenth birthday Richard refuses to submit to medical examination: 'For in Richard's bosom *a fate was working*, and the shame of the insult, as he thought it, rankled' (42, my italics). He escapes with Ripton from the festivities, offends Farmer Blaize, provokes the firing of the farmer's rick, and, when finally apologizing for the episode, meets (though he does not acknowledge the farmer's niece) – Lucy Desborough. When Sir Austin overhears the boys discussing their crime, the same language is in operation: 'A sensation of infinite melancholy overcame the poor gentleman: a thought that he was fighting with a fate in the beloved boy.' This is his fourteenth birthday. Once more his mother had secretly visited him, causing the spying Clare to faint. On this birthday he first meets Lucy, though no significance is attached to the meeting as yet. Richard continues to grow up in the Paradise that Sir Austin has created, a Paradise in which he is kept totally ignorant of the 'meaning' of woman. But while he is kept pure, his father dallies with Lady Blandish and Richard who, unknown to his father, witnesses the flirtation, imitates him in a childish way. Sir Austin, still posing as a suprasexual creature, as perfect 'providence', refuses to see the significance of his own behaviour; he feels all is well with Richard:

> No augury could be hopefuller. The Fates must indeed be hard, the Ordeal severe, the Destiny dark, that could destroy so bright a Spring! But bright as it was, the Baronet relaxed nothing of his vigilant supervision. He said to his intimates: 'Every act, every fostered inclination, almost every thought, in this Blossoming Season, bears its seed for the Future. The living Tree now requires incessant watchfullness (130. 'The Tree' is capitalized as Sir Austin previously referred to Richard as 'a Tree of Eden').

Richard, however, released into a knowledge of sex by seeing Sir Austin kiss Lady Blandish's hand, in his father's absence now falls in love with Lucy Desborough. Meredith's irony is immediately at work: here in Sir Austin's Paradise, the brave new world is actually recaptured. Richard and Lucy, without the knowledge, and against all the efforts of Sir Austin, are 'Ferdinand and Miranda', perfect man and woman, regaining Eden for mankind:

> He had landed on an Island of the still-vexed Bermoothes.
> The world lay wrecked behind him. . . . What splendour in the Heavens! What marvels of beauty about his enchanted head!
> And, O you Wonder! . . . Radiant Miranda! Prince Ferdinand is at your feet.
>   Or is it Adam, his rib taken from his side in sleep, and thus transformed, to make him behold his Paradise, and lose it! . . .
>   The youth looked on her with as glowing an eye. It was the First Woman to him.
>   And she – mankind was all Caliban to her, saving this one princely youth (149–50).

The tragic irony is overt: 'The way the System triumphed, just ere it was to fall'; but the more private ironic reversal is also present. As later Richard is 'widow Ann' and Bella Mount Richard III, here Lucy is the more normally educated Ferdinand and Richard, the unique Miranda. This is another aspect of Meredith's turning of the conventional and the expected on its head. It also is an illustration of his use of sexual role-reversal to make thereby an egalitarian statement.

Meredith makes it quite certain that Lucy is the 'right girl'; in the language of the novel, she is the Cinderella that Richard finds by instinct, whilst his father is scientifically trying the glass slipper on ugly sisters. But the instinctual Paradise Lucy and Richard inhabit shares with the scientific concept of Sir Austin the delusion of its nature:

> Pipe, happy sheep-boy, Love! Irradiated Angels, unfold your wings and lift your voices!
> They have outflown Philosophy. Their Instinct has shot beyond the ken of Science. Imperiously they know we were made for this Eden: and would you gainsay them who are outside the Gates, and argue from the Fall? (194).

From his own romantic predicament, Richard falls into his father's illusion. Lucy and Richard are spied on by Heavy Benson:

'Enchanted Islands have not yet rooted out their old brood of Dragons. Wherever there is Romance, these Monsters came by inimical attraction.' Beneath this inflated language, Meredith makes it quite clear that Benson is nothing but 'a dirty old man' indulging in voyeurism. (This deflation-technique parallels that employed in making the Apple-Disease at times stand for venereal disease.) Most critics have taken these passages as straight lyricism and consequently seen the tragedy as being caused by Sir Austin's harsh separation of his son from his wife. This is to miss completely the gentle, indulgent and yet precise ironizing of romanticism.

It is also to misread the story. Richard, after his illness, does bury his love for Lucy, but, hearing of the possibility of rescuing her from a debasing marriage, his love painfully revives. His subsequent wooing and marriage to her are beset with anti-romantic incidents: he forgets the house where he has lodged her, 'Betrayed by his instincts, the magic slaves of Love!'; he seems to pine for love, 'Lucy wept for the famine-struck hero who was just then feeding mightily' (321); he loses the wedding-ring; his best man, Ripton, becomes grotesquely drunk at the wedding-breakfast and betrays the marriage to Adrian. There is no doubt that Meredith, without therefore condemning it, regards the marriage as a rash one, and Richard as still living in a world of romantic illusion:

> The Alps! Italy! Rome! and then I shall go to the East,' the Hero continued. 'She's ready to go anywhere with me, the dear brave heart! Oh, the glorious golden East! . . . I dream I'm Chief of an Arab tribe, and we fly all white in the moonlight on our mares, and hurry to the rescue of my darling! And we push the spears, and we scatter them, and I come to the tent where she crouches, and catch her on my saddle, and away!
> ——' (320).

The Ordeal is shifting from the generic to the personal; Richard's Ordeal is his marriage: 'Complacently [Sir Austin] sat and smiled, little witting that his son's Ordeal was imminent, and that his son's Ordeal was to be his own.' Sir Austin's notion of divine Fate and Meredith's psychological reinterpretation of this coalesce at this climactic point in a chapter entitled 'In which the last act of a comedy takes the place of the first':

> . . . each man has, one time or other, a little Rubicon – a clear
> or a foul, water to cross. . . . Be your Rubicon big or small,
> clear or foul, it is the same: you shall not return. On – to
> Acheron! – I subscribe to that saying of THE PILGRIM'S SCRIP:
>   'The danger of a little knowledge of things is disputable:
>   but beware the little knowledge of one's self!'
> Richard Feverel was now crossing the River of his Ordeal. . . .
> his life was cut in two, and he breathed but the air that met
> his nostrils. His father, his father's love, his boyhood and
> ambition, were shadowy. . . . And yet the young man loved
> his father, loved his home: and I dare say Caesar loved Rome:
> but whether he did or no, Caesar when he killed the Republic
> was quite bald, and the Hero we are dealing with is scarce
> beginning to feel his despotic moustache. Did he know what
> he was made of? Doubtless, nothing at all. But honest passion
> has an instinct that can be safer than conscious wisdom . . .
> His audacious mendacities and subterfuges did not strike him
> as in any way criminal. . . . Conscience and Lucy went
> together (330–1).

Richard in marrying Lucy is guilty of intensely and unwittingly
wounding the devoted Clare. The pain for Clare is brought out
with full pathos in the scene where she finds Richard's lost wedding-
ring, finds it fits her finger and is teased by her mother and cousins
about having found her future husband. Richard is guilty, but his
guilt is part of the larger social structure: happiness, says Meredith,
is like money, the rich take from the poor: 'Who knows the Honeymoon that did not steal somebody's sweetness? Richard Turpin
went forth, singing: "Money or life" to the world: Richard Feverel
has done the same, substituting "Happiness" for "Money",
frequently synonyms. The coin he wanted he would have, and
was just as much a highway robber as his fellow Dick. . . . His coin
chinks delicious music to him. Nature, and the order of things on
earth, have no warmer admirer than a jolly brigand, or a young
man made happy by the Jews' (386).[6] Meredith treats Lucy's and
Richard's marriage realistically. Although they are happy and still
in love,[7] Richard is frustrated, ambition has replaced 'Love', and
there are minor quarrels and dissatisfactions between them. Adrian,
in a semi-seduction of the one through cookery, and Lady Judith
Velle, in a semi-seduction of the other through romantic philanthropy, play into the vague dissensions of the couple. It is not just

Sir Austin who is responsible for separating the newly-weds and hence indirectly for Richard's infidelity: Fate is other people, but the protagonists make themselves receptive to it.

Separated from Lucy, Richard undertakes the reformation of the fallen women of London. He sees them as 'clever, beautiful, but betrayed by Love'. Where his father has seen men as victims of women, Richard sees women as men's victims. Just as he is righting his father's injustice, he is seduced by Bella Mount (the name is a literary and 'earthy' pun) thus proving his father's theory:

> 'When we're young we can be very easily deceived. If there is such a thing as love, we discover it after we have tossed about and roughed it. Then we find the man, or the woman, that suits us:– and then it's too late' [Bella].
> 'Singular!' murmured Richard, 'she says just what my father said' (483).

Of course, what Sir Austin and Bella have in common are their truistic utterances.

Meredith treats Richard's infidelity with as much realism as the marriage; there is no immediate contrition; he writes to Bella: 'Come, my bright Hell-star! . . . You have taught me how devils love, and I can't do without you.' After Bella has refused, and Clare, married to an old but kindly man, has committed suicide, Richard, despairing, leaves for Germany. He has lost none of his romanticism, where once he dreamt of Arabian adventures, of saving the women of London, now he wants to liberate Italy. He is in the company of Lady Judith, who, as Austin Wentworth says, is 'a sentimentalist'.

In the forest thunderstorm, filled with the glory of his newly-discovered paternity, Richard has a supramundane experience. First it is purely physical; it 'communicated nothing to his heart', but penetrated all through his blood. It turns out to be caused by the licking of the leveret he is carrying. Once Richard knows the reason, his *heart* is touched. All Richard's previous glorious moments have been attributed by Meredith simply to instinct, to 'blood'; now he has passed beyond this to the heart,[8] and thence to the spirit – seeing a small forest chapel he is suffused with a sense of universal love:

> Vivid as lightning the Spirit of Life illumined him. He felt in his heart the cry of his child, his darling's touch. With shut

D

eyes he saw them both. They drew him from the depths; they
led him a blind and tottering man. And as they led him he
had a sense of purification so sweet he shuddered again and
again (558).

But Meredith treats this only as momentary inspiration. In
London, *en route* home, Richard receives Bella's letter. All his life
he has felt subjected to other people's plots, and now he learns that
his desertion of Lucy and seduction by Bella was a further plot.
After he has challenged Lord Mountfalcon,[9] he delays till evening
his return to Raynham. There he discovers his real Ordeal is to
abandon his son and wife for possible death:

O God! what an Ordeal was this! that tomorrow he must
face Death, perhaps die and be torn from his darling – his
wife and his child (582).

And his father discovers *his* Ordeal in the possible death of his son.
Lady Blandish writes:

His Ordeal is over. I have just come from his room and seen
him bear the worst that could be (587).

Love and Death are the Ordeal.

III

'There are women in the world, my son!' – Sir Austin Feverel
(224).
 Women came into the world to tempt men. Sir Austin literalizes
this conventional concept, thereby making it abnormal and hence
available to laughter and ridicule. But Meredith does not simply
prove him wrong – love and sex *are* the ordeal, but not exactly as
Sir Austin means them.
 Who is this woman of ill-omen?
 'Mrs Malediction', who visits the child Richard, disturbs Sir
Austin by kissing his son:

Sir Austin had listened with a pleased attention to his boy's
prattle. The mention of the Lady changed his face.
 'Kissed you, my child?' he asked anxiously (23).

'Mrs Malediction' is, in fact, Lady Feverel. She visits again before the next crisis. Lady Feverel is the orphan daughter of an Admiral who educated her on his half-pay;[10] her adultery with Diaper Sandoe is discussed at the beginning and near the end of the novel. But Richard, who, until his adulthood, knows nothing of his mother's history, with an uncanny 'fatality' always quotes Sandoe's poems just before he makes some false move. The poems' fatuous sentimentality (praised by Richard) thus runs as a disturbing motif through the novel. Richard has a number of relationships with older women who are seen explicitly as mother-substitutes. Lady Blandish (admirer of Austin Wentworth as well as of Austin Feverel), personified first as 'the Bonnet' then as the 'Autumn Primrose', first awakens Richard to sexuality – 'Emmeline Clementina Matilda Laura, Countess Blandish' he rhapsodizes in response to Ralph Norton's love-lorn musings on women's names. But part of her own flirtation with Sir Austin is her assumption of an adoptive parenthood of Richard. When there is the prospect that she might actually become his stepmother, Richard is perturbed with all the jealousy of the boy for his father who has 'won' his 'mother' sexually. Lady Blandish is also linked with Bella Mount: 'She honestly loved the boy. She would tell him: "If I had been a girl, I would have had you for my husband." And he with the frankness of his years would reply: "And how do you know I would have had you?" causing her to laugh and call him a silly boy, for had he not heard her say, She would have had him? Terrible words, he knew not then the meaning of!' (124). Lady Judith Felle: 'A second edition of the Blandish', according to Adrian, 'kissed Lucy protectingly and remarking on the wonders of the evening, appropriated her husband' (413). Mrs Bella Mount, his seductress, is directly linked with Lady Feverel (and, of course, with Austin Wentworth's wife, thereby underlying the parallel roles of the two Austins once more). Richard decides to rescue his mother from her adulterous union, in this act making a confidante of Lady Blandish. He arranges to house his mother with Mrs Berry, but Mrs Berry has seen Richard with Bella Mount in the Park and thinks that 'the lady' who he is to bring is this 'Beller Donner', as she calls her:

'I want you to keep your rooms for me – those [Lucy] had. I expect, in a day or two, to bring a lady here——'
  'A lady?' faltered Mrs. Berry. . . . 'But I ain't a house of Magdalens.' . . . In the evening she heard the noise of

wheels stopping at the door. 'Never!' . . . He ain't rided her
out in the mornin', and been and made a Magdalen of her
afore dark?' . . .

'Mr. Richard! if that woman stay here, I go forth. My house
ain't a penitenteary for unfort'nate females Sir——' . . .

He clapped his hand across her mouth, and spoke words in
her ear that had awful import to her. She trembled, breathing
low: 'My God, forgive me! Lady Feverel is it? Your mother,
Mr. Richard?' (469–71).

The evil woman, then, is the sexual mother; and it is against her
that Sir Austin's energies are ultimately, if unconsciously, directed.
A statement in 'The Pilgrim's Scrip' reads: 'To withstand women,
must we first annihilate our Mothers within us: die half!' It is his
child's mother in Lady Feverel that Sir Austin attempts to
annihilate by not allowing her to exist for Richard. He tries to make
a perfect mother of Lucy, his daughter-in-law, and by his strictures
causes her death. (Richard realizes the murderous implications of
his father's position at the time of Clare's death.)

An important aspect of Meredith's sexual egalitarianism is his
refusal to draw a sharp line between men and women. We have
seen this already in his role-reversal imagery for Lucy and Richard
and Bella and Richard; the women, though utterly 'feminine',
have masculine attributes. In the two Austins, Meredith displays
the importance of femininity in men. Of Sir Austin he writes: 'The
poor gentleman, seriously believing Woman to be a Mistake, had
long been trying to annihilate his Mother within him. Had he
succeeded he would have died his best half, for his mother was
strong in him' (10). It is Sir Austin's suppression of tenderness and
assumption of a mask that is his undoing, as it is his real femininity
that is his glory and that wins him Meredith's approval. Mrs Berry,
the former indiscreet housemaid, 'Polly Acton', utters the truth
about him late (too late) in the novel:

'—I'll say his 'arts as soft as a woman's . . . . That's where
everybody's deceived by him. . . . It's because he keeps his
face, and makes ye think you're dealin' with a man of iron,
and all the while there's a woman underneath. And a man
that's like a woman he's the puzzle o' life! We can see through
ourselves . . . and we can see through men, but one o' that sort–
he's like somethin' out o' natur'. Then I say . . . what's to do
is for to treat him *like* a woman, and not for to let him 'ave his

own way–which he don't know himself, and is why nobody else do' (473).

Austin Wentworth is what Sir Austin should have allowed himself to be: ' . . . he was extremely presentable: fair-haired, with a smile sweet as a woman's: gentle as a child: a face set with the seal of a courageous calm: so pure a face that looking on it you seemed to see into his soul' (30). Transparency *versus* a mask: both are models for Richard. Austin Wentworth twice brings spiritual bliss to Richard: first when he enables him to face the confession of arson ('Feelings he had never known streamed in upon him, as from an ethereal casement: an unwanted tenderness: an embracing humour: a consciousness of some ineffable glory: an irradiation of the features of humanity' (88)) and for a second time when he brings the news of Richard's son. There, *nursing* the leveret, Richard discovers his masculinity in the release of his femininity. It is, however, too late: he was 'too British to expose his emotions', the women are killed, Richard has a motherless son, the mask has triumphed:

Have you noticed the expression in the eyes of blind men? That is just how Richard looks, as he lies there silent in his bed – striving to image her on his brain (592*f*.).

IV

Alceste is the Jean-Jacques of the Heart

Meredith, *Essay on Comedy*

Before his wife's adultery, Sir Austin lives in an imagined Golden Age ('He had bid [Lady Feverel and Diaper Sandoe] be brother and sister, . . . and live a Golden Age with him at Raynham'); his educational system is an attempt to regain for his son that lost Eden. He is even tempted towards a prospect of a renewed Utopia on his own account with Lady Blandish:

. . . was not here a woman worthy the golden Ages of the world? one who could look upon man as a creature divinely made, and look with a mind neither tempted, nor tainted, by the Serpent! (127).

But because he has lost his original Paradise he has sunk into misanthropy: '. . . like Timon, he became bankrupt, and fell upon bitterness'. Meredith later considered *Le Misanthrope* as the

greatest comedy written. Sir Austin has much in common with
Alceste.

All are corrupt; there's nothing to be seen
In court or town but aggravates my spleen
(*Le Misanthrope*, I, 1.)

For Meredith, Molière's Alceste and Molière's great critic, Jean-
Jacques Rousseau, have much in common: both are egotistical
misanthropists; as Mackay[11] puts it, '*la chute du Misanthrope
implique la chute de Jean-Jacques*'. If Sir Austin shares certain
characteristics with Timon and Alceste, could it not follow that he
bears some resemblance to Rousseau?

As yet, there is no absolutely certain evidence that Meredith was
deeply acquainted with Rousseau's work; but his general culture,
his education in Germany, where Rousseau was of far greater
importance even than in France and England, and a later letter to
Morley (1875) congratulating him on his biography of Rousseau,
all strongly suggest that he was. Within the novel Austin Wentworth refers with approval to *The Confessions* (85). But, of course,
if Meredith did have Rousseau in mind as a partial model for Sir
Austin, it is as the author of *Emile* that he is most relevant. Sir
Austin's basic premise reads almost like a simplified version of
Rousseau's position: Man is not born evil (nor absolutely good),
but he has only forfeited Paradise through the corruptness of the
societies he has formed, he *chooses* evil, his aim should thus be to
regain his state of perfection. Both Rousseau and Sir Austin thus
strive towards a Utopia of the future based on a Golden Age in the
past. Meredith demonstrates the fundamental Manichaeism
involved – he may well have felt this about Rousseau (another
'eulogist of Nature') as well as about Sir Austin:

> . . . A Manichaean tendency, from which the sententious
> eulogist of Nature had been struggling for years (and which
> was partly at the bottom of the System), now began to cloud
> and usurp dominion of his mind. As he sat alone in the forlorn
> dead-hush of his library, he saw the Devil.
> . . . and the Devil said to him. . . : 'your object now, is to
> keep a brave face to the world, so that all may know you
> superior to this human nature that has deceived you. For it
> is the shameless Deception, not the Marriage, that has
> wounded you. . . . And your System:– if you would be brave

to the world, have courage to cast the dream of it out of you: relinquish an impossible project; see it as it is – dead: too good for men!'

'Ay!' muttered the Baronet, 'all who would save them perish on the Cross!' (390).

Sir Austin sees Richard as worse than the drunk, pornography-reading Ripton. Meredith, like Molière, believes in the basic good of human nature; what he is criticizing in Sir Austin/Rousseau is the romantic, idealist reinterpretation that finds its source and its conclusion in its obverse – misanthropy. Sir Austin shares with Rousseau his misogyny; Rousseau considers women decidedly inferior and, despite the fact that he does not theoretically regard women as the source of all evil, he makes Sophy's infidelity the cause of Emile's misery, as Lady Feverel was the cause of Sir Austin's.

Many critics of *Richard Feverel* have claimed that Meredith based his notion of the 'System' on Herbert Spencer's contemporary educational theories, published in the *Quarterly Review* (1858). Critics of Spencer thought that he had based his proposals on *Emile*, causing Spencer to claim he had never read a line of Rousseau.[12] Of one thing we can be certain: the cosmopolitan Meredith would not have been guilty of Spencer's complacent philistinism. As there is much in common in the character and in the general theories of Sir Austin and Rousseau, so there is much in common between his 'System' and that of *Emile*.

Rousseau's pupil, Emile, is a boy of pure (upper-class) blood and good health. The father is 'the ideal tutor', but Emile is in fact an orphan, so a tutor takes over. He gives the boy apparent freedom, but in fact operates a system of constant espionage. This is precisely the position Sir Austin adopts: 'the possession of his son's secret flattered him. It allowed him to act, and in a measure to feel, like Providence; enabled him to observe and provide for the movements of creatures in the dark' (71). It is precisely this posturing as 'Providence' that Meredith criticizes in Sir Austin (while Lucy and Richard are Ferdinand and Miranda, we are told Sir Austin is no Prospero). The basic aim of both Rousseau's and Sir Austin's systems is to combine absolute health of body with truth of soul and thus produce 'Valour' (Sir Austin's aphorisms are the skeleton of Rousseau's decomposed circumlocutions). Both believe in early maternal care and in breast-feeding. Both think of education in essentially 'progressive' terms – the child is not an empty vehicle to be filled, but a growing, developing person; hence the notion of stages of growth. Rousseau divides his pupil's life into four stages: 1 to 5 years, 5 to 12, 12 to 15, and 15 to the early twenties. The first stage is purely physical: Emile learns to eat, walk and talk; the second is 'negative': he is not taught truth, but is shielded from vice; hardihood, strength and courage are developed in the intercourse with Nature; little is learnt; there is no punishing and no rewarding. The next stage concentrates on Emile's intellectual growth, the stress here being on discovery and natural curiosity rather than constraint. Up till this point Emile has been a complete individualist and egotist, for self-love is the source of all passions; now begins his moral and spiritual education: from love and feeling are developed virtue and morality. Emile, who has been brought up entirely in the country, is now shown the town, whilst a bride, as pure as himself, is sought for him. He meets this girl, Sophie, but is then separated from her while he spends two years abroad. The final section of the book is devoted to a description of Sophie's education. But Rousseau wrote a 'misanthropic' sequel, *Sophie and Emile*, in which, after marrying and having children, disaster hits the couple: Sophie is unfaithful and Emile is captured and enslaved by Tunisian pirates.

Sir Austin's 'System' differs in a number of details (Richard, but not Emile, studies history, Emile, but not Richard, learns a manual craft, etc.), but imitates many of the broad outlines of Rousseau's plan. Thus Richard's growth is seen as a series of stages; and stages which, though they have slightly different ages for their demarcation lines (Sir Austin's are more blurred) have a similar educational content though redirected solely to Richard's future relationship with 'Woman'. Many statements are clear echoes:

> In Sir Austin's Note-book was written: 'Between Simple Boyhood, and Adolescence – The Blossoming Season – on the threshold of Puberty, there is one Unselfish Hour: say, Spiritual Seed-time? (121–2).

Many aspects seem to bear an extraordinarily strong resemblance: education according to Nature, education for perfection, progressive education through stages, the move from country to town, education right through to marriage, the separation of the lovers and so on. The basic tenets (and the basic character) are far closer to those of Rousseau than to those of Spencer.[13]

Sir Austin follows Rousseau in believing that the primary egotism of man can be transmuted into social conscience and the general will (in Rousseau's case this notion is developed more fully in *The Social Contract* than in *Emile*). There are two ironies deployed by Meredith here: Richard, like Emile, is personally doomed by his efforts at public philanthropy; but above all Rousseau and Sir Austin are arch-egotists. Just as their theoretical Utopia is based on personal misanthropy, so their visions of altruism find their source in an obsession with the self. (The true altruist is, of course, Richard's 'good angel', Austin Wentworth, the man without misanthropy and without a system.)

Sir Austin is not an absolute or a straight portrait of Rousseau, but often he is his essence and his parody. He is also, of course, an 'updated' version. 'Created' in the same year as *The Origin of Species*, he is a 'scientific' humanist (in fact he is neither scientist nor humanist). Rousseau's 'natural man' has been literalized, so that romantic Richard is shocked to discover that in his kinship to the animals is supposed to lie the source of his nobleness.

The upbringing of Richard Feverel is not a direct imitation of the education of Emile, but the overall pattern is strikingly similar and the tone and mood yet more so. In a remarkable review in 1864, Justin McCarthy wrote:

People in general do not now, I think, read Rousseau's *Emile*; but those who are familiar with that masterpiece of a dead philosophy will probably agree with us as to the profoundly unsatisfactory and disheartening impression which its catastrophe leaves on the mind. Was it for this, the reader is inclined to ask, that science and love do their utmost to make one path smooth, one human existence bright, and noble, and happy? Was Emile from his birth upward trained to the suppression of every selfish thought, to the scorn of all ignoble purpose, to an absolute devotion for truth, courage, purity, and benevolence, only that he might be deceived in his dearest affections, and that the crowning act of his existence might be the abnegation of self which we can scarcely even regard with admiration? The author had a right to shape his moral and deal with his creations as he would, yet we feel pained and shocked that he should have deemed it right to act thus harshly towards the beloved offspring of his system.

Something of this surprise and disappointment fills the mind

D*

when we have reached the close of Richard Feverel's ordeal, and find that he has left his brightest hopes and dearest affections dead and buried behind him. The book closes with a sharp snap or crash; we feel as if something were suddenly wrenched away with pain and surprise; a darkness falls upon the mind (*Westminster Review*, July 1864, 31–2, in series 'Novels with a Purpose').

Is it another of his ironic reversals (and a wish to raise the status of women) that makes Meredith have Richard (Emile) unfaithful and not Lucy (Sophie), and Lucy show an 'abnegation of self which we can scarcely even regard with admiration'? Whether or not this is so, McCarthy certainly captures the subject-matter of the novel and the tone of the tract perfectly: tragic without being tragedy, misanthropy passing through idealism has produced a concrete cause for its own disillusionment; egotism has met its just but sad reward in isolation; Utopia may come, but not with the Devil's advocate nor through faith alone.

Notes

1 Meredith made a number of omissions and a few very brief additions for the edition of 1878. Most importantly he reduced the first five chapters to two and omitted details of Mrs Grandison's upbringing of her daughter. He thus shifted the novel away from its earlier stress on education, 'the system' and the Ordeal. As these are precisely the aspects that interest me, I have used the 1859 ed., reprinted by the Modern Library, New York, 1950, throughout. Critical reaction in 1859 tried to unravel the meaning of the novel by over-concentrating on the 'system'; it was doubtless partially in response to this that Meredith underplayed it in the second edition. The second edition is generally felt to be more coherent, but also more elliptical and enigmatic.

2 *The Times* (loc. cit.) wrote that this is 'a catastrophe in defiance of poetical justice – this is neither the ancient nor the true method'. This opinion is reiterated by later critics, e.g. J. Moffatt, *George Meredith: a Primer to His Novels*, 1909.

3 E.g. J. W. Beach, *The Comic Spirit of George Meredith*, 1911, calls it a '*comédie manquée*' in which the comic idea is somewhat obscure and the tragic interest takes over, making it 'something nobler than comedy'.

4 Joyce completed for Meredith his work of building up an internal 'conversation' within literature by quoting the above aphorism in *Ulysses*, 1960, 255.

5 Sir Austin's stress on 'pure' blood and his visits to doctors to discover the physical condition of the families of Richard's prospective bride certainly suggest that the Apple-Disease is V.D. 'What terrible light [Dr] Bairam had thrown on some of [those families]! Heavens! in what a state was the blood of this Empire. . . .

Before commencing his campaign, he called on two ancient intimates, Lord Heddon, and his distant cousin, Darley Absworthy, both Members of Parliament, useful men, though gouty, who had sown in their time a fine crop of Wild Oats, and advocated the advantage of doing so, seeing that they did not fancy themselves the worse for it. He found one with an imbecile son, and the other with consumptive daughters. . . . Both . . . spoke of the marriage of their offspring as a matter of course, "And if I were not a coward," Sir Austin confessed to himself, "I should stand forth and forbid the banns! This universal ignorance of the inevitable consequence of Sin is frightful . . .,'" etc. (178–80).

Reference to V.D. was prevalent in pornographic fiction (see Marcus, *The Other Victorians*, 1969, 238).

If an obvious reference to V.D. was Meredith's intention, it makes this an even more extraordinary novel for a period in which there was a fairly rigid distinction between 'high' and 'low' literature – the treatment of sexuality being one of the main demarcation lines between the two.

6 It is this sort of passage – which, strangely, he omits – that justifies Lindsay's claim that Meredith is inserting a politically radical message into his novel. Unfortunately, I cannot go along with his political redefinition of 'egotism', though much of his analysis is pertinent. J. Lindsay, *George Meredith: His Life and Work*, 1956.

7 This is conveyed in a most striking passage in which they eat nine eggs for breakfast. The amount of eating in this novel, which has as one of its main themes the efforts of an upper-class family to sublimate sexuality, is extraordinary; it is actual and metaphorical, e.g.: 'So, without a suspicion of folly in his acts, or fear of results, Richard strolled into Kensington Gardens, breakfasting on the foreshadow of his great joy, now with a vision of his bride, now of the new life opening to him' (332).

8 John Henry Smith, in *Hiding the Skeleton*, Lincoln, 1966, traces through Meredith's intricate structure of blood, heart and spirit.

9 This conclusion was suggested earlier by the cypress tree – another omen of Fate: the fourteen-year-old Richard sees this pointing at him as it did at his ancestor, Sir Pylcher, before he dies in a duel.

10 There is, of course, an uneasy similarity in the backgrounds of Richard's mother and bride: Lucy is the orphan daughter of a naval lieutenant.

11 M. E. Mackay, *Meredith et La France*, Paris, 1937, has an excellent chapter on Meredith and Molière; unfortunately, she makes no further use of his observations on Rousseau.

12 This is according to W. H. Hudson, in *Rousseau and Naturalism in Life and Thought*, Edinburgh, 1903.

13 Although personally convinced of the association, I feel some hesitation in asserting the parallel, not only because of the lack of direct evidence, but also because I have found only one critic in French, German and English who makes an explicit connection. This may well be oversight on my part. The critic is Sencourt, who writes '*Richard Feverel* was a new *Emile*. But unlike *Emile*, he was to prove the excellence of the education according to nature, by showing the tragedy of education according to a system' R. Sencourt, *The Life of George Meredith*, 1929, 63. And that is all. To suggest that Meredith is using Rousseau is not to deny that he was referring to the theories of Spencer and Mazzini, for instance. Quite the contrary.

'Snips', 'Snobs' and the 'True Gentleman' in *Evan Harrington*

Margaret Tarratt

In *Evan Harrington* Meredith appears to strain towards some kind of social and psychological equilibrium. The author's attitudes can be separated into two seemingly contradictory strands, those of the contributor to the *Ipswich Journal*, the 'Tory' Meredith of Lionel Stevenson[1] and Norman Kelvin,[2] and those of Jack Lindsay's[3] left wing (if occasionally erratic) Radical. Few novelists can have received more contradictory interpretations than Meredith. This seems to be owing to some confusion about his objects of attack, not only on the part of the critics, but on the part of Meredith himself. This conflict of the intellect and the instinct provides a keynote to critical discussion of *Evan Harrington*.

Margaret Goodell[4] and L. T. Hergenhan[5] have both suggested that, paradoxically, Evan's behaviour as a 'true gentleman' (in a moral sense) leads him away from the upper-class society of Beckley, whilst Jack Lindsay, expressing a similar line of thought contends that Meredith is critical of the illusion of 'rising' in a class world. Evan's moral recognition of this is demonstrated by his return to the honest world of work. René Galland[6] saw the novel as Meredith's attempt to exorcize his own irrational desire for acceptance in high society, whilst Norman Kelvin's interpretation is related to Meredith's personal conflict, and he sees the novel as an attempt to work out the desire of Meredith/Evan to win Janet Duff-Gordon/Rose, whilst retaining his moral purity.

For all the surface humour of its mock-heroic mode, this novel is impregnated with a troubling sense of latent conflict. Meredith's attitude to his hero's dilemma is not immediately clear. As L. T.

Hergenhan suggests, 'The theme is assimilated into the whole work and the reader must deduce it for himself'.[7]

Before discussing this novel in detail, it is useful to restate certain pertinent facts concerning Meredith's own life and social attitudes. Both his grandfather and father were Portsmouth tailors with a taste for life amongst the upper classes. His grandfather, Melchizedec Meredith (the original Great Mel), mingled flamboyantly with the local gentry. His father, Augustus, unfitted for his tailor's calling, attempted a similar social feat with considerably less effect. Encumbered by his late father's debts, Augustus became bankrupt and moved to London to become a journeyman tailor. Nevertheless, he declared himself 'gentleman' on his second marriage certificate. George Meredith himself inherited a strangely ambivalent attitude towards the class issue. Nicknamed 'Gentleman Georgy' in his early schooldays, he was, throughout his life, reticent concerning his origins. On his wedding certificate he gave his father's profession as 'esquire'. Similarly, in the 1901 Census, he had himself entered as a man of 'private means' rather than as 'author'. He was also unwilling to disclose his real birthplace, entering 'Near Petersfield'.[8]

Writing to Janet Duff-Gordon in 1861 he reveals a sensitivity on this score:

> H— is a good old boy. He has a pleasant way of being
> inquisitive and has already informed me, quite agreeably, that
> I am a gentleman, though I may not have been born one.
>
> Some men are always shooting about you like May flies in
> little quick darts, to see how near you they may come. The
> best thing is to smile and enjoy the fun of it. I confess a
> private preference for friends who are not thus afflicted and
> get the secret by instinct. As my Janet does, for instance——[9]

In 1886 he was still writing on the same theme, this time to an American, which accounts perhaps for the more aggressively egalitarian tone:

> In origin I am what is called here a nobody, and my
> pretensions to that rank have always received due
> encouragement by which, added to a turn of my mind, I am
> inclined to Democracy.[10]

It seems likely that Meredith also experienced this kind of emotion, considerably repressed, when involved with Janet Duff-Gordon and her *milieu*. The tone of her relationship to him is summed up in the somewhat patronizing epithet 'my poet' liberally scattered throughout her memoirs – an affectionate acceptance of him as someone set apart from her other acquaintances.

Writing to Lucas, Editor of *Once a Week*, towards the end of *Evan Harrington*'s serialization in that periodical, Meredith makes some revealing comments on his feelings towards the work:

> I maintain that the story is true to its title (*Evan Harrington or He Would Be a Gentleman*) and that I avoided making the fellow a snob, in spite of his and my own temptations. Hence probably the charge of dulness; but this comes of an author giving himself a problem to work out, and doing it as conscientiously as he could. The ground was excessively delicate. This is too late to dwell upon; but I shudder at the thought of the last number.[11]

Certain words and phrases here strike a surprising note: Meredith's emphasis that it was not merely Evan's but his own 'temptation' to 'make the fellow a snob'; 'the ground was *excessively delicate*'; 'I *shudder* at the thought of the last number'. At one level, *Evan Harrington* must be seen as a novel involving a fantasy structure of selected elements of Meredith's own life. Meredith, by identifying himself with his hero's temptation, gives only one indication of this. Quite apart from our knowledge of Meredith's source for the Great Mel, we know that Mrs Mel and the Harrington sisters can be seen to be based on Meredith's mother and aunts. An interesting reaction to the novel's publication was that of Meredith's father, Augustus, who was reported to have remarked: 'I am very sore about it. . . . I am pained beyond expression as I consider it aimed at myself.'[12] The portrait of Evan was not a flattering one. Janet Duff-Gordon, on the other hand, eagerly claimed the novel as 'hers':

> *Evan Harrington* (which was first called *He would be a Gentleman*) was *my* novel, because Rose Jocelyn was myself. (Sir Frank [sic] and Lady Jocelyn were my father and mother, and Miss Current was Miss Louisa Courtenay, a very old friend of my parents, who often stayed with us at Esher.)[13]

More significant was Meredith's own letter to Janet Ross of 17 May 1861, writing of his friend, Captain Maxse:

You would like him. He is very anxious to be introduced some day to Rose Jocelyn. I tell him that Janet Ross is a finer creature. . . . Talking of Rose, did you see the Saturday? It says you are a heroine who deserve to be a heroine. And yet I think I missed you.[14]

It is notable that Meredith is prepared to discuss his heroine as a portrait of Janet, using their names almost interchangeably. It is important to remember that Janet Duff-Gordon's engagement to Henry Ross, a middle-aged banker, took place while Meredith was writing *Evan Harrington*, and it seems likely that Meredith himself was in love with her at this time.

The delicacy of the ground and Meredith's 'shuddering' at the thought of the last issue becomes comprehensible if the novel can be seen in the light of a more direct revelation of his social situation and ambition than he appears to have been willing to make in real life, particularly the final episode with the rupture of Rose's engagement to the boorish wealthy aristocrat, Laxley, and her acceptance of Evan, the tailor, as a husband.

Yet this novel is no mere wish-fulfilment; it poses a moral problem from which its structure is derived. Where, we are asked, does Evan's duty lie – in returning to his father's shop and learning the tailor's trade in order to pay off the parental debts or in continuing his career in some unremunerative post consonant with the position of a gentleman and pursuing his emotional involvement with the upper-middle-class Rose Jocelyn? This is basically a problem of class identification: the division of identification with the class into which he is born and the class to which he feels an affinity. The real problem Meredith sets his reader is to gauge the bias of the novel through the narrator's attitude towards the hero's moral dilemma and hence towards the British social structure.

In the following pages I intend to pursue this area of discussion by examining the novel in the light of its three dominant motifs: clothes and the tailor's role (the 'snip'), the snob and the gentleman. From such a discussion, Meredith's primary concerns and emphasis emerge with considerable clarity. To make such an examination, it is necessary to outline the literary context in which the novel appears. *Sartor Resartus*, *The Book of Snobs* and the continuing debate concerning the nature of the 'true gentleman' as canvassed by Dinah Mulock in *John Halifax, Gentleman*, Ruskin in Volume V of *Modern Painters* or Newman in *The Idea of the*

University, throw light on the terms within which *Evan Harrington or He Would Be A Gentleman* is composed.

At one point in *Evan Harrington*, Drummond Forth, referring to the history of the Great Mel, comments that there is 'material enough for a Sartoriad' (279).[15] This reference to Carlyle is not fortuitous. Many of the concerns of *Sartor Resartus* have been incorporated into *Evan Harrington*. Meredith's suggestions of possible titles alone would indicate this:

> What say you to these titles? 'The Substantial and the Essential'. (Bad, but better than 'Shams and Realities'.)[16]

In Book II of *Sartor Resartus*, Teufelsdröckh, considering the calculation of a 'Statistics of Imposture' asks:

> Can any one, for example, so much as say, What moneys, in Literature and Shoeblacking are realized by actual Instruction and actual Jet Polish; what by fictitious-persuasive Proclamation of such . . . . If for the present, in our Europe, we estimate the ratio of Ware to Appearance of Ware so high even as at One to a Hundred . . . what almost prodigious saving may there not be anticipated, as the *Statistics of Imposture* advances, and so the manufacturing of Shams (that of Realities rising into clearer and clearer distinction therefrom) gradually declines, and at length becomes all but wholly unnecessary![17]

In *Evan Harrington* Meredith concerns himself with just these 'Statistics of Imposture' and with his own attempt to separate and analyse the 'Shams' and the 'Realities'.

Carlyle's short section on the tailor in *Sartor Resartus* throws considerable light on the tailoring motif in *Evan Harrington*. Teufelsdröckh:

> undertakes no less than to expound the moral, political, even religious Influences of Clothes; he undertakes to make manifest, in its thousandfold bearings, this grand Proposition, that Man's earthly interests 'are all hooked and buttoned together, and held up, by clothes'. He says in so many words, 'Society is founded upon Cloth.'[18]

Clothes may lend the wearer a symbolic aura of authority or reverence, yet beneath them he remains Falstaff's 'forked Radish with a head fantastically carved'. In *Evan Harrington* Jack Raikes is the most extreme example of this, since he holds a regular income at the whim of the eccentric Tom Cogglesby only if he wears a tin plate inside his trousers. Miss Louisa Carrington uses dress as a concealment of a disfiguring skin disease which she hopes will pass unnoticed by her fiancé until after they are married, whilst Caroline Strike hides the marks of her husband's brutality by a careful arrangement of her draperies. On his first appearance in the novel, Evan too is 'disguised':

> You might have taken him for a wandering Don, were such an object ever known: so simply he assumed the dusky Sombrero and dangling cloak, of which one fold was flung across his breast and drooped behind him (31).

Whilst Rose Jocelyn, also dressed in the Portuguese style, changes into 'quiet English attire' as they approach England, Evan attempts to retain his classless outsider's identity through the foreign garb. Such pretensions are demolished when 'a man of no station' in 'a long brown coat and loose white neckcloth, spectacles on nose, a beaver hat with broadish brim on his head' approaches Evan holding out his hand. He is Goren the tailor, claiming an old and familiar acquaintance with Evan. 'I cut your first suit for you when you were breeched' suggests an unwelcome intimacy (46).

Traditionally, the tailor has held a low social position for centuries as one-ninth of a man (a notion taken up in *Evan Harrington*), but in *Sartor Resartus*, Teufelsdröckh maintains that 'The Tailor is not only a Man, but something of a Creator or Divinity':

> For, looking away from individual cases, and how a Man is by the Tailor new-created into a Nobleman, and clothed not only with wool but with Dignity and a Mystic Dominion, – is not the fair fabric of Society itself, with all its royal mantles and pontifical stoles, whereby, from nakedness and dismemberment, we are organized into Politics, into nations, and a whole coöperating Mankind, the Creation as has here been often irrefragably evinced, of the Tailor alone! – What too are all Poets and moral Teachers, but a species of Metaphorical Tailors?

The tailor, sitting 'on crossed legs' (the ultimate humiliation for Evan), is exhorted to 'Look up' and 'Be of hope!'

> With astonishment the world will recognize that the Tailor is its Hierophant and Hierarch, or even its God.[19]

In this 'Shelleyan' defence of the tailor lies the interpretation of his social stigma. The tailor is the piercing eye, the man who cannot be deceived by the social pretensions of his 'betters'. He is the creator of the basic symbols used by Society to indicate and support the hierarchical structure. As such his knowledge and skill place him in the position of Shelley's poet, and the analogy, as we have seen, is also reversed when poets and moral teachers become a 'Species of Metaphorical Tailors'. An awareness of this transference of role is, I believe, crucial to the understanding of Evan's (and indeed Meredith's) position. I shall return to this later.

If *Sartor Resartus* is a work that should be seen in close relation to *Evan Harrington* as a source for interpretation of the tailor's roles, similarly, Thackeray's *Book of Snobs* appears to provide a key to understanding the use of the term 'snob' in this novel. The Jocelyns and their circle use the term about the Great Mel in the sense of 'A vulgar or ostentatious person' (*O.E.D.*). Meredith's fears concerning Evan's characterization must revolve round the idea of 'One whose ideas and conduct are prompted by a vulgar admiration for wealth or social position' (*O.E.D.*). In his *Book of Snobs* Thackeray contends that snobbery is a vice common to all classes. He lashes his reader's complacent acceptance of a society in which 'this diabolical invention of gentility . . . kills natural kindliness and honest friendship',[20] and claims in a rhetorical denunciation:

> You who despise your neighbour, are a Snob; you who forget
> your own friends, meanly to follow after those of a higher
> degree, are a Snob; you who are ashamed of your poverty,
> and blush for your calling, are a Snob; as are you who boast
> of your pedigree, or are proud of your wealth.[21]

And he arrives at the conclusion that 'it is impossible in our condition of society, not to be sometimes a Snob'.[22]

A comparison between two passages from *The Book of Snobs* and *Evan Harrington* respectively suggests that Meredith was keenly aware of Thackeray's work. In *The Book of Snobs* Thackeray comments on how the term ' "Snob" has gained increased currency to an extent that even young ladies' are aware of its usage:

> You seldom get them to make use of the word as yet, it is
> true; but it is inconceivable how pretty an expression their
> little smiling mouths assume when they speak it out. If any

young lady doubts, just let her go up to her own room, look at herself steadily in the glass, and say 'Snob'. If she tries this simple experiment, my life for it, she will smile, and own that the word becomes her mouth amazingly. A pretty little round word, all composed of soft letters, with a hiss at the beginning, just to make it piquant, as it were.[23]

In *Evan Harrington* Meredith puts the following speech into the mouth of Rose's maid, Polly Wheedle, describing to Evan how Rose had asked her what the common nickname for a tailor was:

> 'Miss Rose was standing sideways to the glass, and she turned her neck, and just as I'd said "snip", I saw her saying it in the glass; and you never saw anything so funny. It was enough to make anybody laugh; but Miss Rose, she seemed as if she couldn't forget how ugly it had made her look. She covered her face with her hands, and she shuddered! It *is* a word – snip! that makes you seem to despise yourself.'
>   . . .What's that the leaves of the proud old trees of Beckley Court hiss as he sweeps beneath them? What has suddenly cut him short? (231).

The words 'snip' and 'snob' are both 'pretty little round words, all composed of soft letters, with a hiss at the beginning just to make them piquant'. They are both pejoratives drawn out of the upper reaches of a self-defensive social hierarchy. When we read the Meredith passage we must be reminded of the Thackeray and of the attitudes the latter brings to the subject. It is a snob who uses the term 'snip'. Such terms spring from a callous reliance on maintaining an exclusive class structure in which the lower classes are dehumanized in the eyes of the upper. The social pre-eminence of the upper classes is maintained by the determined rejection of interlopers ('snobs'), who try to thrust their way in. By repeating the word 'snip', Rose Jocelyn tests her feelings for Evan against the values of her class. Through this distorting mirror such affections appear perverse, but the ugliness which the word 'snip' brings to her features is the moral ugliness of using such a term. This is emphasized by the maid's comic reflection of her mistress's inherited snobbery. The 'hiss' at the beginning of the 'pretty' word 'snob' which renders it 'piquant' to the young lady, becomes the 'hiss' of contempt to Evan, dismissed by polite society as a 'snip'.

Thackeray's satiric awareness of the battle for status, the tension between those of rank and those with wealth, and above all the inability of any member of society to escape unsoiled from such a condition seems comparable to Meredith's own conflicting emotions concerning Society, which he both criticizes and longs to join. It is in this sense that snobbishness becomes his own and Evan's temptation.

If Thackeray minimizes pride of birth in favour of wealth as a necessary adjunct of the 'true gentleman' (like Meredith, who in tailor's metaphor declares, 'Money is the clothing of a gentleman,') (69), his attitude seems to be echoed by the pulp novelists of the mid-nineteenth century who made riches the basic criterion for establishing social position.[24] Almost diametrically opposed to this kind of thought were writers such as Ruskin and Newman, who gave elaborate and reverential treatment to the subject. Whereas Newman refines his definition of 'the true gentleman' down to the premise that 'he is one who never inflicts pain',[25] Ruskin asserts that 'Its prime, literal and perpetual meaning is "a man of pure race"; well bred in the sense that a horse or dog is well bred'. Although the gentleman can be discerned in a cluster of moral and social attributes ('sensitiveness', 'sympathy', 'the desire for truth-fulness', etc.), Ruskin emphasizes that the probability of finding such a man 'is always in favour of the race which has had acknow-ledged supremacy, and in which every motive leads to the endeav-our to preserve their true nobility'.[26]

John Halifax, Gentleman takes its place in this kind of debate in the form of fiction, and appears to be directly relevant to Meredith's use of the idea of a 'gentleman' in *Evan Harrington or He Would Be a Gentleman*. He had at one time suggested the title *All But a Gentleman* to the Editor of *Once a Week*:

This, I think, hits the mark, all but— Say? In this title
'Gentleman' is shown differently. Thus the hero has proved
he has fine noble qualities, but with the stigma that clings
to him there is one drawback. He is *all* but a gentleman.[27]

In *John Halifax, Gentleman* Dinah Mulock introduces her eponymous hero as a waif whose outstanding moral character compels respect from those with whom he comes into contact. From his first regular employment as a menial in the tanner's yard, he steadily mounts the social ladder to become the husband of a lady, despite opposition from an aristocratic rival. As a wandering orphan, his sole possession is his Bible, in which his father's name is inscribed – 'Guy Halifax Gentleman'. No attempt is made to check the authenticity of his pedigree and it is an open question as to whether his moral qualities, which eventually win him social recognition, derive from his being the son of a gentleman or whether they are the consequence of a determination to rise in the world through his own conviction that he is one. Like Ruskin, the narrator, Phineas Fletcher, extols the 'commonsense doctrine of the advantage of good descent', but unlike Ruskin he takes the practical line of admitting, if only in passing, environmental influences in the case:

> Since it is a law of nature, admitting only rare exceptions that the qualities of the ancestor's should be transmitted to the race;— the fact seems patent enough that even allowing equal advantages, a gentleman's son has more chances of growing up a gentleman than the son of a working man.[28]

John Halifax, somewhat in the manner of Evan Harrington, displays on his first appearance 'a mind and breeding above his outward condition'.[29] Contact with trade cannot soil him, he feels, since he is a gentleman by birth. His situation here is that of Evan in reverse, since Evan fears that the tailor's life is one which must deprive him of all he values. The gentlewoman loved by John Halifax comes to realize: 'You have . . . showed me what I shall remember all my life – that a Christian only, can be a true gentleman.'[30] With characteristic irony, Meredith places just this sentiment in the mouth of the arch-hypocrite, the Countess de Saldar, at the end of the novel. Vanquished in English Society, she finds another element within which she can exist and in which she can regain status and self-respect – the Roman Catholic Church:

> It is the sweet sovereign Pontiff alone who gathers all in his arms, not excepting tailors. . . . I am persuaded of this; that it is utterly impossible for a man to be a *true gentleman* who is not of the true Church (569, 572).

Evan's confrontation with the tailor Goren crystallizes the problem facing him on his return to his native land. Significantly, we do not see him as a child in the tailor's shop at Lymport. Unlike John Halifax, Evan's condition appears to be superior to that of his origins in terms of his place in the social hierarchy. When he asks Rose for her definition of a gentleman she replies: '"Can't tell you, Don Doloroso. Something you are, sir," she added, surveying him' (45). The meeting with Goren shows Evan that he must come to terms with the social status he can assume in his own country. Just as the Poles in *Sandra Belloni* are forced to confront the outrageous Irishwoman, Mrs Chump, upon whose wealth their social position rests, so Evan's disguise is penetrated by the plebeian Goren, who offers to take him on as his apprentice. Yet Evan's problems of class-identification are not his alone. Most of the characters in *Evan Harrington* are forced to come to terms with it and are seen to react in different ways. The class-preoccupation of the Great Mel, 'the gallant adventurer tied to his shop' (281), is also the legacy of Mrs Mel, who relinquished her own claims to gentility, married for love and voluntarily assumed a tradesman's identity. Through 'advantageous' marriages, Evan's three sisters move away from the small shopkeeping environment, dissociating themselves from their social origins. Jack Raikes, by birth a gentleman, whose dress and mannerisms root him firmly in the tradition of the comic servant of the picaresque tradition (a part considerably expanded in the serialized version of the novel) drops his absurd social pretensions by the end of the novel, marries a servant and takes over Evan's tailoring business. As the Countess aptly remarks, it is a case of 'natural selection'. His career is the direct antithesis of that of Evan. Even the Jocelyns, with whom Janet Duff-Gordon so eagerly identified, possess some dubious attributes. The aristocratic pretensions of Rose and Harry are upheld by ignoring Lady Jocelyn's plebeian origins. Her family have made their money in oil, and Beckley Court itself is no ancestral home, but the product of a successful speculation. Sir Franks has lived 'a score of years anticipating the demise of an incurable invalid – his mother-in-law' (361) in order to gain the fortune for which he married his wife, and it is the family desire for Harry Jocelyn to marry the crippled heiress, Juliana Bonner. If she inherits, 'he must be at hand to marrry her instantly' (361), Rose's fortune, on the other hand, is 'calculated upon the dear invalid's death' (182). Her father hopes she will marry the uncouth Ferdinand Laxley, who alone rejoices in birth and money. The situation illustrates Meredith's cynical belief that the aristocracy has sold itself to the middle class.[31]

In addition, or perhaps as a result of the bartering of blood and wealth which controls the marriages of the aristocracy and the upper middle class, there is some suggestion of an accompanying exploitation of sexuality. Harry Jocelyn's hollow protestations of love for his crippled cousin run counter to a penchant for local conquests among the servant class. The plight of Susan Wheedle, abandoned and in labour in the road suggests that this licence is not to be taken lightly. When Harry eventually thinks of marrying her, the family sends him away. Caroline Strike's status is dearly bought by the physical brutality she must endure from her husband. Mrs Evremonde is pursued by an insane husband – 'a smart little figure of a man in white hat and white trousers, who kept flicking his legs with a cane' (410). Even the qualities of a Lady Jocelyn can hardly compensate for the heartless decadence of such a Society.

Nevertheless, to understand its significance for Evan it is essential to examine the presentation of the 'honest world of work' in the novel. Its most notable feature is the peripheral position it plays in the drama proper. The bulk of this novel centres round the upper classes or those who instinctively identify with the upper-class way of life. As I have mentioned previously, Evan himself is never shown to be part of the tradesman's society. We are told that 'Tailordom was not a portion of his being, hard as Mrs Mel struck to fix it' (197). The supreme advantage of life in Lady Jocelyn's household is Evan's sense that 'He stood upon his merits in that house' (196). Rose's objection to her 'trade' relations as being 'quite sordid and unendurable' (232) is one peculiarly relevant to his own view. It is an image to some extent shared with the Countess, although for her it becomes an apparition of myth-ological horror. For the Countess trade belongs to 'the gloomy realms of Dis' and tailordom itself becomes her 'Demogorgon':

> She explained to him [Evan] what Demogorgon was in the sensation it entailed. 'You are skinned alive,' said the Countess (216).

This is exposure in its most extreme form: the loss of the ultimate protective outer garment – the skin.

Evan looks at his inherited trade embodied in 'the squalid shop, the good stern barren-spirited mother, the changeless drudgery, the existence which seemed indeed no better that what the ninth of a man was fit for'. This hopeless and claustrophobic existence is opposed to his dreams of the days of the Douglas and the Percy in the childhood picture:

It was a happy and a glorious time, was it not, when men lent each other blows that killed outright; when to be brave and cherish noble feelings brought honour; when strength of arm and steadiness of heart won fortune; when the fair stars of earth-sweet women wakened and warmed the love of squires of low degree (86).

But these dreams are irrelevant to the immediate choices society offers him. By accepting his role of tailor, Evan rejects:

the smiles of turbaned matrons; the sighs of delicate maids; genial wit; educated talk and refined scandal, vice in harness, dinners sentineled by stately plush (509).

Superficially, the loss would not appear to be significant, and it is made clear that Evan in no way loses his 'self-respect' by his acceptance of a tradesman's role. Nevertheless, the Countess's image of the tailor's role also generates some truth for him:

'Oh Evan! the eternal contemplation of Gentlemen's legs! Think of that! Think of yourself sculptured in that attitude' (430).

The dilemma which faces Evan and his instinctive preference for the higher social stratum is akin to the humiliating situation of Fanny Price returned to her family in *Mansfield Park* – moral values being equal, the life of upper-class spaciousness, with its illusion of a potential corresponding self-development is preferable to the honest drudgery, cramped environment and the exclusion of 'genial wit', 'educated talk' and 'sighs of delicate maids' (or, more specifically, the love of the woman he loves), and above all the processes of the imagination. Goren's 'humanization' in Evan's eyes in the final pages of the novel is too slightly portrayed to carry much weight. In spite of its apparent contempt for rank and appreciation of humble virtue, the novel contains an honest wish-fulfilment for Evan in its end – the donation of a fortune and a marriage for love into the upper classes.

Indeed, the novel has a stronger emotional bias in this direction than would appear from the surface image of the conventional upper-class attitude towards 'tailordom' and its all-pervasiveness in *Evan Harrington*.

Both the Great Mel and the Countess de Saldar play roles which subvert the adoption of glib, conventional attitudes to the class conflict on which *Evan Harrington* is built. Each had a distinct yet related function in the novel. The death and debts of the Great Mel initially cause all the problems which Evan and the other Harringtons must face. Although the Great Mel is not, strictly speaking, a living protagonist, his influence is diffused throughout Evan's history. He is a figure of single-minded, almost anarchic aspiration. As a genuine romantic – 'the gallant adventurer tied to his shop' – he earns the grudging sympathy and admiration of both neighbours and creditors. Since he is heedless of their maxim that 'It's no use trying to be a gentleman if you can't pay for it', they in turn 'with one accord hoist him on their heads, and bear him aloft, sweating and groaning and cursing, but proud of him!' (12). His real betrayer is his faithful and industrious wife, who marries him for love but transfers her emotional involvement from him to his business. Just as Falstaff is the poet creator of his own image, so Mel defies the mean conditions of his existence and succeeds in transforming himself, not merely into Epic hero, but (in the words of Lady Jocelyn) into 'an epic' itself. Hence Mel is the source of all heroic imagery, classical references and epic overtones with which *Evan Harrington* is drenched. By reputation, for Lady Jocelyn, he is

'the light of his age. The embodied protest against our social prejudice. Combine – say, Mirabeau and Alcibiades and the result is the Lymport Tailor: – he measures your husband in the morning: in the evening he makes love to you through a series of pantomimic transformations. He was a colossal Adonis' (277).

Retaining his identity as tailor, he is simultaneously actor and potent hero of myth. It is an existence in which the fashioning of new clothes leads naturally into the fashioning of fluctuating roles and images, where the pantomimic merges with the heroic. Here is the embodiment of Carlyle's tailor/poet whose poetic creation is his own style of life and enduring reputation. Even the Countess has a genuine admiration for her father and finds difficulty in hiding her grief at his death. Ironically, he is castigated by the aristocrats as 'prince of snobs' in its sense of ostentatious plebeian by those who in the Thackerayan sense are more guilty of this offence.

The Countess de Saldar wages a feminine continuation and modification of her father's course. She is as much the central protagonist of the novel as Evan. Like her father, she has her place in mythology. An 'escaped Eurydice', she flees 'the gloomy realms of Dis' disguising her 'close relationship to Pluto' (19). Unlike her father, she inters her tailoring origin, defying even the recognition of those she has known in her youth, and re-emerges as a Portuguese noblewoman. Nevertheless, she finds, like most of Meredith's characters, that the true field of action lies in one's native environment. Her motives are described by Meredith:

This was nothing more than the simple desire to be located, if but for a day or two, on the footing of her present rank, in the English country house of an offshoot of our aristocracy. She who had moved in the first society of a foreign capital – who had married a Count, a minister of his sovereign, had enjoyed delicious high-bred badinage with refulgent ambassadors, could boast the friendship of duchesses, and had been the amiable receptacle of their pardonable follies; she who, moreover, heartily despised things English:–this lady experienced thrills of proud pleasure at the prospect of being welcomed at a third-rate English Mansion. But then that mansion was Beckley Court. We return to our first ambitions as to our first loves (174).

With more duplicity, but with greater discipline and subtlety, she recreates her own identity and stages a social revolution.

Who could suppose this grand lady with her coroneted anecdotes and delicious breeding the daughter of that thing [trade]. It was not possible to suppose it. It seemed to defy the fact itself (26).

With the Countess as with the Great Mel, reality bows to the power of the imagination. Her error of insight is to expect that Evan can make a transformation as complete as her own. Hence she is unable to believe that her brother has publicly declared himself a tailor 'because he was nothing of the sort' (175). On another level, her vision of fact is more accurate than that of Evan himself, since he has at this point in no real sense taken on the tailor's role.

In spite of the Countess's unscrupulous nature, her consistent vitality seduces the sympathies of the reader towards her aims. Her 'dedication to the class struggle' is Machiavellian and total. 'She relinquishes the joys of life for the joys of intrigue. This is her element' (170). She is 'the most potent visitor Beckley Court has ever yet embraced' (176). In the 'Battle of the Bulldogs' sequence, the image of the Countess as a warrior in defence of a 'poetic' ideal of individual control over identity and environment appears at its most explicit. The battleground is composed of the two hills 'Olympus' and 'Parnassus', and in these scenes the Countess is presented, albeit ironically, as the poet of her own manœuvres.

> I confess that the hand here writing is not insensible to the effects of that first glass of champagne. The poetry of our Countess's achievements waxes rich in manifold colours: I see her by the light of her own pleas to providence (398).

And 'The Countess stood alone: it is ever thus with Genius' (408). The contempt felt by Rose Jocelyn for her prospective sister-in-law is not shared by Lady Jocelyn, whose attitude is one of fascinated incredulity – the attitude, it would seem, of Meredith himself. Whatever the hypocrisy and snobbery of her pretensions to rank, the Countess is more subversive than her flamboyant father. The Great Mel demanded the right to live openly within the two spheres of tradesman and gentry. The Countess de Saldar insists on total identification with the class to which she feels the greatest affinity whilst retaining a cool and accurate perception of the vulnerability of its pretensions. In her own way, she too is the tailor/poet of *Sartor Resartus*:

> Accept in the Countess the heroine who is combating class-prejudices and surely she is pre-eminently noteworthy. True, she fights only for her family, and is virtually the champion of the opposing institution misplaced. That does not matter: the Fates have done it purposely: By conquering, she establishes a principle. . . . Issuing out of Tailordom, she a Countess, has done all this (394).

Meredith's ironic tone here, as elsewhere in this novel, comes very near to the brand of humour maintained by Carlyle in discussing Teufelsdröckh's Philosophy of Clothes. There is an element of seriousness in Meredith's appreciation of the Countess as a subversive force, however much she can be seen as prey for the conventional satirist.

The Countess's eventual flight to Rome and the 'arms' of the 'Sweet sovereign Pontiff' and her revelation of the real nature of the 'true gentleman' suggest that such a code, pushed to its logical extreme, is divorced from ethical thought and behaviour and needs

only the sanction of society and religious corruption for its main-
tenance. Through the Countess, Meredith attacks the mystique of
the 'gentleman' which bears no relation to current social conditions
and individual ambitions.

The absurd pride which motivates Evan's behaviour as a 'true
gentleman' (as opposed to the 'real' gentlemen, such as Lord
Laxley and Harry Jocelyn) is his closest and most dubious link with
the aristocracy. Each time Evan takes upon himself to behave in
true gentlemanly fashion in defiance of social mores he appears
somewhat ridiculous. His haughty avowal of his tailoring origins
at the inn is countered by Tom Cogglesby's 'You're a hot-headed
young fool, sir: . . . You a tailor! Who'll believe it? You're a nobleman in disguise' (150). When he takes upon himself the Countess's
guilt at Beckley and loses Rose's regard after his 'confession', he
finds 'now that he had plunged into his pitch-bath, the guilt
seemed to cling to him' (450). Just as Rose learns to reject her
snobbish prejudices, Evan learns from her to reject 'the baseness
of his pride which has supported him?'. Evan's idea of honour has
been a force which almost destroys, not only his own happiness,
but that of Rose.

Nevertheless, the most natural and sympathetic environment for
Evan is that of the upper classes. In this respect nothing is changed
by the end of the novel. After his brief sojourn in the midst of
tailordom, he is once more transported to Beckley Court, *Arabian
Nights* fashion. This is no betrayal, since he has all along been
shown as someone whose social and financial condition in life
conflicts sharply with his education. The case of 'natural selection'
illustrated by Raikes could as well be applied to Evan himself.

Evan's salvation does not lie in becoming a tailor, but in a fearless acceptance of his origin and of the members of the tradesman
class as human beings. He must recognize that Goren's 'Balance of
Breeches' is neither more nor less ludicrous than Melville Jocelyn's
'Balance of Power'. He must not take upper-class society at its own
valuation.

Nevertheless, Evan himself does not appear as a revolutionary
any more than his father or his sisters:

Rather he seemed to admit the distinction between his birth
and that of a gentleman, admitting it to his own soul, as it
were and struggled simply as men struggle against a destiny
(290).

In this 'chronicle of desperate heroism' Evan, as the hero of the comedy, is allowed to triumph over his logical destiny and to retain conservative principles whilst profiting from social mobility. A more realistic view of the situation is to be found in Meredith's own comment:

> In this struggle with society I see one of the instances where success is entirely to be honoured and remains proof of merit. For however boldly antagonism may storm the ranks of society it will certainly be repelled, whereas affinity cannot be resisted; and they who against obstacles of birth, claim and keep their position among the educated and refined, have that affinity. It is on the whole rare, so that society is not often invaded. I think it will have to front Jack Cade again before another Old Mel and his progeny shall appear (425).

This seems to be Meredith's only allusion to the 'convulsion' of society which he mentions in a letter as a cathartic process. Nevertheless, his choice of Jack Cade as a revolutionary figure is significant, since Cade was himself an example of a poor man marrying into the gentry and changing his name to the noble one of Mortimer before he led his revolt. Meredith's reference to the rarity of 'Old Mel and his progeny' suggests that in a pre-revolutionary era he is weaving a tale of wish-fulfilment.

Evan Harrington appears to be an exploration of contradictory reactions towards a similar social conflict taking place in Meredith the tailor/poet. He himself is Carlyle's metaphorical tailor who sees through the pretences and protective garb of the upper classes, but he is also the tailor who cannot gain acceptance into the environment which, for all its flaws, is still so desirable.

Notes

1 *The Ordeal of George Meredith*, New York, 1953.
2 *A Troubled Eden: Nature and Society in the Works of George Meredith*, Edinburgh and London, 1961.
3 *George Meredith: His Life and Work*, 1956.
4 *Three Satirists of Snobbery*, 1939.
5 'The Reception of George Meredith's Early Novels', *Nineteenth-century Fiction*, December 1964.
6 *George Meredith: Les Cinquante Premières Années*, Paris, 1923.

7 Op. cit., 228.
8 Much of the preceding information is derived from S. M. Ellis, *George Meredith*, 1920, and Lionel Stevenson, op. cit.
9 *Letters*, collected and edited by his son, 1912, i, 47.
10 Ibid., ii, 387.
11 *Catalogue of the Altschul Collection of George Meredith in the Yale University Library*, compiled by Bertha Coolidge, New Haven, 1931, 83.
12 Ellis, op. cit., 138.
13 Janet Ross, *The Fourth Generation*, 1912, 50–1.
14 *Letters*, 24.
15 The text used is that of the Memorial ed.
16 Catalogue of the Altschul Collection, op. cit., 82.
17 Standard ed., 1904, II, iii, 77.
18 Op. cit., I, viii, 35.
19 Op. cit., III, xi, 196–7.
20 *Book of Snobs*, 1852, 274.
21 Ibid., 278.
22 Ibid., 26–7.
23 Ibid., 275.
24 Margaret Dalziel, See *Popular Fiction of 100 Years Ago*, 1957, 137.
25 *The Idea of a University*, 1873, Discourse viii, 208.
26 *Modern Painters*, New edn., Smith & Elder, 1873, V, vii, 266.
27 Catalogue of the Altschul Collection, op. cit., 82.
28 1st ed. 1856, i, 11.
29 Ibid., i, 11.
30 Ibid., ii, 43.
31 *Letters*, i, 191.

On Re-reading *Evan Harrington*

J. M. S. Tompkins

'As readable as Dickens',[1] says Jack Lindsay of *Evan Harrington*. This description would have puzzled still more the already puzzled readers who groped through the instalments of the novel in *Once a Week*, and it would hardly have pleased the intellectuals who built up Meredith's reputation as 'an heroic spirit', a 'poet philosopher, realist and idealist in one'[2] in the generation before 1914. Even now, when the subtle is more readily assimilated than the simple, when 'naïve', on the one hand, and 'rewarding complexity' on the other, indicate clearly what has been lost and gained in the reading skills of today, we may pause on the comparison. There are plenty of contacts between Dickens and Meredith in the area of their serious concerns, and streaks of similarity, too, in their temperaments, in their secrecy over their origins and in their bent for fantastic farce, shown in the book under consideration in the gambols of the brothers Cogglesby and the antics of Jack Raikes. But does the 'Battle of the Bull-dogs' (xxx and xxxi) slip down with the relishing ease and spontaneity, the narrative lucidity of Dickens' concerted scenes? The comic energy, strong and luxuriant as it is, has by this time assembled so many tasks, is responsible for the motives and movements of so many creatures, that the reader begins to share the anxiety of control, timing the comic collisions and keeping tabs on their multiple agents. The scene is a great exhibition of intellect, and, like so many of Meredith's exhibitions, built up not only round comic situations – the Countess's tactics and Jack Raikes's victimization – but also round centres of strong, natural human feeling – Mrs Mel's terrible love for her son, the young love of Evan and Rose, the unhappy Caroline's inclination to the Duke of Belfield – and these must be perceived to give off warmth even in the cool, astringent climate of comedy. To point this out is not to say that *Evan Harrington* is not readable, even in the knotted scene which I have unfairly chosen, but the reader needs to sympathize with the writer as such, to be interested in his problems and procedures, and this is not necessary for the enjoyment of Dickens, though it deepens it.

The 'Battle of the Bull-dogs', however, comes at the climax of the 'fourth act' of *Evan Harrington*; it is the delusive victory, snatched against cruel odds, which is to be reversed by nightfall; the earlier chapters, though rich and full, move more easily. Siegfried Sassoon, who, like the present writer, first made acquaintance with Meredith in the rich afterglow of his somewhat belated fame, when to taste his work, however negligently, was an obligation upon any young man or woman inclined to literature, describes his reaction on re-reading *Evan Harrington* after some twenty years. After the seventh chapter – this is the one in which Evan, under the weight of his mother's expectations, accepts the duty of paying his dead father's debts by the only way open to him, that of becoming a tailor – he decided that the novel 'was so far a classic performance; clear narration in ripe and sound English; rich material; the characters introduced with precision and with controlled gusto: and a sense of being conducted by admirably unhastened stages towards the development of events. At the end of the twelfth chapter I was feeling as comfortable as ever.' And he sums up his impression of the book with the words, 'a vintage flavour and the mellowness of an old master'.[3]

The twelfth chapter describes the annual supper which Tom Cogglesby gives at the Green Dragon at Fallowfield to the locals and all chance-come visitors. We stand on the threshold of the Countess de Saldar's campaign at Beckley Court and of Evan's ordeal there, which cover the middle three acts of the comedy. Already the texture is thickening. We meet a number of characters not, as all previous ones have been, clearly connected with the Harringtons. They are the future agents and instruments of the family fate – Susan Wheedle, Drummond Forth, Harry Jocelyn and the Honourable Ferdinand Laxley; they are placed prospectively in position, but their relevance is not yet discerned; they are not yet fully identified, least of all to Evan. Retrospectively, we seem to have had hints enough, but at first reading they may well be submerged in the elaboration of the rural festivity and the characteristic accumulation of pressures – innate pride, general and immediate situation, chance, and large potations of good ale – that bring the hero to declare himself publicly the son of a tailor. By now the reader perceives that his pleasure is dependent upon his alertness.

The proliferation of sub-plots in Meredith's fiction is sometimes ascribed to the predominance of the three-volume novel. Certainly, the state of the novel market at the time cannot be ignored. He was not obliged, however, to fill the volumes with such an intricate concatenation of interests. Trollope did not do so. The ample provision of space and the reader's expectation of copious material encouraged the over-development of something that was radical in his attitude to his art, the passion for accounting fully for all that happens. 'This cursed desire I have haunting me to show the reason of things is a perpetual obstruction to movement,' he complained in a letter to Samuel Lucas, editor of *Once a Week*, during the concurrent writing and serialization of *Evan Harrington*. '. . . My principle is to show the event flowing from evident causes. To naturalize them to the mind of the reader.'[4] It was the 'cursed desire', more than the requirements of the novel market that made it impossible for Meredith to write a plain story. He was to begin *Rhoda Fleming* with a limited number of characters and a classically simple situation. But the development required that a young man should act cruelly and caddishly who had not been conceived as a cruel cad. He can do so only under multiple pressures; but the 'haunting' does not stop at that. How do the pressures come to be exerted? What were the motives of those who exerted them? They, too, are individuals in particular situations, not mere embodiments of social conditions. The answers are given; the psychological blur, which the author will not tolerate, recedes to the edge of vision; the foreground is filled with a tangle of crossing threads; and the story ceases to be plain.

Evan Harrington is better managed as a narrative than *Rhoda Fleming*, but the intricacy is of the same kind. The house-party at Beckley Court and their friends in the neighbourhood have a great many functions to fulfil. In bulk, they are the social world with which Evan feels an affinity and in which the Countess manœuvres for a lodgement; but it is as individuals, linked to each other in various ways, that they come into play. They have to offer handles for the Countess's ingenious dispositions, and standards by which Evan is measured, or measures himself. They have to provide means by which the local memories of the Great Mel and his daughters are channelled into the talk of the house-party and exposed to different judgments – hence the Uplofts and Coppings – and means by which these channels are temporarily obstructed. They have to generate from individual sources the opiates that keep Evan from complete realization of his false position at Beckley Court; for his blindness is not a simple submission to the delightful activities of this summer life, to the riding, music, dancing, dining and conversation, nor even to his love for Rose. The approval of the elder men, the companionship and rivalry of the younger, the unshadowed acceptance of him on his merits by Lady Jocelyn, the renewed opportunity to prove his usefulness as Melville's secretary, the reassuring presence of his brother-in-law, known to all as a tradesman, as a guest at Beckley Court, the revelation of his sister Caroline's unhappiness – all these are needed to blunt the stabs of consciousness. All these bear on different aspects of a character which, as Meredith often reminds us, is still unformed, and all these effects have themselves to be traced to the natures and situations of those who produce them. There are some thirty ladies and gentlemen in the Beckley Court scenes. In addition, the servants have some importance. Evan is measured by his conduct to the Wheedle sisters as well as by his conduct to Rose Jocelyn and Juliana Bonner.

It would seem, then, that the reader's pleasure in the middle section of *Evan Harrington* is greatly increased on re-reading. The threads now lie, without disorder, in his hand, and he perceives how few of these figures could be spared. They are not only vivid, typical and variously entertaining, but of multiple use. Lady Roseley, for instance, illuminates both Melchisedec and his wife by her visit of condolence to the tailor's shop at the beginning of the book; through her eyes we see their son's young handsomeness, never described, and his likeness to his father; her silent complicity with the Countess, her absorption of the potentially dangerous George Uploft's services to keep him from Beckley Court, give that arch-conspirator time; and all this falls into place when we can refer it to the anecdote, told at the dinner in ch. xxii, of the magnificent footman at Bodley Race-ball, who fired a curtain to carry away the lady. At this dinner, through which stalks the figure of Old Mel, Caroline, his elder daughter, faints, and is recognized. At first reading, the drama of the exposure may well obscure the exact nature of the strain. When Caroline faints, she has just heard from George Uploft of her father's honourable refusal to traffic in her beauty when she was a girl, and of the fortune it cost him. She herself is on the brink of accepting the Duke of Belfield's proposals. It is the shock of the contrast that causes her collapse, and we do not fully estimate the weight of her distress until we have met her husband, Major Strike, months after the house-party has broken up.

It is perhaps a pardonable fault in a classical novel, which by definition requires re-reading for full appreciation, if the full bearing of its incidents is not immediately apprehended. It is a pleasure to discover more and more, and to follow Meredith's invention as he completes the Harrington spectrum with this kindest, weakest and most beautiful of the sisters. But it is certainly a help in following its involutions in these middle scenes, if we are clear in our heads about the nature of Evan's and Jack Raikes's contracts with Tom Cogglesby, the election at Fallowfield, and the distinction between Admiral Harrington, who was, in truth, a relation of Mel, and Sir Abraham Harrington, who was not, but was boldly annexed by the Countess, in the face, as she comes to fear, of Providence. It must also be admitted that the density of the subsidiary material that presses round Evan's crisis leaves Meredith too much to spin off in the last fifth of his book. That we have to 'see in the dark' when Evan is working in Mr Goren's shop is no great disadvantage. We can discern as much as is necessary for understanding. The partial obscurity stimulates, as it does when we are briefly told that, after a week at Beckley Court, Evan first began to examine of what stuff his brilliant father was composed, and fell into the gloom of the disenchanted; we have to apprehend this veiled stage of the hero's moral development, and grow better acquainted with it thereby. But final obscurity of fact is always irritating. The turns in the Strike-Belfield situation are not elucidated by Andrew's indignant exclamations in ch. xli or by the sprightly allusions in the Countess's concluding letter. Did the Duke set out to abduct Caroline, or was the appearance part of Major Strike's blackmailing plot? How did the Major die? Meredith knows, but he is too busy with Evan, Rose, Juliana, Mr Raikes and his friends, the Countess's inclination to Rome and Andrew's mock-bankruptcy to tell us. He does not, I believe, aim at mystification, in spite of the need to keep up the interest at the end of each serial instalment. He aims at piquancy, at raising a tingling interest in his reader by oblique indications; or he reserves a full statement until the fact confronts his hero, as he reserves the full statement of Caroline's plight to break Evan's self-control in Mr Goren's shop. He does not intend to baffle, but bafflement can result.

The final settlement of the minor characters is a Victorian convention. Here it is touched with originality, because we hear of it from the Countess, a wishful thinker, too much occupied with manœuvring her family to understand them well. She makes constant mistakes. She talks airily about trading Andrew Cogglesby's vote. She tells her sister that Evan 'makes the right use of Portugal'. Are we to believe that Mrs Mel's establishment as Tom Cogglesby's housekeeper is, after all, '*prospective*'? Will Caroline, the Countess's second card, really become Duchess of Belfield? If so, it is a pleasant irony that the most passive of the sisters, the least disturbed by the tailor's shop, should be propelled to the most conspicuous height. But we are not sure. One situation is left entirely open. The Countess is planning to reconcile that provincial Don Juan, Harry Jocelyn, to the Church of Rome. The coyly adumbrated enterprise – 'No; he shall have another wife, and Protestantism shall be his forsaken mistress!' – is full of the keenest comic and satiric possibilities – too keen for Meredith to handle; for, though he has been quite clear, and often very funny, about the Countess's religion, he has carefully preserved an ironical decorum; and how could any decorum survive a theological discussion between the Countess and Harry? We are left, however, with the conviction that life will go on as valiantly for the Countess in Rome as in Hampshire. Meredith cannot quite lay her on the shelf. He continues to have ideas about her.

It is, however, certain that Evan is attaché at Naples and married to Rose. This ending does not commend itself to all modern critics. To Jack Lindsay it is an evasion, and 'the whole bias of the book . . . runs counter to it'. The whole bias of the book, as he discerns it, is towards a 'savage' and 'merciless' criticism of the world of power and privilege, and a condemnation, 'bitter' with personal experience, of the 'illusion that there was anything morally good in the effort to rise in the class-world by accepting that world's values'. In this scheme Evan represents 'the spirit of honesty, the world of honest work opposed to the world of parasitism and exploitation'. After he has left Beckley Court in disgrace, 'his pride and bitterness . . . are sharply set against the world of power and privilege into which he sought to enter; they lock him solidly in with the world of work which he previously despised. They express fundamentally a class-antagonism. . . . His rejection of the Beckley estate is the correct expression of his new position.' But, and how disappointing this is, 'Meredith still feels unable to work out the direct political consequences of such a position.' So he falls back on 'the romantic formula of love triumphant with a bag of gold . . . and blows out the conflicts he has defined'.[5] Evan, in fact, should have been left in the tailor's shop, without Rose.

This is a good example of the press-gang, by which I mean the forcible removal of an author from his own background and way of thought, and the subjection of him to a service and a drill in which he did not spontaneously engage. It is sometimes a costly process. In this case it costs Meredith's honesty as a writer and the wholeness of his conception of his book. This is, in fact, *Evan Harrington* as Lindsay thinks it should have been written. Perhaps it should; but it was not. To make out that it was, the critic has to overleap, foreshorten and even misstate some of the facts of the story. To take one point: he writes: 'The Jocelyns' opposition to Evan [*sc.* as Rose's husband] crumbles when they learn of his cash-prospects.' Not at all. They know of his cash-prospects (Tom Cogglesby's offer of a thousand a year, if Rose marries him, and as much to their eldest child) before he leaves Beckley Court; they regard them with a glum respect, as possible sweeteners of a nauseous draught, if Rose sticks to her choice; but the knowledge does not disarm their opposition, and when Evan has accepted responsibility for his sister's forgery, the cash-prospects do not count at all. He has broken their code, and shown himself an outsider. When the cash-prospects are again referred to, it is after Evan has convinced Sir Franks that he has indeed 'the soul of a gentleman'. The phrase is now unacceptable; but Meredith does not propose Sir Franks as a moral judge, nor, of course, does he throw any doubt on the money-mindedness of the 'Elburne brood', which he has analysed with ironical understanding (xxix), or on their social prejudice. What he shows, by timing Old Tom's offer when he does, is that the code of gentlemanly behaviour counted for something with the Jocelyns and their like, however inadequate it may have been as a system of values.

In quibbling over this small point of the action I am quite impenitent. It is the duty of scholars to quibble, since much truth resides in particulars. A small mismeasurement becomes a large

error, when the lines are protracted into the realm of generalizations. Details of plot and story (as distinct from 'structure') are
now often ignored or devalued – and hence not infrequently
misstated. They can be, however, usefully stable points of reference, not much subject to personal, political or period reassessment,
and, within their limits, they can be applied to check the findings
of more imaginative and comprehensive critical approaches. They
can be applied, for instance, to estimate just how solidly Evan, in
Mr Goren's shop, is 'locked in with the world of work, which he
previously despised'.

Evan Harrington is about social prejudice. Meredith uses the
phrase three times. It is in confronting social prejudice that Evan
begins to make his character. Through his stung pride, he preserves his self-respect, quickens his critical judgment, and addresses
himself to accept his fate. It does not come easily to him. He thinks
of enlisting as a private soldier. He accepts the secretaryship of
Major Strike's company, and relegates his study of tailoring to the
evening hours. His moment of despair comes when the door of
escape back to his own world, opened by the Duke's offer of the
post of bailiff, is slammed immediately after by Strike's gross
insinuations about Caroline. It is then that he weeps for his sister
and himself. When we see him later in the coach, going down to
Lymport and his duty, he has stiffened his back and his lip; his
neck, indeed, is still a little too stiff for a mature posture. Meredith
allows a shimmer of amusement to play over his sympathy and
approval, spreading from the inflated terms in which he paraphrases the young man's self-conquest. The self-conquest is real
and praiseworthy; the rhetoric of rejection and encouragement
which Meredith confers on it has tones of friendly sarcasm. Evan
has still to take his moonlight rides, and show his mother a face
which she declares not 'fit for business'.

It is never Meredith's fault to over-simplify, and his work
refuses simplification. *The Shaving of Shagpat* was, without doubt,
an allegory of social revolution. *Evan Harrington* is a historical
novel, set 'in a time before our joyful era of universal equality', as
Meredith writes, with complex satire. There are likenesses between
Shibli Bagarag, the barber, and Evan Harrington, the tailor's son,
notably in the multivalence of their ruling passions. Shibli Bagarag's vanity imperils and betrays him, but without it he would never
have undertaken his tremendous task. Evan's pride is mixed with
baser elements, but without it he would not have survived the

purgatory of the last breakfast at Beckley Court and the months in Mr Goren's shop. Evan's laughter at his day-dream duel is a modest echo of Shibli's at the reflection of his crowned self. For both heroes the ape is a significant image. But a novel is not a fable; and we cannot assume that because Shibli Bagarag was told to 'cleave to his tackle', and because, in consequence, the Sword of Aklis becomes in his hands a gigantic razor to shave Shagpat, it was ever intended that Evan should cleave to his shears. Evan's real tackle is his pen and his head for affairs. Tailordom is for him an enforced masquerade. The reader notes with some amusement that Evan is never exhibited in the shop, except for the brief moment when he leads Caroline out of it into Mr Goren's parlour. We are told that he stands at the counter and handles the shears, but we never see him do so. It is another young man who, at Lymport, is negligently adorned with a tape-measure. Evan is always on the stairs or in the living-rooms, or has just ridden out.

If we allow the shape and detail of the novel to make their statements, undisturbed by anachronistic harmonies or memories of different performances, we shall find that what they say is not very different from the conclusions of the humanists who debated the nature of the gentleman in the Renaissance. The gentleman is Nature's product; but breeding helps. Meredith, well aware of Nature's secret laboratories, is specific about Evan's 'notable sire' and dam, of whom, he tells us, Evan was the 'best mixed compound', but goes no further back, and consigns 'Powys chieftains' to satire and the Countess. As for breeding, Evan was designed and prepared for the Army, passed through the house and office of a rising political *bourgeois*, and was polished at the Portuguese court. As a tailor he is denatured; and that is why Meredith cannot show him behind the counter. When he submits to be locked (in the other sense of the word) in the world of work – which is for him specifically a tailor's shop – it is, as Lindsay shrewdly remarks, in a spirit of *noblesse oblige*, rather different from his mother's practical rectitude. During this confinement, he rectifies some of his faulty suppositions about that state; but it is a liberation to him when he can return honourably to the world of his affinities. This is the likely result of his temperament and his training. Within the novel, the Jocelyn kind cannot be reduced, like Shagpat, to an Illusion. They are a highly imperfect but confident and tenacious governing class. Evan joins them; it is, within the novel, the best he can do.

This is what we should expect from the biographical context of the book. The extent to which Meredith drew on his family history was not suspected when the novel came out and was praised for the originality of its subject. Readers were not embarrassed, as they sometimes are now, by seeming to discern, under the brilliant surface, old sores, open wounds and remembered bruises. It is probable that Meredith was tougher-minded about social prejudice than we are, as the eighteenth century was tougher-minded about lunacy and the sixteenth about taming shrews. He had, moreover, made his passage. Past unpleasantnesses could be triumphantly turned to the service of fiction, and oppressions, if he still felt any, aerated by laughter. We may deduce some element of self-purgation from the keen liveliness and high mettle that result from the disburdening. The chip, if it exists, seems negligible upon so athletic a shoulder. It is with tolerant satire that he touches on the origin of the sense of social injustice in a young man's personal experience. 'I incline to think that the more ale he drank the fiercer rebel he grew against conventional ideas of rank, and those class-barriers which we scorn so vehemently when we find ourselves kicking against them' (xii). Sassoon thinks that Meredith chose to build his novel on the characters of his relations for the good reason that they were such rich material for a novelist. Their social range was unusually large, extending from tailors and innkeepers to personal friends of royalty and a minister of state, from supposed medieval Welsh princes to a shop in Portsmouth. He thinks also, that, in writing, Meredith ceased to care about his own situation and became 'controlled by the spirit of romantic comedy. . . . Naturally, he had found it a nuisance to be "the son of a snip". But he was now taking advantage of the situation, and doing so with relish.' This seems to me, if not the whole of the truth, at least the most useful part of it. It tallies with what I believe to be the prevailing tone of the book. We need not assume that the purgation was final and complete; a book is not a man.

It is not, in fact, Meredith's savagery and bitterness that comes uppermost to my taste, as I once more peruse (with a mind as flexible to fresh impressions as is possible to the elderly) his picture of the company in a 'third-rate English mansion' in Hampshire a few years after Waterloo (he stresses the period explicitly by several light touches of clothes and manners), and of the social and moral plight there of a young man of good brains and admirable presence, whose background is trade, and for good measure a trade that still carried a special stigma of ridicule. At times I hear the twirl and cut of the satirist's lash. The young men, Harry Jocelyn and Laxley, are specimens of the faults of their class. Harry is irresponsible and sometimes brutal, and Laxley, to whom on one occasion the monkey-image is applied, is arrogant and empty-headed. This is, no doubt, why Meredith added the smiling and inoffensive William Harvey to the cast. Sir Franks, an excellent husband and father, dislikes and evades 'bother', and the Countess thinks his ideas are few; he has, however, travelled in the East with his wife and Drummond Forth, of whom Lady Jocelyn says that she would trust her daughter with him in a desert. Mrs Shorne is unpleasant, and Louisa Carrington after a husband. Melville Jocelyn is open to the Countess's wiles – a diplomatic hazard. We have to add the witty and philosophical spinster, Miss Isabella Current; Rose, for whom the testimony of her maid, breaking into her skilful attempts at flirtation with Evan – 'Miss Rose has my respect' – is enough; and Lady Jocelyn, who speaks to Evan's 'secret nature', so that he 'rose to his worth in the society she presided over'.

What is this group but a normal display of various human beings, living in a state which permits the development of certain valuable qualities – courage, independence, intellectual curiosity, high personal honour – and encourages the overgrowth of certain dangerous faults – arrogance, irresponsibility, a blind limitation of sympathies, and a consequent measure of brutality, ranging from the genial to the violent – and, between the two extremes, has established an ample form of life, where characters can ripen to their full potentiality, and a standard of conduct is maintained, which Sir Osbert Sitwell considers 'very high',[6] and which cannot honestly be dismissed as mere hypocrisy. They are a privileged class and, like all such classes, tenacious of their property and privilege, and insistent on their differentia of breeding. They play politics after the fashion of their time, with a strong eye to personal advantage. They drive nothing to fanaticism, except in self-defence. The Countess, from outside the pale, is more fanatical than anyone inside it; after her, Ferdinand Laxley, who has no brains and no curiosity about anyone unlike himself. The hardest things said are dramatic, a little muted by the strain under which they are said or thought. Evan, after apologizing to Laxley, 'towered in his conceit considerably above these aristocratic boors, who were speechless and graceless, but tigers for their privileges and advantages'; and Juliana, diseased, and torn with love for Evan and jealousy of Rose, tells him that he does not know the brutal cruelty of people of birth. These things have a loading of truth, but they are not Meredith's final verdict. The older men and some of the women recognize quality; and Evan, though known to be the son of a tailor and the impecunious and undesired lover of Rose, is treated as 'one of their own rank' until he is believed to have broken their code. The Countess does not share in this quasi-adoption.

If Meredith, as a political thinker, thought worse than this of the landed gentry, his book is not affected by it. He is writing natural history with a sort of affection for the splendid specimens he records. Here is George Uploft, pinned out on the page:

> a fat-faced, rotund young squire – a bully where he might be, and an obedient creature enough where he must be – good-humoured when not interfered with; fond of the table, and brimful of all the jokes of the county, the accent of which just seasoned his speech.

He is a natural product of the countryside, not without his standards, and capable of speaking up for Old Mel at the Beckley dinner with some kindness and concern for justice. We have to acknowledge that Meredith felt some attraction towards this masculine, confident life. This is amusingly put by Sir Osbert:

> I think Meredith genuinely loved an aristocrat: he liked the robust speech of the great Victorian ladies, so different to the caged-in, mincing ways of the contemporary bourgeoisie, he liked the pride and generosity of the men: their swift return to old habits, their inclination to fight duels, and the facilities offered them by Club steps for public horsewhippings: opportunities of which contemporary novelists took full advantage.[7]

This is said of Meredith's whole opus, but most of it applies to this early work. To describe the Harrington invasion of Beckley Court, as Norman Kelvin does in *A Troubled Eden* (1961) as 'a war in which the upper classes are mercilessly pilloried' is to impoverish the book and flatten the idiosyncrasies of the novelist and his creatures.

Meredith's irony, sympathy, amusement and satiric precision play over his whole subject-matter in shifting lights, but particularly over the Great Mel and what he represents and bequeaths. If we want a consistently punitive display of snobbery, we must turn to Thackeray with his 'mean admiration of mean things'. This does not define the motive force of Melchisedec or his son; I would not contend for the Countess. From the time when we see his portly body laid out in his old dragoon's uniform, split at the thigh, with Jacko, the monkey, cowering eclipsed under the monstrous helmet, and the impressed Lymport tradesmen wondering how their accounts with him stand, and why, to the time when he becomes the topic at the Beckley Court dinner, the Great Mel appears variously as genuine and pretentious, dignified and a buffoon, foolish and admirable. Lady Jocelyn calls him 'the embodied protest against our social prejudices', 'a robust Brummel, and the Regent of low life', and 'the Prince of Snobs'. His tastes were those of the gentlemen present at her table. 'I prefer him infinitely to your cowardly democrat, who barks for what he can't get, and is generally beastly'; and she concludes with more humanity and less boldness of wit: 'The stuff was in him, but the fates were unkind.' His son had admired his father's barbaric virtues, and his daughter, the Countess, considers her father, whom she huddles out of sight, the finest gentleman she has seen; but Evan was very young and the Countess's taste is suspect: she admires Jack Raikes when she thinks him a rich young man. The lights change – and are still changing – over his legacy to his son. He has indeed brought the boy up as a gentleman, but omitted to provide him with a profession; he has taught him to raise his sights above a practicable mark, and plunged him by his gentlemanly extravagance unprepared into tailordom. Even the ape is not a stable symbol or, rather, the snobbery he symbolizes is not a stable thing. Something is to be said for the effort to assimilate ourselves to what we think is above us, even if we say it jocosely. The ape who strives to copy the lion, says Lady Jocelyn, is an ape of judgment. What is the upshot? We cannot generalize. Nature and Fortune play too large a part. Within the book the upshot is an attaché at Naples; in its biographical context, Meredith, artist and gentleman.

The Jocelyn world is obsolete; and its characters and the stories they move in are likewise extinct, says Sir Osbert. What remains is the emotion; 'the love, the hatred, the pity . . . strong as the scent of wood or mountain, still comes up from the words'. It is one of the pleasures of the historically-minded reader to find these fully human emotions moving in obsolete forms and, sometimes, at obsolete promptings. It is another pleasure to come on the situation and reaction that stand free of their context, authenticate themselves, and need no socio-historical commentary. We can find both kinds in *Evan Harrington*. The 'manners' of Evan's love-passages with Rose, the value she attaches to a kiss, Evan's chivalrous abstention that defers their first embrace to the end of the book and reserves for it a conclusive importance – these modes of courtship, if not wholly out of knowledge, are so remote from today's expectations that they are often simply dismissed as 'romantic'; but Evan's anguished nights in Mr Goren's shop, the unconscious cruelty with which he follows Rose in the park, are quite independent of their social and moral frames. His crucial contest, which is not between snobbery and honest work, but between love and self-love, is universal in its nature and particular in its form. It is not a simple romantic issue. Self-respect that has kept him true to his standards, upright in his despair and independent in his tailor's shop, is a product of self-love. Evan's progress has been to claim to be a gentleman, to feel himself a better gentleman than Harry or Laxley, and to prove himself, in fact, too good, too theoretic a gentleman, by honouring a code at the expense of Rose's love and courage. This he has now to perceive and recant, and he does so in the simplest and most immediate way. Rose's physical presence, alone with him in the room above the shop, confronts him with the individual reality that is the touchstone of what is true and false in his pride. Her touch breaks through the artifice of his self-defence. He will accept help to be true to her. This is his full maturity.

Sir Osbert describes the Meredith territory as 'a country full of ennobling love, and one where the human relationships revealed have a peculiar value never quite to be assessed to the full extent'. I do not find much on this aspect of his art among modern critics, and Sir Osbert's words may well seem to have an old-fashioned ring. Not obsolete, however. This was the aspect emphasized by my elders, when – not quite so young as Sir Osbert, who thinks he must have been about twelve – I entered, stumbling, the Meredith country; and this is the aspect which continues to give out radiance at each re-reading, even when the reader is a little weary, as he may sometimes be, of the high intellectual feats and the tricky irony. These relationships are of many kinds and between all ages. They sometimes issue in tragedy, and are often exposed to the scrutiny of the Comic Muse. They work in a state of human imperfection, and generate there a sense of the beauty and capacity of life. *Evan Harrington* is not so rich in this respect as some of Meredith's later books. It has nothing to match Lord Ormont and his sister, Lady Charlotte Eglett, in *Lord Ormont and His Aminta*. Yet everywhere there is the flow of human affection, irrigating the social territory. This flow is so continuous, that it is perhaps the arid spots that are most noticeable. Poor Juliana, diseased in mind and body, is essentially unlovable to the robust Jocelyns. Only Caroline, accustomed to sorrow, and not quite pure in her motives, since she has Evan in mind, does her best.

Those scenes of affection that I have in mind are neither romantic nor heroic; they are the common stuff of life. Sir Franks and Lady Jocelyn, defending themselves against the bother of Rose's love of Evan by reading French memoirs together, exchanging choice bits in assured conformity of taste, until the calm wife has seen her husband read himself into tranquillity, is a pleasant picture, focusing a partnership that has worn well. Meredith spends some care on a partnership that has been dissolved before the book starts. Mrs Mel, who stands gazing down with 'benignant friendliness' at the splendid man she married for love, 'aloof, as one whose duties to that form of flesh were well-nigh done', has accepted his infidelities, carried him upstairs when he came home drunk, and picked up the pence while he squandered the guineas. The physical fascination of her youth never left her. 'In her heart she hardly blamed him.' She is a silent woman. It is Meredith who, for a moment, opens to us the nature and the depth of her experience when she comes to Beckley Court with the 'terrible determination to cast a devil out of the one she best loved . . . to speak publicly, and disgrace and humiliate, that she might save [her son] from the devils that had ruined his father'. It is one of Meredith's thrilling moments of serious passion. Mrs Mel's words are few, plain and controlled, but her life is behind them.

The observations of a reader who comes back once more to a familiar book are not likely to be concerned with its obvious merits. I yield to none in admiration of the Countess de Saldar. What I have noticed this time, however, has not been her brilliance and glittering obliquity, but the exchange of ghostly anecdotes with her mother, which economically illustrates the Countess's conscious adaptation to low society (though her ghosts are all titled), her superstition, and the curious ties of family likeness. Such ties can be followed through all the Harringtons. Evan's quietness, so often distinguished, is his mother's. Meredith had a most thorough-going humane imagination. Here he may be working from, and varying, known facts; but his books are full of such material, restless and rewarding with constant observation and speculation, abundant in substantiating and subtle detail. He offers an almost inexhaustible field of quiet discovery. It is a charm that outlasts other pleasures and outweighs irritations.

Notes

1 See *George Meredith, His Life and Work*, 1956, 352.
2 See Dixon Scott, 'George Meredith's Letters', *Manchester Guardian*, 1912.
3 See *Meredith*, 1948.
4 Undated; in the Altschul Collection, Yale University Library. Quoted from L. T. Hergenhan, 'A Critical Consideration of the Reviewing of the Novels of George Meredith from *The Shaving of Shagpat* to *The Egoist*' (unpublished thesis, London, 1960).
5 See Jack Lindsay, op. cit., 105–7.
6 See Presidential Address to the English Association, 1947.
7 See Sir Osbert Sitwell, op. cit.

Rhoda Fleming:
Meredith in the Margin

David Howard

'Help poor girls.' The last words of *Rhoda Fleming* (1865), the words of the dying Dahlia Fleming, are often what is most remembered from the novel. And when they are quoted it is usually with the same meaning and context for the word 'poor' in mind: help fallen girls. *Rhoda Fleming* belongs to fallen-girl fiction, it is part of that intense Victorian concern for 'the great social evil'. Meredith, of course, is on the generous, liberal side: the seduced Dahlia should be helped, not blamed or punished. It is the plain moral to 'my plain story'.

But these can hardly be the last words on these last words. *Rhoda Fleming* is a novel about three 'girls' and there is a sense, not an uncommon one in Meredith, that all women are to be pitied. Dahlia stands for her sex rather than for her depraved sisterhood.

But more importantly for doubts about the plainness of the story its last paragraph hints that Dahlia is really talking about her sister Rhoda, the intransigently 'pure'. One rightly, I think, suspects a pun, and also a double sense of 'pure', the same Hardy was to use in his *Tess of the D'Urbervilles* sub-title: morally pure, and more interestingly the suggestion of fundamental womanliness, which in this novel involves an attraction to the superficial and (the two are closely connected) the purposive and brave. Both Rhoda and Mrs Lovell demand 'manly' action and this demand is part of a general concern in the novel with 'purity 'of action, as I shall indicate.

However, the meaning I would want to stress now is the most obvious one – 'lacking money'. 'Everyone wants money,' says Algernon Blancove at one point. *Rhoda Fleming* is a novel preoccupied – one could say obsessed – with money, particularly with the lack of it. 'The money-demon' is early introduced and from then on scene after scene invokes him: Rhoda embracing Anthony's stolen gold, Rhoda and Robert breaking into the trivial savings of the servants, Algernon with his dwindling £1,000 – these are obvious instances of what is a continual manifold concern in the novel; and, of course, what was particularly obsessing Meredith at the time of writing it. He was more than usually desperate for money, anxious to write what could be sold, a short popular ('plain') novel, through a popular publisher, Tinsley. As the novel expanded under his hand, as the attempt at popular appeal became more and more ironic, he realized that this was not the novel to make him a millionaire, as he had planned. The guilt and bitterness of trivial treasure trove haunt the book: everyone is about to be dunned. The novel and poor girls be damned – God help poor novelists.

The novel in general then supplies this meaning for 'poor' and so does the scene immediately before Dahlia's brief deathbed. This is a conversation between Percy Waring and Mrs Lovell discussing her prospects, where she reveals she is bankrupt and is going 'to marry a bank-balance', Edward's father, in fact. In an earlier scene, where Waring proposes to her, she asks him in reply how much money he has. We have this poor girl recently in mind then when we meet Dahlia's sentimental injunction at the end of the book.

Meredith seems set to destroy his gently tearful ending; indeed, he seems set almost from the beginning to destroy his own novel. There is an urge to set up appealing moments which are then avoided, destroyed, or heavily penalized.

In many ways *Rhoda Fleming* seems to be a mess. The plot is often awkward and incredible, although this would matter less if the writing wasn't so careless. But, apart from this awkwardness and perfunctoriness which are obvious enough, particularly if one were to concentrate on the use of Sedgett, there are two striking characteristics of *Rhoda Fleming* – two markedly irritating characteristics. They are characteristics of Meredith's work in general, and they are particularly obvious in this 'plain story'. We have to remember that Meredith is the most irritating novelist of the nineteenth century, and if we ignore that capacity to irritate we are inventing a safe Meredith to argue about.

The two characteristics – which in the end are probably one and the same – are, firstly, what I will call for want of a better word

peripheralism, and, secondly, the concern with mistaken identity
(particularly marked in *Rhoda Fleming*) and the connected sense of
confusion and ignorance. By peripheralism I mean Meredith's
habit of concentrating on trivial incident and character to the
exclusion of and often in place of major event and character. I take
it this is what Henry James was talking about in his remarks on
Lord Ormont and his Aminta:

> not a difficulty met, not a figure presented, not a scene
> constituted – not a dim shadow condensing once either into
> audible or visible reality making you hear for an instant the
> tap of its feet on the earth!

The second characteristic frequently leads to the response: I
don't know what's going on, I don't know who is who. This was
and still is the at least initial reaction, for example, to 'Modern
Love'. And, of course, the two irritations can combine into an
overwhelming single irritation: first nothing happens and then
everything happens at once, but usually somewhere else.

To elaborate the second element in *Rhoda Fleming* a little.
Mistaken identity is crucial to the plot: Algernon Blancove must be
confused with Edward Blancove. This is the main cause for the
manifold confusions that arise in the novel, but Meredith continually tops it up in other ways. The landlady of the Pilot Tavern
thinks Robert Armstrong might be her son at one point; we are
made to believe until the last in the final conversation between Mrs
Lovell and Peter Waring that she is going to marry Algernon; and,
most baffling moment of all, in ch. xxx, 'The Expiation', we over-
hear with Robert a plea to Dahlia which could be from Sedgett, or
from Edward, or from some unknown 'gentleman'.

As well as mistaken identities, the novel seems full of double
identities. There are respectable thematic ones like Edward as
gentleman and Edward in his treatment of Dahlia and Robert;
similarly, Algernon being forced to allow his sinister double,
Sedgett (also a double for Edward), as his companion in gentlemanly pursuits. But the moral certainty of such doubles (which
isn't, after all, so certain – if one tries to work out how Robert
actually got beaten up, for example) can't be carried over into the
presentation of major figures like Dahlia, Robert and Mrs Lovell.

Their doubleness supports only the theme or the obsession of
doubleness itself. We are given inconsistent or contradictory
impressions of them – compare the early vain Dahlia with the later

one, try to compare and sort out the many Mrs Lovells. With Mrs Lovell there does seem the possibility of a consistent and subtle portrait of this 'spur to black energies', a convincing presentation of a particular combination of 'bravery' and 'brains', of convention and unconvention, which would substantiate rather than extend the general atmosphere of duplicity. For a conventional reading she is attractive and interesting enough to be the secret heroine of the novel, the real 'poor girl'. But she is too often the cipher of reversals, not a suitably complex embodiment of them.

There is much point, of course, in talking of changes of heart here – the novel is manifestly about obduracy and change of heart, change of heart too late. But – and it is here that in talking about one characteristic we inevitably talk about the other – the point is one does not witness the process of change: one merely comes across the fact of doubleness – it jumps into one's carriage or touches one's sleeve in the street. We are not there when it matters – hence we come round to the primary irritation of Meredith's peripheralism.

One scene can serve to give brief illustration of these and other irritations – in ch. xv the visit of Farmer Fleming and Robert to Squire Blancove to accuse the latter's son, Algernon, of seducing and hiding Dahlia. It is a curiously pointless scene haunted by the ghost of something much more decisive and dramatic (every scene in the novel appears to have its possible double in this way). Of course, Algernon is the wrong man, and Squire Blancove doesn't really care whether he is or not, not thinking much of his son and being more interested in his gout. The Squire talks directly only to Fleming, so that the interventions of the more articulate and forceful Robert operate in a kind of vacuum. He is given a powerful denunciation of Blancove's class, but that can't really count – just as, in pulling Algernon off his horse he has the wrong man, the dramatic stroke is ludicrous and ineffective. Everything, including a potentially powerful class confrontation, has been shifted off centre.

Of course, there are many more obvious cases of peripheralism in *Rhoda Fleming*. Most of the main characters are missing for long stretches of the narrative – Rhoda, for example, is only briefly glimpsed after the opening section of the book. Similarly, the relationship between Rhoda and Robert is set up as something complex and interesting – particularly in the scene when he tries to force himself on her ('devil is what I want in a woman' xiv), but this complexity is not maintained. Indeed, the undercutting of such possibilities is already going on in the scene mentioned: 'You really can defend yourself. That's all I was up to.'

This damping-down of compulsions seems an important element in the relationship. Theirs is an agony of postponed confrontation, a relationship which frustratingly expresses itself through the problems of others. So in this scene Robert has to disguise his love-making as a test of Rhoda's virtue, a test, moreover, parasitic on the 'fall' of her sister, whom she is off to find. Of course, if she passes the test they can't love, and she does. Nevertheless, the intricate process of contact and loss of contact hinted at here doesn't return until the end of the novel. The relationship is signed off with 'That's all I was up to', and because of this lack of elaboration we are almost forced to take this straight, to consider Robert as the faithful, virtuous lover, carrying out the moral task enjoined by his mistress.

Again, much of the important action happens offstage: Robert's attack on Algernon, the attack on Robert, his illness and near-death, Dahlia's brain-fever and the plan to marry her off to Sedgett, the marriage itself, Edward's illness and his nursing by Mrs Lovell. When an important scene does appear, as I have already indicated, its effect is often diminished in some way. Typically at the end of the book, when Edward makes his apologia to Farmer Fleming, the scene is partly presented through Rhoda listening and trying not to listen at the top of the stairs.

Throughout the book information of such scenes is conveyed both to character and reader fleetingly, confusedly, grudgingly. Moreover, to the forefront of the novel come elaborations of minor characters and their lives. In particular, we seem to be continually shifted off on to Algernon Blancove and Anthony Hackbut. Or we get inflated scenes like that at the Pilot Tavern. Frustration, delay, periphery – it is continually a very irritating novel.

There are many ways in which Meredith's peripheralism might be explained. One could simply assume that this is a poor novel, that Meredith is a poor novelist: that he always came reluctantly to fiction, that he could not sustain or control fundamentals of plot, character, theme and tone. There is certainly supporting evidence in the letters that *Rhoda Fleming* got out of control, that it was written hastily, and the prime motive in writing it was quick money. Coupled with this, Meredith was deliberately trying to write a plain, popular novel, trying, in fact, to write down, and hence perhaps making a mess of it. Lionel Stevenson has shown[1] the connection between the novel and an earlier attempt Meredith made to write a popular story for *Once a Week*. He concludes that *Rhoda Fleming* is a success because its subtle and credible characterization triumphs over the cruder, 'popular' original. This is true in so far as the novel is better than the early story, but as one can imagine little worse than that it doesn't take us very far. And I find Stevenson's statement that what I am calling peripheralism is less apparent in *Rhoda Fleming* frankly incredible.

Surely the 'popular' elements in the novel are insistent, indeed blatant. And just as obvious in the novel is the pressure to defeat popular expectation and popular stereotype, not, I would suggest, through deep characterization, because, as I have indicated that too, and the expectation of it, has to go. All expectations are defeated, all norms of fiction, not simply of popular fiction, defied or made a mess of. One of the things Meredith does contrive to do until the end is keep you guessing about what will happen, and an essential part of that is refusing to go very far in characterization. Even Sedgett remains an option. In a curious way, Meredith has learnt the Wilkie Collins lesson of suspense, has applied it here to peculiar self-destructive ends, so that the stereotype defeat of stereotype is itself defeated.

But I ought to give examples of the handling of popular stereotype in the novel. The obvious elements have already been pointed out by Stevenson, and naturally have much to do with the fallen-girl type of fiction. Edward the seducer is not presented as a villain. The poor who fight to get justice from the seducer's class are not presented as heroes or heroines. The repentant villain does not get the girl back; the girl does not succeed in killing herself ('lift her up tenderly'); the villainess (Mrs Lovell) repents and does not get her faithful lover back; Hackbut doesn't have a lot of money in the bank. The good gentleman hero turns out to be just as ineffective as the good (though drunken) poor hero. The servants haven't miraculously saved a fortune between them.

What a catalogue like this (which could be much extended) doesn't sufficiently indicate is the way in which the novel, having upset an obvious popular expectation, goes on then to defeat subtler expectations. There is not the clearing away of debris of stereotype allowing the subtle centre to emerge more strongly, as in a novel like Austen's *Northanger Abbey*. The note is sounded in introducing Edward's letter to Algernon in ch. xxviii:

As there is a man to be seen behind these lines in the dull
unconscious process of transformation from something very
like a villain to something by a few degrees more estimable,
we may as well look at the letter in full.

There is a similar tone in handling Robert's attitude to Dahlia in
ch. xxx – this is what we have to put up with as foreground figures
and we 'may as well' get on with it: 'The young man who can look
on them we call fallen women with a noble eye, is to my mind he
that is most nobly begotten of the race, and likeliest to be the sire
of a noble line. Robert was less than he. . . .' The stale, aristocratic-
heroic language is characteristic here too.

We can look at this note of periphery in another way if we consider Meredith as writing a popular novel in a different sense –
that is, writing a novel of the people. The two senses of popular
overlap: the gentleman seducing the country girl is a popular
stereotype in both senses. Meredith is interested in *Rhoda Fleming*
as a treatment of class struggle and exploitation, and in the treatment of the exploitation from the viewpoint of the exploited.
Again, this approach may merely serve to illustrate the weakness of
the novel. Meredith seems much more at home in the country-
house scenes than in (say) the Pilot Tavern. And, partly because of
the confusion about the identity of the seducer, the class conflict is
always muffled, it never emerges clearly.

It would be some sort of defence to argue that through this
confusion Meredith is able to conflate two kinds of exploitation
(banker and squire). But it is far more important to realize that in
the context of class struggle this muffling peripheral effect begins
to look effective in a much more interesting way. For what the
novel illustrates again and again is the inability of a lower class to
make contact with their superiors. I do not mean by this the merely
static matter of one class not understanding the speech, habits, and
manners of another. It is a question in *Rhoda Fleming* of the
exploited class trying to catch up with the exploiters, trying to
bring them, or the guilty ones, to account; and of the evasive
tactics used by the exploiting class in response.

The novel is a pattern of flight, pursuit, and abortive contact, it
is meaningfully a novel of frustration. I know of no other nineteenth-century novel which catches so often the desperation and
exasperation of a lower class, and the apprehension and condes-
cension of an upper class. The fundamental tactic in this class

conflict is to avoid contact. In this context the adventures of Algernon Blancove begin to acquire their true significance: more than simply the pursuit of him by the Flemings and his lower-class double, Sedgett, they involve his election by his own class as buffer and substitute, as hero of the periphery.

Nevertheless, this won't completely do. Surely one has to reverse the terms and see Meredith using class to illustrate frustration rather than vice versa. Is a class analysis much help in dealing with the frustrated relationships of Rhoda and Robert, Mrs Lovell and Percy Waring, for instance? Class frustration is hardly appropriate to Master Gammon's dumplings. And although they may be there because of Meredith's delicate digestion and Rossetti's breakfasts, they seem also to play their part in the accumulation of different kinds of frustration. I almost wrote 'minor part', but it is just that sense of major-minor, periphery-centre one is talking about. If one dismisses the dumplings, one may have to dismiss Dahlia's champagne, and one can't afford to because the whole periphery would collapse. We are really not quite in the territory of Mr Woodhouse, whose existential boiled eggs are firmly if tenderly relegated. It is after all a major move in the development of fiction to elevate the importance of the trivial and the low. This is one of the defences we have for plot. Like all Meredith's novels, *Rhoda Fleming* accumulates plot almost manically. It accumulates it probably because of an obsession with plot as the key to popular success – witness the famous advice to Thomas Hardy – but perhaps for another purpose as well. The pace and proliferation of Meredith's plotting produces a kind of exhilaration (indeed, all of Meredith's novels feel better as they lengthen), which can be related to his theory of comedy in which plot exists to defeat ego.

The accumulation of frustration, the pressure of non-revelation, these seem to move us into the familiar Meredith territory of the 'ordeal' (also, I would think, very much into Browning territory. Nothing happens in Browning's poetry, but certain moments get missed or elected). Meredith had already written three novels of ordeal centred on two heroes and a heroine. Already in *Feverel* this centring was in question, but it is in *Rhoda Fleming* that the ordeal is spread – democratized, one might say. In this way the novel plays an important part in the transition from the novel of the ordeal of an artistic sensibility in middle-class England (*Emilia in England*) to the novel of the ordeal of the birth of a nation (*Vittoria*).

The question remains whether what usually gets attached to the ordeal in discussions of Meredith – namely, his concern with blindness and egoism, and his 'idealism', should be attached to *Rhoda Fleming*. The general question of the presence in Meredith's work of the moral placing of egoism and salvation through suffering is a large one, and I shall confine myself to *Rhoda Fleming*, merely repeating that in this matter as in others I don't find the novel 'atypical'.

Rhoda Fleming, then, can be read as a novel of conflicting egoisms, of multiple blindness, of class, family, and person. Again 'conflict' misleads somewhat because through egoism everyone misses the point, no one knows himself or the world outside himself, peripheries are inevitable. Anthony Hackbut steals the bank's gold, but not to save Dahlia. A lifetime obsession moves to its climax brought on by his brother-in-law's mistaken belief in his riches. This final result of his egotistic pursuit of his reputation coincides with the necessity to buy off Sedgett. The coincidence operates ironically against the neater and inegotistic possibility that he would steal to save his niece.

Meredith, then, allows the novel itself to be peripheral by allowing it to be taken over by minor egos, which then exist as satirical doubles for the major ones. And this attack on central character and central event inevitably becomes an attack on the ego of the reader – the expectation of what is due to him. He goes through his therapy of ordeal just as Mrs Sunfit does waiting for Gammon to finish his dumplings.

But what kind of moral dimension is involved in this? We could plot the novel in terms of gradual escapes from self and of possibilities of escape that are missed. But then one inevitably comes up against the persistent way Meredith distributes ego on both sides of the question. This extends from the obvious irony of the exploited being as egotistic as the exploiter, Rhoda and her father forcing the detestable marriage on Dahlia becoming a worse crime than the original seduction; to the ironies of repentance in Edward's case, where the egotism of submission replaces the egotism of arrogance. We can obviously suppose a hierarchy, a progression through levels of self-love, the purgatorial ordeal, with all kinds of slipping back and 'dull transformations'. But if we do suppose that, I think we are half-way to the spiritual or idealist Meredith; we also couldn't then account for the way in which the novel retains its respect for vanity, self-display, bravery, money until the end; and, most important of all, we would be avoiding the peripheral experience. We do after all only glimpse the ordeals, and one is continually substituted for another. It seems almost as if the notion of an individual moral ordeal and progression were in itself too egotistical.

Similar worries would arise if one did give an idealist account of the novel. Meredith here as elsewhere sometimes seems to speak directly in support of such an interpretation: 'Can a man go farther than his nature? Never, when he takes passion on board' (xlviii). The novel is concerned with victories or attempts at victories over passions and the flesh, with the release of the spirit. Dahlia 'had gone through fire, as few women have done in like manner, to leave their hearts among the ashes; but with that human heart she left regrets behind her. The soul of this young creature filled its place' (last paragraph of the novel).

'Taming the brute', although it has its ironic place as part of a title for the episode where Mrs Lovell deceives and puts off Robert Armstrong, is something the book appears to insist on. Armstrong's violence and drunkenness seem to fit here, as does the familiar Meredith preoccupation with military life and duelling. Mrs Lovell both tames the brute and enrages him. And three of the main characters go through purgatorial illnesses to become possessed of tamer, more spiritual selves. Dahlia loses her lovely golden hair.

And yet, again, we can't be sure. Those illnesses happen off-stage. And this has the effect of minimizing their importance. Because we don't see Robert or Edward 'going through the fire', they seem much the same after as before. Meredith doesn't exhibit the spiritual Dahlia: he does exhibit Dahlia after her first illness, caught in the agonies of regret and repentance, still wanting her lover and abhorring Sedgett. And, of course, the repentance is tied to her love of her sister. The love of Edward might be more 'spiritual' than marrying the brute Sedgett, but this misses the point of Meredith's arrangements. The possibility of Sedgett makes her love for Edward even more intense, just as his love gains impetus from the abhorrence of Mrs Lovell. What gets hinted are the intricate threads of motivation and the persistence of ordeal and frustration even in apparent progression. The escape to the centre, morally or spiritually, never really takes place. That is another ghost of egocentric fiction. 'Do you care to find the Holy Grail, Fred?' Meredith asked his friend, Captain Maxse, weary of Tennyson's ideal medievalism.

It is, of course, a general problem with Meredith's idealism that he wants it to be of the 'earth', that it has in some paradoxical sense to be materialistic, especially when matched with a 'sentimental' vision, a vision ignoring and corrupting the appetites of earth. But whatever the hidden dialectic involved, what seems obvious in this novel is that both sides of it are diminished. We know Squire Blancove is doomed, not because he doesn't care about his son's morals, but because he can no longer relish his port. And this lack of relish, material and spiritual, is characteristic of the novel. Its scenes of lost interest are its most typical ones, although they are in easy competition with scenes of revived interest. The novel is engaged in 'stripping the bloom from life'. Its epitome is the chapter entitled 'An Indicative Duet in a Minor Key' – which is partly memorable because of its affinity with Victorian story-painting – where the dwindling of Edward's love for Dahlia is worked through tepid greens and flat champagne, and includes a tepid revival of interest. There has been no attempt to represent this love in its bloom, no attempt that is to repeat the early pages of *The Ordeal of Richard Feverel*.

I should briefly add that although I have used the word 'ironic' of some of Meredith's effects, the peculiar nature of his idealism and the insistence of frustration do not allow, here at any rate, any finality or elopuence of irony.

I began by considering *Rhoda Fleming* as incompetent or reluctant popular fiction, and I have moved towards regarding it as subversive fiction. Subversive technically, that is, undermining the norms of fiction – not simply the norms of popular fiction, but the norms of fiction itself – in particular its centralities of action and protagonist, its revelations and climaxes. And subversive socially, not so much because of its fallen-woman theme (the respectable are more guilty than the fallen), but because of its class sympathies, and because of its challenge to ideals of individual moral and spiritual development through ordeal and suffering.

I do not want to argue that *Rhoda Fleming* is anything but unsatisfactory, although the word 'unsatisfied' would be nearer my sense of it. But the quality of its impatience is arresting and is illuminating for the quality of Meredith's work in general.

I want finally to give a more extended example of its 'subversion'. The following passage comes from ch. xxxvi, 'Edward Meets His Match', where Edward is beginning his 'ordeal' of trying to win back Dahlia. He encounters Robert and Rhoda:

She stood watching them striving to divine their speech by their gestures, and letting her savage mood interpret the possible utterances. It went ill with Robert in her heart that he did not suddenly grapple and trample the man, and so break away from him. She was outraged to see Robert's listening posture. 'Lies! lies!' she said to herself, 'and he doesn't know them to be lies.' The window-blinds in Dahlia's sitting-room continued undisturbed; but she feared the agency of the servant of the house in helping to release her sister. Time was flowing to dangerous strands. At last Robert turned back singly. Rhoda fortified her soul to resist.

'He has fooled you,' she murmured, inaudibly, before he spoke.

'Perhaps, Rhoda, we ought not to stand in his way. He wishes to do what a man can do in his case. So he tells me, and I'm bound not to disbelieve him. He says he repents – says the word; and gentlemen seem to mean it when they use it. I respect the word, and them when they're up to that word. He wrote to her that he could not marry her, and it did the mischief, and may well be repented of; but he wishes to be forgiven and make amends – well, such as he can. He's been abroad, and only received Dahlia's letters within the last two or three days. He seems to love her, and to be heartily wretched. Just hear me out; you'll decide; but pray, pray don't be rash. He wishes to marry her; says he has spoken to his father this very night; came straight over from France, after he had read her letters. He says – and it seems fair – he only asks to see Dahlia for two minutes. If she bids him go, he goes. He's not a friend of mine, as I could prove to you; but I do think he ought to see her. He says he looks on her as his wife; always meant her to be his wife, but things were against him when he wrote that letter. Well, he *says* so; and it's true that gentlemen are situated – they can't always or think they can't, behave quite like honest men. They've got a hundred things to consider for our one. That's my experience, and I know something of the best among 'em. The question is about this poor young fellow who's to marry her today. Mr. Blancove talks of giving him a handsome sum – a thousand pounds – and making him comfortable——'

'There!' Rhoda exclaimed, with a lightning face. 'You don't see what he is, after that? Oh!——' She paused, revolted.

'Will you let me run off to the young man, wherever he's to be found, and put the case to him – that is, from Dahlia? And you know she doesn't like the marriage overmuch, Rhoda. Perhaps he may think differently when he comes to hear of things. As to Mr. Blancove, men change and change when they're young. I mean, gentlemen. We must learn to forgive. Either he's as clever as the devil, or he's a man in earnest, and deserves pity. If you'd heard him!'

The mixture here is typical: the odd energy of it, which manages to be both frenzied and weary, and issues in a language and speech which is both forceful and stale; the characteristic device or habit of doing things indirectly, so we get a report of Edward's explanation, not the explanation itself. There is a rapid appearance of some of the persistent preoccupations of the novel: with class and the expectation of class, with manly, vigorous action, with the possibility of repentance, with the trust in words, with money, with moral righteousness. And most of these, of course, conveyed through the reluctant go-between figure, Robert, who has to argue with the girl he loves using someone else's language – that someone else abhorrent to her.

But, of course, one is not getting complexity except of a nominal kind. There is enough complication to defeat any clear, dramatic possibility and enough gestures at the latter to make the complications seem forced, regretted. There is a kind of momentum of redundancies. It's a scene like many in the book which refuses itself full articulation. And perhaps significantly the next chapter begins with a cool account of Edward's eloquence.

Nevertheless, there is an achievement of sorts here. It might be more clearly indicated by referring back to the novel's concern with class frustration. For once again Meredith presents the baffling and untrustworthy figure of the gentleman, puzzling and attempting to persuade his victims, and once again deference, resistance, and obtuseness combine in his reception. And I would suggest that here that sense of the gentleman combines with the more general sense of frustration and periphery in the novel, that sense of substitution and evasion I have been arguing for as the most persistent characteristic of the work. 'They've got a hundred considerations to our one.' The point is made, if made minimally, the 'considerations' which can disguise exploitation must also be offered, reluctantly, as the sign of a necessary complex consciousness and understanding. Just as the single-mindedness of Rhoda is offered as a sign of a necessary strength of will and conduct.

Something like the same point is made through Mrs Lovell (again one would have to insist, made minimally). There is a similar scene to the one just quoted, which I have already referred to, where Robert is taken in by Mrs Lovell, but where too the idea of the necessity of 'considerations' escapes from its connection with trickery and with the class of gentlemen, just as Robert's simplicity and persistence, taken to by Mrs Lovell, escapes its connections. And, of course, Mrs Lovell to some extent, with her combination of 'brains' and a respect for manliness, carries both sides of the argument.

As is often the case with Meredith, the question of feminine development and independence becomes joined with the question of an inferior and subjugated class, and joined too with the question of the terms and the possibilities of communication and explanation and impingement – '[he] says the word' . . . 'Well, he *says* so.' One thinks of the discussions in *Beauchamp's Career* of the language and imagery of explanation of politics to women, of the connection of the feminine artistic voice with the political voice in *Sandra Belloni* and *Vittoria*. And that is the final point here: What kind of plainness, what kind of complexity, can the novel afford? Can it achieve, what is so obviously frustrated in *Rhoda Fleming*, an art which is both plain and complex, and suggesting through that art a life possibility? 'There is the democratic virus secret in every woman' (xxii). Could the novel make an honest woman of itself?

Note

1 'Meredith's Atypical Novel: a Study of *Rhoda Fleming*', in B. H. Lehman, and others, *The Image of the Work: Essays in Criticism*, 1955.

Emilia in England and Italy[1]

Ioan Williams

Although they share the same heroine – the half-English, half-Italian *cantatrice*, Emilia Alessandra Belloni – *Sandra Belloni* and *Vittoria* are strikingly dissimilar novels. Originally they were to have been more closely related. Meredith seems to have planned the later novel as a sequel to the earlier and to have changed his mind during the long process of writing and rewriting so as to make *Vittoria* not only independent of its predecessor, but a contrast in style and structure.[2] This change of mind seems partly to have resulted from a desire to make a more popular appeal by increasing and clarifying the narrative interest. More powerful motives were Meredith's dissatisfaction with *Sandra Belloni* and his desire to experiment with new techniques in order to create a more satisfactory medium for his thought. In *Sandra Belloni* Meredith tried to combine the presentation of an individual case with an extended analysis of a whole society. In *Vittoria* he attempted a similar task with different techniques and came closer to success. In neither of the novels did he achieve complete fusion of both aspects of his subject matter in artistic form, but together they show a developing technical maturity and represent an important phase of the novelist's struggle to realize in one fiction the full complexity of his vision of human life.

Meredith described *Sandra Belloni* as 'a contrast between a girl of simplicity and passion and our English sentimental, socially-aspiring damsels'.[3] The girl of simplicity and passion is the heroine, Emilia Belloni, poorly brought up and educated, but endowed with a beautiful voice and a passionate devotion to music and to the cause of Italian freedom. The English damsels are the three sisters,

Arabella, Adela and Cornelia Pole, daughters of a speculating merchant. They aspire to create a nation-wide 'Circle', radiating from their recently acquired country estate, Brookfield. Emilia's naturalness, freshness and spontaneity contrast with their striving for refinement and sophistication and this contrast is the basis of Meredith's commentary on English society. The Pole sisters are representative of wealthy English youth, who, Meredith explains in deflatory terms, owe their existence 'to a certain prolonged term of comfortable feeding' (i).[4] Arabella, Adela and Cornelia are sentimentalists who claim to have reached a level of existence higher than is possible for the common herd and are disappointed in their efforts to raise Emilia to the same level of refinement. During the action both they and Emilia have to endure experiences which test their pretensions and strength of character. The sisters come under pressure from elements in external reality whose existence they refuse to recognize, and are eventually brought low by fundamental weakness of character. Their collapse demonstrates the truth of Meredith's assertion that growth to a higher nature than the ordinary is possible only on the basis of the acceptance of the reality of human character, including its cruder elements. Emilia emerges from her ordeal with greater maturity and integrity because she never attempts to evade reality or to pretend that character and circumstance are other than they are.

Meredith's attack on sentimentalism, more consistent in *Sandra Belloni* than in his previous works, is qualified by his awareness that it plays an important part in the development of the race.[5] He points out that if 'we mark the origin of classes, we shall discern that the Nice Feelings and Fine Shades play a principal part in our human development and social history' (i).[6] Sentimentalism as illustrated by Merthyr Powys and his half-sister, Georgiana Ford, is not an unhealthy condition. Merthyr's devotion to the cause of Italian freedom and Georgiana's devotion to him are largely produced by refined emotionalism. Georgiana and Merthyr are no closer to the primitive simplicity of life than are the Pole sisters or their brother, Wilfrid, but they differ from sentimentalists of a lower order in their willingness to recognize facts. The brute power of Austrian military force in Italy is an accepted reality to Merthyr, though he believes in the power of the Italian people to overcome it. He and his sister sometimes shrink sensitively from particularly unpleasant circumstances, but they never attempt to evade them nor to use their principles as masks for selfishness or sensuality:

> A sentimental pair likewise, if you please; but these were
> sentimentalists who served an active deity, and not that
> arbitrary projection of a subtle selfishness which rules the
> fairer portion of our fat England (xiviii).

Without an 'active deity', the Pole sisters direct their energy
towards maintaining a false image of themselves and their circumstances. Fundamental to their creed is the determination to act as
if they are independent of crude financial reality, and it is this
which brings about their downfall. They persist in offending their
father's friend, the elderly and vulgar Mrs Chump, in spite of
ample evidence that their own financial security is somehow bound
up with her peace of mind and continuing friendship. Gradually
they are forced to realize that the woman whom they have insulted
and forced from their home is the victim of their father's financial
speculation and that the only way by which they can prevent his
ruin and disgrace is to keep her allegiance by encouraging her idea
that she is to become their stepmother.

Mr Pole himself is a suitable father of sentimentalists. Unable to
bring himself to plain speaking, he is tormented by his secret and
becomes obsessively concerned with the idea of marrying his
children well before his financial ruin. When Emilia, with naïve but
relentless insistence, forces on him the responsibility of preventing
her marriage with Wilfrid, his pathetic attempts at evasion and
denial culminate in an attack of nervous paralysis – a fitting disease
for one in whom 'feeling was almost physical'.[7]

While their father's grasp of health remains tenuous and he
continues on the verge of further attacks, the situation of the three
Pole sisters becomes intolerable. They, who 'supposed that they
enjoyed exclusive possession of the Nice Feelings and exclusively
comprehended the Fine Shades' (i), are obliged to equivocate, to
lie and to endure the familiarities of Mrs Chump in order to
preserve his health. Mrs Chump in herself they could accept, but
she is a distressing reminder of their too-recent emergence from
the City of London and of the vulgarity of their early life:

> As a mere animal they passed her by, and had almost come to
> a state of mind to pass her off. It was the phantom, or rather
> the embodiment of their First Circle, that they hated in the
> woman (xxvii).

Forced into actions and situations which make it impossible to preserve their image of their own spotless refinement, their morale breaks. Under pressure from sordid reality, they revert to their natural characters. Arabella, the eldest, retreats into household cares; Adela, the youngest, becomes 'fast' and begins to behave with scarcely concealed vulgarity. For Cornelia, who has the strongest pretensions to true nobility of soul, a worse fate is reserved.

Cornelia drifts into a sentimental friendship with Purcell Barrett, an impoverished gentleman who is employed for some time as an organist at Brookfield's local church. Their relationship develops into sentimental love, in spite of domestic circumstances at Brookfield and growing familial pressure on Cornelia, which is urging her to accept the hand of a wealthy and boring suitor. Afraid to refuse him outright because of her father's nervous condition, Cornelia keeps Sir Twickenham Pryme waiting for an answer and allows herself to get further involved with Purcell. Ironically, though she prays for the poverty which would bring her together with Purcell, she is forced to do everything that she can to avert it by preserving appearances before Mrs Chump. Purcell's father dies, leaving him nothing more than a title, and although he is given the chance of accepting an income from his uncle he cannot bring himself to put the proposal before Cornelia until it is too late. When the time for plain speaking comes they pay the penalty for having wrapped themselves in folds of sentiment and for having refused to recognize what they are and what they are doing. Meredith's narrator comments; 'So it is when you play at life! When you will not go straight you get into this twisting maze' (lv). Like Sir Austin Feverel, they succumb to the temptation of masking their real feelings behind refined and noble pretences. Purcell becomes annoyed because Cornelia will not step down from the pedestal on which he has placed her and make his situation easier for him. Cornelia, subjected to growing pressure at home and forced into degrading situations, is resentful because he will not divine the difficulty of her circumstances and rescue her. He finds relief in railing at Destiny; she in a feeling of martyrdom. In a state of morbid despair, the product of repressed irritation and a determined habit of blaming circumstances for his own difficulties, Purcell asks for a last interview with Cornelia. The night before he charges one of a pair of pistols, returns them both to their case and before starting out the next morning selects one at random with a mournful dependence on Providence. When Cornelia fails to appear he takes out the pistol and places it against his heart. His body is carried by those who discover it to Cornelia's home.

In sharp contrast to this pair of sentimentalists who choose to evade reality rather than adapt to it, Emilia never sinks into despair. Her simple instinct tells her that the way out of the trap into which they have fallen lies in direct action on Purcell's part. But Emilia is regarded rather as a lower animal by the possessor of Nice Feelings. The sentimental members of the Pole circle find it hard to reconcile her lack of sophistication with her possession of a magnificent voice. Purcell, in discussion with her, receives clear evidence of her lack of the higher mental qualities:

> 'I have always thought sadness more musical than mirth,' said he. 'Surely there is more grace in sadness!'
> Poetry, sculpture, and songs, and all the Arts, were brought forward in mournful array to demonstrate the truth of this theory.
> When Emilia understood him she cited dogs and cats and birds, and all things of nature that rejoice and revel, in support of the opposite view.
> 'Nay, if animals are to be your illustration!' he protested. He had been perhaps half under the delusion that he spoke with Cornelia, and with a sense of infinite misery he compressed the apt distinction that he had in mind. . . .
> 'But such talk must be uttered to a *soul*,' he phrased internally, and Emilia was denied what belonged to Cornelia (xxxviii).

In place of the 'soul' of the sentimentalists, however, Emilia has the capacity for real passion. Coming into the Brookfield circle by chance, she resists all attempts to refine her and falls wholeheartedly and trustfully in love with Wilfrid Pole. In spite of appearances, she believes that he returns her love until she hears him deny it himself. It is then that her ordeal begins. The shock of witnessing the interview between Wilfrid and Lady Charlotte, in which he is brought to declare that he has never loved her, is followed by a drastic loss of confidence. This is increased past bearing by the consequent disappearance of her voice and by the brutal behaviour of Antonio Pericles, the wealthy devotee of opera who was to have paid for her training in Italy. Emilia leaves from the interview with Pericles stunned and bewildered. Suffering a deep sense of bereavement and anguish, she approaches, but does not reach, despair.

From this state of desolation Emilia is rescued by Merthyr Powys, who tries to win her back to self-respect by awakening her to consciousness of her own beauty. Her recovery is furthered by the knowledge that Wilfrid does in fact love her, and is completed by the realization that she has attracted the love of Merthyr himself. Almost simultaneously with this discovery, Emilia learns of the Italian insurrection. Merthyr hurries to Italy, but she remains in England, refraining from any participation in Italy's fate, at first because she has given her promise to Wilfrid to remain in England, but later because she has come to realize that she is still immature. By the end of the novel she has decided to subject herself to the discipline of her art in order to achieve strength of mind and character. Her voice having returned, she signs a contract with Antonio Pericles to study for three years at the Conservatorio. The novel ends with the letter in which she informs Merthyr of her decision and which marks the completion of the first phase of her spiritual growth:

> I am a raw girl. I command nothing but raw and flighty hearts of men. Are they worth anything? Let me study three years, without any talk of hearts at all. It commenced too early, and has left nothing to me but a dreadful knowledge of the weakness in most people: – not in you.
>
> My misery now is gladness, is like the rain-drops on rising wings, if I say to myself 'Free! Free!, Emilia!' I am bound for three years, but I smile at such a bondage to my body. Evvivia! my soul is free! Three years of freedom, and no sounding of myself – three years of growing and studying; three years of idle heart! (lix).

Wilfrid Pole, the cause of so much of Emilia's trouble, is incapable of such development. Nor is he capable of that passion which, though a destructive force, Meredith describes as the disorder of a strong and healthy organism: 'noble strength on fire' (xliv). He is a creature deluded by the fumes of sentiment into thinking himself stronger than he is and made the victim of a fierce internal conflict. Wilfrid is what Meredith's Philosopher calls 'a double man'. Divided between heart and head, he is incapable of understanding himself or of following a straight path to achieve his own desires. He is the product of his education and his environment, awaiting the fiery ordeal of circumstance which will prove his real worth – meantime, as Meredith warns, he is not to be despised: 'All of us are weak in the period of growth and are of small worth before the hour of trial' (xviii).

Wilfrid's trial comes through Emilia. Though he is enchanted by her freshness, simplicity and straightforward responsiveness, he is one 'whose soul thirsted for poetical refinement and filmy delicacies in a woman' (xviii). Consequently, the first phases of his relationship with Emilia are marked by alternate attraction and repulsion on his part. During the incident which follows from her promise to sing at a meeting of a working-men's club, his attraction seems to deepen into love. In the morning, painfully embarrassed by a swollen face and with a faint memory of the smell of tobacco in her hair, he sees Emilia in another light and leaves Brookfield in the hope that the events of the night will be forgotten. Emilia waits for him trustingly. Meanwhile, he involves himself with Lady Charlotte Chillingworth, a mature and common-sensical spinster to whom he is attracted in admiration for her firmness and clarity of speech and action. From then on Wilfrid is the shuttlecock between two battledores, fluctuating between attraction towards Emilia and admiration for Lady Charlotte. Intending to break with Emilia, he allows himself to fall into a 'pitfall of sentiment' and gives her the impression that he is prevented from marrying her only by the severity of a cruel father. In attempting to break off with Lady Charlotte, he again takes a sentimental pose and ends the scene with a declaration of love and a betrayal of Emilia. Once the latter is lost, however, she becomes immeasurably precious. Sorrow makes her a fitter object of adoration, and frustrated sentiment hurries Wilfrid away into violent action. In a state of self-induced excitement resembling hysteria, he rushes to Monmouth, where Emilia is recovering with Merthyr and his sister, to snatch a clandestine interview and assure her of his love. When she is back in London he tries to win her over again. Finally, he answers her request for a meeting at night in the romantic setting of a wood, receives his final dismissal and is made the instrument of her revenge on Lady Charlotte Chillingworth. All this time, in subjecting himself to the internal struggle between conflicting impulses, he has, as the Philosopher puts it, been 'fining himself down', ultimately to emerge from his trial a stronger man, capable of discerning the impulse to right action.

Wilfrid reappears in *Vittoria* among the group of characters taken over from *Sandra Belloni*, as indecisive as ever, but, though his vacillation between the transformed Emilia and the Austrian, Countess Lena Von Lenkenstein, is of importance to the plot of the second novel, he is no longer an important focus of interest in himself. The plot of *Vittoria* centres on the relationship between Vittoria herself and the Italian, Count Carlo Ammiami, but it is played out against the background of historical events in which all the characters are involved. The fate of individuals is interwoven with the fate of the emergent Italian nation so as to express Meredith's conception of the laws governing individual and national life. *Vittoria* suggests that certain qualities are essential to the successful development of the individual and the nation – internal harmony, clearness of vision and firm devotion to a purpose – that for those who are unwilling or unable to meet these conditions disaster is inevitable, but for those who can the sharpest adversity is no more than a schooling for further efforts which will ultimately lead to complete self-fulfilment.

The story of the novel is complex, perhaps at times confusing. It concerns Vittoria's relationship with Carlo Ammiami, a young Italian nobleman who is passionately devoted to the national cause. The action begins with a number of scenes which immediately precede and follow a meeting near the summit of Monte Monterone, where several of the Italian conspirators discuss with Mazzini the circumstances of the Lombard revolt against Austrian domination. Vittoria is chosen to give the signal for the beginning of the revolt by singing a patriotic song at the end of an allegorical opera which has somehow passed the Austrian censorship. On the way back from this meeting, however, she encounters a group of English tourists, among whom are Adela Pole (now Mrs Sedley) and Captain Gambier, and she leaves them a warning to avoid Milan on the date planned for the revolt. Later she corresponds with Adela and Wilfrid, who has now followed his uncle in seeking a career in the Imperial Army. Word of her apparently treasonable correspondence comes to Barto Rizzo, a powerful and fanatical conspirator, who brings about the postponement of the insurrection and has Vittoria publicly marked as suspect. In spite of these circumstances, Vittoria decides to continue with the task she has been given. She avoids certain manœuvres of Antonio Pericles to spirit her away, is rescued from the confusion which follows her singing and is whirled away from Milan. There follows a breathless sequence in which she is hunted, captured and rescued – hunted by

Captain Weispreiss, most noted swordsman of the army of occupation, and rescued by Angelo Guidascarpi, Carlo Ammiami's cousin and a hunted man himself.

The next phase of action takes place at Meran, where Vittoria incurs the animosity of the Lenkenstein sisters and is forced to manipulate Wilfrid and bring him into disgrace in order to effect the escape of Angelo Guidascarpi from his pursuers. From Meran Vittoria goes to Piedmont, where she becomes involved with the cause of King Carlo Alberto. There follows a series of misunderstandings between her and Carlo Ammiami, who, since the night of the opera at Milan, has been her accepted lover. Following the Piedmontese troops during the first successful campaign, Vittoria meets Carlo, and in the few moments that they have together they agree that she will join his mother, the Countess Ammiami, and wait for him. After the Piedmontese and Lombard defeat and the Austrian return to Milan new sources of misunderstanding arise. Vittoria, obliged to remain in Milan while Merthyr Powys recovers from a dangerous wound, cannot obey her lover's summons to join him in order that they may be quickly married. By the time that she does join him it is, for the time being, too late. Carlo, disappointed by defeat and thirsting for a quick revenge, is taken up in conspiracy with the Countess Violetta D'Isorella, who works, as he is well aware, for her own benefit between both sides, but whom he hopes to use. What he does not know is that in opposing his immediate marriage on the grounds that Vittoria is still under suspicion among the patriots, Violetta is motivated by the bribery of Anna von Lenkenstein, who wishes to injure Vittoria. Anna also contrives to bring Carlo to a meeting with Captain Weispreiss and so procure his death. In spite of these difficulties, the marriage does eventually take place and some months of happiness ensue. Carlo, however, continues to plot a new revolt. Instead of fleeing to Rome, which is still free under Mazzini and the Republicans, he encourages and organizes a second Lombard insurrection which is doomed to defeat even before it is betrayed to Anna Von Lenkenstein by Violetta D'Isorella. By this time Carlo is fully aware of the situation, but considers himself bound to go to his death with the patriots who have followed his lead. The outbreak of the revolt marks the beginning of the last phase of the action.

Gradually, as more of the circumstances surrounding the desperate uprising are revealed, the persons about Anna and

Vittoria become aware of the full extent of Carlo's danger. Anna, passionately devoted to her country, had associated Vittoria with the idea of revolt against the Empire and with the death of her brother. She had become the victim of a passionate aversion which clouded her intellect and distorted her character. Justifying hatred by patriotism, she had sacrificed half her fortune to learn the details of the conspiracy in which Carlo was involved, and, in spite of her love for Captain Weispreiss, had promised her hand in marriage to a man she despised as a reward for the death of Vittoria's husband. A confrontation between the two women at this point restores Anna to her natural character, and she explains the circumstances of the plot, sending messengers to intercept her agent.

The action which follows amounts to a bitter parody of a common type of novel ending. The desperate remnant of the insurgents, including Carlo and Angelo, fly to the mountains, pursued by half a regiment of Austrian troops. Behind them come Wilfrid and Anna's brother, who carry an official order for the surrender of the prisoners to them, and Captain Weispreiss, who bears a commission from Anna to save Carlo from death and herself from the consequences of the bargain. Vittoria herself, accompanied by Merthyr, follows at a further stage, waiting hour by hour for news of her husband's capture, escape or death. Wilfrid, Count Karl and Weispreiss come up with the pursuing forces just after the capture of Carlo and Angelo Guidascarpi; the former two retire so as to leave Weispreiss free to take over the command. Weispreiss does this, then takes Carlo aside to tell him that he is safe, but that Angelo will meet the death of a common murderer. Enraged, Carlo throws away his chance of life. Impelled by affection for his cousin and a fatalism which has developed through the previous months of hopeless conspiracy, he insists on a duel with Weispreiss and kills him. At that moment Barto Rizzo and two other insurgents burst out upon the soldiers surrounding the prisoners 'and not one Italian survived the fight' (Epilogue).

The history of Vittoria, Carlo and Anna is a history of growth from weakness and confusion to true self-understanding. Their story involves a favourite theme of Meredith's – the extent to which human fate is dependent upon character. Yet, although they bear responsibility for their own tragic circumstances, Meredith does not subject them to the comic treatment which he reserves for other of his characters who are responsible for their own downfall.

In dealing with Sir Austin Feverel, with Alvan and Clothilde in *The Tragic Comedians* and with Cornelia, Purcell and Mr Pole in *Sandra Belloni*, Meredith conveyed his assessment of their apparently tragic circumstances by means of a superficially incongruous comic treatment, thus reminding the reader that their plight was not to be dignified with the name of tragedy. Vittoria, Carlo and Anna, like Meredith's tragic-comic characters, set in motion trains of circumstances which they are later incapable of stopping. But though they fail until it is too late to conquer the lower elements which compose human nature and to free themselves from passion, Meredith refrains from labelling them tragicomic. He represents them as potentially noble and unselfish people who have the tragic misfortune of growing to full maturity among circumstances which press too heavily upon them.

During the course of the action which leads up to the final catastrophe, Vittoria acts confusedly both in relation to Carlo and to the political circumstances. With what Meredith calls 'a craving for idealistic truths', she seizes on the cause of King Carlo Alberto (xxxi) and supports it in spite of Carlo's Republicanism. She acts thoughtlessly in warning her English friends of the coming revolt in Milan and in failing to obey Carlo's request for her to leave Piedmont and join his mother, meanwhile partially deceiving herself as to the motive for her actions. Her tendency to act with obstinacy and inconsistency encourages her husband to believe that she is unreliable and emotional. Her worst mistake follows her marriage, when, instead of insisting that her husband abandon a pointless conspiracy, she allows herself to be silenced by his charge that she is jealous of Violetta D'Isorella – a charge which both she and Carlo know to be false. Later, when the conspiracy is fully formed she insists on intervening. In a last meeting of the conspirators she urges them to abandon their plan. Her attempts meet inevitable failure and she reports bitterly to Merthyr, admitting her responsibility for what has come about: 'I have helped to teach him that I am no better than any of those Italian women whom he despises. I spoke to him as his wife should do at last. I saw his error from the first: and I went on dreaming and singing; and now this night has come!' (xliv).

Carlo too comes to realize his own responsibility for his situation when it is too late to alter it; 'I have woven my own web.' In a moment of bitter self-knowledge, when he knows that he has been betrayed, he analyses his previous conduct, exposing the vanity which had impelled him:

> But I, sir, I, my friend, I, Merthyr, I said proudly that I would not abandon a beaten country: and I was admired for my devotion. . . . Vast numbers admired me. I need not add that I admired myself. I plunged into intrigues with princes, and priests, and republicans. A clever woman was at my elbow. In the midst of this, my marriage: I had seven weeks of peace; and then I saw what I was. . . . I cannot draw back. I have set going a machine that's merciless. From the day it began working, every moment has added to its force (xliv).

Yet even after this moment – even up to the instant of his death – Carlo is free to withdraw, except that his bitter self-reproach, working on a nature never quite free from vanity, engenders a mood of cloudy fatalism in which he is capable of marching to his own execution.

Considered merely as the lover of Vittoria and the hero of a carefully analysed love-plot, Carlo is a noble youth capable of great self-devotion, who grows to self-knowledge through painful suffering and who cannot, even at the end of his life, free himself entirely from some of the elements of his lower nature which have been strengthened by his class and his nationality. Meredith, however, wishes him to be seen against the background of the historical events which are related in the novel and to be considered as representative of certain factors in the circumstances of his nation. Carlo himself emphasizes this aspect of his role when he appeals to Merthyr not to judge him by his own standards: 'Do not judge me by your English eyes: – other lands, other habits; other habits, other thoughts' (xliv). Like many other characters in *Vittoria*, he has to perform a double role and be at once individual and type.

Vittoria traces a stage in the development of the Italian nation, not in terms of conventional political analysis, but by treating it as a corporate body, subject to the laws that govern individual life. Italy's struggle for freedom was immensely important for Meredith. In early youth his devotion to the cause had been enthusiastic and passionate. In age he referred to it as 'the main historical fact of the 19th Century'.[8] Yet he claims impartiality in his depiction of the insurrection and in his analysis of the condition of Italy under Austrian domination:

He who tells this tale is not a partisan; he would deal equally
with all. Of strong devotion, of stout nobility, of unswerving
faith and self-sacrifice, he must approve; and when these
qualities are displayed in a contest of forces, the wisdom of
means employed, or of ultimate views entertained, may be
questioned, and condemned; but the men themselves may not
be (ii).

Meredith sees the emergence of the Italian nation in terms of
mankind's continuing evolution towards a higher nature. He
presents the Austrian army as a superbly efficient machine, the
ultimate defeat of which in course of time was inevitable. Incapable of growth or change by the very rule of its existence, an
army is powerful only while 'the password is MARCH and not
DEVELOP' (ix). In contrast, Italy, though habituated to servitude,
torn from within and uncertain of its aim, had still to gain maturity
and strength. Meredith saw the events of 1848–9 as the first phase
in the growth of Italy from weakness to inevitable victory:

> In the end, a country true to itself and determined to claim
> God's gift to brave men will overmatch a mere army, however
> solid its force. But an inspired energy of faith is demanded of
> it. The intervening chapters will show pitiable weakness, and
> such a schooling of disaster as makes men, looking on the
> surface of things, deem the struggle folly (ix).

Vittoria chronicles some of the 'intervening chapters' which come
between the awakening of the spiritual life of the nation by
Mazzini and the fulfilment of the task ten years after the death of
Carlo and the Brescian volunteers. The action of the central
characters is seen against a background which gives the detail of the
larger political action in which they are involved. The factors
affecting their fate are seen to be identical with those determining
the fate of Italy.

Meredith attempts to unify the two aspects of his subject
partly by sheer plot-manipulation, partly by making the main
characters typical as well as individual, and partly by surrounding
them with other characters and groups of characters who are
themselves suggestive of certain aspects of the political situation.
The Guidascarpi brothers, Angelo and Rinaldo, illustrate the way
in which Meredith relates the love-plot to his historical analysis.
As the cousins of Carlo Ammiami and prominent patriots, they are

closely involved in the events which affect the fortunes of the hero and heroine. Their importance, however, is far greater than their relationship with Carlo and Vittoria would suggest, and it depends largely on an incident which is supposed to have occurred before the action related in the novel. Angelo and Rinaldo, imaginative and idealistic, are fanatically devoted to the liberation of their country, considering themselves, with some reason, to be marked by Fate for a special role. They find their younger and much-loved sister involved with Count Paul Von Lenkenstein, and present her with the alternatives of suicide or withdrawal to a convent; she chooses the former, and it is in the presence of her corpse that they kill Count Paul in a duel which is conducted according to the strict rules of honour. They are considered by the Austrians to be common murderers, by the Italians extreme patriots. To the narrator they embody certain aspects of the newly awakened life of their country. Fanatically single-minded, extreme to the point of obsession, they illustrate the effect of passionate self-devotion without the sense of proportion which comes only from a clear and rational understanding of both external and internal forces.

Vittoria contains a large number of characters who are of importance primarily for the analysis of the state of Italy. Many of them may be placed in one of three groups – Austrian, Italian or Austro-Italian. These groups contain a number of minor characters, like the spy Luigi, Beppo, Lorenzo and his wife, Jacob Baumwalder Fechelwitz and Johann Spellmann, who contrast with each other and fill out the details of Meredith's analysis by embodying aspects of Austrian and Italian character. Of greater significance is the large and colourful group of Italian patriots, headed by the shadowy figure of Mazzini himself, who hardly functions as a character in the novel, but whose influence is felt throughout the action and in the thought which lies behind it. Among these are Colonel Corte, Marco Sana, Luciano Romano, Count Medole, Agostino Baldini. Prominent among them is Barto Rizzo, who has won great authority among the people by his strength, daring, cunning and vigilance. Barto, however, though unceasing in his activity on behalf of the cause, has learnt in a lifetime of conspiracy and betrayal to trust too much in his own powers, to mistrust everyone around him and to involve himself in a network of plot and counterplot. Eventually defeat and self-doubt bring him close to insanity and it is he who sparks off prematurely the ill-fated Brescian uprising. He is a striking realization of those factors in the revolutionary movement which tend to perpetuate internal dissension and weakness in a long-protracted struggle.

Laura Piavenni, Vittoria's close friend, is another patriot devoted to the cause. She and her father, Count Serabiglione, are studies in Old and Young Italy. The Count, a member of a class which is 'traditionally parasitical', runs the gauntlet between Austrian authoritarianism and patriot devotion, inveighing against both and increasingly isolated in a world which he has ceased to understand: 'The count would speak pityingly of the poor depraved intellects which admitted the possibility of a coming Kingdom of Italy united: the lunatics who preached of it he considered a sort of self-elected targets for appointed files of Tyrolese jagers. . . . The detested title "Young Italy" hurried him into fits of wrath. "I am," he said, "one of the Old Italians, if a distinction is to be made" ' (xi). His daughter, in contrast, is patriotic beyond the bounds of self-consideration. To gain an immediate end which will benefit the cause she will stoop to any means and employ any machinery. She acts from emotional impulse rather than clear determination, from the burning passion which Meredith considers characteristic of an early stage of development. He contrasts her with the ageing Countess Ammiami, who had also learnt to love her country through the love of a husband and, like Laura, had also lost him at the hands of the Austrians. The Countess, however, preserves her mental balance and clear-sightedness even in the deepest concern for her son. Laura, their different circumstances set apart, resembles the Austrian, Anna Von Lenkenstein, whose own emotionalism leads her to be untrue to herself and to destroy the man she loves.

In writing *Vittoria* Meredith took every opportunity of developing characters like Laura, the Countess and Barto Rizzo, and of contrasting them with each other beyond the point strictly justified by their relationship with the action involving the central characters. If he had been primarily interested in the political events, he would have been obliged to subordinate his main characters. If, on the other hand, he had wanted merely to write a story about Vittoria and Carlo, he would have had to reduce the dimension of the historical material and to present it as the background to an intrigue. Because he was interested in both and wished to relate them so as to imply an overall vision of life, he attempted to preserve a balance. He expanded certain elements in the novel which might have been of minor importance and by these means achieved a much more effective unification than in *Sandra Belloni*. Yet *Vittoria*, too, falls short of complete success. Both novels represent stages in Meredith's struggle to mould his highly complex material. Neither is a completely balanced and aesthetically pleasing fiction.

Sandra Belloni went through several processes of drastic revision and gave Meredith more trouble than any of his previous novels.[9] There are signs of this in the published version of the novel – as, for example, the vestigial or embryonic character of Mrs Lupin. This lady, as the aunt to the Pole sisters and superintendent of the household, would seem to have deserved proper introduction to the reader and might have been expected to feature in that part of the action which is concerned with domestic activities at Brookfield. She is, however, never introduced, though in ch. iii she appears in a short clause: 'Then they spoke with their aunt, Mrs Lupin, and went to their papa.' Then in ch. xv 'Wilfrid took his father's seat, facing his aunt Lupin . . .', and in ch. xvi Mr Pole ends a sentence addressed to Adela by saying, 'I have all the bills, or your aunt has them.' Her only appearance in anything like a proper person occurs in ch. xxvii, where it is not unfair to say that she is dragged in to strengthen the comedy surrounding Mrs Chump and to add to the social criticism. There we learn that Mrs Lupin is an insignificant little woman with an insuperable tendency to detect and to laugh at the slightest double meaning and that she suffers agonies in attempting to restrain herself. Consequently, the narrator informs us, she 'was one of the victims of the modern feminine "ideal" ', and he is able to use her in order to stress the artificiality of the image which the Pole sisters would present: 'She was in mind merely a woman; devout and charitable, as her nerves admitted; but radically – what! They did not like to think, or to say what. . . .'

Sandra Belloni does not as a whole lack consistency of characterization. Mrs Lupin is no more than an indication of the possibility that a long process of revision and rewriting had prevented Meredith from having a very clear idea of what the novel he had written was actually like. More serious is the structural weakness which arises from the novel's lack of evenness and balance. The action begins with the encounter between Emilia and the Pole sisters and continues with a number of scenes at Brookfield, during which the attention of the narrator alternates between the sisters on the one hand and Emilia and Wilfrid on the other. With the development of the relationship between these two a train of events is begun which breaks the unity of scene and action maintained up to that point. The basic contrast between Emilia and the Poles is weakened as more characters are introduced to thicken the texture of the novel and extend the picture of contemporary English society. This process continues as Emilia strikes out on her own, leaving Brookfield and its inhabitants behind her. Gradually, moreover, the sisters develop separate relationships – Cornelia with Purcell and Sir Twickenham Pryme, Adela with Captain Gambier and others – and gradually the narrator begins to treat them separately. Eventually the novel is held together only by the machinery of the story-plot.

The process of disintegration really begins with Emilia's flight to London to interview Mr Pole. This incident and those which lead immediately from it take up three chapters (xxiv–xxvi). Emilia does not appear again until ch. xxxvi, when she is allowed by Lady Charlotte Chillingworth to hear Wilfrid's renunciation of her, but ch. xxxvii-xli are taken up entirely with her flight, her interview with Pericles, her wanderings about London and her rescue by Merthyr. Although there is an abrupt return to Brookfield in the next chapter, to describe the defection of Mr Pericles from the circle and the further development of the relationship between Cornelia and Mr Barrett, we visit Brookfield after this only in ch. liv, though we hear a good deal about it indirectly. Other sections of the novel are taken up with the antics of Wilfrid (xliii-xlvi), the situation of Emilia, Merthyr and Georgiana (xlvii-lii) and the suicide of Purcell (lv).

Throughout the later part of the novel the scene is constantly changing, with bewildering rapidity, from Brookfield to London, to a yacht at sea, to Dover, to Devon, to London, to Monmouth and back again to London, and finally to the woods where Emilia sings. Change of focus is equally abrupt and unprepared for, sequential connections are sometimes clumsy, parts of the action are given undue prominence and some chapter divisions are incomprehensible. Ch. xxxv, for example, 'Mrs Chump's Epistle', has a rather small function in providing comic relief and is useful in preparing us for the transition from Brookfield and the Pole sisters to Devon, Wilfrid, Lady Charlotte and Emilia, but in itself it contributes very little to the action or to the statement of the novel. On the other hand, certain incidents which are clearly necessary to the conduct of the plot are poorly managed. Ch. xlii, for example, 'Defection of Mr Pericles from the Brookfield Circle', contains a very important incident which is insufficiently motivated. Mr Pericles is beaten by Wilfrid because he traduces Emilia. He has it in his power to ruin the Poles and shows a tendency to do so. It is important that we appreciate his alienation and that it is presented in such a way as to leave the sisters in some doubt as to its cause. Accordingly, Meredith introduces a scene in the local church during which the girls discover Mr Pericles in the company of their rivals, the Tinleys. This is an efficient piece of plotting, but leaves the reader unsatisfied. We know Mr Pericles as an eccentric Greek millionaire with a passion for the opera and as the business partner of Mr Pole. We see him as a guest in Brockfield and at his London office. We appreciate his reaction to Wilfrid's treatment of him. On the other hand, we are provided with no reason for his appearance in the Tinleys' pew during a service for which he has scant respect. We may presume that this is a deliberate action intended to annoy the three girls, but we are not told that it is so, and if we were we should find it hard to reconcile with what we know of his character from scenes like that in which he insults and rejects the voiceless Emilia. We are ultimately obliged to accept the incident as a piece of machinery which means nothing to us in any other sense.

Vittoria shows a greatly increased power of management and a keener sense of the proportionate value of incidents than *Sandra Belloni*. The later novel contains brilliant manipulation of action and character and frequently shows a fine sensitivity for details of technique. Thus, while the narration remains throughout in the hands of the narrator, the last scenes are reported from the point of view of Merthyr Powys. It is from his detached but deeply sympathetic viewpoint that we see the events leading up to the final catastrophe, and by this means Meredith permits himself not only to maintain a fine suspense, but also to preserve the impression of inextricable confusion of character and circumstance which is so important a part of his statement. In the Epilogue we receive an objective account of the death of Carlo, but before this, in ch. xlvi, 'The Last', we follow the events with Merthyr as he approaches the scene of action. The end of the chapter comes with great force.

Yet *Vittoria* gives an overall impression of unevenness of texture and imbalance which prevents the complete fusion of its separate parts. Meredith's method of alternately shifting the focus from the general picture of Italy to the situation of his main characters is not quite successful. A clear example of the kind of interrelationship which he was attempting is given by the chapters describing the scenes preceding, during and following the opera at Milan. These scenes reflect Vittoria's character as patriot and *cantatrice*, contain incidents vital to our understanding of her later career, give a brilliant impression of the relationship between the occupation forces and the population, and at the same time contain (in the text of the opera itself) something closely approaching Meredith's own analysis of the state of the country. Elsewhere in the novel there is rarely an equal degree of fusion. Some chapters are taken up entirely with the introduction of characters (xi, 'Laura Piavenni'; vi, 'Barto Rizzo'; xvi, 'Countess Ammiami'). Others are almost exclusively concerned with the relation of historical events (xxix-xxxv, 'Episodes of the Revolt and the War'). Occasionally the reader is presented with a long scene which seems to have little importance to either of the main sources of interest. Thus, one of the longest of the earlier chapters (xvi, 'At the Maestro's Door') describes the scene outside the door of Rocco Ricci, the progress of Pericles' intrigue to get Vittoria out of danger before the night of her début, the counterplots of the spy, Luigi. Other chapters, like the one that follows this (xvii, 'Ammiami through the Midnight'), preserve their relevance, but appear in contrast to the slow-moving scenes at the beginning of the novel, or to others which are taken up with concentrated incidents or interviews, to be scattered and scrappy. Others again bring the action to a halt without developing it, except by the introduction of a new character, and in these Meredith sometimes reveals an eye for the less relevant details of scene which is disconcerting.[10] In complete contrast, other sections of the novel are fast-moving to the point of breathlessness.

All this, however, is only to say that in 1865 Meredith had not achieved the degree of control over his material which he did achieve later. *Sandra Belloni* and *Vittoria* embody his mature and fully consistent vision of life, show deep penetration into human character and into the nature of social and political organisms. Their plotting is complex and consistent and their partial failure results rather from the choice of an unsuitable type of structure than from any incapacity to handle the highly original material for which Meredith was seeking a fictional form. In *Harry Richmond* (1871) Meredith succeeded far better in what he was attempting, and in *Beauchamp's Career* (1874) he succeeded completely. In this novel, as in *Sandra Belloni* and *Vittoria*, Meredith aimed to show the social forces around the individual, 'to put the destinies of the world' around the flesh and blood of the individual history – 'like an atmosphere out of which it cannot subsist'. With Nevil Beauchamp he had a hero who was typical of a class, and with his subject – Nevil's attempt to move the political and social forces of England – he had a subject which allowed naturally for a wide social observation. Meredith's career between 1861 and 1874 may be seen as a search for such a form, which would allow him to dramatize his conception of the vital relationship between the individual and the society and the operation in the lives of both of certain immutable laws. In this process *Sandra Belloni* and *Vittoria* were of great importance. In them Meredith first realized the full width of his subject-matter. In attempting to solve the problems which they presented he gained valuable experience which later enabled him to find complete and aesthetically satisfying expression for his most mature convictions.

Notes

1 *Sandra Belloni*, Meredith's third novel, was published under the title of *Emilia in England* in 1864: it was followed by *Vittoria*, Meredith's fifth novel (*Rhoda Fleming* had intervened), which was originally to be called *Emilia in Italy*, but was published with its present title in the *Fortnightly Review* from 15 January to 1 December 1866 and in three vols. in 1867.
2 See *Letters of George Meredith*, ed. W. M. Meredith, 1912, 129–30, 132, 145, 147, etc.
3 Ibid., 130.
4 Bracketed roman numerals refer to the chapter numbers of the respective novels.
5 Though Meredith several times defined sentimentalism, the prevailing evil in English society, his definitions were particular in their application. It may generally be defined as it appears in his work as the attempt to impose on reality a pattern which is more attractive to the subject than that which actually exists. It may therefore be the result of crude egoism in refined disguise, or, on the other hand, stem from a genuine sensibility and lead to a sincere and honest attempt to achieve improvement of circumstances.
6 Meredith's phrase 'the origin of classes' sounds like a deliberate Darwinian echo: and it is in *Sandra Belloni* that his analysis of individual and social evolution, which were formed years before the

publication of *The Origin of Species* (1859), were first expressed in Darwinian terms.

7 This sentence belongs to a passage which Meredith excised from editions of *Sandra Belloni* after the first; it remains an apt description of the excitable but inarticulate merchant.

8 *Letters* . . . , 1912, 529.

9 See *Letters* . . . , 1912, 75, 79, 82, 103, etc.

10 See, for example, xvi, where we are told that Carlo and Luciano 'fell hungrily upon dishes of herb-flavoured cutlets, and Neapolitan maccaroni, green figs, green and red slices of melon, chocolate, and a dry red Florentine wine'.

The Adventures of Harry Richmond
—*Bildungsroman* and Historical
Novel

Margaret Tarratt

Although *Harry Richmond* is a work that may be easily read and
absorbed at a superficial level, it can have a bewildering effect,
since it does not follow any clearly recognized formal lines. A
stream of characters and incidents are introduced, dropped and
occasionally reintroduced in the arbitrary tradition of the picaresque. The novel combines this element with a heterogeneous
assortment of fiction genres – the fairy tale, Ruritanian romance,
confessional autobiography and Goethean *Bildungsroman* which
may well disconcert the reader's expectations. It cannot sensibly
be read outside these traditions.

A survey of the most important critical responses to *Harry
Richmond* suggests the complexity of the problems of interpretation. Few critics have prepared to look at it with any formal
considerations in mind. Barbara Hardy, in her essay in *The
Appropriate Form*,[1] comes nearest to such an examination. Her
contribution is a description and discussion of certain recurrent
images prefaced with a warning that Meredith's imagination works
in a less ordered manner than that, for instance, of James or
Proust, and that his imagery cannot usefully be made to conform
to some schematic structure. She sees the novel as a typical
Bildungsroman, the central theme of which is Harry's awakening to
the 'real' world and his rejection of what his father stands for. Yet
such an account ignores Harry's mixed feelings towards the Squire
and his 'impossible' choice between Janet and the Princess Ottilia.
Most important, it brushes off the burning of Riversley as a mere
example of Roy's 'heroic futility'. Jack Lindsay also sees this novel
in terms of Harry's rejection of the delusory romantic view of Roy,

but adds that Harry 'does not accept the Squire's egoist greed as a solution'.[2] He criticizes the novel on the grounds of its lack of constructive ideas and its ending, which he sees as a 'shallow formula of reconciliation'. Norman Kelvin finds that Meredith in this novel asserts the value of living rationally, i.e. in harmony with the laws of society. He suggests that in this context, 'illusions' signify an absence of moral awareness and 'maturity' its presence.[3] Walter Wright alone makes a distinction between the value of the resources of Roy's imagination and his 'glamour', suggesting that 'the story is really of a youth's education in romance'.[4]

In the following pages I intend to discuss this novel in terms of autobiography, *Bildungsroman* and historical novel, since these aspects appear to illuminate certain of the problems of interpretation to which the work is subject. Through such an examination, I intend to show that *Harry Richmond* bears a closer affinity to *Wilhelm Meister* and the German *Bildungsroman*[5] than to any contemporary English 'autobiographical' novels. At the same time, it is not a mere imitation of such a genre, but an interpretation and comment in terms that are related to the state of British society and the dilemma of the young Englishman looking for a field of relevant action. It is in this context that we must look at Meredith's developing personal involvement in this novel and observe the elements from his own life which are caught up in the web of narrative. In this sense *Harry Richmond* can be regarded as a contemporary historical novel in the terms applied by Gyorgy Lukács in *The Historical Novel*.

Harry Richmond's hybrid nature may owe something to the apparent changes which developed over a period of several years in Meredith's own conception of the work. In a letter to F. Maxse of 1863 whilst gathering material for *Vittoria* and planning 'an English novel' – *Rhoda Fleming* – he makes his first reference to a projected 'Autobiography'.[6] By May 1864, writing to William Hardman, the 'Autobiography' seems to have become the 'Autobiographic Tale',[7] whilst a letter of the same month to Augustus Jessopp is more explicit:

> I have also in hand an Autobiography and 'The Adventures of Richmond Roy and his friend Contrivance Jack: Being the History of Two Rising Men' and to be a spanking bid for popularity on the part of this writer.[8]

This was the last reference to 'Autobiography' or 'Autobiographic

Tale'. By 1870 'The Adventures of Richmond Roy and his friend Contrivance Jack' and the 'Autobiography' had become one work – *The Adventures of Harry Richmond* – and Meredith was clearly unable to sustain his effort to win popularity:

> I fear I am evolving his personality too closely for the public, but a man must work by the light of his conscience if he's to do anything worth reading.[9]

The novel was out of his hands by July 1870 and a letter to Captain Maxse at Christmas 1870 mentions the completion of

> The History of the inextinguishable Sir Harry Firebrand of the Beacon, Knight Errant of the Nineteenth Century, in which mirror you may look and see – my dear Fred and his loving friend, GEORGE MEREDITH.[10]

From this it seems clear that the 'Autobiography' or 'Autobiographic Tale' had been assimilated into the original picaresque romance of his early conception and that both elements had been subsumed into a contemporary historical framework.

Writing to Jessopp in October 1871, Meredith gave his most detailed account of his aims and method in *Harry Richmond*. In a later letter to Hardman, he displayed some earnestness in his instructive comment:

> Don't speak of Richmond till you have read the whole. When you have done that say what you like. I shall be glad of criticism. Consider first my scheme as a workman. It is to show you the action of minds as well as of fortunes – of here and there men and women vitally animated by their brains at different periods of their lives – and of men and women with something of a look out upon the world and its destinies – the mortal ones. The Divine I leave to Doctors of Divinity. Let those far-sighted gentlemen speak on such subjects.[11]

For all the novel's flamboyance, Meredith maintained that he had 'resisted every temptation to produce great and startling effects'.[12] He also complained of being

> hand-tied too by gentlemanly feeling in relation to the reigning Royal House, Sweet Tory Tuck! or I should (and did on paper) have launched out. The speech at the City Banquet would have satisfied a Communist Red originally.[13]

Between 1863 and 1870 Meredith's work seems to develop from the forms of the popular picaresque and the novel of autobiographical relevance into a study of the socio-political structure examined through the psychology of individuals. Meredith deliberately chooses to study situations and events through the filter of a specific consciousness and he was to observe with some insight that 'much of my strength lies in painting morbid emotion and exceptional positions'.[14]

As an 'Autobiographical Tale' *Harry Richmond*, like *Evan Harrington* and to some extent *Richard Feverel*, can be related to sources in Meredith's own life. It was his first novel to deal with the hero's childhood since *Feverel*, and the writing of *Harry Richmond* coincided with the adolescence of the neglected son, Arthur Meredith – a period punctuated by George's sententious, fussy and slightly guilty letters to him discussing his educational development and possible future career. The onset of the Franco-Prussian War gave rise in these and other letters to reflections on German national characteristics, revealing a considerable degree of sympathy and admiration for that nation, combined with a strong consciousness of the contrast which the Germans presented to the British. This contrast of national characteristics is an important feature of *Harry Richmond*. Lionel Stevenson[15] has suggested that Meredith's acquaintance with Bonaparte Wyse and a visit to his mother's house (a daughter of Napoleon) may have influenced the presentation of Richmond Roy's grandiose aspiration to royalty. Stevenson also mentions the case of two brothers in 1842 who claimed to be legitimate grandsons of Bonnie Prince Charlie and were accorded royal privileges in Bohemia. This may well have been in Meredith's mind when he created Richmond Roy. It is generally accepted that Meredith's legendary grandfather, Melchizedek Meredith – the original 'Great Mel' – and Janet Ross are at least partial sources for Richmond Roy and Janet Ilchester.

Harry Richmond derives its structure from the growth of a central character; this in itself is not unusual in English fiction. *David Copperfield*, *Great Expectations* and *Pendennis* are only three notable examples of this kind of novel. Yet *Harry Richmond* cannot usefully be seen as part of this group. Unlike them, it does not immediately make plain its moral premises. In *David Copperfield*, for instance, which *Harry Richmond* resembles in certain incidents and character groups (particularly in the sections relating to Steerforth and Heriot, Little Em'ly and Mabel Sweetwinter, Traddles and

Temple respectively) the growth of David's maturity is in some measure to be gauged by his replacement of the child-bride, Dora, by the upward-pointing Agnes as a female ideal. Similarly, Arthur Pendennis can find stability only when he has spontaneously rejected the meretricious charms of Blanche Amory for the admirably moral Laura Bell. Torn between the conflicting claims of the fiery, tradition-bound Squire Beltham and the romantically ambitious 'outsider', Richmond Roy, between the robust and wholesome Englishwoman, Janet Ilchester, and the intellectually and morally aspiring Princess Ottilia, Harry Richmond is allowed no easy path towards a 'right choice' and consequent accolade of 'maturity'. The hunger and power of emotion and imagination so strongly featured in the early parts of *David Copperfield* and so singularly absent in the final sections are driving forces throughout *Harry Richmond*, forming an integral complication in Harry's moral dilemmas. Moreover, unlike the other novels, *Harry Richmond* ends on an almost surreal note of uncertainty, leaving us with a sense that little has been established.

This emphasis on the protracted search and the tentative open-ended conclusion in *Harry Richmond* suggests that a more fruitful field of comparison lies in the Goethean *Bildungsroman*, which is also characterized by these qualities. It is to *The Apprenticeship of Wilhelm Meister* that we must turn for this purpose. This novel of Goethe's was, through Carlyle's translation, the main filter through which the *Bildungsroman* influenced the English novelists. However, the quality of Meredith's appreciation of Goethe differed considerably from that of Carlyle:

I do worship the splendid stature clothed with wisdom only I claim the right to smile now and then.[16]

Bracketed alone with Shakespeare, Goethe was cited by Meredith as a man 'to whom I bow my head'. Although most of his references to Goethe are in the letters to Lady Ulrica Duncombe which were written towards the end of his life, listing his 'readings of the formative kind' in 1906, he declared:

They were first, the Arabian Nights, then Gibbon, Niebuhr, Walter Scott; then Molière, then the noble Goethe, the most enduring.[17]

During the years when we know *Harry Richmond* to have been in Meredith's mind, there are two minor references to Goethe. He is a Realist '*au fond*' who has 'the broad arms of Idealism a command'. He gives us 'Earth, but it is earth with an atmosphere'.¹ In a letter of 1865 to Captain Maxse he declares: 'Goethe' Elective Affinities – the *Wahlverwandtschaften* – would deligh you.'[19] We have already seen that Captain Maxse was associate with Harry Richmond in Meredith's mind.

It is more than pure coicidence that the Princess in *Harr Richmond* shares the same name as the heroine of *Elective Affinitie* Like Natalia in *Wilhelm Meister*, the Princess Ottilia is reported '*schöne Seele*' – the term initially used by Schiller to describe a typ of Platonic spiritual beauty, and used also in *Wilhelm Meister* in th diary of Natalia's aunt. Harry, on his way to a midnight rendezvou with the Princess, finds himself humming the '*Zigeunerlied*' – point which is emphasized by repetition – and Ottilia, in he attempts to bring Harry and Janet together near the end of th novel, sends him 'one scrap from the playful *Xenien* of Ottilia' favourite brotherly poets of untranslatable flavour':

> Who shuns true friends flies fortune in the concrete:
> Would he see what he aims at? Let him ask his heels.
>
> (1, 65)

These Goethean associations surrounding Harry's relationshi with the Princess cannot be overlooked. In the following para graphs I shall comment in more detail on certain aspects o *Wilhelm Meister* which seem to provide relevant points of compari son with Meredith's novel.

Wilhelm Meister is a prosperous merchant's son. As a child, th unexpected puppet-show in his home disrupts his mundan existence with overpowering effect, firing a dormant imagination Unwittingly, his mother introduces into the house a model for a system of values opposed to those of mercantile existence. At th age of fourteen he writes a poem in which

> the Muse of tragic art and another female form, by which I personified 'Commerce', were made to strive very bravely for my most important self. . . . How repulsively did I paint the old housewife . . . and how differently advanced the other! What an apparition for the over-clouded mind.[20]

As I have mentioned above, Harry Richmond, like Wilhelm Meister, is from childhood torn between opposing values in life – values which the child sees initially as *bourgeois* conventionality *versus* the life of the imagination, and in the first chapter heading, 'I am the Subject of Contention', he is seen as a pawn in the opponents' hands. From the first chapter of *Harry Richmond* Squire Beltham, his grandfather, is associated with the power with which his wealth endows him. Roy seems to come from nowhere. He is the sudden quasi-magical irruption into Harry's life which the puppets were to Wilhelm, and he demands a place as of right in Harry's consciousness. Several times Roy is shown as an actor. The games to which he introduces Harry are games of fantasy which he renders real by his ability to enact. The regular Punch and Judy show he orders for the child lacks all zest when he is not there to give an imaginative commentary. He is seen a little later acting some of the incidents of the *Arabian Nights*, and when Harry rediscovers his father in Sarkeld it is to find him like a kind of court jester impersonating a statue of Prince Ernest's ancestor.

Just as Wilhelm Meister learns to reject the world of actors as a medium through which his dreams of self-development can be realized (they show themselves to be narrow in aims and achievement and narcissistic in temperament) so Harry learns to criticize and reject the actor in his father. The bronze-coated Roy is both horrifying and ludicrous and it is some time before Harry can renew his relationship on the old footing. Although Roy does not immediately lose his place in Harry's imagination, Harry's aim is no longer the romantic yearning towards his company, but instead a desire to 'unite' his father and grandfather 'on terms of friendship'. The Squire is now included in his schemes. He has reached a stage similar to that of Wilhelm Meister, who looks back on his childhood allegory of Commerce and the Tragic Muse and meditates: 'The one no longer looks so pitiful as then; nor does the other look so glorious.'[21]

Both Wilhelm and Harry are under pressure many times in their lives to return to a financially stable environment, and those who urge this are not mere cogs in such a system. The wandering Clara Goodwin, Harry's 'fairy Peribanou' of the *Arabian Nights*, predicts a curious destiny for him, but still urges him to desert Roy and return to Riversley and the Squire. Similarly, in *Wilhelm Meister* the child Mignon, a figure embodying the irrational and intuitive emotions, protests when Wilhelm signs up as an actor. In both Goethe's and Meredith's novels the heroes are at some point compelled to realize that 'to work effectively' a man stands 'in need of outward means'.[22] This point is emphasized in *Harry Richmond*, where Roy's failures are seen to be largely owing to a constitutional inability to handle money.

For both Wilhelm and Harry the life of the imagination involves an incessant wandering and ultimately, perhaps, such wandering is enforced upon them. Jarno in *Wilhelm Meister* associates the life of actors with that of gypsies. Harry Richmond hopes at one point to be a gypsy king and feels that 'houses imprisoned us . . . a lost father was never to be discovered by remaining in them' (i, 81). Yet he is himself betrayed for money by gypsies and his own deepest moment of duplicity in his relationship to the Princess Ottilia is marked by the 'gypsy burden' of the '*Zigeunerlied*'. In both works the fascination of gypsy life is regarded with suspicion.

Both implicitly and explicitly throughout *Wilhelm Meister's Apprenticeship* Wilhelm's aim has been towards some kind of self-culture which can absorb the aims of his imagination. He asks and answers his own question:

> What is it that keeps men in continual discontent and agitation? It is, that they cannot make realities correspond with their conceptions, that enjoyment steals away from among their hands, that the wished for comes too late, and nothing reached and acquired produces on the heart the effect which their longing for it at a distance had led them to anticipate.[23]

The direction his life has taken is analysed:

> The cultivation of my individual self, here as I am, has from my youth upwards been constantly though dimly my wish and my purpose.[24]

And Theresa comments later:

> The description of his life is a perpetual seeking without finding; not empty seeking, but wondrous, generous seeking; he fancies others may give him what can proceed from himself alone.[25]

The pursuit of inward cultivation which begins for Wilhelm through following the life of the imagination and develops into a concrete ambition to found a National German Theatre, by the end becomes a metaphysical search, reflected with significant variations in *Harry Richmond*. Harry's alternation between Riversley and the wanderer's life is more intuitive than planned, although his search for his lost father (a figure vital to the life of the imagination) is consciously undertaken. The framework for his aspirations, however, is initially a conventional one of patriotism. Such 'patriotism' involves a schoolboy sense of 'honour' and is bound up in being a 'gentleman'. A legendary image of England's history has been present for Harry from the period of early childhood spent with his father, when he is given a choice of heroes, Nelson, Shakespeare and Pitt, and later lives in a house decorated with stained-glass windows depicting the kings of England. The effect of this is such that, when he is searching for his father, supposedly in 'the Bench', he imagines its walls

> in the middle of a great square and hung with the standard of England drooping over them in a sort of mournful family pride (i, 136).

This is a childish version of Wilhelm Meister's youthful nationalism.

Beyond hoping to effect a reconciliation between his father and grandfather, Harry seems innocent of personal aspiration. His father makes no secret of his ambitions for Harry's future and Harry confesses that 'his visions of our glorious future enchained me' (i, 229). Such aims are never made explicit, although they involve the establishment of a position of high social prestige. The 'glorious' future does not imply moral development. We are told that Harry, a true Englishman, 'hated speculation' in history and philosophy. Consequently, although he studies voluntarily at a German university, he is completely out of his element in the context of the intellectual life shared by Ottilia and Professor von Karsteg. Both are figures who, in attitude, might have stepped from the pages of *Wilhelm Meister*.

Both question Harry as to his 'aims' and the part they play in the course of his life, but, unlike *Wilhelm Meister*, *Harry Richmond* is concerned not merely with the individual in his own country, but with the confrontation of two different cultures and the applicability of the Goethean ethic to the young Englishman. They point out the minimal part which the life of the intellect plays in English society, and Von Karsteg asserts the 'exact stamp of the English mind . . . is, to accept whatsoever is bequeathed it' (i, 313). Ottilia is concerned to know whether Harry makes his aims a part of his life, and, like Theresa in Goethe's novel, claims that 'Well I know a man's field of labour in his country' (i, 308). There is a further parallel in *Wilhelm Meister* in a discussion of the implications of

Lothario's travels, through which he had hoped to 'accomplish something':

> 'I recollect the letter which you sent me from the Western world,' said Jarno, 'it contained the words: "I will return, and in my house, amid my fields, among my people, I will say: *Here or nowhere is America.*" '[26]

Von Karsteg, questioning Harry about his 'scheme of life' (xxix),[27] sees through his hypocritical temptation to display himself in the light of 'Shakespeare's book; or Göthe's, in the minor issues'. But he assumes that Harry by nature of his position of material influence must have some 'object' in view. Harry's vague hope of 'doing Good' with his wealth brings down upon him the Professor's scorn. Von Karsteg sees English society as stagnant, remaining in a 'past age'. The aristocracy, since it neither governs nor takes a lead in the arts of military science, is parasitic upon the materialistic middle class: 'You work so hard that you have all but one aim, and that is fatness and ease!' The British are a frogs' chorus of critics at the German pattern of 'striving, failing and striving on'. They are unable to appreciate 'aims that don't drop on the ground before your eyes'. Harry's tentative suggestion that his aims would be to 'endeavour to equalize ranks at home, encourage the growth of ideas' is further food for the Professor's contempt. The individual effort in England is useless in such a programme. The country needs 'blasting'. Harry as a 'heroic' figure would most resemble 'Laocoon in the throes' with the aims he has adopted. At last he is forced to confess that he has no aim beyond longing in a mystified fashion to be 'of some service'. His imagination clings to the image of Ottilia, as does that of Wilhelm to that of the 'Beautiful Amazon', Natalia.

Yet, temperamentally, he is not another Wilhelm. His aim, in order to appear meaningful to him, must be embodied, since this is the only way in which he can 'make his aims a part of his life'. It is in the associations surrounding the Princess Ottilia, their embodiment, that confusion continues to reign. Having won the Princess's love, Harry torments himself with the realization of his 'bewildering incapacity to conjure up a vision of Ottilia free of the glittering accessories of her high birth' (i, 329). His acquiescence in Roy's scheme to trick her into a solemn betrothal marks his falling away from the moral goal he has set himself, being

tired of seeming to be what I was not quite, of striving to
become what I must have divined that I never could quite
attain to. So my worthier, or ideal, self fell away from me
(ii, 377).

Harry's thoughts turn to Janet Ilchester, for in her society

I was sure to be at least myself, a creature much reduced in
altitude, but without the cramped sensations of a man on a
monument. My hearty Janet! I thanked her then for seeing
me of my natural height (ii, 393–4).

As a child, Harry had thought of the gods as statues. Roy's descent
as a statue from his pedestal was the first crack of disillusionment in
Harry's godlike image of him. Ottilia's rarefied image of Harry
causes him to identify unconsciously with his posturing father
sooner or later to be shown up as a fraud. He has made the mistake
against which Ottilia implicitly warned him – that of 'shooting at a
false mark' through lack of self-knowledge. Contrary to Goethe,
who sees Natalia's treatment of people as if they always lived up to
their nobler natures as a positive encouragement to behave in such
a fashion, Meredith demonstrates the destructive quality of self-
disgust which may issue from an over-wearisome attempt to live up
to exalted expectations. In the *Wanderjahr* Wilhelm Meister's
separation from Natalia, the woman he loves, is shown to be
spiritually enriching. Harry's separation from Ottilia sends 'the
whole structure of my idea of my superior nature . . . crumbling
into fragments' (ii, 467).

Although visions of a life with Janet at 'peaceful Riversley' no
longer seem hateful to him, Harry is unable to wean himself
from his obsessive striving towards the hopelessly unattainable
moral and metaphysical goal which Ottilia has become for
him!

My strivings were against my leanings, and imagining the
latter, which involved no sacrifice of the finer sense of honour,
to be in the direction of my lower nature, I repelled them to
preserve a lofty aim that led me through questionable ways
(ii, 511).

What does repel Harry about Janet Ilchester is her lack of sentiment and imagination. Her strength lies in her association with a
traditional mode of English life.

I thought of Janet – she made me gasp for air; of Ottilia, and she made me long for earth. . . . To strangle the thought of either one of them was like the pang of death; yet it did not strike me that I loved the two: they were apart in my mind, actually as if I had been divided (ii, 575–6).

Harry's dilemma is Wilhelm Meister's situation in reverse. Wilhelm, betrothed to the practical Theresa, yearns towards the spiritually elevated Natalia, but Meredith's hero has a more complex choice to make. In *Wilhelm Meister* Theresa points out that men choose practical wives because of common sense, although with their imaginations they long for other qualities. Harry, betrothed to the lofty Ottilia, cannot stifle a desire for the practical, the stable, the concrete.

In a letter to Captain Maxse, Meredith had already stated his own attitude: 'Between realism and idealism there is no natural conflict. This completes that.'[28] The development of a friendship between Janet and the Princess is an expression of their compatibility – the compatibility of air and earth. Each has qualities the other admires as wanting in herself. 'Spice of the Princess's conversation' flavours Janet's speech by the end of the novel, whilst the Princess praises Janet's quality of extraordinary courage. It is Ottilia who engineers their marriage whilst resuming her place in Harry's imagination: 'The home is always here where I am, but it may now take root elsewhere' (ii, 673).

The child Janet and the Janet of the final chapters are different women. The course of the narrative shows her growing away from her youthful greed and selfishness towards a heroic restraint of personal feeling. This reaches mistaken heights in her 'pride's conception of duty', which forces her to attempt to go through with her marriage to Edbury. But by the final chapters she has conquered the delusion that 'what she was she must always be because it was her nature' (ii, 648). Like Harry, and unlike the Squire or 'the unteachable spirit of Roy', she proves herself capable of moral and emotional development. The development in her characterization is witness of this, and it is for this reason that Harry, unlike Wilhelm Meister (and indeed David Copperfield), does not end his history by attaching himself to an upward-pointing figure of moral aspiration. 'Leanings' should be as important as 'strivings' is the implication of his marriage choice.

Ottilia is a figure from another culture, another social sphere.

Harry, dazzled by her rank, educated to an inferior degree with his roots deeply embedded within an English tradition, can attempt to win her only at the price of destruction of his natural personality, of his self-respect and – last but not least – by using his personal fortune as a kind of investment, with Ottilia as the dividend. He reflects that 'A life caught out of its natural circle is as much in danger of being lost as a limb given to a wheel in spinning machinery' (ii, 523). This is not mere acquiescence to the reactionary traditionalism of Prince Ernest, as Harry suspects.

Criticisms of the notions of destiny and free will are common both to *Wilhelm Meister* and *Harry Richmond*. Within the framework of a desire for self-development, Goethe develops his ideas on destiny and on the influence of the experiences of childhood. A speculative conversation on the existence of destiny between Wilhelm and the Abbé is biased heavily against the validity of such a concept. Yet at one important level destiny can be said to have a real meaning in terms of the events, actions and decisions of one's life, which 'by their incessant movements weave a web, which we ourselves, in a greater or a less degree have spun and put upon the loom'.[29] Wilhelm is warned: 'Let no one think that he can conquer the first impressions of his youth',[30] and the clergyman brought in to help the Harper's insane condition remarks: 'Everything that happens to us leaves some trace behind it, everything contributes imperceptibly to form us.'[31]

In *Harry Richmond*, as in Goethe's novel, man's fate is shown to be deeply involved with his past history. Harry reflects from the narrator's mature standpoint:

> If a man's fate were as a forbidden fruit, detached from him, and in front of him, he might hesitate fortunately before plucking it; but, as most of us are aware, the vital half of it lies in the seed-paths he has traversed. We are sons of yesterday, not of the morning. The past is our mortal mother, no dead thing. Our future constantly reflects her to the soul. Nor is it ever the new man of to-day which grasps his fortune, good or ill. We are pushed to it by the hundreds of days we have buried, eager ghosts. And if you have not the habit of taking counsel with them, you are but an instrument in their hands (i, 132).

Harry's choice of action at any given point is influenced by his own unravelling history. Freedom only has a meaning within this context. Hence, Janet, tempered by the influence of Ottilia, becomes both the practicable and the ideal wife for Harry. It is in this sense that in Wilhelm Meister's terms 'realities' can be made to 'correspond to conceptions' and the 'continual discontent and agitation' is dissolved. Harry by the end of the novel appears to have reached a point of equilibrium indicated by Jarno in Goethe's novel. His 'vague striving' has now 'itself marked out its proper limitations'.[32]

Like Goethe, Meredith rejects any concept of destiny other than as a term to describe the influence of past events and actions upon the present. The character most closely concerned with ideas of Providence and destiny is Roy, who complains of his birth stars and predicts a brilliant destiny for Harry. This attitude, imparted by his father, is something which Harry must fight. For Roy destiny is both something which is given by the stars and also the individual's assumption of control over his own fate. 'We have a rich or a barren future, just as we conceive it', he maintains, and Tamburlaine-like urges Harry: 'I have my hand on the world's wheel and now is the time for you to spring from it and gain your altitude' (ii, 408–9). His analysis of the situation is proved false when, like Wilhelm Meister, he discovers that to a large extent his life has been guided indeed, but by a hidden *human* agency. Harry and Roy also have their 'Tower Watchers'. They live to see the actions they thought of as Providence revealed as the work of human hands. The sum of money deposited 'providentially' for Roy is not the opportune payment from a guilty royal house, but an offering of love from Dorothy Beltham. Harry's seat in Parliament and his voyage round the world are not divinely ordained 'accidents', but the consequences of Princess Ottilia's concern for him: 'Ottilia was still my princess; she my providence' (ii, 673). Captain Bulsted's contempt for the belief that accidents can exist without cause triumphs. Harry, near the conclusion of his history admits:

> I was still subject to the relapses of a not perfectly right
> nature, as I perceived when glancing back at my thought of
> 'An odd series of accidents!' which was but a disguised
> fashion of attributing to Providence the particular concern in
> my fortunes: an impiety and a folly! (ii, 680–1).

What he wishes to understand as 'Providence' is the result of human action – the Princess's ability to assess character and to realize 'what could be wrought out of me'.

Many of the ingredients of the *Bildungsroman* as described by Roy Pascal[33] also hold good for *Harry Richmond*, including the absence of a static set of values and the indeterminate conclusion 'comparable with the indeterminateness of life'.[34] Pascal's description of the archetypal hero of the *Bildungsroman* excellently sums up the relation between Harry and the narrative structures in Meredith's novel:

> The hero is not a man of action or will, he does not influence the march of events. He is interesting above all for his disposition, his moral views and sentiments, his moral personality. In the midst of apparently fortuitous occurrences, he gives the latter a unity within his disposition, he 'moulds' them, though he does not cause or control them. . . . There is no fatal clash between circumstances and character; the outcome is inherently there in the character from the beginning. Hence . . . a moral meaning is given to the outer world however haphazard its scenes and occurrences may appear.[35]

Nevertheless, *Harry Richmond* is in one important aspect significantly different both from *Wilhelm Meister* and from Pascal's generalized description of the *Bildungsroman*:

> The 'Bildungsroman' leads up to the decision to take part in social life, but halts at the threshold, or deals summarily and feebly with the later fortunes of the hero . . . the problems of actual social life are not here.[36]

In *Harry Richmond* the social and even geographical setting is of crucial importance in influencing the course of his moral development. The application of the Goethean ethic to the hero of nineteenth-century England is put to the test. The initial conflict between the world of upper-middle-class stability and the Bohemian imagination is speedily transformed into a social conflict in which the settled order is threatened by an overblown Byronic individualism identified with no specific class. The Goethean moral and metaphysical aspiration of the Princess Ottilia is entangled in discussions on differences in national characteristics between the English and the Germans. Harry's uncertainty arises from his inability to envisage an abstract aim and his consequent need to find an embodiment for his moral aspiration in the figure of the Princess. Such embodiment leads to practical confusion, as

G

we have seen. Moreover, neither can offer the other a meaningful life in terms of their own environment. Nevertheless, Harry cannot accept the 'easy' alternative of a retired life of an English squire at Riversley with a wife chosen for him by his grandfather, since he has extended himself too far in the spheres of imagination and emotion to be able to indulge in the national vice of accepting what has been bequeathed.

It is this practical element which is absent from *Wilhelm Meister* and the German *Bildungsroman*. To complete a satisfactory analysis of Meredith's concerns and positions in *Harry Richmond* we must refer back to Meredith's letter to the Radical Captain Maxse, in which he speaks of this novel as 'The History of the inextinguishable Sir Harry Firebrand of the Beacon, Knight Errant of the Nineteenth Century in which mirror you may look and see – my dear Fred and his loving friend, GEORGE MEREDITH'.

This novel is not a record of a youth's personal development within a timeless context. Bearing in mind the somewhat passive role of the hero, the description of him as 'the inextinguishable Sir Harry Firebrand of the Beacon' is initially surprising. 'Inextinguishable', 'Firebrand' and 'Beacon' appear to link him with some kind of unquenchable revolutionary activity. As 'Knight Errant of the Nineteenth Century', Harry would appear to be in Meredith's eyes a hero, in the chivalric tradition, in search of a cause. Such a notion is not without precedent in Meredith's novels. Richard Feverel attempted to live in the tradition of the medieval knight-errant, Evan Harrington bemoaned the impossibility of such a course of action, Merthyr Powys in *Sandra Belloni* attaches himself too impetuously to a moral and political cause before the time is ripe for action. It is not until *Beauchamp's Career* that Meredith endows his hero with the genuine contemporary cause of Radicalism with which he must wrestle. The avowedly autobiographical strain in *Harry Richmond*, including the reflection of Maxse, is significant here in connection with Meredith's support for him as a Radical candidate.

Meredith's concerns in *Harry Richmond* are not directed towards detailed social description and analysis of the kind to be found in *Felix Holt* or *Great Expectations*, although he is involved in an attempt to establish certain social values. Perhaps the most illuminating way of discussing Meredith's concern with the 'Knight Errant of the Nineteenth Century' is through Lukács' comments on the nature of the historical novel.[37]

For Lukács what distinguishes the genuine from the 'so-called' historical novel is the 'derivation of the individuality of characters from the historical peculiarity of their age',[38] and he traces the development of the 'classical' historical novel involving events of past ages (epitomized by Scott) to the achievement of Balzac in establishing the 'continuation of the historical novel, in the sense of a consciously historical conception of the present',[39] a description which could as aptly be applied to *Harry Richmond*. As we have seen, Meredith claimed Scott as one of his formative influences. For Lukács an important and distinguishing characteristic of Scott as 'historical novelist' in his use of the 'middle of the road hero' as a central figure in his novel:

> It is their task to bring the extremes whose struggle fills the novel, whose clash expresses artistically a great crisis in society, into contact with one another. Through the plot, at whose centre stands this hero, a neutral ground is sought and found upon which the extreme, opposing social forces can be brought into a human relationship with one another.[40]

The 'mediocre' hero with his somewhat shapeless personality is expressive of the non-partisan element in human nature and becomes a feature of the classical historical novel – and following this the great realistic contemporary novel.

Meredith's letters during the period in which *Harry Richmond* was being produced are closely concerned with his theories on the evolution of his own society and on the possibilities of appropriate or relevant action for the individual within such a framework. Re-echoing through such letters is an assertive confidence in the traditional 'middle way':

> You fancy all things as immensities; you cannot understand the value of an intermediate measure.[41]
>
> Hitherto human nature has marched through the conflict of extremes. With the general growth of reason it will be possible to choose the path mid-way.[42]

Harry Richmond is a clear instance of a 'middle of the road' linking hero. From the novel's opening chapter he is the passive object in a clash between the Fieldingesque Squire Beltham, epitome of established order and landed wealth, and Richmond Roy, would-be Byronic hero, socially rootless, a compulsive wanderer, obsessed in the Gothic/Romantic tradition with his own origins, possible royal parentage and restoration of his 'rights'. The argument between them concerning Harry's mother rapidly develops into a battle over the child Harry, a symbol of the future. Both grandfather and father seek to have him recognized as their respective heir. That he should be heir to both appears to be an impossibility, and the Squire threatens to disinherit him completely should he become identified with his father. Harry's early rejection of the Squire's environment as an emotionally satisfying *modus vivendi* in favour of the life of the imagination offered by his father is counterbalanced by the gradual displacement of Roy as an ideal. His youthful hopes that grandfather and father can be reconciled are doomed to failure, since each stands for an opposing order, symbolically expressed by the Squire's refusal to allow Roy into Riversley.

The collision in *Harry Richmond* is between two figures who are presented very much as 'set pieces', who are allowed no philosophical or emotional development. Such change as we are able to witness in their portrayal is really the change which occurs in Harry's developing perception of these key figures in his life, the Squire, his grandfather and Roy, his father. Both are reminiscent of the eighteenth century. Squire Beltham is not far removed from the literary type of Squire Western in *Tom Jones*. Only the emphasis on his capitalist prosperity roots him in the nineteenth century. Roy is a more complicated amalgam of a later-generation Regency beau and Byronic hero pursued by 'natal furies'. He claims an unspecified royal duke as father and is a somewhat incongruous figure dabbling in the nineteenth-century capitalist world. He looks hopefully towards a revival of aristocratic leadership in England in which he and Harry can figure. He is a natural incendiary, an *agent provocateur*. Both Roy and the Squire are driven by ambition for the future of their mutual heir, Harry – a name epitomizing 'Englishness'. His other names, Lepel, Richmond, Beltham, suggest the confusion of elements in his ancestry.

The development of the novel suggests with some insistence the irreconcilability of aims and interests of Roy and the Squire. For each the other is insane. The Squire accuses Roy of responsibility for his daughter's madness, whilst Roy suggests that such insanity is her inheritance from her father. The Squire, continually associated with his established estate and home, Riversley, is shown to bear a paranoid antipathy towards the nomadic Roy, who is frequently associated with the perils of fire.

In the first chapter the Squire, awakened by Roy's knocking, leaps to the conclusion that Riversley is on fire and, in Harry's words, 'the robbers had come at last most awfully' (i, 1). It appears to the Squire that all the town's bells are ringing – a traditional sign for warning of an invasion. Harry, searching for his father in 'the Bench' is confronted instead by a fire which at first seems to be the Bench itself. In the Squire's house smoking is strictly forbidden. He would have 'no waving of flags and lighting of fireworks in a matter of business' (ii, 460), and describes Harry, under Roy's influence, like Nero dancing while Rome burns. Of Roy he declares, 'I'd as lief hang on to a fireship' (ii, 477). Harry's own reaction to Roy when he sets fire to the library curtains at the Lake Palace is to have 'a touch of fear of a man who could unhesitatingly go to extremities . . . by summoning fire to the rescue' (ii, 392). He shares this nervousness with the Squire, and sees the fireman's role to be comparable to that of slaying a dragon. Yet Von Karsteg insists that Harry's role as heir to the Squire's wealth is that of the dragon himself, squatting upon his hoard. The two roles are incompatible.

On his way to the Isle of Wight Harry passes 'Riversley station under sombre sunset fires' and is 'saddened by the fancy that my old home and vivacious Janet were ashes' (ii, 576). It is a fancy at this time, but in the final chapter, with Squire Beltham dead and Janet and Harry married, returning to claim Riversley as their home, Roy, at last allowed to live in the house, unwittingly destroys it. The description of this ultimate fire is pregnant with significance: a dark sky 'ominously reddened over Riversley' – 'funeral flames' of the 'old Grange', a blow that was 'evil, sudden, unaccountable':

> Fire at the heart, fire at the wings – our old home stood in
> that majesty of horror which freezes the limbs of men,
> bidding them look and no more.

The Squire's room is seen ablaze, and with the death of Roy a 'human' is added to the 'elemental horror' of the destruction of the 'doomed old house'. The fire suggests more than the mere burning of Harry's and Janet's 'old house'.[43] In this conflagration, unknowingly caused by Roy, his own destruction is effected, together with the symbol of the inheritance bequeathed by the Squire. 'He was never seen again' (ii, 685). Harry had attempted to inherit from the Squire and to cherish his father. Squire Beltham's instinctive sense of the incompatibility of such elements is vindicated. Each destroys the other. Simple inheritance of the acquisitions and values of a former generation is shown to be impossible. In Von Karsteg's view, it is, in any case, undesirable.

The character of Von Karsteg seems so heavily drawn as to verge upon a kind of caricature. Yet in a considerable number of instances in his own letters Meredith seems to reiterate Von Karsteg's opinions. The Professor's brief against the English is that they are a materialistic nation, pioneers of civilization only inasmuch as they led the world at a time when 'the earth had to be shaped for implements and dug for gold' (i, 306). In his eyes the wealth of the country is drained by the rich 'pumpkins' – an alliance of aristocracy and merchant class without responsibilities or talents. 'Merchandized' aristocracy and 'married clergy' are 'coils' and 'ivy about your social tree' (i, 316), whilst 'the exact stamp of the English mind'

> is to accept whatsoever is bequeathed it without inquiry whether there is any change in the matter (i, 313).

Meredith's own views on the social and political situation as expressed in letters to Maxse between 1866 and 1870 are similar:

> The aristocracy has long since sold itself to the middle class; that has done its best to corrupt the class under it. I see no hope but in a big convulsion to bring a worthy people forth,[44]

and

> The Parsonry are irritating me fearfully, but a non-celibate clergy are a terrific power. They are interwound with the whole of the Middle class like the poisonous ivy. Oh! for independence that I might write my mind of these sappers of our strength.[45]

Regarding to Democracy, he had earlier suggested:

> I take no interest in Reform. I see no desire for it below. If there were, I would give it. . . . Democracy must come. . . . We say – Democracy, as if it were some deadly evil; whereas it is almost synonymous with Change. Democracy never rests. The worst of it is that it can be violent in its motion.[46]

He seemed acutely aware of the English dislike of change whilst himself believing, like Von Karsteg, in the logical necessity of such social and political disruption. It seems reasonable to assume that much of what Von Karsteg asserts about the British nation reflects Meredith's own views – including the Professor's rejection of Harry's muddled ambition to work towards the democratization of the social structure. The Englishman's love of the *status quo* must remain unsatisfied, since the process of continual change continuously affects any given situation. This is probably the most important lesson that Harry has to learn. The 'explosion' in Harry which Von Karsteg awaits is analogous to the 'convulsion' looked for by Meredith to herald the nation's moral regeneration.

The 'convulsion' and the 'explosion' find their reflection in the destruction of 'the doomed old house', Riversley, a symbol throughout the novel of an illusory established social order. In reality the destruction is written into its existence. This ending is not haphazard and arbitrary, as Jack Lindsay suggests, but is integral in the novel's structure. Harry, at last married to Janet, returning to claim his inheritance, appears to have chosen the Squire's values and to have rejected those of Roy. He has done neither. Just as Harry's image of Ottilia differs radically from Roy's view of her in that he learns to see her primarily as a moral guide, so Harry's Janet Ilchester of the final pages differs from the unimaginative Englishwoman 'bought' by the Squire for his grandson. We have seen that a crucial element in her characterization has been her ability to develop and her susceptibility to the rarefied influence of the Princess Ottilia. Ottilia admires Janet's courage above all which could 'bear the ordeal of fire' (ii, 688). It is this quality which makes her eminently suited to be Harry's wife, since as an Englishwoman in English society, the 'ordeal of fire' ('convulsion', 'explosion') is inevitable. Her marriage with Harry highlights this novel's concern with the evolution of the British social order. The Princess, a German, associated with elements of sea and air, may condition Harry's response to the situation, but it is only Janet, associated with earth and fire, who can share this ordeal.

It is crucial to the import of this novel that it ends on this note of disruption juxtaposed against the new and hopeful marriage of Harry and Janet. The rapidly shifting action and scene warns us to be prepared for any eventuality. Above all, the references to the fall of Troy provided us with an analogy.

As a boy, Harry in search of his father sees himself as Ulysses and Telemachus alternately, and he and Temple make frequent allusions to the legend. Yet Von Karsteg bluntly suggests that

Harry's heroic role in terms of bringing order to his native land is that of 'Laocoon in the throes' (i, 316), unable for all his efforts to prevent the inevitable destruction of Troy by fire. One mode of civilization inevitably gives place to another.

Meredith's reference to 'Sir Harry Firebrand of the Beacon' seems less unexpected if we read the novel in this way. Clearly, *Harry Richmond* is concerned in general terms with the destruction of the eighteenth-century social order and the social and political evolution in England brought about by developing industrialization. It would appear to have been influenced by the Hegelian interpretation of history. Harry and Janet, marked by their experience of the Princess Ottilia and the metaphysical speculative tendency of German intellectuals, are figures drawn in terms of the Hegelian concept, in which man is seen as 'a product of himself and of his own activity in history'.[47] They are involved in continual change and modification, and are seen as potentially capable of incorporating the 'ordeal of fire' or destruction of former structures, values and ideas into their own developing mode of existence. They recognize and are attached to their roots in the past, but, Meredith seems to imply, they are able to face a future of conflict and uncertainty.

Notes

The text of *Harry Richmond* is taken from the 1st ed.

  1 'The Structure of Imagery: George Meredith's *Harry Richmond*', in op. cit., 1964.
  2 *George Meredith: His Life and Work*, 1956.
  3 *A Troubled Eden: Nature and Society in the Works of George Meredith*, Edinburgh and London, 1961.
  4 *Art and Substance in George Meredith: a Study in Narrative*, Lincoln, 1953.
  5 *Bildungsroman* – 'the story of the formation of a character up to the moment when he ceases to be self-centred and becomes society-centred, thus beginning to shape his true self', Roy Pascal, *The German Novel*, 1956, 11.
  6 *Letters of George Meredith*, collected and edited by his son, 1912, hereafter referred to as *Letters*, i, 115.
  7 Ibid., i, 142.
  8 Ibid., i, 143.
  9 Ibid., i, 204.
 10 Ibid., i, 220.

11 *Catalogue of the Altschul Collection of George Meredith in the Yale University Library*, compiled by Bertha Coolidge, New Haven, 1931, 90.
12 *Letters*, i, 229.
13 Ibid., i, 229.
14 Ibid., i, 171.
15 *The Ordeal of George Meredith*, New York, 1953.
16 *Letters*, ii, 525.
17 Ibid., ii, 577.
18 Ibid., i, 157.
19 Ibid., i, 169.
20 Goethe, *Wilhelm Meister's Apprenticeship*, translated by Carlyle, 1842, i, 29.
21 Ibid., i, 318.
22 Ibid., ii, 243.
23 Ibid., i, 88–9.
24 Ibid., ii, 12.
25 Ibid., ii, 291.
26 Ibid., ii, 177.
27 The phrases that follow are all taken from this chapter of *Harry Richmond*.
28 *Letters*, i, 156.
29 *Wilhelm Meister*, ii, 304–5.
30 Ibid., i, 132.
31 Ibid., ii, 166.
32 Ibid., ii, 314.
33 *The German Novel*.
34 Ibid., 13.
35 Ibid., 23–4.
36 Ibid., 28–9.
37 *The Historical Novel*, tr. Hannah and Stanley Mitchell, 1962.
38 Ibid., 19.
39 Ibid., 81.
40 Ibid., 36.
41 *Letters*, i, 185–6.
42 Ibid., i, 67.
43 Quotations immediately preceding, taken from *HR*, ii, 683–5.
44 *Letters*, i, 191.
45 Ibid., i, 201.
46 Ibid., i, 198.
47 Lukács, op. cit., 28.

Beauchamp's Career

Arnold Kettle

Meredith published *Beauchamp's Career* in 1876. Like several of his novels, it is a deeply political book – not merely in the more superficial sense that its main characters are politicians, but in the more important one that it is conceived in political terms: the human issues it discusses, even when they are personal and private in form, are presented as fundamentally political ones. The characters of the novel are all, though the setting is contemporary, seen as characters in history: they are individualized men and women, but they are always presented – consistently and in-sistently – as, in Aristotle's sense, political animals, social creatures inconceivable in any social setting save that of England of the 1870s. And England itself is seen, as few nineteenth-century English novelists see it, as part of Europe: an eccentric part, no doubt, with the British Navy (in which Lieutenant Beauchamp serves) turning the Channel into something more than a moat, but concentric too, never wholly isolated by those fogs and mists with which Dickens and Emily Brontë only too plausibly shroud their more insular island.

Behind *Beauchamp's Career* lie two specific events, as well as a longer train of development. One is a by-election at Southampton in 1867 in which Meredith had spent two months working for his friend, F. A. Maxse, recently retired from the Navy, who was standing as Radical candidate. Maxse was beaten and Meredith was convinced that the principal cause was bribery, direct or oblique:

> It is a very corrupt place [he wrote], it has been found by experience of the enlarged franchise that where there are large labouring populations depending upon hire (especially in a

corrupt and languishing town like Southampton) they will be thrown into the hands of the unscrupulous rich. . . . It is one of the evils we have to contend against until the poor fellows know . . . where their own interests lie and the necessity for their acting in unison.[1]

The other event is the Paris Commune, to which Meredith, like other positivist Radicals of the day (Frederic Harrison is perhaps the classic example), responded with a deep sympathy for the Communards, clearly expressed by Maxse when he wrote (in a lecture published in 1872) of

> that terrible week in May, when an ignorant soldiery entered Paris, on behalf of religion and order, and rioted in the bloodshed of Paris workers and their families, while the clerical journals hounded them on to massacre; and one of them indignantly demanded why only 40,000 Communists had been killed . . .
>
> We may dragoon, sabre and shoot down democracy in the manner they have been doing recently in Paris; we may invent any hideous epithet wherewith to deprecate those who labour for the collective improvement of mankind, still . . . will men be found, some madly but others wisely, to devote themselves to an incessant struggle for radical change.[2]

I have quoted the passage at length because of its direct relevance to *Beauchamp's Career*, and because it breathes the very spirit of what in Britain in the 1870s was meant by the word 'Radicalism'. For Nevil Beauchamp the hero of Meredith's novel is a Radical, and his career, though not, of course, in literal detail, is clearly based on that of F. A. Maxse.

Beauchamp's Career is an extraordinarily brilliantly conceived novel. E. M. Foster has called Meredith the finest contriver that English fiction has ever produced:[3] but contrivance is not an adequate word to do justice to this book. For though the plot is a very different sort of thing from that of, say, a Dickens novel, such as *Bleak House*, a matter essentially of a number of carefully planned and well-prepared scenes, it has the merit of all good plots – that of being beautifully at one with the novel's total meaning.

Beauchamp's Career is not, of course, the only novel of this period whose subject is Radicalism. We have only to cast our minds over a decade either way to recall *Felix Holt* (1866) and *The Princess Casamassima* (1886). Yet to compare the effect of Meredith's with George Eliot's novel is immediately to be aware of an essential difference. *Felix Holt* is about Radicalism, but what we tend to remember is not so much its 'subject' as the personal stories of Mrs Transome and Harold, of Esther and Felix, and the two centres of interest, the personal and the political, never quite unite, except in the very opening chapters. With *Beauchamp's Career* there is no such duality. Whether one says that the novel is about Radicalism or about Beauchamp makes little difference, for the two elements within the conception of the book, the general and the particular, the politico/social and the personal, are inseparable. Nevil Beauchamp is interesting because he is a romantic Radical: romantic Radicalism as a human and historical phenomenon is interesting because the presentation of Nevil Beauchamp's career makes it so.

It might be inferred from this that Meredith's, as opposed to George Eliot's, is in a narrower sense a political novel, that unity is achieved by a process of abstraction more thorough-going so that non-political irrelevances are not allowed to creep in. But the inference would be false. The canvas of *Beauchamp's Career* is not narrower than that of *Felix Holt*, the conception of politics not less broad, the characters not less concerned with the most varied problems of moral, personal and intellectual life. Although the title speaks of Beauchamp's career, it is not a political career in the specialized sense that is implied. Beauchamp's career is not one aspect of his life, but his life itself.

Meredith has left us his own account of his intentions in the novel:

> It is philosophical-political, with no powerful stream of adventure; an attempt to show the forces round a young man of the present day in England, who would move them, and finds them unutterably solid, though it is seen at the end that he does not altogether fail, has not lived quite in vain. Of course this is done in the concrete. A certain drama of self-conquest is gone through, for the hero is not perfect. . . . And I think his History a picture of the time – taking its mental action, and material ease and indifference, to be a necessary element in the picture.[4]

It is a surprisingly objective description. 'An attempt to show the forces round a young man' gives a good idea of the sort of book this is. Meredith is very conscious – as conscious as Disraeli – of 'forces' in the historical sense. But he tackles the problem of their representation in concrete terms on a far more serious artistic level than Disraeli had any conception of. Nevil Beauchamp is a young aristocrat. The 'forces' round him work both externally and internally. He is a character in history, coming to consciousness in a specific situation – against the background of the French scare whipped up by Palmerston in 1858, the Crimean War, and the extension of the franchise in Britain. He starts as a romantic nationalist patriot and becomes a Radical democrat and republican under the impact of external influences: the Crimean War itself, the reading of Carlyle, the condition of the poor, the influence of the Radical Dr Shrapnel. At the same time the development of his personal, as well as his public life is revealed, largely through his relations with three women: the French aristocrat, Renée, the *bourgeois* Tory heiress, Cecilia Halkett, and the Radical Dr Shrapnel's ward, Jenny Denham, who is not much of a Radical but something of an intellectual.

Meredith on the whole succeeds remarkably well in achieving a sort of continuous interplay of public and personal forces. It is the revelation of corruption and inefficiency in the Crimean War, the utter division between the ideal and the actual, that directs Beauchamp's high-principled romanticism into Radical political channels. But he remains at this stage romantically enraptured with the aristocratic Renée. All Meredith's resources are brought into play for the achievement of an appropriate glamour: the original meeting in Venice could not be more propitious, for the gallant Beauchamp has saved the life of the young woman's military brother. The conflict between chivalrous romance and the unromantic realities of feudal marriage-arrangements is fought out against a backcloth of the sun-tipped Alps on the Adriatic. The glamour is highly theatrical and, on the level on which Meredith is working, effective. Nevil Beauchamp's progress is dramatized in a series of significant scenes and episodes, linked together by a certain amount of connecting narrative and observation, the point of which is to provide the reader with necessary background information. The first chapter – the farcical episode of the young man's personal challenge to the insolent French upstarts – establishes the high-flown romanticism which is Beauchamp's starting-point and also the nature of his relationship with Rosamund

Culling, the lady whose position in his uncle's household is to be the focal-point of such plot as the novel has. A fuller insight into the romantic Beauchamp is provided by the longer Venetian episode, his capitulation to the brittle, aristocratic but vivacious charms of Renée, who is able to combine (since she is French) the classic attractions and rigid social standards of the feudal damsel in distress with the high sophistication of an anti-Puritan culture. Renée is lost, not because Beauchamp is insufficiently romantic, but because the family ethic of the landowning French aristocracy is too strong for him. But because his romanticism remains untarnished, albeit unsuccessful, he retains the glamorous idealization of Renée in his heart.

Between the episode in Venice and the next major episode, the wooing of Cecilia Halkett, comes the development of Beauchamp's Radicalism, the seeds of which have already been sown by the disenchanting experience of actual war (an interesting reversal of the situation described in Tennyson's *Maud*) and the reading of Carlyle. At first his Radicalism is almost purely romantic – the outraged response to the shattering of his ideal conceptions of honour and integrity against the material world of British *bourgeois* philistinism. 'Manchester', the embodiment of the nightmares of his uncle, the Whig landowner, is for Beauchamp, too, the villain of the piece. At first his attack on 'Manchester' is from the point of view of an idealized feudal past:

> The inflated state of the unchivalrous middle, denominated Manchester, terrified him' (iii, 24).[5]

But under the influence of the Radical Dr Shrapnel it changes. Shrapnel attacks 'Manchester' from a different standpoint:

> . . . The people are the Power to come. Oppressed,
> unprotected, abandoned; left to the ebb and flow of the tides
> of the market, now taken on to work, now cast off to starve,
> committed to the shifting laws of demand and supply, slaves
> of Capital – the whited name for old accursed Mammon. . . .
> '. . . . Now comes on the workman's era' (xxix, 271, 273).

Beauchamp casts in his lot with Shrapnel and becomes the Radical candidate for Bevisham (Southampton).

The chapters (xviii, xix) on election canvassing in *Beauchamp's Career* are something of a *tour de force* on Meredith's part, an extremely difficult, directly political episode, carried through with a good deal of *brio* and insight. But the centre of attention in the part of the novel which involves the election is Beauchamp's simultaneous personal crisis – his relations with Cecilia Halkett and his response to Renée's peremptory summons to her château in Normandy.

Cecilia Halkett is rich, beautiful (her 'English' beauty is remarkably well evoked) and a Tory. She likes and admires Nevil Beauchamp, but is repelled by his ideas. He admires her beauty and respects her quality of mind, a respect which Meredith's presentation admirably reinforces. Cecilia is not 'converted' to Beauchamp's Radicalism, but she is considerably affected by it. When she has to choose between his, to her, mistaken integrity and the unprincipled manœuvring of her father's Tory friends, she is on Beauchamp's side. For a time it seems as though she may 'come over', and it is one of Meredith's achievements to convey the complex interpenetration of ideas and feelings in this relationship. It is not a simple matter of a conflict between 'love' and 'reason'. Meredith, for all his tendency to conceive his situations somewhat abstractly, knows very well that life is more complex and richer than that. Cecilia's 'ideas' are also 'feelings': her Toryism is largely instinctive and class-determined, nor can her affection for Nevil be separated from the 'ideas' involved. If Nevil were ignoble, she would not wish to love him; and the revelation (through personal experience) that Radicalism is not ignoble must affect her judgment of its intellectual and moral validity. From Beauchamp's side the interplay of public and private attitudes is also complex. He recognizes that the charm of Cecilia is linked with her way of life, her wealth. In a splendid passage, unmatched in its way in Victorian fiction, he watches Cecilia's yacht, the *Esperanza*, carry her on the Solent:

> He was dropped by the *Esperanza's* boat near Otley ferry, to walk along the beach to Bevisham, and he kept eye on the elegant vessel as she glided swan-like to her moorings off Mount Laurels park through dusky merchant craft, colliers, and trawlers, loosely shaking her towering snow-white sails, unchallenged in her scornful supremacy; an image of a refinement of beauty, and of a beautiful servicelessness.
>
> As the yacht, so the mistress: things of wealth, owing their graces to wealth, devoting them to wealth – splendid

achievements of art both! and dedicated to the gratification of
the superior senses.

Say that they were precious examples of an accomplished
civilization; and perhaps they did offer a visible ideal of grace
for the rough world to aim at. They might in the abstract
address a bit of a monition to the uncultivated, and encourage
the soul to strive toward perfection in beauty: and there is no
contesting the value of beauty when the soul is taken into
account. But were they not in too great a profusion in
proportion to their utility? That was the question for Nevil
Beauchamp. The democratic spirit inhabiting him, temporarily
or permanently, asked whether they were not increasing to
numbers which were oppressive? And further, whether it was
good for the country, the race, ay, the species, that they should
be so distinctly removed from the thousands who fought the
grand, and the grisly, old battle with nature for bread of life.
Those grimy sails of the colliers and fishing-smacks, set them
in a great sea, would have beauty for eyes and soul beyond that
of elegance and refinement. And do but look on them
thoughtfully, the poor are everlastingly, unrelievedly, in the
abysses of the great sea . . . (xv, 129–30).

It is a passage which well illustrates Meredith's method. My
immediate point is to note how uncompromisingly he breaks
through the *bourgeois* convention that the private and the public
life are separable and that emotion is properly the province of one,
'reason' the other. The Beauchamp–Cecilia love relationship, the
Radical–Tory political relationship and the popular–*bourgeois* class
relationship entwine themselves into an inseparable fusion, expressed most successfully in images like that of the yacht and the
colliers in which visual and social significance are united.

Beauchamp's failure with Cecilia is due to reasons altogether
more complex than his failure to win Renée. The immediate cause
may be Cecilia's conviction that she cannot replace the French girl
in his heart, but the underlying reasons are subtler and more
important. Fundamentally, Cecilia cannot draw herself sufficiently
out of her class life. Like Renée, she submits to her father's social
attitudes, superficially in order not to hurt him, more basically
because they are her attitudes too. And here Meredith establishes a
subtle point. Had the battle been simply between Beauchamp and
his cousin Baskelett (a Tory candidate) and such representatives of

Toryism as Grancey Laspel (the renegade Liberal) or even her father, Beauchamp might well, on the strength of his superior integrity, have triumphed. But there is another Tory in the picture, Sumner Austin, and it is he who most influences Cecilia, providing through his intelligent cynicism a haven of enlightenment within the ruling-class camp. 'Austin's a speculative Tory, I know, and that's his weakness' (xxxvii) is Colonel Halkett's comment when he learns that his friend has been putting forward to Cecilia views which give Nevil Beauchamp credit for sincerity and treat his Radicalism with respect. Halkett thinks Sumner Austin is selling out to the enemy, but in truth the old lawyer is wiser from the Tory point of view than the true-blue Colonel. For it is he who gives Cecilia the strength to resist Beauchamp.

The decision, however, is not entirely Cecilia's. If she is drawn into marriage with the sound, dull Blackburn Tuckham, it is not simply her own lack of moral courage that is to blame. For there have been reservations about the relationship on Beauchamp's part too, and it is these reservations which not quite consciously lead him to postpone his proposal of marriage until it is too late. For he from his side clearly recognizes the conflict between Cecilia's attachment to Tory ideas and his own Radical aspirations, and lacks full confidence that he could in fact carry her with him. The fact that he wants money to start a Radical newspaper and that Cecilia has money increases his scruples. And the attraction of Renée – now married to an elderly French *roué* – though less important by this time than Cecilia imagines, remains in Beauchamp's mind a compelling force, an incompletely subdued area of romantic irresponsibility.

How compelling it can be is illustrated by the episode of the sudden summons to France which Beauchamp, in the midst of the election campaign, chivalrously answers, thereby decisively contributing, through the ensuing scandal which his opponents are able to imply, to his defeat at the polls. Beauchamp responds unhesitatingly to Renée's call of distress, only to find that it was, rather, a whistle to a faithful dog, a display of power and a result of boredom. But again Meredith's contrivance is of unusual subtlety, for he suggests very successfully the real distress, the actual desperation which the Frenchwoman's triviality of life conceals. So that the episode at Tourdestelle, while it has the effect of underlining for Beauchamp the impossibility of reconciling Renée and Radicalism and of undermining – still unconsciously rather than overtly – his romanticism, also enables Meredith to develop further his image of the anachronistic decadence of the aristocracy and to prepare the ground for his next great episode for Renée, her flight to England.

By the time Renée is sufficiently desperate to throw herself upon Beauchamp's chivalry Beauchamp has changed. This episode – the arrival of the Frenchwoman in London, the high comedy involved in the averting of scandal, the realization by Beauchamp that he no longer wants what he has romantically built up over the years, the consequences in pain and humiliation for Renée herself – all this is carried through triumphantly and tied up by one of Meredith's most brilliant strokes: the marriage of Beauchamp's uncle, Everard Romfrey, now Lord Avondale, to his lady housekeeper, Rosamund Culling.

This marriage is precipitated by the conjunction of a most complex series of events and motives. It represents at once the old aristocrat's revenge on his erring nephews – Beauchamp and Baskelett – his appreciation of the quality of Mrs Culling's devotion to his interests, the triumph (and at the same time frustration) of her efforts on behalf of her beloved Nevil, and the culmination of the social game that has been played with such sophistication around the flight, and return to conjugal humiliation, of Renée. To see such a moment primarily in terms of Meredith's unique technical skill with a plot is to do the novelist much less than justice. The moment is, technically, a triumphant one precisely because the strands of the plot have represented and involved so many real and relevant forces – psychological and social – which do indeed unite to form an episode of a significance which, like all good artistic images, is at once as complex as life itself and as concrete.

So complex indeed (though not troublesome or fussy) is the structure of this novel that there has meanwhile been going on, alongside the development of the Beauchamp–Renée relationship, another development equally important, which involves Cecilia, but in which Renée is not implicated – the baiting and horse-whipping of Dr Shrapnel.

Shrapnel is a slightly absurd and not wholly sympathetic figure, even though he represents the Radical point of view which is throughout the novel the political standpoint from which Meredith writes. The good doctor is a windbag. He has absorbed more of Carlyle than his critical ideas. And besides being a crank and a bit of a bore, he is hopelessly out of touch with many political realities, so that one of the problems of the Bevisham Radicals is to keep him out of the way during the election. But at the same time Shrapnel's integrity and the nobility and essential rightness of his ideas are emphasized; so that when Everard Romfrey, representative of the old world of feudal ideas, egged on by the unscrupulous Cecil Baskelett, and half-unwittingly encouraged by Rosamund Culling herself, is persuaded (quite falsely) that his lady housekeeper has been insulted by Shrapnel and takes his horsewhip into Bevisham, the full horror of the half-farcical episode comes home. It would be hard to find a better example of the strength of Meredith than the whole conception of this episode. Everything about it is magnificently integrated. The assault itself is not described. We see Romfrey departing for Bevisham, whip in hand; at once Beauchamp's view of the old Radical is reiterated, he is planning to take Dr Shrapnel for a voyage for the sake of his health; we hear of what Romfrey has done through Colonel Halkett's telling Cecilia, a method which allows us at once to grasp, through Cecilia's horrified comprehension, all its appalling implications, and at the same time to record the Colonel's complacent approval. A fuller description of the assault comes almost immediately, through a minor character, 'an Admiral of the Fleet and ex-minister of the Whig Government', who gives what might be called the public, ruling-class view of the outrage. Meanwhile, Beauchamp is still ignorant of what has happened, and the next time we see him is when he arrives at Steynham to face his uncle.

What makes the episode so striking, so much more than an ingenious melodramatic contrivance, is its *rightness* on so many levels. As a symbolic illustration of the conflict between past and future, this particular encounter of Beauchamp's two guardians is magnificently right. A horsewhip has for centuries been an emblem of class–domination, as a famous Marx Brothers' joke ('If I had a horse I'd horsewhip you') reminds us. Everard Romfrey's motives are chivalrous, his action barbarous and his understanding entirely erroneous. He allows himself to be misled because of his political prejudices, and the misleading is itself wonderfully convincing, for though it is Cecil Baskelett, the conscious mischief-maker, who lights the trail, it is Rosamund Culling, sincere and conscientious, who has laid it. The whole description of Mrs Culling's reactions to Dr Shrapnel, her deep class prejudices, her desire to prevent Nevil from falling into the old man's clutches, her half-conviction that she has been insulted, her horror on the discovery of what her self-deception has led to, all this is superbly done. One is reminded, perhaps, of E. M. Forster's treatment of the Adela Quested part of *A Passage to India*: but a comparison leads to conclusions so much in Meredith's favour that one is surprised that so scrupulous a writer as Forster should not seem more aware of his own great debt to the older novelist.

The horsewhipping of Dr Shrapnel emerges with a kind of high artistic inevitability out of the main general themes of *Beauchamp's Career* as well as out of the detailed personal relationships of its plot. It symbolizes, as I have suggested, the underlying conflict between the old ruling class and the groping popular movement, and does so with remarkable justice because the personal psychological basis of the episode corresponds so exactly to the general social movements involved. As a central, climactic situation, it poses to the individual characters involved choices which are at the same time private and public, personal and general: each is forced to take a personal moral position which involves in practice a class position. For some of the principal contenders the first choices are simple, spontaneous. Everard Romfrey's ruling-class friends, Whig or Tory, rally instinctively to his side, even though some, like Sumner Austin, see the folly and brutality of his action. And to Beauchamp and the Radicals, Dr Shrapnel's entourage, there is no conflict of loyalty whatever: the moral issue is simple – as indeed objectively it is. The two people most agonized by the situation are the two women who love Beauchamp, but belong by birth and feeling to the ruling-class party – Cecilia Halkett and Rosamund Culling; and Meredith's account of their reactions is masterly. Once again it is not, with either of them, a simple conflict of 'feeling' *versus* 'reason' or 'love' *versus* 'prejudice'. Because Cecilia values Beauchamp she cannot see the assault on Dr Shrapnel as her father sees it, retribution richly deserved. To her it is barbarous; she is in no doubt about that. Where she falters is in her judgment about its fundamental wrongness, its total dishonour-ability:

> Grieved though she was on account of that Dr. Shrapnel, her captive heart resented the anticipated challenge to her to espouse his cause or languish (xxxii, 306).

Cecilia stands by Beauchamp, but with reservations. She goes with him to Bevisham, but stays outside when he visits the sick Shrapnel.

Her heart is captive, imprisoned by her class allegiance, which is stronger than her feeling for Beauchamp or her respect for truth.

Rosamund Culling is, within her limitations, more courageous, for she, unlike Cecilia, feels a personal responsibility for the shameful assault, and this leads to an examination of conscience, meticulous and sincere, which has, most convincingly, the effect of raising her whole moral stature and – a brilliant touch this – of making Everard Romfrey see her differently and, indeed, marry her. The marriage involves a move into the final reaches of the book, in which Romfrey and Shrapnel are, personally, reconciled. It is Rosamund who restores honour to the Romfreys, rather in the way (though the means are utterly unlike) that in *Bleak House* honour comes back to Sir Leicester Deadlock in his defeat.

The closing chapters of *Beauchamp's Career* are, in terms of the story the book has told, almost arbitrary. Renée and romantic irresponsibility have been rejected; Cecilia has married her dull Tory dog; Rosamund Culling has brought about the reconciliation of Romfrey and Shrapnel; Nevil Beauchamp has recovered from an almost fatal illness. How is his career to develop now that the conflicts which have served to express its essence have been, in some sort at least, resolved? We are left with a series of images, none of them as fully developed as the central scenes and conflicts of the book: the image of Beauchamp's marriage to Jenny Denham, an unromantic but apparently happy one, of his cruising around the Mediterranean studying Plato and rejecting Dr Shrapnel's compulsive insistence to return to the political fray, and, finally, of his jumping into the Solent to save a boy from drowning and in doing so drowning himself. The final image is clearly intended as, in the least ambiguous sense, symbolic. A working-class child's life is saved at the expense of Nevil Beauchamp's:

> This is what we have in exchange for Beauchamp!
> It was not uttered, but it was visible in the blank stare at one
> another of the two men who loved Beauchamp, after they
> had examined the insignificant bit of mudbank life remaining
> in this world in the place of him (lvi, 527).

This is evolution, the survival of the fittest, the way the world progresses.

That final page of Meredith's novel recalls, perhaps, the close of two other novels, one written fifty years before *Beauchamp's Career*, the other fifty years later. In Stendhal's *Armance*, the young

Byronic hero, Olivier, believing himself to be impotent, dives to death in the Aegean. The hero of Erich Kästner's novel, *Fabian*, a name which also tells its story, lives impotent through the chaotic, cynical, doomed days of the dying Weimar Republic and jumps into the river to save a child from drowning:

> The little boy swam ashore, howling. Fabian sank.
> Unfortunately, he had never learned to swim.

One remembers, too, the end of Jack London's *Martin Eden*, and the actual death of Hart Crane, and the significance of Madame Sosostris's advice to fear death by water deepens.

Beauchamp's Career is, I have hoped to suggest, a novel of remarkable interest and one greatly underrated in current literary criticism. I am also conscious that, in writing about Meredith's book, I have given the impression of its being better than it actually is. This is because the conception of the book considered in general terms, the idea behind it and the ideas involved in it are in fact more impressive than the book itself. It is, one might almost say (though this would be unfair), a better book to talk about than to read.

It is not easy to substantiate this view except on the basis of the rather unsatisfactory, subjective assertion that one does not sufficiently care about anything that happens in *Beauchamp's Career*. For all the interest it evokes, one is seldom touched. There are, it must be added, important exceptions to this statement. The whole presentation of Rosamund Culling seems to me admirable; the canvassing episode at Bevisham is brilliantly done; the rejection of Renée is genuinely moving. And yet, by and large, what one admires about the novel is, I think one has to say, more fully expressed in the word 'conception' than 'achievement'; so that Forster's own word, 'contrivance', does have, even in this – one of Meredith's undoubted successes – a certain pejorative force, even though it seems to me so much less than just.

I would suggest that the reason why *Beauchamp's Career*, for all the qualities I admire in it, does not move or delight me as much as I feel it ought to, lies in a failure in style rather different from the sort of thing Forster indicates in *Aspects of the Novel*. One might put it this way: a novelist (whatever the particular quirks or intricacies of his vision or his philosophy) always has to present his situations either from the inside or from the outside. This is a social as much as a literary matter. I do not say he may not be able to do both, and I am not passing any value-judgment as to the relative merits of the two methods. Jane Austen among English novelists pre-eminently represents the one method, Fielding the other. I do not think Meredith manages either approach. He does not get so deep and close, so far *within* a situation, that it dramatizes itself, so to speak, convincing us utterly of its authenticity by making us share the vibrations of the characters who are acting it out. We very seldom (in this context) know sufficiently what his characters *are*; the precise quality of their feelings at the lived moment is not conveyed to us. We never really know, in that sense, what Beauchamp feels about Renée any more than (to change novels) we know what Lucy feels when Richard Feverel leaves her stranded at Cowes. For social reasons, Meredith cannot allow himself to work from inside.

Now this wouldn't matter at all if he had found some other way to bring his people fully to life, to give to a situation that breath of living significance (or significant living) which convinces us of artistic authenticity. But unfortunately, having opted for the 'outside' method, the method of Stendhal and E. M. Forster, he fails to establish for himself a sufficiently firm vantage-point from which to operate. This question of 'point-of-view' seems to me, in any analysis of Meredith, the fundamental one. What is his relationship to what he is describing? What is his relationship to his reader? On what is his observation, his judgment, his artistic sensibility, his *style*, based?

I think it is the expression of an intelligence which is remarkably acute, deep and far-ranging, but essentially abstract and lacking in real confidence, self-confidence, the artist's secure yet perilous poise. I think this is at bottom due to Meredith's isolation, his inability to identify himself with any social force or developing cultural tradition from which he might draw strength and the best kind of self-confidence. No British writer of his time – Dickens once dead – had so deep an understanding of the Victorian world and the way it was going. No contemporary novelist, not even George Eliot, got on to something so deep and promising and contemporary as Meredith's apprehension of what he, like Balzac before him, called 'egoism', the essence of nineteenth-century *bourgeois* man. No novel of its decade – the decade following *Our Mutual Friend* – says so much that is acute and penetrating about Victorian England as *Beauchamp's Career*. The trouble is that it says it – to such an extent – *abstractly*, rather than in the concrete terms of art. For the consequence of Meredith's failure to break through his social isolation is his taking refuge in a style in which a false rhetoric clothes an insecure irony.

The elements of this rhetoric – the juxtaposition of archaisms with colloquial speech; the heavy reiterated biblical phrases with their persistent 'cometh's' and 'goeth's'; the ridiculous inversions which would allow a sentence like 'Drove she ducklings to the water, every morning just at nine' to pass as prose; the tricks of Parliamentary oratory; the deliberate 'poetic' phrases; the coy confidences whispered *sotto voce* like the calculated indiscretions of Millamant's tea-table – what they amount to is a desperate attempt to cover up the actual insecurity of Meredith's own position: and they dominate the scene to the extent that he fails to find a stand-point which can give him real sustenance to back and fill out his real perceptions. Meredith is a vulgar writer precisely because he is afraid to be vulgar. Where Dickens, at his best, draws so effectively on the popular culture of his day – the fairy tales and nursery stories, the music-hall and melodrama, the popular songs and lampoons – and above all on the actual speech of the common people, Meredith falls back on a cultural *mélange* which he himself can only half respect.

The key-figure behind Meredith, for better and for worse, is undoubtedly Carlyle. It was from Carlyle, more than from anyone, that he gained his insight into the British world of his time – his sense of the corrupting power of the cash-nexus, of the social movement from the world of Sir Austin Feverel and Everard Romfrey to that of Manchester and of the consequences of this in human alienation and impoverished relationships.

The strength of Carlyle lies in his insights into *general* social and historical phenomena. He has a good deal of Hegel's sense of the nature and universality of process. The movement of things, the development of ideas, a sense of the revolutionary nature of reality: these perceptions impregnate his work. And he is shrewd too. He sees the tremendous significance of Chartism, the fundamental fraudulence of the business-men's enthusiasm for 'democracy'. But because he is so incorrigibly, in the philosophic sense, an idealist, his most potent insights are seldom disciplined by that concrete analysis which is the basis of the artist's perceptions. Of course, it is not difficult to see (with our rather smug hindsight) why Carlyle took refuge in heroes and rhetoric and romanticism in the pejorative sense and has to be seen, historically, as a forerunner of Nietzsche rather than of William Morris. It was extraordinarily difficult, in the first half of the nineteenth century, for the *bourgeois* intellectual, however shrewd and even revolutionary, to commit himself to an actual social movement, to become engaged in the realist's way in the down-to-earth grappling with concrete human problems. Carlyle's great contribution to the development of the novel was an indirect one – he helped men to see themselves as characters in history.

The Ordeal of Richard Feverel is even more closely connected with Carlyle than *Beauchamp's Career*. And whereas in the later novel, through its strong framework of political actuality, the problems Carlyle raises are elucidated, rendered more concrete, carried forward even (that last image of Beauchamp drowned in the Solent tells us a great deal about heroes and hero-worship), in *Feverel* the Carlylean cloudiness is mirrored rather than dispersed. Because in *Feverel* politics appears only on the sidelines (like the information that Austin Wentworth is a republican) the Romantic elements in both Carlyle and Meredith are given freer play. Sir Austin's 'system', which, more than anything, the book is 'about', is never really artistically defined. For that we have to wait for *The Egoist*. Here it is swamped in irony. And when, at the very end of the book, Lady Blandish grasps the full horror of it, the revelation is unsatisfactory, hysterical, abstract. All the positive forces of the novel depend on an objective definition, within the terms of art, of Richard's and Lucy's romantic love. But this never comes. The relationship is never 'placed'. It would be nice to take the novel as an extended comment on Carlyle's advice to the young to abandon Byron and take up Goethe. But in fact it is so full of the paraphernalia of Byronism that Goethe never really gets a look in. I think Meredith's *intention* in *Feverel* is fairly clear. As he himself put it: 'The moral is that no system of the sort succeeds with human nature unless the originator has conceived it primarily independent of personal passion.' In other words, 'To change anything you first have to be objective'. Meredith goes on (analysing the public response to his book): 'My fault is that I have made the book so dull that it does not attract a second reading.' He ought to have said: 'My fault is that I have myself failed in creating an objective world of art and have stuffed it instead with Romantic verbiage.'

This sounds unsympathetic. I do not mean it to be. Romanticism in its various forms and aspects and implications is the great critical problem of English nineteenth-century literature, and it is a problem precisely because the Romantic impulse contains at the same time all that is best and worst in the literature of the time. If Meredith – or Carlyle – had drunk less deep of the Romantic draught they would certainly not be the writers they are; but it is also doubtful whether they would have been writers at all.

Notes

1 *Letters of George Meredith*, edited by his son, 1912, I, 194.
2 *The Causes of Social Revolt*, 1872.
3 *Aspects of the Novel*, 1927, 121–2.
4 *Letters of George Meredith*, I, 242–3, Letter to M. D. Conway.
5 The text is taken from the edition of 1897.

The Egoist: Anatomy or Striptease?

John Goode

Yes! Mr. Meredith is the Harvey of the Ego.

Le Gallienne

Four species of idols beset the human mind, to which (for distinction's sake) we have assigned names, calling the first Idols of the Tribe, the second Idols of the Den, the third Idols of the Market, the fourth Idols of the Theatre.

Bacon

I

Criticism is a game played to throw reflections on the literary work in order to exhibit the way in which it deals with human nature. But *The Egoist* seems to be an inward mirror: it throws its own reflections, so that, for example, to discover that the willow pattern or the symbolic status of hands are important is to do no more than restate what the author, and, indeed, his protagonists, tell us. How do we muscle in on a game of patience? The novel states its own terms, works itself out in perfect accord with those terms, and the critic either paraphrases (Beach), makes doubtful analogies with life (Priestley) or becomes something else, a metacritic questioning the terms themselves.

Thus Gillian Beer. She measures the achievement of *The Egoist* against works not so committed to a specific aesthetic, notably *The Tragic Comedians*, and she sees it finally as a *parenthetical* work in which Meredith works out schematically the role of authorial distance before he moves on to the later novels, 'in which Meredith shows an enhanced tenderness toward his characters and a willingness to move through the emotions and not only through the head'.[1] I don't really know what *The Egoist* 'moves' through if it is not the generation of an emotional commitment (think only of the way in which Meredith links Clara, Crossjay and the wild weather). But, more importantly, Gillian Beer's placing seems to me to demolish the novel altogether. She sees it as an experiment in a deliberately enclosed form: 'in contrast with *The Egoist*, *The Tragic Comedians* derives from real life, not from literature.[2]' It explicitly is such an experiment, of course, but the enclosure has no point unless it enables the novel to relate more vividly to life. It invokes 'the embracing and condensing spirit', and thus to argue that it derives, more than most other literary artefacts, from 'literature', is to condemn it outright. Meredith is claiming a definite social role for art in the Prelude ('Art is the specific'), so that the only way we can evaluate the novel is to evaluate its terms and the claims those terms make to offer a meaningful impression of the actual.

II

The very title seems to reduce the 'original psychological notation' which is the most recognizable development in later-nineteenth-century fiction, to a simple moral typology. George Steiner's history of the words 'egoism' and 'egotism' concludes that, on the whole, they 'betray the survival of a neo-classical façade long after Rousseau and Romanticism had subdued the feelings which had originally animated these words'.[3] If he is right, and if *The Egoist*, therefore, is merely the elaboration of a pre-Romantic psychology, its theme is anachronistic, and its extensive exploration within the formal terms of the novel is gratuitous. For the most successful realizations of pre-Romantic characterization depend precisely on their allusive brevity. We are alerted to the complexity of Atossa, for example, because we recognize that the moral framework of *The Moral Essays* demands a rhetorical process of typification through epigram and pictorial fixity. *The Egoist* seems to be trying to create a profound world out of that highly achieved surface.

But Steiner is inaccurate, at least about the latter half of the nineteenth century. He fails to make any real distinction between 'egotist' and 'egoist', and yet the *N.E.D.* would have told him that *The Saturday Review* saw Meredith's use of the French orthography as an adoption of 'the current slang'. Although the word was used in the eighteenth century as a philosophical term, the most extensive use of it in the 1870s in that way was by Henry Sidgwick, who was concerned to take it seriously as a possible moral attitude, so that he hardly conceals a neo-classical anti-individualism. Its most important use, however, is as a biological/psychological term, with, to be sure, moral implications, by Spencer and Comte. 'Egoism' belongs to a technical context, and we can gauge how technical if we note that whereas Comte himself uses the word in a fairly general way (it does, of course, have a consistent history in French) when he says, for example, '*Le Positivisme conçoit directement l'art moral comme consistant à faire, autant que possible, prévaloir les instincts sympathiques sur impulsions égoistes*',[4] the English translation renders this last phrase as 'selfish instincts'[5] and uses 'egoistic' in the specific context of the section on biology. What I am emphasizing is that 'egoist' re-enters the English language between the mid-fifties and mid-seventies with a renewed connotative force – linking it with the attempt to find a basis for human conduct in empirical scientific discourse. And with this renewed force, it is connected not with attempts to resurrect pre-Romantic attitudes, but with attempts to find post-Romantic ideas, ideas which would cope with that aspect of human experience which is not coherently explained in terms of individual consciousness. Such an attempt dominates the speculative thought of the mid-Victorians. It pervades, for example, Leslie Stephen's *Thought in the Eighteenth Century*, in which he speaks for the generation reflected in Meredith's novel when, commenting on Hartley, he writes: 'The purely selfish solution . . . has a terrible plausibility, especially when all philosophy is obliged to start from the individual mind, instead of contemplating the social organism.'[6] 'Egoism', through its links with Comte and Spencer, becomes involved with the movement to create sociology – that is, to confront fully the romantic self and to transcend it in social terms. Positivism is the most influential system to cater for this desire, but Bradley, in his own terms, was also engaged in affirming extra-personal forces which motivate individuals as social beings. We shall see that *The Egoist* needs to be referred to all these contexts, and that, consequently, it is at the pulse of its own epoch.

The Prelude rejects the scientific description of human nature, but to reject it is not to dismiss it. *The Egoist* echoes in its title and in the connotations of its theme Comte's biological account of human emotion, the theory of cerebral functions. Comte analyses the cerebral functions in terms of a progressive scale moving from egoism to altruism, a scale which exists statically in the mind of every individual and dynamically in individual growth and social evolution. The fundamental law of the scale is that 'cerebral functions are higher in quality and inferior in force as we proceed from behind forwards'.[7] He categorizes the egoistic functions in three stages, moving progressively towards the individual's awareness of and involvement in society. At the base are the defensive instincts – self-preservation and procreation; above them are the instincts which make for self-improvement, military (destructive) and industrial (constructive). Intermediary between these purely egoistic instincts and the social affections are pride (which is defined as love of power) and vanity (love of approbation). Both of these 'are essentially personal, whether in their origin or in their object. But the means through which these instincts are to be gratified give them a social character, and render their tendencies far more modifiable'.[8] One final relevant point is made by Comte, and that is that the organism which provides the bridge between egoistic instincts and social affections is the family:

> If, on the one hand, domestic life is that which prepares us best to feel the charm of living for others, on the other hand it places us in the situation that best enables each of us to abuse this power over others . . . For Society continually acts in purifying the leading characteristics of Family.[9]

The Egoist is not, of course, a Positivist manifesto; on the contrary, as we shall see, much of its didactic impetus is directed against Comte's seductive and dangerous complacency. Nor does it reflect Comte schematically: it is rather that it is saturated with the Comtist ambience. The implicit way it tends to find itself in the novel is best exemplified in the episode of the rumour about the widow 'who had very nearly snared him' (iii, 18). It requires an aggressive act on the widow's integrity in order to quash it:

> Sir Willoughby unbent. His military letter I took a careless glance at itself lounging idly and proudly at ease in the glass of his mind, decked with a wanton wreath, as he dropped a hint, generously vague, just to show the origin of the rumour, and the excellent basis it had for not being credited (iii, 19).

Marriage at this point is an act of self improvement: 'His duty to his House was a foremost thought with him' (iii, 18) and he has moved in 'his admirable passion to excel' (ii, 15) from hunting to the pursuit of Constantia Durham. The constructive act of building the new generation has to be preceded by the military training of the hunt (which Meredith explicitly links to a stage in society in which the State demands no personal service, just as Comte makes the modification of egoism dependent on the ability of society to exert its influence), and it is thus natural that, in this description of Willoughby's exertion to the destruction of the threatened snare, he should use Comte's adjective 'military'. Comte is important for *The Egoist*, not because of a deliberate commitment to or confrontation with that philosopher in particular, but because the general tenor of his thinking pervades so much English thought in the 1870s (the decade of the official translation and the heyday of figures like Beesly and Harrison).

In a general way, therefore, the structure of egoism in the novel has to be related to this biological scheme. The most important point (and this is true as well of Herbert Spencer) is that Comte maintains an air of moral neutrality about the word – egoism is the starting-point of what transcends it. Up to a point, which we shall have to define precisely, *The Egoist* shares this neutrality. The Book of Egoism is the Book of the Earth. 'The Egoist is our fountain-head, primeval man' (xxxix, 476) and thus, without irony, Meredith can go on to say he is 'a sign of the indestructibility of the race'. This is why it is a grand old Egoism that built the house: it is not endorsed in absolute terms, but it is granted its role: man's instinct for self-preservation, which Comte defines as nutrition and which is both affirmatively and ironically imaged in the novel as Crossjay's appetite and Dr Middleton's gastronomic vulnerability, is what has created the society whose finest manifestation is the Comic Spirit. The primitive force which determines Willoughby is a potential for good, and Clara's own rebellion begins with a necessary self-assertion: 'She preferred to be herself, with the egoism of women' (vi, 54). It is those who deny themselves for Willoughby's sake who are the perpetrators of the social ill-health which enables him to remain unexposed – the Patterne ladies, Lætitia and, to a very large extent, Vernon. For Willoughby is a *degenerate* egoist essentially. What he seeks in love is not self-preservation, but something more, 'the pacification of a voracious aesthetic *gluttony*' (xi, 131). This implies that in one sense he is retarded, so that, for example, the procreative instinct is perverted to a narrower appetite: 'Miss Middleton was different: she was the true ideal, fresh gathered morning fruit in a basket, warranted by her bloom' (v, 45). But equally he is, in the Comtist perspective, highly advanced, a *social* egoist whose main motives are pride and vanity, which, as Comte says himself, are the most difficult to modify for two reasons: first, they are in 'perpetual antagonism' with each other, and, second, the most developed society has a tendency to stimulate both.

Egoism ceases to be a morally neutral word in Meredith's novel as soon as it becomes involved with a social structure, particularly that of the family. In the first place, it becomes linked to competitiveness – Willoughby uses a Darwinian vocabulary of natural selection about Flitch or Vernon (they are 'extinct' if they thwart him). Secondly, its involvement with property – property that is not built, but inherited and used as an instrument of power and a claim to applause (this emerges in Willoughby's patronage of Vernon) – provides not a modification of the beast, but a protective cover. Willoughby's jealousy is defined as 'the primitive egoism seeking to refine in a blood gone to savagery under apprehension of an invasion of rights' (xxiii, 277). George Woodcock, in his excellent Introduction to the Penguin edition of *The Egoist*, says that Meredith may have been aware of Stirner (and that Stirner was known in England at this time is confirmed by F. H. Bradley's use of him to admonish Henry Sidgwick). And if that is the case, he would have read (I'm quoting here from Woodcock's book, *Anarchism*, 94):

> He who, to hold his own, must count on the absence of will in others is a thing made by those others, as the master is a thing made by the servant.

Certainly Willoughby, because of his competitive and property-based sensitivity, is finally exposed as a thing, a leg, we may say, whose life consists of dancing to the tunes and leaping the obstacles provided by those over whom he has power.

But this makes the novel a very radical challenge to Comte's version of social evolution. For in so far as Willoughby grows away from primitive egoism, he clearly grows not towards society, but towards a more inexorably alienated relationship to it. Comte's assertion that pride and vanity require social *means* is endorsed by the novel, but that this makes them more accessible to modification is exposed as absurd. In fact, the very title implicitly attacks the

Comtist (and equally Spencerian) biological/ethical relation through the concepts of egoism and altruism. Strictly speaking, for Comte, though there is egoism, there can be no Egoist, for egoism is merely a part of the pattern which is in all of us at various phases of growth: it is an element in an evolutionary process, and hence cannot be a fixed attribute. That Meredith should use the phrase 'social egoist' and make his consummate example embody not so much the basic features of egoism, but the intermediary features, pride and vanity, is a direct challenge to Comte's social faith. For what the 'scientific' explanation of ethics fails to account for is the divorce between self and self-communication. The Carlylean clothes image is invoked only briefly in the Prelude, but it is enough to alert us to the special claims of insight which art makes in the face of sociology (and this is one reason why we have little to learn of apes). Self-consciousness, which is what differentiates pride and vanity from the other egoistic instincts, is not the same as self-awareness. Art offers an 'inward mirror'. It is the psychology of the social egoist that matters, not just his position in the evolution of society.

We should recall here that one of the earliest uses of the word 'egoist' in England was by Thomas Reid, and that Reid used it in an epistemological framework to describe those (unspecified) philosophers who were trapped in a post-Cartesian solipsism. In the 1870s it is Henry Sidgwick who devotes most coherent attention to the egoist world-view, this time within a discourse on ethics. Both Reid and Sidgwick assume that 'egoist' defines a tenable and permanent *attitude*. Meredith could hardly have been unconscious of Sidgwick at least (and if he was, Stephen would have sufficiently evoked self-interest as a possible consciously held attitude). He commits himself neither to the simply biological nor to the overtly ideological uses of the word, but the coexistence of the two demands psychological dramatization of the interaction of biologically enforced will and ethically based idea. It is the rationalization of the first by the second which becomes the most obvious theme of the novel, and it is this that commits him to take account of egoism at precisely the point where it accounts for itself in terms of 'the world', in pride and vanity.

Willoughby himself uses the word 'egoist' in a traditional pejorative sense. Nevertheless, his most explicit *idea* is hatred of the world: 'up in London you are nobody,' he says, '. . . a week of London literally drives me home to discover the individual where

I left him' (xi, 122). His enemy is the world, but this means only, of course, that the world has to be continually squared. This is the simplest paradox of the novel, and Clara rapidly recognizes it. In Comtist terms it should make Willoughby ripe for modification, but the novel sees the psychology of self-consciousness primarily in terms of reflection and therefore of enclosure. Given the epistemological and ethical connotations of the word, it becomes possible for pride and vanity to become motives which not only use society as a means of personal gratification, but which attempt to transform the means themselves into functions of the egoistic mind. This is why to be a social egoist is to be 'arcadian by the aesthetic route'. The golden world of grand old egoism (Meredith is, of course, using 'arcadian' with ironic undertones) is recovered through the assimilation of the outer world into personal images. The dominant motif of the novel has to do with mirrors (which are servants both of vanity and art): 'In his more reflective hour the attractiveness of that lady which held the mirror to his features was paramount' (iii, 20). The image undergoes many repetitions and variations until it enters explicitly into his calculations about Lætitia, with an almost insanely obsessive intonation: 'It would be marriage with a mirror, with an echo; marriage with a shining mirror, a choric echo (xxxvii, 464). The point is that pride and vanity, so far from being intermediate in the evolution from egoism, are its terminus ad quem; they formulate, as long as they are not completely antagonistic to each other, an enclosed world from which there is no escape. Thus Meredith uses the motif to encapsulate an immediate reflex action springing from an apparently selfless concern:

> He sprang to the ground and seized her hand. 'Lætitia Dale!' he said. He panted. 'Your name is sweet English music! And you are well?' The anxious question permitted him to read deeply in her eyes. He found the man he sought there, squeezed him passionately, and let her go. . . . (iv, 29–30).

It is a reflex, but it is the reflex of the reflective man. Most of his reflections, it is true, are mediated by sentimental stereotypes: he accuses Clara of seeing the world through popular romances, but his hilarious projections of the ruined and penitent Clara are, of course, all highly literary, and Meredith makes it quite explicit 'as his popular romances would say' (xxiii, 271). The mirror works both ways: in order that society should reflect Willoughby, Willoughby has to shape himself to society. Comte is ironically half right. But the primary concern is with the process of reflection itself, so that the mirror motif enters into his carefully chosen language: 'You hit me to the life' (iv, 41) he says to Lætitia, and, later: 'Where I do not find myself – that *I* am *essentially* I – no applause can move me' (xxxi, 376). It is because he seeks a mirror that he is so anxious to reveal himself first to Clara and later to Lætitia: 'But try to enter into my mind; think with me, feel with me' (vi, 60).

The image is linked, as a phrase such as this suggests, to another motif which equally embodies the enclosed psychology of social egoism, and which manifests itself in terms of the imprisonment of the reflected image. At the end of ch. ix, Willoughby reflects with a systematic aesthetic gluttony which looks forward to that of Will Brangwen, on the physical beauties of Clara. In the following chapter he makes a decisive bid to appropriate her mind by 'revealing' his fault in a way which makes him into a Darwinian natural force and a 'fallen archangel'. Clara realizes that she is now in 'the inner temple of him'. He rejects the bid Vernon is making for independence because it threatens the walls of 'our magic ring'. 'One small fissure,' he says, 'and we have the world with its muddy deluge' (x, 107). Later in the chapter Willoughby supplies his own title, and by the end of the episode Clara feels herself trapped:

> The idea of the scene ensuing upon her petition for release, and the being dragged round the walls of his egoism, and having her head knocked against the corners, alarmed her with sensations of sickness (x, 116).

The temple, externalized as the house itself, becomes an image of the reflective mind, again making for an extreme scepticism about Comte's theory. For this image finds a parallel on a narrative plane, when Willoughby, to secure Dr Middleton, Clara's social guardian, takes him to the inner cellar of Patterne Hall. On this level, the procedure works. Pride is able to exploit social means to its own end. What prevents it ultimately from asserting domination is not society, but the opposing *self* of Clara's egoism – courage to be dishonourable. Mirror and cave are total defences against the social world they respond to. What happens, of course, is that the enclosed, reflective mind destroys itself. The key image modulates from mirror to web: 'And this female, shaped by that informing hand, would naturally be in harmony with him, from the centre of his profound identity to the raying circle of his variations' (xi, 129). This image has overtones both of mirror ('raying') and web. Once Clara has broken out of the house, Vernon has placed him with the zoological image:

> His insane dread of a detective world makes him artificially blind. As soon as he fancies himself seen, he sets to work spinning a web, and he discerns nothing else. It's generally a clever kind of web; but if it's a tangle to others it's the same to him and a veil as well (xxx, 370).

Willoughby is no longer in an inclusive world of self: there are other spiders, and Clara's flight makes him feel 'as we may suppose a spider to feel when plucked from his own web and set in the centre of another's' (xxxix, 355). Pride and vanity are henceforth at war.

These images are not substitutes for the dramatic realization of the process. The gyrations Willoughby gets caught in in the attempt to preserve the mirror-cave are manifest in the outstanding moments of the novel – the interviews with Lætitia, the pursuit of Clara and the struggle with Clara for Dr Middleton's mind. What the images do is to transpose the biological source of egoism into a psychological drama growing out of an ethical and epistemological commitment. It is not biological growth that transforms egoism; it is a fundamental intellectual error that exposes it – through very love of self himself he slew. Sidgwick argued that empirical hedonism (which is the 'method' of egoism) was likely to be self-defeating, and went on to say 'that a rational method of attaining the end at which it aims requires that we should to some extent put it out of sight and not directly aim at it . . . [is] . . . the "fundamental Paradox of Egoistic Hedonism" '.[10] Stephen made a similar, slightly positivized point in his commentary on Bishop Butler.[11] The comedy of *The Egoist* grows out of the 'twists of the heart', the ironic contradictions which are inherent in the relationship between the idols of the tribe and the idols of the den, and it is given moral depth by the careful placing of moral discriminations at the point at which the human mind, in its self-realization, is confronted with a choice between being directed outwards towards love or turning in on itself to form a cave of possession in which there is no fissure.

III

I don't think I need to insist on its value in these terms. George Woodcock argues that Meredith gives us not just two-dimensional characters defined simply by inward feeling and pretension, as do Fielding, Congreve and Wilde, but manifests 'a probing complexity' which presents the comic victim in process. But though this may be enough to make us read the novel, it clearly isn't enough to make it a great or even good one. Woodcock's comparatives are significant: two minor dramatists and an eighteenth-century novelist do not offer much of a challenge. The critical question is whether *The Egoist* doesn't fade into insignificance beside *Middlemarch* and *The Portrait of a Lady*. Fade because Willoughby may seem to be only a stylized, and therefore harmless, version of Casaubon and Osmond. Dorothy Van Ghent compares the novel at some length with *Portrait of a Lady*, and the comparison becomes the most damaging attack on *The Egoist* which has been written. She points out that although Willoughby ought, on the face of it, to be a characterization which offers meaningful insights into human psychology (he demonstrates, as she points out, 'the fetal and infantile proclivities of the adult'),[13] he remains so distant that our response is at best admiration for Meredith's cleverness, and in the end an inevitable indifference. The distance is not merely the result of the comic form (though I think that, implicitly, she is querying the validity of the conventions), but comes from the fact that Willoughby has no dramatized causal connection with the world he inhabits – he is without 'internal relations' with the society he dominates, like the giant in 'Jack and the Beanstalk'.

I don't think we can escape the fact that there is, on the face of it, a good deal of confusion between what Meredith claims the form of the novel to be and the themes that he proposes to handle within that form. Both the 'Essay on Comedy' and the 'Ode to the Comic Spirit' show that Meredith was very conscious of the particular social context of comedy. The comic spirit is the sword of common sense; it is the dramatization of 'our united social intelligence'. In the past, therefore, the best comedy, like that of Molière, appears when society is one wherein 'ideas are current and the perceptions quick'. It depends on the assumption that 'our civilization is based on common sense' because, for example, 'Molière's comedy . . . appeals to the individual mind to perceive and participate in the social'. Meredith is surely right about Molière. The social criticism voiced within the plays can be devastating, but it never queries the structure of society because it sees social evils as deviationist. Thus Philinte is, if anything, more bitter about the world in which he finds himself than Alceste: but he knows that to criticize society is as deviationist and ridiculous as any of its vices '*Le monde par vos soins ne se changera pas*': Alceste is absurd because he judges society by social criteria (those of the *honnête homme*), and then tries to become free of it. The social status of Molière's comedy can be defined by the end of *Tartuffe*, in which, after a devastating portrayal of hypocrisy, the exposure is brought about by the King himself, and the constable he sends identifies the King with the comic spirit: '*Nous vivons sous un prince ennemi de la fraude.*' Comedy reflects the social artifice of good government. Both simplify human relationships sufficiently to affirm a normative code which guarantees the triumph of reason.

'Comedy' is the first word of *The Egoist*, and its predicate acknowledges its artificiality: it will exclude the dust and more of the outside world. It will be played in the drawing-room, not because Meredith is concerned with a particular social class, but because he wishes to create a social paradigm, which will hunt 'the *spirit* in men' and therefore the spirit in society. That spirit is 'the Book of our Common Wisdom'. The rhetoric doesn't make it clear whether this Book is different from the Book of Earth, but clearly Egoism and Common Wisdom are the concepts which do battle with one another.

There are two points to be made here. The first is that it is difficult to know what in *The Egoist* is meant to stand for 'Common Wisdom'. Is it merely the author himself? In which case it seems very abstract and tenuous. Or is it the society at large? It cannot be the latter, because most of the characters who surround Willoughby are either social cast-offs, such as Vernon, Crossjay and finally Clara; or they are fools – the Patterne ladies, Lady Busshe and Lady Culmer, and, though at a somewhat different level, Mrs Mountstuart Jenkinson and De Craye (who turns out in the end to be 'a Willoughby butterfly'). We may say perhaps that it is the grouping of these characters at the end which exposes Willoughby, but it isn't true, since it is the combined assertiveness of Clara and Lætitia, aided by the elements which *create* the situation. And in any case when Willoughby finds himself in the jaws of the world, he seems much less ridiculous than the out-rageous crowd who are waiting to consume him. We have already seen that *The Egoist* offers a radical challenge to the most accepted ideology of social man in the late nineteenth century. It is difficult to see how Meredith proposes a different order or a different ideal.

The trouble is that Willoughby is the consummate product of the social structure, not merely a moral type it yields. Mirror, temple and web are motifs which imply social relationships, but they are of a very general kind: they define only the attitude of man to woman, man to family and man to 'the world'. In this way Willoughby's social status is merely paradigmatic: Meredith chooses a country gentleman because this enables him to present these relationships uncluttered by economic pressure or class antagonism. Indeed, for a moment, in ch. xxiii, when Wil-loughby assesses his position after Clara's flight and return, there is a perfect coalescence between the particularity of Willoughby's position and the generalizations it is meant to bear: although it defines 'the feelings of a man hereditarily sensitive to property', we are conscious that the egoism is conditioned only by biological and cultural determinations: 'The capricious creature probably wanted a whipping to bring her to the understanding of the principle called mastery, which is in man' (xxiii, 268). The difficulty is that Willoughby's feelings are not seen to be com-pletely subjective, and hence they cannot be characterized as an abnormal development of normal traits. Another of the major motifs in the novel *is* very specifically social, and as such is deterministic:

> The little prince's education teaches him that he is other than you, and by virtue of the instruction he receives, and also something, we know not what, within, he is enabled to maintain his posture where you would be tottering (ii, 16).

It is true that 'something, we know not what, within' alerts us to the portrayal of Willoughby as a moral type, but the whole image emphasizes the differentiation (the use of 'you' here is crucial) in social terms. A social determinism heightens and grants cover to the moral individuality. Metaphors suggesting a German prince or the sun-king pervade the novel, and are linked inextricably with the voracious aesthetic appetite for applause and devotion: 'At least I have you for my tenant,' he tells Lætitia, 'and wherever I am, I see your light at the end of my park' (iv, 40). And later, speaking of Vernon, he says: 'Feudalism is not an objectionable thing if you can be sure of the lord. You know, Clara, and you should know me in my weakness too, I do not claim servitude. I stipulate for affection' (ix, 99). The social structure, the great house giving power to the central figure, becomes thus the agent of Willoughby's sentimentality. At the end of the novel the Patterne ladies, themselves hard-drilled soldiery of the proper emotions, ask Dr Middleton:

'Is it Self that craves for sympathy, love and devotion?'
'He is an admirable host, ladies' (xliv, 552).

Middleton's reply is not merely bathetic: it is importantly true. Craving for sympathy is what the self of the little prince, the host of the great house, is educated to. Lætitia is not wrong when she says, 'the excuses of a gentleman nurtured in idolatory may be pleaded' (xlix, 619).

This cannot be explained away by saying that the social contains inherent dangers which have to be moderated by the sword of common sense. For it depends for its very existence on the egoism it creates. In dramatic terms, Willoughby is the centre and linchpin of the social world. Vernon recognizes this when he says to Lætitia:

'We none of us know what will be done. We hang on Willoughby, who hangs on whatever it is that supports him: and there we are in a swarm' (xviii, 209).

The hold Willoughby has over Dr Middleton is not merely the hold of sensual pleasure over an epicure: 'A house having a great wine stored below, lives in our imagination as a joyful house fast and splendidly rooted in the soil' (xx, 228). It is the house which holds also Vernon, Lætitia and all of the characters who do not specifically break out. The power the house has over others is its rootedness, and its rootedness is epitomized in the inner cellar which is itself related to Willoughby's egoism. It is thus not enough to say that the social order permits egoism – egoism is the social order.

This is made explicit in the opening passage of the novel proper:

There was an ominously anxious watch of eyes visible and invisible over the infancy of Willoughby, fifth in descent from

Simon Patterne, of Patterne Hall, premier of this family, a lawyer, a man of solid acquirements and stout ambition, who well understood the foundation-work of a House, and was endowed with the power of saying No to those first agents of destruction, besieging relatives. He said it with the resonant emphasis of death to younger sons. For if the oak is to become a stately tree, we must provide against the crowding of timber. Also the tree beset with parasites prospers not. A great House in its beginning, lives, we may truly say, by the knife (i, 6).

It is a passage which leads us to expect a much greater social specificity than the terms in which we have seen the novel so far (moral drama based on biological and cultural universals) allow for. For it points very precisely to the *bourgeois* foundation (the lawyer) of a paternalistic social structure (the gentry). And, more importantly, it draws attention to the Hobbesian reality behind the Burkeian affirmation of an organic society (the tree prospers by pruning). As the novel progresses, such precision comes to seem irrelevant. But we are reminded of it again when Willoughby rejects marriage to the aristocracy when, with un-conscious irony, he describes the Americans as the sons of Round-heads, and when he has to forgo the *ancien régime* role of 'the Gallican courtier' for that of the more *bourgeois* 'model gentleman'. The specific bases and limitations of egoism are not on the surface, but they are stubbornly recurrent.

To note this is to offer some kind of answer to Van Ghent's criticism. Willoughby is not only related to the social context; he is, in his major characteristic, the very essence of the social structure. But this only moves the question on to a different plane. In the last chapter Meredith is drawing attention very emphatically to the theatrical basis of the novel – 'the curtain falls', 'so the knot was cut'. But immediately after this latter phrase, Mrs Mountstuart Jenkinson, with her habitual helpless shrewdness, says, 'and the policy of the county is to keep him in love with himself, or Patterne will be likely to be as dull as it was without a lady enthroned' (i, 625). Willoughby's egoism has to be preserved because that is what an ordered society (the swarm) is based on. It is the trans-fixed spectators of Willoughby's exposure who compel him to preserve his egoism intact. And his most loyal tenant, seeing through him, nevertheless sacrifices herself to this preservation. Patterne Hall closes its gates. The swarm loses two or three bees,

H*

but re-forms itself. If the knot has been loosened; it has not been cut.

What, then, we ask, is the comedy trying to achieve? In this perspective, it seems that it wishes only to define egoism, so that it challenges not the principle itself, but merely the folly of its trying to transcend itself. Willoughby has to learn to be a model gentleman, obedient to the limited social contract, rather than a *grand monarque*. He must acknowledge liberty of mind. He must choose his own tenant to preserve the house, and not make conquests beyond his property. In this odd way, the comedy seems to bid self-love and social be the same. This is how Meredith saw Molière, but it hardly fits with the 'probing complexity' with which Willoughby is presented as a moral type, for that doesn't allow for the *reform* of egoism towards social accommodation. The comedy seems thus to retreat from a full confrontation with the social implications of egoism. On the one hand we see egoism as an extension of biological self-assertion into the realm of social relationships in which it plays what is fundamentally an anti-social role. On the other we see it as the essence of the social order. The paradox is not an impossible one, but it is difficult to see in what way comedy can expose it and resolve its tensions. For comedy asserts the social order, but here the social order seems to depend on what it is asserted against. It is as though Tartuffe should turn out to be Louis XIV in disguise: the comic scapegoat, so far from rushing off the stage with exasperation like Alceste, or being carried off to gaol like Tartuffe, turns out to be the instrument of order.

Le Gallienne praised Meredith as the Harvey of the ego, but in the end we have to ask the question whether the unmasking of Willoughby is anatomy or striptease For anatomy uncovers something about the structure of all of us, and offers the possibilities of cure. Whereas striptease is a process we go through to reassure us of our own clothing – the stripping happens to someone else. And we are not concerned with the nakedness so much as with the clothing: clothing is what matters because it relates us to everyone else. And equally striptease stops short at the g-string, for what is important is that finally the real animal truth shouldn't be revealed, should remain intact. The plot finally resolves itself to recover Willoughby before the final exposure. The exposure he has been submitted to comes to seem a reassurance: the curtain falls, we may feel in the end, not because the comedy is complete, but because finally it is ashamed of the nakedness it has hinted at. We seem bound to come away feeling either that Willoughby has never stood a chance, and so that his stripping is almost authorial sadism (the view that Meredith was relentlessly, almost hysterically, punishing himself is enticing), or that he is so harmless, the stooge that society creates and ultimately cherishes with a sceptical smile, that the analysis is superfluous. Both views depend on seeing the novel as comedy, artificially limited to establish a paradigm and affirming our united social intelligence against abnormality. But I think this simplifies the novel too much. Comedy is only one of the perspectives it uses. We have seen how Meredith builds a psychological drama out of the relationship between the idols of the tribe and the idols of the den. It is a drama which seems to be distanced for the sake of the idols of the market-place. In so far as he is a representative type, Willoughby is stripped, but he is also a proprietor, and he must be recovered. He is indeed, made to perform 'a monstrous immolation for this laughing empty world' (xlvi). But this is Meredith's phrase and Willoughby's consciousness. Such a self-evaluation compels us to look more precisely at the comic structure.

IV

Clara, Vernon and Lætitia between them offer the most radical challenge to Willoughby's safety. Within the comic structure, they clearly establish norms of right imagination, right temper and right vision. But Meredith makes them perform much more complex dramatic roles. Comte, as we have seen, places egoism opposite altruism, and Steiner says that 'Meredith enlarged the definition [of "egoist"] by applying it to a man incapable of altruistic emotions'. But this is clearly a grotesque simplification since, given the intense scepticism the novel displays about the evolutionary process, and given that altruism is usually seen as a development out of self-centredness through self-knowledge, it is hardly likely that the novel contrasts 'egoism' with 'altruism'. In fact, altruism is precisely what the normative characters have to grow out of in order to challenge Willoughby's power. Clara, in fact, encounters the George Eliot solution very early in the novel: 'We must try to do good; we must not be thinking of ourselves; we must make the best of our path in life' (ix, 95). Meredith's adjective for such thinking is 'infantile'. Doing good here, the going out of self towards the world, means marrying Willoughby. Vernon too withdraws from self-assertion, and as long as he does it is a withdrawal into an honour which is false. He pursues Clara to the railway station and tries to persuade her to go back. His reflections afterwards are definitely opposed to the concept of duty:

> He had also behaved like a man of honour, taking no personal advantage of her situation; but to reflect on it recalled his astonishing dryness. The strict man of honour plays a part that he should not reflect on till about the fall of the curtain, otherwise he will be likely sometimes to feel the shiver of foolishness at his good conduct (xxvii, 330).

The impotence of moral rectitude is made farcically obvious when Lætitia and Vernon insist on praising one another for their constancy, each hating the praise. Because it is clear that the concept of social being which issues out of so much mid-Victorian theory is simply confirmative in the world realized in the novel. When Lætitia accepts Willoughby she says simply, 'I will do my duty by him.' In the whole context of the novel we have to register a moral horror. Both Clara and Vernon have to learn to 'be brave enough to be dishonourable' (x, 111). The rejection of duty is related to a rejected structure of being. When Clara is again trying to use duty as an accommodating concept (A plain duty lay in her way') she thinks of Vernon: 'he had not failed of self-control, because he had a life within. . . . Can a woman have an inner life apart from him she is yoked to?' (xxi, 239). The answer, Laetitia's decision to marry, implies that it can, but Clara learns that it cannot. To have a life of one's own is to reject the accommodation society offers. And though Vernon is rational and worthy, he is, dramatically, ineffective. It is Clara's wild flight which gives meaning to his existence.

The moral norms these characters offer become meaningful only in so far as they are related to and finally transcended by their own self-assertion. This is because, as we have seen, the egoist is not merely a moral type but the representative of a whole way of knowing endorsed by the social structure. The battle becomes one between kinds of knowledge. Clara threatens Willoughby from the first because she has eyes that do more than reflect: 'She took impressions of his characteristics' (v, 49). A little later she can picture him as an identifiable type: 'Surprise . . . stretched him with the tall eyebrows of a mask – limitless under the spell of caricature' (vi, 55). What Clara's imagination can do is to distance Willoughby, so that, for moments at least, he seems no longer the centre of the universe:

> He found himself addressing eyes that regarded him as though he were a small speck, a pin's head, in the circle of their remote contemplation. They were wide; they closed (ix, 91).

The kind of knowledge is important because it is so different from Willoughby's: it is a knowledge of perception rather than reflection, a shrewd insensitiveness as opposed to a blind sensitivity. But it is, at this stage, merely an agency of retreat, of 'the frost to kill her tenderest feelings'. It is not until Clara sees Vernon under the cherry tree that it becomes a knowledge capable of action. It is for Clara a moment of awareness without reflection. And when reflection does come, it contracts her vision to a moral affirmation. There is not much doubt about what the tree embodies. Earlier Crossjay has presented Clara with a bouquet 'and rising out of the blue was a branch bearing thick white blossom' (ix, 89). Middleton's description of it is absurdly ironic (he calls it the vestal of civilization). The blossom recalls the Alps, and in the next chapter Vernon and Clara imagine themselves climbing: 'If you speak so encouragingly I shall fancy we are near an ascent' (xii, 139). The important point is that Clara sees Vernon thus framed in an image of his sexual potency *asleep*. Conscious, Vernon is the honourable man, and the sexual bond between himself and Clara is built up indirectly through their mutual interest in Crossjay, the child of ambiguous age who runs truant, pays exaggerated devotion to Clara, and whom Willoughby tries to assimilate by spoiling. Vernon and Clara are united via Crossjay as doctor and nurse, but it is clear that he stands for a physical knowledge which Patterne Hall cannot accommodate. Clara finally recognizes that her escape from Willoughby will be effected only through love: the knowledge she comes to is a triumph over reflective knowledge because it is a genuine, unsentimental knowledge of that which is outside her, not as something separate but as something she relates to. Considering how much she has to rely on men, on Crossjay, on De Craye, on Vernon, it is ironic that feminists found it cheering.

We might go on to say that such knowledge comes to another kind of common sense which doesn't belong to a particular social world but to the operation of the universal within the one. In many ways this novel, which we have just defined, both in its attitude to duty and in its affirmations about knowledge as very anti-Kantian, seems to reflect the thinking of a writer unlikely to be appreciated by Meredith, F. H. Bradley, whose *Ethical Studies* is a highly conservative version of the Hegelian concrete-universal. Bradley asserts first that individuals do not exist, and what we call 'individual man' is 'what he is because of and by virtue of community' (166). He expands this in a way which is very close to Meredith's novel:

> The soul within his is saturated, is filled, is qualified by, it has assimilated, has got its substance, has built himself up from, it *is* one and the same life with the universal life, and if he turns against this he turns against himself; if he thrusts it from him, he tears his own vitals; if he attacks it, he sets his weapon against his heart (172).[14]

Bradley uses this kind of argument initially to advocate a social quiescence. But what is important is that he does not try to define community in terms of a social structure, but in terms of a universal life. He is defining a basis for morality which escapes both egoism and 'duty for duty's sake', and he does this first by exposing the absurdity of egoism and then by ridiculing the self-centredness of 'conscience'. Moral action is seen in immediate judgment ('an intuitive subsumption') which is best manifested in women. 'Conscience,' he goes on to say, 'is the antipodes of this. It wants you to have no law but yourself, and to be better than the world' (199).[15]

Bradley is useful because the structure of his ideas enables us to make more sense of the way in which Meredith uses such terms as Comic Spirit, Common Wisdom and Comedy. If we see Common Wisdom as a universal struggling to manifest itself in the concrete world of social relations stylized by the comic mode, we begin to cut through the apparent contradiction between the moral drama and the theatrical exhibition of a triumphant social order. But clearly this process cannot go on within the simple terms outlined in the Prelude. In fact, I believe, what we have at the centre of the novel is a radical transformation of the comedy by its momentary negation.

Comedy contains 'no dust of the struggling outer world, no mire, no violent crashes to make the correctness of the representation convincing' (Prelude). Willoughby, the victim of the comedy, also strives to exclude 'the world with its muddy deluge'. Vernon, on the other hand, comments on the world: 'One might as well have an evil opinion of a river: here it's muddy, there it's clear; one day troubled, another at rest' (viii, 85). The images are performing different functions, but they irresistibly make us aware that Willoughby's exclusiveness is closer to the ideal of comedy than Vernon's 'common sense'. Van Ghent argues that the style of *The Egoist* is as self-regarding as the egoist himself, and she may be right, and it may be a deliberate authorial strategy. At any rate, Willoughby is in firm control of the drawing-room. He loses Clara because she breaks out. The weaknesses in his armour are indicated by his rejection of Lieutenant Crossjay, whose chief claim to attention is the struggle with the outer (indeed, outermost) world, and by the banishment of the ever-recurring Flitch, who with nine children and an alcoholic tendency, surely brings to Patterne the dust and mire. Flitch also causes the violent crash which the in objective correlative of Willoughby's image of Clara is smashed.

These are only clues. Chs xxv to xxviii, which occupy the centre of the novel, take the plot decisively outside the drawing-room. The weather itself, of course, is thunderous and mire-inducing – the point is emphasized with an absurd detail when Willoughby sends 'word for his man Pollington to bring big fishing boots and water-proof wrappers' (xxv, 310). He is forced to confront what separates him from Clara with the defences of civilization. But although, as the opening of Ch xxvi makes clear, this episode portrays the invasion of the drawing-room by natural vitality ('Rain was universal'), it is not as simple nor as sentimental as that. For we become aware, too, in this chapter of the presence of a social world not contained within the drawing-room, so that what has seemed to be offered as *paradigm* is now placed as *section*. And this places not only Willoughby, but also Vernon, who is at one with Nature, as he demonstrates when he leaps the stile at a vault. The tramp meaningfully scales down the gesture: 'That's what gentlemen can do, who sleeps in their beds warm,' moaned the tramp. 'They've no joints' (xxvi, 317). Momentarily we seem to see both sides of the comedy, the excessive and the normative, as *irrelevant* to the hard facts of the outside world. Comedy seems to become both gratuitous and inadequate. As he pursues Clara just after his encounter with the tramp, Vernon meditates in terms which confirm this perspective:

> But Willoughby's obstinate fatuity deserved the blow! – But
> neither she nor her father deserved the scandal. But she was
> desperate. Could reasoning touch her? If not what would? . . .
> Yesterday he had spoken strongly to Willoughby . . . a man
> so cunning in a pretended obtuseness backed by senseless
> pride, and in petty tricks that sprang of a grovelling tyranny,
> could only be taught by facts (xxvi, 317).

The opening sentence belongs to a context like *L'Ecole des femmes*,
but what follows is a concern with the messiness in real life of the
just comic *dénouement*. Vernon retreats to reason, but not the reason
of the comic norm which Willoughby has already defeated:
rather it is the reason of Jane Austen's grimmer realism. And he
quickly realizes too that this, in such a context, is unrealistic.
Reason will neither enlighten Willoughby nor curb Clara. All that
will be effective is the intrusion of facts. And it is facts, sexual,
natural and social, that we are made aware of in this world beyond
the park. Patterne Hall, the drawing-room, is no longer capable of
dealing with human nature.

Comedy is negated by universal life, but this is only an interlude.
Built into Clara's flight is an absurdity which will finally bring her
back to the drawing-room. Before the flight, but in a chapter in
which Meredith has warned us of the coming crash of the outer
world ('Thunder was in the air, and a blow coming'), Clara,
reflecting on her coming rebellion, acknowledges both the explosive
force within her and places it: 'She was in action, driven by
necessity, between sea and rock. Dreadful to think of! She was one
of the creatures who are written about' (xv, 180). The high point of
the rebellion is the glass of brandy, which is meaningful in what it
signifies (a kind of communion between herself and Vernon), but
silly in its form:

> They were to drink out of the same glass; and she was to
> drink some of this infamous mixture: and she was in a kind of
> hotel alone with him; and he was drenched in running after
> her: – all this came of breaking loose for an hour (xxvii, 322).

It is surely ironic, and surely places Clara's mind in the realm of
the novelette. Finally, the rebellion is brought to an end by the
comic accident of her being found by De Craye. De Craye's vision
of Clara is important here. It is a limited vision because he is
capable only of *classifying women*, but in this episode Clara classifies

herself. He has seen her as a Diana figure: 'Her cry of loathing: "Marriage!" coming from a girl, rang faintly clear of an ancient virginal aspiration of the sex to escape from their coil, and bespoke a pure cold savage pride . . .' (xxii, 266). And the flight, linked as it is to her confidence in Lucy Darleton, and her use of the *boy* Crossjay is precisely one of virginal aspiration. But he has equally seen her, in her love for Crossjay, as a Venus Genetrix: 'and he felt her love of the boy to be maternal, past maiden sentiment' (xxii, 263). It is another classification, but it recognizes Clara's sexuality, which is what she does not recognize by her flight. And De Craye pursues her because he achieves one of the many reductive images that he shares with Willoughby: 'Then a thought of her flower-like drapery and face caused him fervently to hope she had escaped the storm' (xxv, 312). She doesn't escape, but she does, on her return, accept for herself the reductive image, 'Both in thought and sensation she was like a flower beaten to earth' (xxviii, 338). Her negation of the comedy is self-assertive, but it is only the self-assertion of the mental woman, and it thus becomes a stereotype – retrievable by the drawing-room. Vernon, too, as we have seen, conforms to his own stereotype.

We settle down, then, to the reaffirmation of the comic mode in the last twenty chapters, and, of course, Meredith creates a deliberate and slowly accumulated *staging* of all the characters for the final trapping of Willoughby. But at the same time the comedy has been exposed to the dust and mire, and it is not the same again. De Craye, triumphantly carrying Clara back to the drawing-room, says, 'Truth and mother-wit are the best counsellors' – which is a basic affirmation of comedy. But truth and motherwit begin to part as the novel progresses. Clara is compelled to play the game within the house as she tries to convince Dr Middleton in the library – '*Invent!* shrieked the hundred-voiced instinct of dislike' (xli, 506); but already she has become detached from the play – 'she *dramatized* them each springing forward by turns' (xli, 506; my italics). Mother-wit is of no service; it is only when she escapes from beyond the park to learn the truth that she can return to demolish Willoughby, and her reaction looks significantly to an order not contained within the social structure: 'heaven forgives me' (xlii, 530). In formal terms, what happens is that the comedy becomes progressively more visible. Most of the image-motifs, mirror, hand, willow pattern, are given explicit voice by the characters on the stage (Willoughby even wonders whether De

Craye isn't punning on his name, so that he almost fictionalizes himself as the author does). And the games which are played at the end are played more and more by Willoughby. It is his mother-wit, not the comic spirit's, which squares the world and reaffirms its order – at least, that is, his blind sensitivity and Lætitia's sighted indifference to her own life. As I have suggested, we witness not the final exposure of egoism, but its victory over its own world. I say its own world, because the visibility of comedy makes for the visibility of the drawing-room – no longer a paradigm, but an enclosed segment playing its own games. The key moment in the comic ordering is when, after Willoughby has decided to relinquish Clara by marrying her off to Vernon, he enters the drawing-room, the comic stage, to find not Clara, but the world: 'One step there warned him that he was in the jaws of the world' (xlvi, 573). It's a moment with great stage potential, but we do not witness it as audience. It is from the wings, from Willoughby's viewpoint, that we see the entry (we have already seen it once from the point of view of the general assembly – it is as though, giving us the stage effect, Meredith wants us to see the staging). Once on the stage, Willoughby can become 'himself', become, that is, the great comedian, fooling Lady Busshe, engaging Mrs Mountstuart Jenkinson and finally sporting with De Craye's fatuous vanity. The comedy serves him well. But we see it very much as comedy. More importantly, so does Willoughby: the game he plays is a monstrous immolation before a laughing, empty world. Meanwhile, the comic spirit, the sword of common sense, withdraws to a world beyond this scene to affirm the poetry of Nature as opposed to the poetry of sentiment. And it is the non-comedians, those who are not on stage at the right time, those who seek truth beyond the drawing-room, who are lifted on to the Alps.

We can see now why Meredith depicts the egoist both as a universal moral type and as the consummate manifestation of a particular social order. The comic spirit is a universal struggling to manifest itself within the particular comedy. Its stage is that which is most accessible to paradigm – the drawing-room in which manners are most clear of historical determinations. But to say 'most clear' is not to say 'free'. The comic spirit operates only up to the point at which the special community can be the vessel of universal life which is 'community'. In the drawing-room egoism can be isolated and exposed to the impressionable intelligence it contains. But the impressionable intelligence can manifest its knowledge only by retreating to an open, flux-dominated world outside the theatre of forms. Or else it can, as Lætitia does, hold its knowledge within itself and participate in the social game to moderate the effects of its motivating force. There is a choice between freedom and articulateness, for Vernon and Clara, committed wholly to their knowledge, can only go away. The only articulate opposition to egoism is Lætitia's kind of altruism, a knowing which is accepting, and which is, within the particular social ideology, merely the force which preserves egoism from total destruction by exerting an irony to forestall over-reaching. 'Duty, that's to say complying.'

And we can see too why, for all that *The Egoist* gave to Henry James, it remains a radically different novel which *The Portrait of a Lady* does not supersede. It is obvious that James gives us a much more profound dramatization of Isabel's consciousness than Meredith does of Clara's. But he can do this because he identifies the world of Isabel's marriage with *the* world. In ch. xlii he is laying the ground for the defeat of her critical imagination. Osmond takes on a metaphysical satanic quality: to *place* him is not to destroy him, for that would be to deny the social and moral order, to deny, by implication, 'reality'. Meredith is charting not merely the exposure of egoistic sterility in the world of forms, but also the potentialities that will realize a new world beyond the forms which are the apparent totality of human relationships. Goodwood's kiss is destructive, but Vernon's holy tree is a liberation. I don't think that this is merely to say that Meredith is optimistic. For, if the comic spirit withdraws from the comedy, it is still the comedy we are engaged with. The Alps are beyond us as well as the minds of the characters. And it may not merely be with laughter that the comic muse compresses her lips: it may also be with a grim recognition that the character who has achieved most self-knowledge in the course of the drama is still there propping up the stage long after the leading actor has discovered, to himself as well as to her, his own essential emptiness. James, we feel, spares Isabel with an admiration of her suicidal embrace of duty because he has postulated only death as the alternative. Meredith postulates life, not as a realized complexity, but as an undeniable but unaccommodated determination. I don't claim that *The Egoist* is a greater novel than *The Portrait of a Lady*, but it is one with larger and persistently challenging perspectives. Meredith would not have stood back from Isabel to admire her decisiveness; he would have stripped her too.

But if this means that it is striptease we witness rather than anatomy in terms of the *characters* in the novel, it also means that we are present – in fact, patients of – a ruthless vivisection of the whole social pattern which relies on the egoist's monstrous immolation for the perpetuation of the games it plays. There is a world elsewhere; we are not of it, but it asserts itself against the forms of our mirroring intelligence.

Notes

1 G. Beer, 'Meredith's Idea of Comedy, 1876–1880', *Nineteenth-century Fiction*, September 1965, xx, 176.
2 Ibid., 174.
3 F. G. Steiner, 'Contributions to a Dictionary of Critical Terms. "Egoism" and "Egotism" ', *Essays in Criticism* (October 1952), ii, 452.
4 A. Comte, *Système de Politique Positive*, Paris, 1851, i, 91.
5 A. Comte, *System of Positive Polity*, tr. John Henry Bridges, 1875, i, 73.
6 L. Stephen, *A History of English Thought in the Eighteenth Century*, 1962, ii, 58.
7 A. Comte, *System of Positive Polity*, i, 559–60.
8 Ibid., 564.
9 Ibid., tr. Frederic Harrison, ii, 178.
10 H. Sidgwick, *The Methods of Ethics*, 1874, 136.
11 L. Stephen, op. cit., 45–6.
12 G. Meredith, *The Egoist*, ed. with an Introduction by George Woodcock, 1968. My text has been taken from the Mickleham edition of 1922.
13 D. Van Ghent, *The English Novel Form and Function*, New York, 1961, 188.
14 F. H. Bradley, *Ethical Studies*, 1874, 172.
15 Ibid., 199.

The Tragic Comedians:
Meredith's Use of Image Patterns

Leonée Ormond

Art thou ambitious? What would my 'golden child' say, if I
led her in triumph to Berlin in a car drawn by six white horses,
as the greatest lady in the land?[1]

The man who wrote these words, in a letter to his fiancée, is
acknowledged by historians as an important predecessor of Karl
Marx. He was a German, Ferdinand Lassalle, the revolutionary
leader of the Social Democrats, whom the proletariat worshipped
as their messiah. Yet the passage quoted above echoes Tamburlaine,
not Marx, and the letter's recipient, the 'golden child', was a
representative of the upper-class world which Lassalle was
committed to destroying. Through Hélène von Dönniges, that
frivolous world attracted and ruined its greatest opponent. Even
his death, at the hands of her official fiancé, Prince Yanko von
Racowitza, was fraught with ironic contradictions. Lassalle, an
outspoken opponent of the barbarous practice of duelling, fell in a
duel which he had provoked, bringing his story to a conclusion
both tragic and comic.

George Meredith had already heard of Lassalle before he read
the account of the fatal love-affair given by Hélène von Dönniges
herself, then the Princess von Racowitza. But it was her book,
Meine Beziehungen zu Ferdinand Lassalle (My Relations with
Ferdinand Lassalle), of 1879, which inspired him to write his novel
about Lassalle and Hélène, *The Tragic Comedians*, of 1880. Such
passages as the one above, quoted by the Princess von Racowitza
in total unconsciousness of their ironic import, appealed to
Meredith's sense of the 'fantastic', while the psychological

complexities of Lassalle presented him with a problem to solve. He had apparently read J. M. Ludlow's article, 'Ferdinand Lassalle, the German Social Democrat', in the *Fortnightly Review* of 1869, but he does not seem to have carried his researches further.

The story, as he found it in these two sources, is as follows: In 1862, Hélène von Dönniges, then a young girl, had met Lassalle at a party in Berlin. He was thirty-six and at the height of his power and influence. The pair fell in love on this first evening; but, paradoxically, their meetings during the next two years were extremely rare. They moved in different worlds, and Lassalle was much occupied by politics and by writing. In the summer of 1864 Lassalle and Hélène met near Lucerne, and became engaged. Hélène's family were horrified at the prospect of such an alliance; in their eyes, Lassalle was a notorious demagogue, a Jew and a womanizer. Faced with overpowering family opposition, Hélène fled to her lover, and offered to elope. Lassalle wavered, and then, in a moment of catastrophic nobility, handed her back to her family, intending to win her by conventional means. Imprisoned, physically maltreated and browbeaten, the weak-willed young woman renounced Lassalle, while, unknown to her, he was making frantic efforts to free her. Driven almost to madness, Lassalle then challenged her father to a duel. The challenge was accepted by Prince Yanko von Racowitza, and in the succeeding duel he shot and fatally injured Lassalle. Soon afterwards Hélène married the victor.

Since its first publication, *The Tragic Comedians* has been frequently criticized as a flawed novel. Meredith is accused of making inadequate researches into Lassalle's life, and of too closely following the Princess's story: the result being a semi-documentary pot-boiler. The novelist laid himself open to criticism by his own remarks on the book. He told William Hardman that his novel was 'history', 'a curious chapter of human nature',[2] and he writes in the Preface: 'Nor is there anything invented, because an addition of fictitious incidents could never tell us how she came to do this, he to do that.'[3] *The Tragic Comedians* is also a short novel for Meredith, written in about six months, and serialized between October 1880 and February 1881 in the *Fortnightly Review*. Joseph Jacobs, reviewing the novel in the *Athenaeum*, lists several passages where Meredith has done no more than translate the original. On the other hand, Jacobs does make a comparison with Shakespeare's use of Plutarch, and adds:

'What remains as Mr Meredith's own is his style, and this, as everyone knows, is peculiarly his own.'[4]

If *The Tragic Comedians* is not Meredith's greatest novel, it is certainly far more carefully written and structured than has usually been suggested. It has no sub-plot, and concentrates almost exclusively on its two major figures. The theme is one of implacable destiny, and the narrative gathers momentum with every page. The developing conflict, and the tragic irony of the last chapters, when the misunderstanding between the lovers becomes almost unbearable, makes *The Tragic Comedians* one of Meredith's most obviously 'dramatic' novels. The love-scene at the opening of the book, when the pair meet and exultantly claim one another, is superbly described, and so too is the confrontation between Alvan (Lassalle) and the mother, Frau von Rüdiger, with Hélène (Clothilde) a desperate and helpless spectator.

Several writers have noticed the 'perfervid atmosphere'[5] of the novel. Siegfried Sassoon writes in his biography of Meredith:

> What possessed him to make this unrestrained – almost daemonic – demonstration about them? . . . It is when the climax begins to develop that the strain on one's nerves becomes distressing. But this overwrought effect, it will be said, was integral to the narrative. It was necessary for Meredith to work himself up to a savage frenzy while dramatizing the havocked mind of Alvan. Nevertheless I am still wondering why the performance seems somehow abnormal, like a symphony scored with diabolic discords.[6]

This overwrought quality of the book in no way derives from Meredith's presentation of Clothilde von Rüdiger (Hélène). With the Princess's text in front of him, he captures her shallow nature with an objectivity which is occasionally brutal. The passion of the opening love-scene is qualified with a savage reminder of Clothilde's feminine artifice:

> 'Who ever loved that loved not at first sight?' And if nature, character, circumstance, and a maid clever at dressing her mistress's golden hair, did prepare them for Love's lighting-match, not the less were they proclaimingly alight and in full blaze (i, 71).

Meredith sums up her character more directly at the end of the book:

Providence then was too shadowy a thing to upbraid. She could not blame herself, for the intensity of her suffering testified to the bitter realness of her love of the dead man. Her craven's instinct to make a sacrifice of others flew with claws of hatred at her parents. These she offered up, and the spirit presiding in her appears to have accepted them as proper substitutes for her conscience (ii, 174–5).

Years later she wrote her version of the story, not sparing herself so much as she supposed. Providence and her parents were not forgiven. But as we are in her debt for some instruction, she may now be suffered to go (ii, 181).

In an article on the alterations made between manuscript and final version,[7] Mrs Gillian Beer has shown Meredith's increasing scorn for Clothilde. In the second passage quoted above, the sentences after 'supposed' were among the last added.

Clothilde von Rüdiger stands apart from most of Meredith's heroines. In *Rhoda Fleming* he had shown sympathy for a woman's weakness, and his subsequent heroines are characterized by an increasing forthrightness and self-awareness. Janet Ilchester in *Harry Richmond* and Clara Middleton in *The Egoist* represent a stage in the progress towards Diana Warwick, Nesta in *One of Our Conquerors,* and, finally, the triumphant mountain girl, Carinthia Jane in *The Amazing Marriage*. At the same time, Meredith's leading men become more and more effete and egocentric. His desire to attack and humiliate the aristocratic male leads to such characters as Sir Willoughby Patterne, Dudley Sowerby and Lord Fleetwood, self-regarding and self-obsessed men, who rely for success on their inherited position alone.

The opposite is true of *The Tragic Comedians*. Lassalle is the new man, the vigorous herald of social change, and the weak and havering Clothilde represents the dying social order. Meredith's ideals and aspirations are expressed in most of his other novels through minor and often unsatisfactory figures like Vernon Whitford and Gower Woodseer, the poor men who hold the true vision of life. His more autobiographical heroes, Evan Harrington and Harry Richmond, are conceived retrospectively and without great depth. In *The Tragic Comedians* Meredith moves the figure of the dreamer and idealist to the very centre of the canvas. It is the identification of his own vague aspirations with those of Lassalle which makes *The Tragic Comedians* an intense and terrible book.

Meredith was sympathetic with Lassalle's political views, but he devotes very little space to them in the novel: 'He [Alvan] was the leader of a host, the hope of a party, venerated by his followers, well hated by his enemies, respected by the intellectual chiefs of his time' (i, 2–3). What primarily concerns Meredith is Alvan's personal failings, not his political status, though the two are inextricably linked. There are, however, two important statements of Lassalle's ideology. The first is the account of Alvan's conversation with Ironsides (Bismarck). This is subtly altered from *Meine Beziehungen* to reveal Alvan's growing opportunism, his inflated belief in his own power and destiny, and his lack of genuine principle. The second example is one of the most moving passages of the book, in which Meredith describes Alvan's early morning walk through Geneva, his last lucid and hopeful moments before his final rejection by Clothilde. He experiences an almost mystical sense of identity with the workmen:

> He listened to the workmen's foot-falls. The solitary sound and steady motion of their feet were eloquent of early morning in a city, not less than the changes of light in heaven above the roofs. With the golden light came numbers, workmen still. Their tread on the stones roused some of his working thoughts, like an old tune in his head . . . These numbers are the brute force of earth, which must have the earth in time, as they had it in the dawn of our world, and then they entered into bondage for not knowing how to use it (ii, 113).

The bond between Meredith and Alvan is obvious in descriptions like this, but there is almost no concrete political detail in the novel. As a result, Meredith was criticized for failing to go deeply into the subject. He had clearly not consulted George Brandes' biography of Lassalle of 1877, nor Bernhard Becker's *Enthüllungen über das tragische Lebensende Ferdinand Lassalle's,* published in 1868. Writing to Clement Shorter on 21 January 1892, Meredith himself said of *The Tragic Comedians*:

> I tried at the time of writing the book to get a portrait of Lassalle, and had so far to write in the dark. For this and corresponding reasons I put a poor estimate on the book, though it was done with honest endeavour to run with the facts.[8]

If Meredith had seen a photograph of Lassalle by 1892, he must have felt that his own portrait of Sigismund Alvan was subtly idealized. The face of the real Lassalle is void of the godlike qualities of Meredith's hero, just as *The Tragic Comedians* liberates itself from the story which inspired it. Meredith's chief interest in writing the novel was to analyse the strangely contradictory elements in Lassalle's character: heroism, conceit, blindness, passion and egoism. He approached the problem as a novelist, not as a historian. Certain aspects of the story are compressed or suppressed; others are highlighted and meticulously detailed. His own position as omniscient narrator and chorus enables him to interject ironic comments and judgments. More importantly still, he formulates the relationship between the lovers through a closely-worked pattern of images and symbols.

Meredith's comments in *The Tragic Comedians* inform us that the lovers fail to understand either each other or themselves. Clothilde has been flattered by her society friends into believing that she is worthy of an Olympian lover. In submitting to Alvan, she places an implicit trust in his strength, and abrogates her own responsibility. Alvan, like Sir Willoughby Patterne in *The Egoist*, wishes to subjugate his fiancée, while preserving her originality.[9] He fails, however, to understand that the apparent strength of Clothilde's attachment is derived entirely from him. Once removed from the hypnotic power of his physical presence, she loses all moral courage and independent will, and becomes the tool of her parents. When she returns his love-letters, he accepts her rejection as genuine, while she expects him to recognize in her final message a plea for help: 'to tell him that she was enforced and still true' (ii, 60).

This fatal misunderstanding is encouraged by the lovers' illusory belief in their own similarity. Lassalle's revealing exclamation on first meeting Hélène (not, in fact, used by Meredith), is characteristic: 'Brunhild, the Brunhild of the Edda . . . the Northern Valkyrie, and he wanted to be the Siegfried of this Brunhild.'[10] Meredith knew of the physical resemblance between the two lovers, but he concentrates more in his novel on their assumption of a spiritual rapport. This is remarked on by their common friends before they meet, who thus prepare them for one another in advance. Clothilde thinks, 'Alvan and she shared ideas. They talked marvellously alike, so as to startle Count Kollin' (i, 39), while Alvan says, 'We use phrases in common, and aphorisms, it appears. Why? but that our minds act in unison' (i, 56). Alvan's desire to be echoed is narcissistic, although he recognizes Clothilde's need to be mastered:

> she required for her mate a master: she felt it and she sided to him quite naturally, moved by the sacred direction of the acknowledgement of a mutual fitness (ii, 14).

Equally, Clothilde demands an ideal in her lover, which he is not capable of fulfilling. In a brilliant image, Meredith exposes their mutual egoism:

> Her gaze was met by nothing like the brilliant counterpart she merited. It was as if she had offered her beauty to a glass, and found a reflection in dull metal (i, 183).

Mirror images are abundant in *The Egoist*, where Sir Willoughby regards himself in the 'glass of his mind'. His attitude to Clara, his fiancée, is similar to Alvan's, in that he refuses to understand her as she is. Clara is to be Sir Willoughby's 'companion picture', 'the female image of himself by her exquisite unlikeness. She completed him, added the softer lines wanting to his portrait before the world.'[11] In the same way, Alvan is looking for his Brunhild, and, misled by Clothilde's golden hair, he attributes to her the qualities of his ideal woman. His pursuit of the dream rather than the reality is fatal:

> Among Alvan's gifts the understanding of women did not rank high. He was too robust, he had been too successful. . . . Their feelings he could appreciate during the time when they flew and fell, perhaps a little longer; but the change in his own feelings withdrew him from the communion of sentiment (i, 157, 158–9).

A successful career and success with women have blinded Alvan to his faults. He is exposed to the temptations of a towering pride: 'A Faust-like legend might spring from him: he had a devil' (i, 2). Obsessed by his thwarted passion for a worthless woman, he loses the self-restraint and admirable lucidity that have made him a great leader, and descends into the abyss. The pattern is that of the medieval wheel of fortune.

Meredith conveys a sense of Alvan's greatness by a careful use of heroic parallels. On his first appearance he is described as the ideal and faultless Jew. Although this recalls Disraeli's Sidonia, the comparison, like many others in the book, is classical:

> This man's face was the born orator's, with the light-giving eyes, the forward nose, the animated mouth, all stamped for speechfulness and enterprise, of Cicero's rival in the forum before he took the headship of armies and marched to empire (i, 37).

The hero's name, Alvan, perhaps echoes Disraeli's *Alroy*, another novel dealing with a Jewish hero betrayed by ungovernable passion. Alvan's first name, Sigismund, however, roots him firmly in Germanic mythology. He is compared, directly or indirectly, to a host of heroes, both mythological and historical. None of them is Jewish, and Meredith does not mention Lassalle's reputation as the new Messiah. A comparison with other novels dealing with the Jewish question, like George Eliot's *Daniel Deronda* of 1876, is therefore tenuous. Instead, an indefinable air of romance is conjured up by references to Alexander, Caesar, Hercules, Zeus, Roland, Siegfried. Meredith's analogy between Alvan and other doomed heroes of legend, such as Oedipus, Phaeton, Hamlet, Orpheus, Pompey, Schiller's Fiesco, the Cyclops and the Titans, prefigures the inevitable fall. Clothilde's name for the love-lorn Prince Marko (Yanko von Racowitza), her 'Indian Bacchus', refers to the story of Ariadne, comforted by Bacchus after her desertion by Theseus.

These classical comparisons are rarely contained in the narrator's own commentary, but usually worked ironically into the thoughts of the characters. Clothilde, looking for a conqueror, rejects her fiancé, Prince Marko, as a mere Adonis, and demands a Caesar for herself, a man whose greatness will glorify her own image:

> Siegfried could not be dreamed in him, or a Siegfried's baby son-in-arms. She caught a glorious image of the woman rejecting him and his rival, and it informed her that she, dissatisfied with an Adonis, and more than a match for a famous conqueror, was a woman of decisive and independent, perhaps unexampled force of character (i, 11–12).

Alvan, in the role of Hercules, regards Prince Marko in much the same light: 'That is he, then! one of the dragons guarding my apple of the Hesperides, whom I must brush away' (i, 102).

These slight but cumulative allusions build up an image of

overwhelming conceit. Yet, cast in the grand manner, they command respect. 'I have a Durandal' (i, 116), cries Alvan, and, more magnificently still:

> You hold a Titan in your eyes, like metal in the furnace, to turn him to any shape you please, liquid or solid. You make him a god: he is the river Alvan or the rock Alvan: but fixed or flowing he is lord of you (i, 115).

Even in defeat Alvan clings to the image of himself as a god among men: 'Well, and do you suppose me likely to be beaten? Then Cicero was a fiction, and Caesar a people's legend' (ii, 25–6).

Alvan's presumption, and his lust of power and glory, are ill-suited to his socialist ideals. Nor is he, Meredith implies, the born leader of men he imagines himself to be. When Clothilde sits listening to Alvan lecturing his friends, he is exploring 'the political advantages of action' (i, 43):

> Action means life to the soul as to the body. Compromise is virtual death: it is the pact between cowardice and comfort under the title of expediency (i, 43–4).

To illustrate inaction, Alvan seizes upon the character of Hamlet: 'How brilliantly endowed was the Prince of Denmark in the beginning!' (i, 45). Clothilde interjects: 'Mad from the first! . . . after the apparition of Hamlet's father the prince was mad' (i, 45). The introduction of Hamlet is deliberately ironic. Alvan, 'brilliantly endowed in the beginning', has just seen the apparition (Clothilde) which is to make him mad. Nor is he unconscious of the parallel. At the end of the evening he asserts that Hamlet was poisoned in the blood by the sight of the ghost, and wittily explains to Clothilde that this would excuse infidelity to an Ophelia of fifty. Even she realizes her role as the serpent, and Alvan's reference to his former mistress, the Baroness Lucie. Hamlet also prefigures Alvan's own last days, when he too suffers from an inexplicable inability to act.

The image of Hamlet is succeeded by that of Alexander and the Gordian knot. Alvan characterizes the barriers which prevent him from marrying Clothilde as 'a gate in the hunting-field: an opponent on a platform: a knot beneath a sword: the dam to waters that draw from the heavens' (i, 74). At the end of the novel Clothilde pathetically waits for someone else to cut the knot, which she and Alvan have been trying to unwind.

The central image of the novel is that of heaven and earth, of soaring into the sky and crashing to the ground. The note is struck before the lovers meet with a typical Meredith aphorism: 'Barriers are for those who cannot fly' (i, 24–5, 65). At the beginning, the lovers are certain that they can fly, and their common faith keeps them aloft. Alvan's mind carries him upwards in Meredith's parallels with eagle, sun-god and towering alp. As fallen Titan, grinning skull, centaur and devil, he is mere human being, whose all-consuming egoism is no protection. In the last chapters of the book, the Baroness takes over Meredith's function as chorus, and draws the images of heaven and earth to a concluding judgment:

> He was a man of angels and devils. The former had long been conquering, but the latter were far from extinct. His passion for this shallow girl had consigned him to the lower host (ii, 139).

The themes of flying and falling are underlined by the heroic comparisons. Meredith conceives Alvan as Phaeton, aspiring to drive the chariots of the sun, and exposing himself, by his monstrous presumption, to the thunderbolts of Jove. Alvan, who naïvely hopes that his noble character will persuade Clothilde's family to accept him, is blind to his inability to control the situation. He sees himself as the sun, to whom Clothilde renders 'the sunflower's homage' (i, 26), and she is like a mirror to his belief: 'He was like summer's morning sunlight, his warmth striking instantly through her blood' (i, 131). 'She wheeled above their heads in the fiery chariot beside her sungod' (i, 62). The sun, with its warmth and brilliance, is a recurring image at their first meeting. Alvan compares Clothilde to the sun-blessed wine which they are drinking: 'Wine of the grape is the young bride – the young sun-bride! divine, and never too sweet, never cloying like the withered sun-*dried*' (i, 69). The lovers hope to reach the sunland of satisfied love beyond the forest of difficulty, but Alvan's assumption of more than mortal power betrays them both. In his passion, his 'charioteering' (ii, 116) becomes wild, and an 'edge of cloud' (ii, 148) obscures him.

Sunlight performs a dual function in the book. It is warmth and love on the one hand, and the false, glittering gold on the other. In *Harry Richmond* Richmond Roy is frequently associated with sun images, which denote false ambition and self-delusion, as in *The*

Tragic Comedians. At one of the climaxes of the latter novel, the lovers climb to the summit of the Rigi Mountain to watch the sunrise. The incident is taken from *Meine Beziehungen*, and perhaps first suggested the sun theme to Meredith. It is prophetic here:

> Sunless rose the morning. The blanketed figures went out to salute a blanketed sky. Drizzling they returned, images of woefulness in various forms, including laughter's. Alvan frankly declared himself the disappointed showman; he had hoped for his beloved to see the sight long loved by him of golden chariot and sun steeds crossing the peaks and the lakes (i, 126).

According to J. M. Ludlow, Lassalle was particularly fond of the colour of gold, and the Princess von Racowitza confirms this in her account of his conversation with Bismarck. To Lassalle Bismarck was the man of iron, while he himself was the man of gold: 'Gold! more powerful than even omnipotent iron: what iron has destroyed, gold builds up again; the rain which seduced the heart of Danae was of gold.'[12] These references suggested to Meredith the source of Lassalle's weakness: his concern with externals in his love of the beautiful yet pliant Hélène. With her glorious hair, Clothilde is Alvan's 'Aurora breaking the clouds' (i, 46). Her hair is also described as falling in golden serpents, and one of Meredith's few factual changes from the original text was to make Alvan's name for her not 'golden fox' but 'golden crested serpent'. The implications of this latter name, with its suggestion of sinuous danger, are underlined by Alvan's comparison of Clothilde to the golden-shining sand. He sees her as a weak and shifting character, but he fails to recognize the danger of trusting himself on such a footing. His golden aurora leads him to a duel, a 'death-dealer who stood against red-streaked heavens . . . grandly satanic' (i, 168).

The audacity and presumption of Phaeton are punished by the hand of Jove, but Meredith's Alvan usurps Jove's functions no less than those of Phoebus. His aquiline features and dominating presence conjure up for Clothilde (as for Hélène) the image of an eagle: 'the strongest, the great eagle of men, lord of earth and air' (i, 12). At their first meeting Clothilde is working with lamb's wool, and Alvan becomes for her, 'her dream in human shape, her eagle of men, and she felt like a lamb in the air' (i, 82). Alvan also assumes the lightning and thunder of Jove:

So vigorously rich was his blood that the swift emotion running with the theme as he talked pictured itself in passing and was like the play of sheet lightning on the variations of the uninterrupted and many-glancing outpour (i, 38).

In contrast to the warm golden sunlight, Meredith introduces the foreboding symbol of the dead tree, which Alvan and Clothilde come upon three times during their walk in the wood. While the other trees are 'golden green in the yellow beams', this is 'dead-black' (i, 136), and covered with lichen 'bearing a semblance of livid metal' (i, 138). As they wander through the trees, the lovers are drawn implacably to this symbol of fate and death. Its colour suggests to Alvan the image of Clothilde as a widow, and he tells her, lightly and ironically, that she is not to wear mourning for him. Mentally, he compares the dead tree to Clothilde's hair: 'The tree at a little distance seemed run over with sunless lizards: her locks were golden serpents' (i, 143). To the shallow and triumphant Clothilde the deadness and darkness of the tree represent her rival, the Baroness. The conversation of the lovers continues on the theme of death and life, winter and summer. Drawing Clothilde away, Alvan tells her:

We will take good care not to return this way again. . . .
That tree belongs to a plantation of the under world; its fellows grow in the wood across Acheron, and that tree has looked into the ghastliness of the flood and seen itself. Hecate and Hermes know about it. Phoebus cannot light it. . . . The shudder in that tree is the air exchanging between Life and Death – the ghosts going and coming: it's on the border line (i, 144).

Through the symbol of this tree, Meredith suggests yet another figure from classical mythology, Proserpine, the goddess who combines the contrasting attributes of Earth and Hades. Although Alvan sees Clothilde as his spring, she is also his winter and death. On his way to her he rejoices: 'No dark bride, no skeleton, no colourless thing, no lichened tree was she. Not Death, my friends, but Life' (i, 163). Yet his dreams reveal his doubts as his hopes turn cold: 'I dreamt last night she was half a woman, half a tree, and her hair was like a dead yew-bough' (ii, 104). The dream haunts his last days; he is Orpheus, and Clothilde is Eurydice or Proserpine 'sitting on a throne in Erebus' (ii, 121).

Doom, death and unsatisfied desire dominate the last chapters of the book. Like Shakespeare in the great tragedies, Meredith conveys his sense of Alvan's physical frustration through animal images. Some of these, like the eagle and the lamb, have a mythological context. Others repeat the theme of Alvan's nobility and strength and the devious frailty of Clothilde. He is a lion and a horse, while she is a bird, a serpent, a lizard, an eel, a timid and fleet hare. The opening sentence of the novel underlines the nature of their conflict:

An unresisted lady-killer is probably less aware that he roams the pastures in pursuit of a coquette, than is the diligent Arachne that her web is for the devouring lion (i, 5).

At first Alvan rejoices in his own capture:

I am he who chased a marsh-fire, and encountered a retiarius, and the meshes are on my head and arms. . . . I have a voice for ears, a net for butterflies, a hook for fish, and desperation to plunge into marshes: but the feu follet will not be caught (i, 120 and 116–17).

In pursuit of her, Alvan imagines himself to be a centaur, quadruped or satyr, pursuing a will-o'-the-wisp. His physical lust for her, conveyed through an amazing range of sexual imagery, gathers intensity as Clothilde slips through his fingers. At the crucial moment, when she offers herself to him, his nerve and his strength give way. His gesture of apparent nobility in handing her back to her family represents a crisis of weakness, of vacillation and sentimentality. In his later novels, Meredith opposes the demands of true love and desire to the compressions which society demands. In bowing to the conventional social morality, Alvan is betraying himself. He is already the outsider, and must act in accordance with the dictates of his own spirit. In an astonishing image of physical energy and desire, worthy of D. H. Lawrence, Meredith describes the true Alvan whom he admires so much:

He waited, figurable by nothing so much as a wild horse in captivity sniffing the breeze, when the flanks of the quivering beast are like a wind-struck barley-field, and his nerves are cords, and his nostrils trumpet him: he is flame kept under and straining to rise (ii, 137).

As Alvan's mind runs to madness in his frustration at losing

Clothilde, the intensity of the narrative becomes agonizing. Meredith's identification with his hero is almost complete by the end of the book. The detached, ironic commentator, who can appreciate the comedy of the situation, has almost entirely disappeared. Meredith has entered into Alvan, and the mood is one of unredeemed blackness.

The plot of *The Tragic Comedians* is predetermined. In choosing to retell 'a well-known story', Meredith allowed himself some flexibility in treatment and emphasis, but he did not alter the main outlines of the narrative. In consequence, it is possible, by comparing the novel with historical accounts, to isolate the creative function of Meredith's style. The one is grafted on to the other, rather than the two developing simultaneously. It is through his position as narrator and commentator and his use of recurrent image patterns that Meredith seeks to turn the love-story of Lassalle and Hélène into a work of art, and to illumine deeper truths than was possible in a purely factual account of their fate.

The complex classical mythology employed by Meredith is not simply an embellishment, but an essential counterpoint to the narrative, at once establishing a mood and a thematic sequence, as deliberate as in an opera by Wagner. Image patterns are woven into the story, and they describe and prefigure that Destiny, with a capital 'D', which hangs over the lovers and impels their actions. If Lassalle is raised from a mundane level to the status of a god, this is partly as he appeared to himself and to his contemporaries. And only by escaping from the limitations of the actual story could Meredith endow it with a form and unity and scale sufficient for his ambitious canvas. It would be wrong to overstress the significance of myth in Meredith's treatment. While at one level Alvan and Clothilde are doomed to part, like Orpheus and Eurydice; at another the failure of their relationship is seen in sharply human terms: they engineer their own destruction through weakness and ignorance. Early in the book Meredith's sympathy for Alvan creates a warm, enriching atmosphere, in which classical allegory remains a mere, persistent echo in the background. It is in human and psychological terms that Meredith draws his novel together and attempts, not altogether successfully, to prevent the reader from hurrying through the book 'for the story'. His understanding of the psychological situation is expressed through imagery far more widespread and complex than the few examples which can be quoted in an essay.

The novel is a considerable achievement, and the reasons for Meredith's partial failure lie more in the nature of the original material than in any weakness as a novelist. In whichever version it is found, the account of Lassalle's last weeks is so harrowing as to dominate the reader's mind to the exclusion of all else. In the second half of Meredith's novel his careful literary analysis verges dangerously on the brink of becoming life and not art. Although he returns to a more objective standpoint at the end, we have been through an experience in which hero, novelist and reader have become hopelessly entangled.

Notes

1 H. von Racowitza, *An Autobiography*, 1910, 111. In *Meine Beziehungen zu Ferdinand Lassalle*, Breslau, 1879, 97, the passage read: 'Bist Du ehrgeizig? – Was würde mein Goldkind sagen, wenn ich es einmal im Triumph in Berlin einführen könnte, von 6 Schimmeln gezogen, die erste Frau Deutschland's, hoch erhaben über Alle?'
2 G. Meredith, *Letters*, ed. W. Meredith, 1912, i, 311.
3 *The Tragic Comedians*, 1880, i, 3–4. All quotations are from this edition.
4 No. 2,776, 8 January 1881, 49.
5 G. Beer, 'Meredith's idea of comedy: 1876–1880', *Nineteenth-century Fiction*, September 1965, xx, 176.
6 *Meredith*, 1948, 157–8.
7 'Meredith's Revisions of *The Tragic Comedians*', *Review of English Studies*, n.s. xiv, 33–53.
8 *Letters*, ii, 446.
9 A fuller treatment of the similarities between the two books will be found in Mrs Beer's article, 'Meredith's idea of Comedy: 1876–1880', *Nineteenth-century Fiction*, September 1965, xx, 165–76.
10 *Meine Beziehungen*, 40: 'Aber Brunhild – und zwar die Brunhild der Edda, ja, die war's! die nordische Walkyre! und er wollte der Siegfried dieser Brunhilde sein!'
11 Constable edition, 1897, xv, 55.
12 *Meine Beziehungen*, 112: 'Gold! – Was das Eisen zerstört hat, baut das Gold Wieder auf; – der Regen, der das Hertz der Danaë verführte, war von Gold!'

Diana of the Crossways:
Internal History and the Brainstuff of Fiction

Jan B. Gordon

> Brainstuff is not lean stuff; the brainstuff of fiction is internal
> history, and to suppose it dull is the profoundest of errors;
> how very deep, you will understand when I tell you that it is
> the very football of the holiday afternoon imps below (i).

A shortcut to the structural development of the English novel in
the nineteenth and twentieth centuries might be provided were the
reader to explore the corners of those 'houses' that dot the fictional
landscape: *Mansfield Park; Waverley; Wuthering Heights; Bleak
House; Bladesover;* even *Howard's End.* Naturally, the question of
legacy and inheritance loom large, as if not only the future of
England, but the very future of the novel as a 'house of fiction' were
at stake. The prospect from some window overlooking a decaying
garden, the scurry of maids whose new-found surliness could only
be attributed to the shadows of the Reform Bill; the dogs beside the
fireplace; the endless moving and resettling of dusty furniture; and
the distant whistle of the locomotive that threatens to disrupt some
ritual fête of springtime – all appear as part of the *rite du passage* by
which the Victorian manor house became a museum of the mind.
Crossways is surely no exception:

> There stood the house. Absolutely empty! thought Redworth.
> The sound of the gate-bell he rang was like an echo to him.
> The gate was unlocked. He felt a return of his queer
> churchyard sensation when walking up the garden-path, in the
> shadow of the house. Here she was born: here her father had
> died: and this was the station of her dreams, as a girl at
> school near London and in Paris. Her heart was here. He

looked at the windows facing the Downs with dead eyes. The vivid idea of her was a phantom presence, and cold, assuring him that the bodily Diana was absent. (viii, 84).

As the reader discovers quickly enough, Diana Warwick is never far distant from the house that stands at a symbolic crossing of two roads, even when she commences her final fictional masterpiece, *The Man of Two Minds* (by the woman of two natures). One road leads to London and its financial houses, anonymous dwellings that endlessly invest in the hope for Britain's future connections, the railroad. The other road leads to Copsley, the twelve-hundred-acre estate of the eminent Sir Lukin Dunstane, recently retired from service in India. As the railroad proceeds outward from London in ever-widening arcs, supported only by the speculative bubble that was to bring panic to Victorian England, so its correlate in the realm of manners, gossip (or as Meredith terms it, 'the sentimental tramways of tragi-comedy'), radiates outward from Copsley, the cowslip-bedecked bastion of retreating British imperialism. Like her mythical ancestress, the huntress, Diana Warwick stands alone at *Crossways*, as if midway between the Old England with its eighteenth-century names and the new 'houses' dubbed 'The Funds' or 'Railholm' (Chapter xl). Having a two-sided nature that encompasses both the goddess of chastity and the attendant spirit who assists at childbirth in Greek mythology, Diana Warwick's internal history is identical to the 'brainstuff' of Victorian fiction, and her existential space reflects the legacy of her own being as well as the condition of England in the 1880s, somewhere between repression and fictional, if not real, connection.

History itself comes to be but another fiction in *Diana of the Crossways*. Not unlike *Middlemarch*, set at the time of the First Reform Bill, though written thirty-odd years later, Meredith's so-called feminist novel is set in the 1840s, long before its initial serial publication began in 1884. Although the historical realist might presume the motive for such temporal nostalgia to lie in its evocation of the financial collapse of railroad entrepreneurs or the pull of the Oxford Movement (Constance Asper is 'saved' from a pilgrimage to Rome by marriage to the Whig minister, Percy Dacier, as if to suggest the ease with which politics co-opted faith in the nineteenth century), Meredith probably had more aesthetically sophisticated motives. In the topsy-turvy world of the novel, historical or incremental time becomes fictional at the same time that our very human fictions, gossip and rumour become historicized. In what amounts to an epigraph of *Diana of the Crossways* Meredith wrote:

> A lady of high distinction for wit and beauty, the daughter of an illustrious Irish House, came under the shadow of calumny. It has latterly been examined and exposed as baseless. The story of 'Diana of the Crossways' is to be read as fiction.

The first sentence purports to be historical fact, while the latter phrase discounts its validity by fictionalizing both the 'lady' and the 'shadow of calumny'. Just as surely as he had done in 'An Essay on Comedy', George Meredith uses a second fiction, the novel itself, to deflect the fiction of Diana's reputation that had been established as an historical *donnée*. The final sentence of the prefatory comment is, in effect, a redundancy. We should realize that every 'story' including the one we are about to read is a fiction, without being so pointedly informed by the narrator or his imps. The impact of the statement is far more intriguing than it first appears, for what Meredith has really succeeded in doing is making the novelist's craft just another extension of the social deceptions that make up Victorian history. That which discounts rumour becomes part of the rumour!

There is presented to the reader then an interlocking infinite regress of 'fiction' corresponding to the Chinese-box structure of so many earlier Victorian novels: the lineage of the lady; the scandal in which she has become involved; the rumour and gossip which feeds the scandal; and finally, Meredith's own 'story', the brainstuff of Victorian fiction, which is thus reduced to the status of merely another improvisation within a larger network of social lies. The reader is thus simultaneously presented with the overlapping of many fictions, each of which evokes a number of different temporal rhythms: the reader's time, reputation's time, the narrator's time, the private time of Diana, and finally the intersubjective field created by the degrees of understanding which the characters share, and which is, somehow, a correlate of 'social time'. In his excellent essay 'Time and Intersubjectivity', J. Hillis Miller has commented on the ways in which the Victorian novel, though by nature an open form, represents human experience as standing outside itself 'as reaching toward an as yet unpossessed totality which will complete it and draw the circle of life closed'.[1] For Miller, the novelist struggles to close down the existential spaces of the narrative so as to make of the intersubjective field a 'word' whose co-ordinates his own voyeuristic stance establishes. In *Diana of the Crossways* the author figuratively at least allows time to stand outside itself by restarting the novel within 'narrative' rather than linear or incremental time, hence the novel struggles to draw the circle of time closed and spatializes the historical events of the novel so as to produce a mass saga. The achieved effect is in essence the Bergsonization of the historical novel, in so far as there is a doubling of durational and real time. This basic mode of discourse involves a doubling of minds which is the analogue in the autobiographical or confessional novel of the 1880s and 1890s of the more usual Victorian style in which an omniscient narrator, standing at a time after the events of the story are over, re-created by indirect discourse some inner experience of the protagonists. Of course, at the centre of all this heightened self-consciousness is Diana herself, writing *The Young Minister of State*, that parody of Trollope's parliamentary novels, and hence writing her own confession (internal history) while completing the political saga of Victorian England. As is true of the spatiality of the three houses in the novel, the issue is really one of interiority and exteriority, of associating fiction and history, space and time, the passive, uncommitted posture of the prick-tease and activist, radical politics – in brief, of getting the mythical two Dianas together. In so far as *Diana of the Crossways* is a parody of Victorian formal conventions, it is a history of a history as well as the fiction of a fiction of which Meredith warns us in his epigraph. And structurally, this is a pattern of concentricity.

The opening chapter of the novel, 'Of Diaries and Diarists Touching the Heroine', introduces the reader to the huntress, Diana, through the medium of a diary, aestheticized interior gossip. It is perhaps the only living being that ever touches Diana Warwick. The diarist, one Henry Wilmers, gives us a sequence of perspectives on the heroine that is partially the product of private vision and partially that of overheard, public opinion, as befits the literary mode. But, if gossip was indeed an early eighteenth-century invention, as at least one structural anthropologist alleges, then we are first introduced to a curiously divided woman by an even more ambivalent art form. The mode, however, is surely suited to Diana for another reason: as a socialized being, she wears a mask that hides some private or inner self:

'One word of her we call our inner I. I am not drawing upon her resources for my daily needs; not wasting her at all, I trust; certainly not walling her up, to deafen her voice. It would be to fall away from you. She bids me sign myself, my beloved, ever, ever your Tony.' (xviii, 173).

The passage cited above, from the chapter entitled 'The Authoress', demonstrates the extent to which Diana quite quickly develops a *persona* as a mode of defence against the hostile world. Her being comes to resemble a fortress which has the effect of immediately transforming the rest of the world into vindictive champions of aggression. Wilmer's diary is a fictional work couched in the language and imagery of social history. As a literary mode, the diary most closely resembles the latter, in so far as both are the vehicles for interior history that, by being revealed, also have a public demeanour. The reader is given the impression of invading privacy in the opening chapter of *Diana of the Crossways*, and the indictment of aggression is accomplished in a way quite similar to that by which Diana tempts the assaults of suitors. Because the diary is essentially a private form, the reader's role must be that of a vicarious participant in the events of the 'fiction' as well as the events of Diana's *affaires du coeur*. As we shall see, even the language of the novel re-enforces the reader's posture as a voyeur. Even when she goes on holiday to the Mediterranean, Diana travels aboard the Esquart's *Clarissa*, a vessel which takes its name from the eighteenth-century epistolary novel which combined repression and gossip within the network of threatened sexual violence. In Richardson's volumes, the temptation to sexual assault perfectly parallels the invasion of imaginatively purloined letters in a manner not unlike that in which the reader of Meredith's novel, by being introduced to the protagonist through a diary, must feel the pressure to turn private spaces into public places. It is a temptation abetted by Meredith's tendency to combine two distinctly different styles: the convoluted prose characterized by parenthetical expressions which invariably overstate and the incomplete, elliptical phrases which allow the reader to construct his own beginnings and endings in a manner not unlike that which typifies the gossips in the story itself.[2]

As early as the first chapter of *Diana of the Crossways*, then, the reader is not only introduced to, but voyeuristically involved in, the central dialectic of the novel: the private or insulated 'self' and a 'self' as exteriorized, communal history. The chapter titles suggest the spatialization of the self (internal history or confession) and various exteriorized fictions: 'The Interior of Mr Redworth and the Exterior of Mr Sullivan Smith' (chapter iii) or 'A Drive in Sunlight and a Drive in Moonlight' (chapter xix). Diana, although a moon goddess, was the twin-sister of Apollo, whose inner and spiritual qualities she was believed to share; hence many of her early appearances in art (particularly as Diana of Ephesus) gives her a strange, hermaphroditic appearance in which qualities of both solar (internal) and lunar (reflectively external) energy are manifest. The novel is replete with internal/external dichotomies: 'the fiction which is the summary of actual Life, the *within* and *without* of us, is, prose or verse, plodding or soaring, philosophy's elect handmaiden' (chapter i). In describing her experience of Copsley, Meredith writes of the bored Lady Dunstane:

> The colour of it taught white to impose a sense of gloom. Her cat's love of the familiar *inside* corners was never able to embrace the *outer* walls. (iv, 38).

In point of fact, *Diana of the Crossways* is comprised of groupings of chapters which typically alternate between self-conscious fictional commentary on social events and the events, or the subjects of those events, presented by themselves. The former clusters do not have subjects, but instead are process-laden gerundive or participial phrases: 'Containing Hints of Diana's Experiences and of What They Led To' (chapter iv) or 'Concerning the Scrupulous Gentleman Who Came Too Late' (chapter v). In this group of chapters Meredith's presence is continually felt; it is almost as if he were keeping a diary and endlessly reminding us that these are subheadings for entries. The social events themselves are headlined in Meredith's other style – precise, brief, but often incomplete: 'The Couple' (chapter vi) or 'The Crisis' (chapter vii). This curious antipodal arrangement of titles would suggest that Meredith, like his heroine, is experimenting with the alternation of exterior and interior chapters, a technique that was to become characteristic of early twentieth-century fiction. For example, the reader is first introduced to Diana mediated by the fictional diary only to have his knowledge filled in later by being present at 'An Irish Ball' (chapter ii). The social events of the novel are thus always posterior to their aesthetic reflection so that history always appears within some framing device. The emblem

ɪ*

for this technique is Miss Paynham's painting of Diana Warwick which lies at the novel's structural centre and functions not unlike those 'imaginary portraits' that reappear in *fin-de-siècle* visual and verbal art.[3]

This design, so evident in *Diana of the Crossways*, is not merely fortuitous; but in the largest sense should tell us something about the structural configuration of Victorian society. The intermediate terms in this dialectic between internal history and the brainstuff of fiction may well be gossip and its formal enactment, scandal. Of course, Victorian novels are filled with figures about whom scandal swirls: Bulstrode, Lady Dedlock, John Jasper, Dr Jekyll, Dorian Gray, Martin Decoud, and Diana Warwick. Upon reflection, the nature of both the gossip and the scandalous behaviour that appear in the novels in or adjacent to the *fin-de-siècle* differ in both quality and quantity from the good old High Victorian scandal detailed in, say, Trollope's *The Way We Live Now*.[4] For one thing, Diana Warwick, like Dorian Gray and Dr Jekyll, clearly enjoys being the object of gossip, and her shallow disclaimers to the contrary, regards the whisper as a liberating breeze:

> 'But, my own dear girl, you never could have allowed this infamous charge to be undefended?'
> 'I think so. I've an odd apathy as to my character; rather like death, when one dreams of flying the soul. What does it matter? I should have left the flies and wasps to worry a corpse. And then – good-bye gentility!' (xii, 109).

She recognizes quite early in her social apprenticeship that gossip has such a dynamic that every defence is but another re-enforcement for the nineteenth century's most unusual art form. Surely there is a relationship between Jane Austen's novel of manners, with its 'unuttered and half uttered statements of human value',[5] and that indicting buzz of rumour that no longer gives evidence of either social class or cultural sensibility, but perhaps a societal norm of even greater interest, as we shall soon discover.

After all, Diana Warwick's pilgrimage is only slightly deflected from the typical nineteenth-century *Bildungsroman*. She is educated into society's expectations; she does mature as an artist through varying genres of increasing sophistication, and she departs from the ancestral home only periodically to return in scenes of defensive *déja vu*. Although not a foundling or an orphan, the status which characterizes the protagonist in most developmental or apprentice

novels, she is an alien from across the sea who is introduced into a
societal field whose contours are gossip. Like the Victorian novel
itself, several of which she is writing, Diana commences her career
at an eighteenth-century social occasion, an aristocratic ball
attended by idle military commanders in full dress. There,
ceremony centres on the image of the minuet where rotation of
partners provides social harmony. As the moon goddess, Diana
steals some of the light from the Apollonian martial hero whose
return the Irish Ball was designed to celebrate. But the theft of
attention is all carefully disguised by the conventions of the dance,
with its pantomimed manners and artificially stylized responses
that do not depend upon verbalization. So totally is the design of
society duplicated in the pattern of the dance that Lady Dunstane's
question, 'Any proposals?' exhibits referential ambivalence in so
far as it alludes to life as an extension of the dance. At the conclusion of her début, she dances alone with the honoured veteran in
the middle of a semi-circle formed by jealous onlookers:

> The block of sturdy gazers began to melt. The General had
> dispersed his group of satellites by a movement with the
> Mayoress on his arm, construed as the signal for procession
> to the supper table. (ii, 28).

The reader of *Diana of the Crossways* senses that the private Irish
Ball with its dance of manners and rigid *a priori* decorum is on the
verge of breaking down: and it will be replaced by another ritual,
the Victorian feast, which suggests that at least one kind of
appetite lurks very close to the surface of manners and gesture. It
is during that prolonged supper that Diana Warwick is exposed to
a viciousness of spoken word that corresponds in intensity to the
ravenous prying of appetite:

> The remark had hardly escaped him when a wreath of
> metaphoric smoke, and fire, and no mean report, startled the
> company of supping gentlemen. At the pitch of his voice, Mr
> Sullivan Smith denounced Mr Malkin in presence for a cur
> masquerading as a cat.
>   'And that is not the scoundrel's prime offence. For what
> d'ye think? He trumps up an engagement to dance with a
> beautiful lady, and because she can't remember, binds her to
> an oath for a dance to come, and then, holding her prisoner
> to 'm, he sulks . . .' (iii, 33–4).

Diana's education moves her from the mediated posture of the eighteenth-century woman who passively provides a focal point for the dance pattern at an Irish Ball to the unmediated attitude of the so-called 'new' woman who appears at the commencement of the twentieth century in the plays of Shaw and the fiction of Forster. Her journey is, in one sense, the cavalcade of the Victorian novel – from the self-reflexive diary entries of a nobleman (which would correspond to the private, patterned dance of the novel of manners), to the playground for increasingly middle-class gossip, to the enactment of that gossip in scandal, complete with an appearance in newspaper columns – from Jane Austen to Oscar Wilde. Diana Warwick comes to have a public, even legendary existence, and hence enters the conscience of the race in a way previously denied to her. This progression in both narrative technique and existential condition is really the movement from private to public, from the patterned dance that begins and ends on cue from some lead musician to a wild chase where all classes have access. As if in synchrony with that rhythm of the novel, Meredith's style moves from measured cadences and periodic sentences to the frenetic ventriloquy of the last three chapters. Even the one bastion of privacy in the novel, the ancestral estate at Crossways, is always on the verge of being transformed into an apartment house whose tenants have little respect for the long corridors of history. But all this threatened transformation private spaces, including Diana's; all this democratization of personal and historical prerogative in *Diana of the Crossways*, results in an enormous cultural and psychic debt.

The metaphor for the social, psychological and physical barriers which tempt the invasion of privacy is the whispering that simultaneously frees Diana from her status as an alien while defending her from real assault. From at least one perspective, Meredith's novel is an exploration of the psychodynamics of gossip and its cultural impact. And since Diana's sexual behaviour is really the focus for surreptitious talk, there is an implicit relationship between pornographic behaviour and the role of gossip as a sort of psychic catalyst. During the course of *Diana of the Crossways*, gossip approaches scandal as its existential limit and, at that point, functions much like the comic sprites of 'An Essay on Comedy':

The comic poet is in the narrow field, or enclosed square of the society he depicts; and he addresses the still narrower enclosure of men's intellects, with reference to the operation of the social world upon their characters. He is not concerned with beginnings or endings or surroundings, but with what you are now weaving. ('An Essay on Comedy', 47)

George Meredith's famous essay on the role of comedy in civilization is actually a utopian document in so far as it envisions a kingdom ruled by the Comic. It is a realm where proper perception of the Comic Spirit gives high fellowship, where one becomes a citizen of 'the selected world'. As in most utopias, there are certain general conditions for election: equality of the sexes; at least a moderate degree of intellectual activity, and the avoidance of heavy moralizing. In this peculiar covenant, the fulfilment of all these conditions means that

You will, in fact, be standing in that peculiar oblique beam of light, yourself illuminated to the general eye as the very object of chase and doomed quarry of the thing obscure to you. ('An Essay on Comedy', 48)

Diana's pilgrimage is the quest for that elusive kingdom where spontaneity and the processes of democratization meet in eternal sunlight.[6] As the victims of Diana's spirit are the mannered minuet and polite disguise, so the targets of Meredith's Comic Spirit are those artificial comedies of manners that had graced continental stages for a century. More importantly, the Comic Spirit is not divorced from the life of the state; but exists in an uneasy, though close relationship with the other forces working towards social equality, much as Diana's tryst with Dacier. During the reign of the Comic Spirit (Meredith sees a sort of dialectic of history operating which insures the alternation of kingdoms), life and art are virtually indistinguishable. It is when the Comic Spirit comes to exist apart from the people as a separate artistic manifestation, that the collapse of the realm is at hand and comedy lapses into irony or satire. Aesthetic organicism is a necessity for the operation of the Comic Spirit, and its precursors are the smaller sylphs who deflate egos through the manipulation of overheard rumour.

Throughout *Diana of the Crossways*, the cast of minor characters, Arthur Rhodes, Danvers, Mr Sullivan, Lady Wathin, continually fill the pages with an overlay of rumour and gossip, all of which centres on Diana Warwick. And beneath those buzzes and winks, the heroine carries on a steady stream of epistolary correspondence with her friend, Lady Dunstane. One can almost imagine some literary critic, generations later, collecting her letters (really a sort of inner, inner chapter of the novel itself) and claiming that they are organically related. And, with every other letter, it seems, the hostess of Copsley dispatches her weary husband to the men's social clubs of London in an effort to abate the gossip which makes the rounds of these masculine haunts with almost the same frequency as the postman. Clearly, Emma Dunstane's marriage is no model of happiness, but any sexual encounter with her husband is deflected by his assumption of the role of the envoy. Through him Lady Dunstane participates vicariously in the sex life that is denied her at Copsley. What is established is a relationship between an almost pornographic interest in Mrs Warwick's difficulties, complete with the usual setting in a male-dominated environment, the man's club, and the gossip that inflates that difficulty. Lady Dunstane, then, uses an intermediary to defend herself against the horrors of the marital life at Copsley in the same way that the civilization uses gossip, to gain access through fictional creation, to that which under normal circumstances would remain private. And, of course, that is a large part of the role of the Victorian novelist.

Perhaps an equation might be of help in understanding the dynamics of the relationship:

$$\frac{\text{Scandal}}{\text{Gossip}} = \frac{\text{Pornography}}{\text{Repression}}$$

Although it would appear that pornography creates repression as a counter-measure and that scandal leads to gossip (either as a counter-measure to deflate its range or as a way of extending its sway over and through the masses), all the force is operative in the other direction: repression tends to lead to pornography as an outlet and gossip to create scandal as its mode of validation. In *Civilization and its Discontents* Freud defined eros in terms of a force through which it was possible to unite any number of people in love as long as they had a common object of aggression. The shift from repression to pornography is often accompanied by the body, which is a repressed subject, introjecting itself as an object of affection. Gossip, whose etymology might suggest that the original gossipers were regarded as 'siblings of God', and hence possessed a kind of foreknowledge, is of course baseless. And, as Heidegger mentions in *Sein und Zeit*, gossip tends to float around the civilization without beginning or ending. Gossip and scandal are not only modes of vicarious or voyeuristic participation in the world, but can be engaged in without running the risk of authorship and hence the blame that accompanies any exercise of authority. It is a way of being both 'inside' and 'outside' all action simultaneously, to borrow my previous metaphor of interiority and exteriority. By simply telling his audience that he overheard the story he is about to tell, the teller diverts the story into the realm of fiction (much the way Meredith did in his epigraph), and in the process converts himself from subject to object and experientially participates in the story over and over again. It is, as it were, the closest we might come to the genuine tradition of an oral fable. Through gossip, we democratize the act of authorship, and each man is capable of becoming an artist by merely adding a bit to the original fiction:

> An odd world, where for the sin we have not participated in we must fib and continue fibbing, she reflected. She did not entirely cheat her clearer mind, for she perceived that her step in flight had been urged both by a weak despondency and a blind desperation; also that the world of a fluid civilization is perforce artificial. (xii).

Structurally, gossip functions to fill in the metaphoric spaces of the culture, as Meredith suggests when he hints that Sir Lukin Dunstane 'had a wallet of gossip that would overlay the blank of his absence' (chapter xxxvi). As the geography of *Diana of the Crossways* shifts from rural England to London with the heroine's increasing involvement in publishing and financial ventures, the spaces become urbanized and with the ensuing tightening down of space, verbal feedback increases. The eighteenth-century Irish anecdotes that had graced tables at Crossways are replaced by another, even more portable art form, which 'unlike the lightning flash . . . will not go into the pocket; they can be carried home, they are disbursable at other tables' (chapter xiv). As pornography provided the lower classes with access to aristocratic bedrooms (hence, according to Leslie Fiedler, there is a long tradition of association between working-class literature and pornography),[7] so gossip provides access to another heretofore private domain.

Were it not for gossip, there would be no way of 'peering beyond the limits' (chapter xx). And, the more free Diana Warwick becomes, the more she comes to recognize the height of those limits. Whereas the gossip-scandal axis has shame as its coordinate, the repression-pornography axis involves guilt, so that to move from one to the other duplicates the psychological progression from shame, which is prior, to guilt, which must be atoned for in some penitential way:

> Marriage might be the archway to the road of good service, even as our passage through the flesh may lead to a better state. She had thoughts of the kind, and had them while encouraging herself to deplore the adieu to her little musk-scented sitting room . . . (xliii).

The final two chapters of Meredith's novel allude to scriptural passages and on the very last page, Diana requests a prayer from her friend.

The relationship between Diana's sexual independence, the increasing volume of gossip, and pornography is, again, inextricably bound up with a blurred barrier between the private and the public domain. The gossip in *Diana of the Crossways* inevitably deals with morals. It is a mode of indulging in fantasy without ever really speaking about it in detail, so that the object of gossip exists at an ambivalent distance from those who would despoil her reputation. We tend to gossip about those who exercise some power over us and hence have a kind of immediate impact upon our welfare. Yet, if the object of gossip is too familiar, the divergence from a truth that is more readily obtainable, is easily detectable, and the mode cannot survive. Like the Comic Spirit, the object of gossip occupies an intermediate realm between naturalism and an allegorical distance that prevents over-familiarity. Again, like pornography, gossip appears as subversive, one of those forces that barbarize civilization. But in reality, the 'hummers and hawers' (chapter v) are constitutive. Not only does gossip move horizontally to disrupt the silence of Copsley and Crossways, but also vertically, for it reaches both the ministerial level of government and filters all the way down, ultimately to involve Danvers and even the dog, Leander. It is the only binding force in a culture being disrupted by that train whose whistle can barely be heard above the other verbal din:

Society is the best thing we have, but it is a crazy vessel
worked by a crew that formerly practised piracy, and now, in
expiation, professes piety, fearful of a discovered
Omnipotence, which is the image of themselves and captain.

(xviii)

The substitute for that omnipotence, the filler for the void that J.
Hillis Miller referred to as the 'disappearance of God', is the
'environment' which gossip creates. It is the perfect metaphor for
an increasingly industrialized society where every utterance is
echoed. As the Victorian novel strives to close down its space
and time, the house of fiction becomes a haunted chamber about
which rumour provides the only circulation. As the metaphor for a
system of feed-back or infinite regress, gossip has a number of
attractive features: it can be joined and exited at will; there is
no responsibility for origination nor author identification;
all referrals are backward in time; and the course of gossip is
predictable.

This is all a way of saying that Diana Warwick's role in the world
of *Diana of the Crossways* is, finally, as therapeutic as the tasks of
her mythological namesake. When she visits the ailing Dannisburgh
and later, when she answers the summons to attend Emma Dunstane in her illness, Diana appears as a nursemaid. And that is
precisely her role in the culture at large; as an object of gossip, she
gives everyone an opportunity to vent repression through mass
artistic activity. Her ability to provide some semblance of a 'cure' is
doubtlessly Meredith's way of approaching the relationship
between gossip and witchcraft, a topic that has lately drawn the
attention of a number of anthropologists.[8] Of course, the nature of
gossip is such that everyone is involved sooner or later, so that
subjects of gossip tend to become objects, and vice versa. Finally,
even Diana falls ill from the curious malady that sweeps across the
pages of the novel, and it is the 'cured' Lady Dunstane who must
enter the sick room to effect a treatment. Symbolically, that event
corresponds to Diana's role in leaking the confidential information
about Dacier's party's role in the upcoming vote on Corn Law
Repeal to the newspapers. Long the object of gossip, even from the
opening pages of Wilmer's diary, she must eventually become its
instigator. Only Andrew Hedger, the hog farmer in Hampshire,
remains exempt from the infection of gossip, and his immunity has
something to do with his spurning of the cities and railroads for the

more open spaces of the country, where the incubation of reflexiveness is impossible.

The movement from the opening diary, to the gossip columns in London newspapers, to the wedding announcement on the last pages of *Diana of the Crossways* parallels the progression to 'bad faith' that Sartre describes in *L'être et le néant*. In the famous chapter in Part I of Sartre's treatise, he gives the example of a woman who has consented to go out with a particular man for the first time. Although she well knows the intentions of the man regarding her and recognizes that sooner or later she will have to make the decision regarding his advances, the woman never recognizes the urgency, electing instead to postpone the reckoning. She concerns herself only with what is respectful and discreet in the attitude of her companion. And she restricts his behaviour to what is in the present, just as Diana, unlike the gossips who surround her, always speaks in the present tense. Even were he to say, 'I find you so attractive', a variant of which is uttered by Dacier, Redworth, Rhodes and Lord Dannisburgh during the course of the novel, the woman chooses to disarm the phrase of its sexuality. The chances are, as Sartre wisely observes, she attaches to the conversation and the speaker only the *immediate* meanings which she imagines as objective qualities. The qualities of all Diana's men become fixed in a permanence like that of *things*; it is no other than the projection in the strict present of the qualities into the temporal flux of her life. She does not lack knowledge, but is, to the contrary, profoundly aware of the desire which she inspires. Yet the desire cruel and naked would always humiliate and horrify her. Simultaneously, she never finds charm in an attitude which would be only respect. Satisfaction is obtainable only from a feeling which is addressed wholly to her personality, i.e. to her full freedom. Diana, like the woman in the chapter 'Bad Faith', does not apprehend the desire for what it is, though; she recognizes it only in so far as it transcends itself towards admiration or respect. Should the man then grasp her hand, the young woman would be forced into an immediate decision – notably, how to defend against disinformed desire. She can neither withdraw her hand (for such is to break the charm of the evening) nor grasp his (for such is to engage herself).

What follows is entirely predictable: she leaves her hand in his while not being conscious of the choice:

She gave him her hand: a lost hand, dear to hold, needing to be guided, he feared. For him, it was merely a hand, cut off from the wrist . . . (xxix).

The woman may, Sartre adds, casually sentimentalize about Life in an effort to achieve some transcendence over the supposed disappearance of choices. In the process she has reduced her 'self' to its essential aspect – a consciousness which neither consents nor resists but creates the illusion of having no choice as part of the defence mechanism. The hand is no longer part of 'her', but has become disembodied, creating a schizoid condition. In the process both partners have colluded in a dehumanizing journey to 'thing-ness', from 'je' to 'moi', to borrow Sartre's terminology.[9] It is a pilgrimage which relates sexuality, freedom and the disappearance of subjectivity in ways strikingly like that accomplished by gossip. In an effort to avoid access to the 'self', Diana Warwick elects to martyrize her nothingness, swapping one form of emptiness for another. Thus Crossways becomes a fortress of desire in the final chapter, containing all the mental refuse of a socialized woman:

And the drawing-room was fitted with her brackets and étagères, holding every knick-knack she had possessed and scattered, small bronzes, antiques, ivory junks, quaint ivory figures Chinese and Japanese, bits of porcelain, silver incense-urns, dozens of dainty sundries. She had a shamed curiosity to spy for an omission of one of them; all were there. The Crossways had been turned into a trap. (xl, 379).

Of course, the trap is of her own creation.

In order to prevent victimization at the hands of her lovers, Diana literally splits her being, resorting to the typical schizoid defences in order to combat the double standard on its own terms. The symptoms of Diana Warwick's illness are very similar to those outlined by R. D. Laing in *Self and Others* and later in *The Divided Self*: the confusion between 'self' (meaning *my* self and no other) and the other; the fear of implosion (the idea that the walled-in self is being invaded and is hence in danger of losing cohesion); and finally the fear of dehumanization that occurs from the feeling of subjection to the constant scrutiny of the 'other'. To refuse the commands of the other is to abandon the self to its own subjectivity:

'What is it to a man – a public man or not! The woman is
always the victim. That's why I have *held myself in* so
long . . .' (xxv, 236).

To admit and obey the will of the other is to become indistinguishable from the other's being, and hence lose the self in a more radically derivative way. In terms of the strategies of the novel, the
pattern of either/or choices has been transformed into the more
closed-circuit dynamics of being/and. The infinite regress of
fictions on the narrative plane corresponds in Diana's life to her
reduction to a metaphoric prison where there is only the *pretence* of
choice. While delaying the decision to elope with Dacier, Diana
recognizes that her education has been merely the acquisition of
pretence:

'What if we had to confess that we took to our heels the
moment the idea struck us! Three days. We may then pretend
to a philosophical resolve. Then come to me: or write to me.'

(xxv)

Her assumption of a mask is suggested throughout the last half
of Meredith's novel. Diana initially fears jumping 'away from her
shadow' (chapter xviii); identifies any notion of settling down
with her projected 'double', Emma Dunstane; fears that 'she was
divided in halves, with one half pitying the other' (chapter xvi);
and finally, completes her fictional career by writing *The Man of
Two Minds* while looking in the mirror 'at the woman likewise
divided' (chapter xxx). In psychological terms she introjects her
own autobiography, making her own interior history part of the
brainstuff of fiction. She never so much surrenders the bastion, but
rather identifies with the aggressor in order to avoid the further
brutality of pretence – a sufficiently cynical view of the projected
marriage:

. . . cherishing her new freedom, dreading the menacer;
feeling, that though she held the citadel, she was daily less
sure of its foundations, and that her hope of some last
romance in life was going; for in him shone not a glimpse. He
appeared to Diana as a fatal power, attracting her without
sympathy, benevolently overcoming: one of those good men,
strong men, who subdue and do not kindle. The enthralment
revolted a nature capable of accepting subjection only by
burning (xl, 381).

It is a sad but, one suspects, wise ending to a tale of liberation. *Diana of the Crossways* concludes at precisely that point where so many nineteenth-century novels began: the orphan, exhausted from the chase, is incarcerated within some prison that poses as an example of domesticity. And surely, that is the scandal that completes all the gossip.

It almost seems as if Meredith realized the final plight of his poor Diana. For in the final two chapters, he, too, tried to get the interior self related to all its false-self systems by bringing together the two types of narrative that had made up the clusters of interior and exterior chapters: 'The Penultimate: Showing a Final Struggle For Liberty and Run Into Harness' (chapter xlii) and 'Nuptial Chapter; And of How a Barely Willing Woman Was Led to Bloom With the Nuptial Sentiment' (xliii). The process-laden diary entries and their respective occasions are brought together in the same chapter title, rather than separated within their own groups, as they had been previously. But even this effort betrays the stylistic adaptation of the *doppelgänger*, a popular icon of the decadent literature of the nineties. Just around the corner chronologically is the ventriloquy of point-of-view narration and the aestheticized impotency of the voyeuristic dandy who engages in ocular gossip while simultaneously becoming the object of verbal gossip, and hence having a double existence, inside and outside action, or fiction, as the case may be. The mythological Diana was worshipped at the Crossways, located in the village of Trivia in central Greece. As its name might suggest, the small community stood at a junction of highways much as does Diana Warwick's ancestral estate. And those highways, all meeting at the societal trivia that we call gossip, demarcate the internal history of women as well as the kingdom of nineteenth-century fiction. With the final sentence of the novel, the reader, like Meredith's Comic Imps, begins to peek over those barriers prefatory to creating his own fictions.

Notes

Quotations from *Diana of the Crossways* are from the edition of 1916. The quotations from 'An Essay on Comedy' are taken from W. Sypher, *Comedy*, New York, 1956, because of its availability.

1 J. Hillis Miller, *The Form of Victorian Fiction*, Notre Dame, 1968, 15.
2 For a similar analysis of the relationship between Meredith's prose

style and the thematic interests, see R. B. Wilkenfeld, 'Hands Around: Image and Theme in *The Egoist*', *ELH*, xxxiv, No. I, March, 1967, 367–79.

3 For a full discussion of the role of the imaginary portrait in decadent literature, see my 'The Imaginary Portrait: *Fin-de-Siècle* Icon', *Windsor Review*, v, No. 1, Autumn, 1969, 81–104. The portrait, with all its attendant reflection, merely suggests the extent to which Diana has confused her real and fictional existence and parallels her assumption of a *persona*.

4 For a discussion of the evolution in the design of Victorian scandal, see Robert B. Martin, *Enter Rumour – Four Early Victorian Scandals*, London, 1962. Lionel Stevenson, *The Ordeal of George Meredith*, New York, 1953, 253–61, feels that *Diana of the Crossways* is a realistic portrayal of the scandal involving Caroline Norton and the Peel government during the debates over repeal of the Corn Laws. Although I would defer from such an overly faithful reading, there is a political dimension to the novel, notably, the uneasy relationship between the Liberals and the Irish that ultimately emerged into a coalition.

5 See Lionel Trilling's brilliant evocation of the mood of the novel of manners in his chapter 'Mansfield Park', in *The Opposing Self*, New York, 1955. His introduction to the Riverside edition of *Emma* continues in the same mood.

6 Diana needs sunlight of course in order to maintain her role as a reflector of light and hence follows the sun across Europe during the course of the novel.

7 Leslie Fiedler, 'Cross the Border and Close the Gap', an unpublished lecture delivered 9 May 1969 at Capen Hall, the State University of New York at Buffalo, New York.

8 Max Gluckman, 'Psychological, Sociological and Anthropological Explanations of Witchcraft and Gossip: A Clarification', *Man*, v, No. 1, March, 1968, 20–34.

9 Jean-Paul Sartre, *Being and Nothingness*, tr. by Hazel E. Barnes, New York, 1966, 97–9.

One of Our Conquerors:
Language and Music

Gillian Beer

One of Our Conquerors is a deliberately experimental work; it lies close to the source of much that has proved most fruitful in the twentieth-century novel. It was serialized in 1890, and first published in three volumes in 1891; its influence can be felt throughout the 1890s and beyond.[1] Joyce, Forster, Lawrence, even T. S. Eliot seem to have drawn something creative from it. It is the apotheosis of the new artistic freedom which came to Meredith as the result of a legacy in the early 1880s. He put this freedom to some curious uses. His late novels often seem cryptic, self-absorbed, baulking our efforts as readers. But on re-reading the crabbedness obtrudes itself far less, the intelligence, the poignant consciousness of human complexity comes fully home.

The novel is part also of that wider movement which tended to displace the common language of society from the narrative of the novel and replace it with the thought processes of an idiosyncratic sensibility. Trollope complained that he had had to read many sentences in *Daniel Deronda* three times. To him this was a self-evident condemnation. Now, I think, we would not be so sure. *Daniel Deronda, One of Our Conquerors, The Wings of a Dove,* each uses what might be called 'introspected melodrama'. Vivid incidents are deliberately blurred and shown to be of significance *only* through the characters' interpretation of them: murder, persecution, betrayal lose their names, and regain them only if one of the characters within the novel risks a definition. Meredith was the first Victorian novelist to demonstrate the possibilities opened by a more 'mandarin' approach. His 'late' period began a number of years before that of Henry James, and in James's wary, impatient admiration of him we can sense the artist's unwilling acknowledgment of a predecessor.

One of Our Conquerors is, self-consciously, a novel *about* language and the limits of language. At times it inadvertently oversteps those limits. At other times, it deliberately explores the territory beyond them. Morally, the novel reveals the responsibilities imposed by language and by the articulated consciousness. Decoratively, it allows Meredith to try out stylistic effects which ignore his readers. There is a paradox here which strikes to the heart of his artistic dilemma. In his late novels Meredith often seems to have lost faith in language as communication. In *One of Our Conquerors* this loss of faith is both a theme and a temptation.

Beyond language lies silence, music, and death. Each of these in turn dominates the novel. But since Meredith is a novelist he must continue to use language, and if the narrative eschews the effect of conversation it may lose dynamism – become merely fusty ornament mirrored endlessly away from us. Though occasionally the style seems frivolously hermetic (a smile: 'like the moral crepuscular of a sunlighted day down a not totally inanimate Sunday London street') the novel overrides such failed effects. In the intense directness of its imagism, its mimicry of diverse consciousnesses, it allows the reader a creative role. We have to make the book, not simply listen to it.

Its scope is grandiose – nothing less than a critique of the whole range of assumptions commonly held in British society in the 1880s. At its centre is the unreflective consciousness of the successful City man, Victor Radnor; the controlling movement is his progress towards understanding and madness. The narrative voice alternates between remote sybilline playfulness and close imitation of the various social speech-patterns of the period. Events never reach us intact; they come refracted through the wishes and dreads of the characters.

Meredith – as so often – starts more ideas than he can work out with any richness. There is a profuse ornamental clutter on the surface of the work – thoughts about politics, London, women's rights, the Alps, the Salvation Army, France, money, the Fall of Man, fallen women, music, the Thames, Wagner, wine, the English language, the Naturalistic novel, conscription, economic theory. Most of these topics are generated by Victor's free play of thought. Some of them penetrate to the depths of the book's meaning. But Victor is not capable of subjecting them to any ordering scrutiny and for much of the book his mind is the medium of perception as well as the principal object of satire. Meredith seems at times to have abdicated from judgment, requiring us as readers to formulate not only the events, but even the attitudes of his work. Like many later novelists, in using stream-of-consciousness, he probably overestimates our willingness to enter his characters' inner being before we have been introduced to them. On a first reading we must strain to construct a story out of hints and allusions; at the same time we are plunged into intimacy with Victor, of whom as yet we know nothing. Victor himself, throughout the novel, is in search of the lost over-arching Idea which momentarily illumines him in the first scene of the novel when he falls in the street.

It emerges in the course of *One of Our Conquerors* that Victor Radnor (now a millionaire, active in the City, with musical tastes) had married in his youth a rich widow much older than he, called Mrs Burman. (Hints about the characters are frequently conveyed in their names.) He fell in love with her young companion, Nataly, and they eloped together. They have lived together as man and wife for twenty years and have a daughter, Nesta. They have never been able to marry, because Mrs Burman, though ailing with a number of diseases, still lives on and refuses a divorce. The deep happiness of their union has been tainted by the need to live a lie. Victor, determined that they shall enjoy the social glories of his wealth and prestige, insists that they live in the full glare of society without acknowledging that they are unmarried. As a result, rumours and scandal circulate and they have been obliged to leave two country homes because of the falling off of their neighbours. Victor believes that it is Mrs Burman who spreads the gossip. It is never clear how far he is right in this. Their married life is lived in the unspoken hope of her death. Nataly would be quite satisfied to live quietly to placate Mrs Burman, but Victor cannot be content except when blazing forth as a 'conqueror'. Nesta is unaware of her illegitimacy.

The novel covers a period of a few months when Mrs Burman's death seems imminent and Victor is chafing to move into the absurd grandiose country mansion he has built, called 'Lakelands', which is his version of the pastoral: 'Well, this is my Sabine farm, rather on a larger scale, for the sake of friends' (I, iii, 44). He is hoping that her death (and that of an ailing Member of Parliament) will make it possible for him to enter the House – the crown of his social ambition. The novel shows Nesta's period of growing to adulthood, discovering the truth of her birth, breaking a socially acceptable, thin engagement to which the unacknowledged needs of her parents have led her. For Nataly the book tracks her withdrawal and the silent growth of her fatal disease – at the end of the novel she dies of breast cancer a few hours before Mrs Burman's death. Victor goes mad. Nesta finally marries her true mate.

These are some of the events of the novel. The novel's *action* is internal. The marriage of Victor and Nataly and its gradual attrition through silence and fear shapes the course and meaning of the book. Running alongside this is the awakening of Nesta, whose innocent, 'implacable intuition read with the keenness of eye of a man of the world'. Meredith observes the silences and estrangements within love. He observes also the accord which has no need of speech.

Running through the book is Colney Durance's ironic fantasy, *The Rival Tongues*, about the claims of various languages to be adopted by the Japanese. This tedious work has the effect of calling attention to the relativity of language, its partial nature, its absurdity, its indispensability. Colney Durance is Meredith's representative within the novel – a brilliantly unsuccessful author working 'in the Idea', opposed both to the 'Brandy' novel of sensation, beloved by the British, and to the 'cacaturient' realism of the French Naturalists. But Durance represents particularly what Meredith learnt to distrust in himself – 'the passion to sting and tear, on rational grounds' (I, ix, 151). Writing to Maxse on 15 January 1888 when he was just starting work on *One of Our Conquerors*, Meredith said that he was 'beset by the devils of satire' when he looked at the English public. 'That is not a good state for composition,' he remarked. The satirist, with his 'unfruitful rod', fails to penetrate to the true depths of other men because satire is imprisoned in its own exaggeration. Much earlier in his career Meredith asserted that 'Between realism and idealism there is no natural conflict' (20 September 1864). *One of Our Conquerors* is his fullest attempt at a realism which will show the continuity between man in society and man in the depths below consciousness. He wants to show the realities of man's mind as well as of his appetites. This full realism must register both the surface of active life and the flux of feeling 'the strange faint freaks of our sensations' which are incapable of expression or action – which cannot, without violence, be translated into words.

The germ of the novel seems to have been a single word. In a portfolio of notes now held at Yale one page lists together a number of remarks he used in *Diana of the Crossways* (completed in late 1883) and two which appear in *One of Our Conquerors*.[2] The first of them is the significant one:

> 'None of your impudence,' the young gentleman observed.
> 'And none of your damned punctilio,' said the man.

The opening scene of the novel shows Victor helped up after a fall by a workman whose dirty fingers mark his white waistcoat. A slight altercation follows:

> 'Ah, well, don't be impudent,' the gentleman said, by way of amiable remonstrance before a parting.
> 'And none of your dam punctilio,' said the man.

Victor is pursued through the novel by this remembered word, 'punctilio'. His obsession has begun. Immediately after this incident 'It was observed in the crowd, that after a few paces he put two fingers on the back of his head.' He is attempting to remember the Idea which came to him as he fell and which was driven away (as it seems to him) by the word 'punctilio'. The word haunts him because it 'renders him portable' – it circumscribes him, classes him.

Victor, at the beginning of the novel, is quite unself-critical. Meredith expresses this by casting the first two chapters as stream of consciousness. Any criticism registered comes as imagined comments from Victor's friends – and these friends are 'characterized' by Victor: Simeon Fenellan's 'explosive repartee', Colney Durance's 'malignant sketches'. Their views seem limited, held in the unbounded flow of Victor's own identity. He feels himself to be a part of London – perhaps even more, he feels that London is an expression of himself. As he looks down upon the river from London Bridge his energy, his eagerness for the sublime, finds its counterpart in the outward scene:

> Down went the twirling horizontal pillars of a strong tide
> from the arches of the bridge, breaking to wild water at a
> remove; and a reddish Northern cheek of curdling pipeing
> East, at shrilly puffs between the Tower and the Custom
> House, encountered it to whip and ridge the flood against

descending tug and long tail of stern-ajerk empty barges; with
a steamer slowly noseing round off the wharf-cranes, preparing
to swirl the screw; and half-bottom-upward boats dancing
harpooner beside their whale; along an avenue, not fabulously
golden, of the deputy masts of all nations, a wintry woodland,
every rag aloft curling to volume . . . (I, i, 12–13).

The prose poem (which endows Victor with Meredith's language)
expresses Victor's capacity for rapture – a kind of selflessness which
is more the expansion of self than its annihilation. The method of
narration in these early chapters indulges Victor's sense of
boundlessness. The distinction between narration and the character's consciousness is deliberately blurred.

Meredith appears, disconcertingly, to be implicated in the
blimpish, anti-Semitic pastoral of Victor's invention. Only
gradually is Victor's ego contained within the bounds of characterization; at first the whole style, the language of the book is impregnated with his assumptions (which express the common
assumptions of unreflective Englishmen of the period). Meredith
set a trap for his contemporary readers, inviting them to relax upon
a stream of narrative composed of their prejudices and then gradually revealing the gap between such values and the values of his
work. Few modern readers are likely to fall into the trap. The
effect is altered. We are more likely to be surprised by the tenderness Meredith shows for Skepsey, Victor's messenger, with his
pugilistic adventures and eagerness to see the country in a state
prepared for war. The fate reserved for him is a happy one – his
drunken wife is killed and he marries the Salvation Army girl,
Matilda Pridden. His life is seen as absurd but admirable.

The shift from Army to Salvation Army is significant. The
whole book is concerned with the change from material values to
spiritual discovery; Skepsey provides a kind of comic descant to
Victor's loss of belief in facts. Magnificent Lakelands, with which
Victor intended to conquer the social world and his wife's mis-
givings, gradually loses all significance for him as the book goes on.
The gigantic material carapace he has constructed for himself
gives way to the obsessive inner search for the 'Idea'. Victor
expresses his new reflectiveness to himself in psychologically
violent terms: 'Since the day of the fall . . . he had taken to look
behind him, as though an eye had been knocked in the back of his
head' (II, iii, 47).

Nataly, Victor's wife, is reflective by temperament, but she is withheld from scrutiny and formulation by her love, and by her fear that she may cease to love. Her consciousness is silent – or impenetrable. Meredith records Victor's impatient generalizing about women's low appetite for facts:

> man's mate the fair, the graceful, the bewitching, with the sweetest and purest of natures, cannot help being something of a groveller.
> Nataly had likewise her thoughts (I, vi, 104).

The chapter ends. The blank half-page provokes imagination. Nataly dreads speech – even inner speech: what is formulated can no longer be ignored. She can face Colney's satire because the language of satire leaves reality intact while mocking the straw figure created by its own exaggeration: 'She could bear the lash from him, and tell her soul that he overdid it, and have an unjustly-treated self to cherish. But in very truth she was a woman who loved to hear the truth' (I, xi, 212).

This is Nataly's dilemma: her dread of judging the husband whom she passionately loves makes it impossible for her to recognize the thrust of guilt within her. Her only means of judgment on herself and on those she loves is physical withdrawal. Nataly feels herself to be Victor's accomplice, not his mate – she feels that 'the deficiency affecting her character lay in her want of language. A tongue to speak and contend, would have helped her to carve a clearer way' (II, ii, 32). As it is, longing for and dreading the power of speech, she chooses unwittingly the more destructive way. 'Unable to find the words, even the ideas, to withstand him', she sleeps apart. They cease to make love (II, v, 105):

> She could have turned to him, to show him she was in harmony with the holy night and loving world, but for the fear founded on a knowledge of the man he was; it held her frozen to the semblance of a tombstone lady beside her lord, in the aisle where horror kindles pitchy blackness with its legions at one movement. Verily it was the ghost of Mrs. Burman come to the bed, between them (II, v, 108).

> Like sculptured effigies they might be seen
> Upon their marriage-tomb, the sword between.
>   ('Modern Love', i.)

The images from 'Modern Love' begin to well up, and with them Meredith's creative knowledge of alienation in the midst of love. On this one topic he can sound tragic depths.

Nataly's withdrawal (fully understood, fully felt within the work) leads her into the wastes of isolation. She is shown to be a rich-spirited and loving woman, yet later in the book she refuses all explanations from her daughter, who has befriended a 'fallen woman' and shuts herself away in her room: 'she felt her existence dissolving to a dark stain of the earth' (III, xi, 228). Her mind is becoming evil, expressing the evil views in society which have caused so much of her own suffering as an unmarried woman. She comes through this isolation capable of 'singularly lucid' thoughts, but secretly, mortally ill. So much does she reject articulation that it is only by her physical gestures – clutching her breast, sensing pain – that we discover or infer that she is dying from cancer of the breast. Neither Victor nor Nesta know. She dies while Victor is addressing a political meeting expecting at any moment to receive news of Mrs Burman's death. The reader is not present at Nataly's death.

Victor, in his madness, believes himself the dead one of the two. He insists on a marriage ceremony. The description comes to us through the thin medium of Dudley Sowerby's experience: Victor 'had a confession for his Nataly, for her only, for no one else':

> He had an Idea. His begging of Dudley to listen without any punctilio (putting a vulgar oath before it), was the sole piece of unreasonableness in the explanation of the idea: and that was not much wilder than the stuff Dudley had read from reports of Radical speeches (III, xiv, 299).

This is the book's last major irony. Victor's Idea remains veiled, despite his struggles to recapture it. But from the many references and hints that we are given as readers we can guess more or less what it was. Victor cannot recall it because he cannot accept its lack of originality. As it came to him it bore the whole weight of his inner life. It was bodied out by his rich sense of identity. When he comes near to remembering it he avoids it because it has lost colour and palpability:

> You would found a new and more stable aristocracy of the contempt of luxury. . . . Was it his Idea? . . . But his Idea had been surpassingly luminous, alive, a creation; and this

came before him with the yellow skin of a Theory, bred, born of books (III, xii, 245).

And:

> His lost Idea drew close to him in sleep: or he thought so, when awakening to the conception of a people solidified, rich and poor, by the common pride of simple manhood. But it was not coloured, not a luminous globe: and the people were in drab, not a shining army on the march to meet the Future (III, xiii, 269).

The Idea returns to Victor 'full-statured and embraceable' once he is mad – but he cannot then communicate its significance.

Victor *becomes* his Idea. The first scene of the book shows the Idea in action as the workman raises him after his fall. But it is driven away by the class tension epitomized in the word 'punctilio'. The book charts the process by which he acts out his discovery of the oneness, the continuity of man with man, rich and poor, Jew and Gentile, past and present, man and beast. Before they visit the dying Mrs Burman, Victor takes Nataly to the Regent's Park Zoo:

> 'After all, a caged wild beast hasn't so bad a life,' he said. – To be well fed while they live, and welcome death as a release from the maladies they develop in idleness, is the condition of wealthy people: – creatures of prey? horrible thought! yet allied to his Idea, it seemed (III, xii, 253–4).

When he goes mad the narrative voice records:

> For awhile he hung, and then fell, like an icicle. Nesta came with a cry for her father. He rose; Dartrey was by. Hugged fast in iron muscles, the unhappy creature raved of his being a caged lion (III, xiv, 300).

The idea can only truthfully exist through action; recorded, it loses all its substance and reverts to bromide.

This, of course, is precisely Meredith's artistic problem. Language defines, and so, inevitably, distorts. Victor finds phrases reassuring; he likes things 'raised and limited'. Within *One of Our Conquerors* the puddingy epigrams of Simeon Fenellan and Colney Durance offer no very satisfying alternative to inarticulateness. And the narrator's stylistic mannerisms too often seem to wince away from the emotion he creates. Skepsey is filled with a pregnant sense of life on his journey to France: 'there was a remarkable fulness, if only he could subordinate it to narrative'. (This quotation also illustrates the way in which Meredith sets the narrative in a no-man's-land between author and character. The third person is retained, the vocabulary is Meredith's, but the tone and *syntax* imitate the character.) The argument about language, experience and action is carried on at varying levels throughout the book.

Nesta, Victor's intelligent young daughter, represents the possibilities of direct, unanalysed responsiveness. Her lack of worldly vocabulary leaves her free from the world's prejudices. She doesn't recognize her friend, Mrs Marsett, as a 'fallen woman'; the word 'mistress' has no significance for her. She responds directly to the individual. Her feelings 'swept her to a fount of thoughts, where the thoughts are not yet shaped, are yet in the breast of the mother emotions' (II, ii, 23). . . . 'Burning Nesta', 'full blooded to the finger tips', as the narrator enthusiastically calls her, is the one ideal figure in the book. She is also the only major character whose consciousness is rarely shown. Instead, Meredith tends to use a medieval romance imagery to describe her – an imagery which comes from the idealizing narrator rather than being generated by Nesta's own thoughts. When, very occasionally, he allows irony to approach her he uses it to bring out the poignancy of a situation which might otherwise appear simply comic. The middle-aged, worthy Rev. Septimus Barmby is the first man to declare his love for her. The pain of lost possibility is expressed in her thought of 'the shimmering woods and bushy glades, and the descent of the shape celestial, and the recognition – the mutual cry of affinity' – all now seen as 'the deceptions our elders tell of!' (II, ii, 37). The 'cry of affinity' comes at last to Nesta, but it comes not as speech, but as sight and touch. She and Dartrey Fenellan wordlessly recognize each other:

> There was no soft expression, only the direct shot of light, on both sides; conveying as much as is borne from sun to earth, from earth to sun. . . . Nesta felt it, without asking whether she was loved. She was his. She had not a thought of the word of love or the being beloved (III, x, 208).

She has no way of knowing if she will ever marry Dartrey.

Nesta represents the possibilities of the growing consciousness as yet unhampered by tired formulations. She does not fear articulate-ness; she is shrewd – her poker-faced fiancé 'slightly crisped under the speculative look she directed on him'. Whereas her father seizes on summarizing phrases and her mother rejects argument, Nesta recognizes language as one possible means of acting and responding. So she can save her father from his barren flirtation with Lady Grace by coming to walk home from the City with him every day precisely because she does it without meditated design. After she has discovered the secret of her birth, she leaves for home: 'She passed into music, as she always did under motion of carriages and trains, whether in happiness or sadness'. . . (II, vi, 125).

Music, in this novel, is the liberating alternative to language. It is vital equally to Victor, Nataly and Nesta. Meredith constantly uses musical imagery to suggest the movement of unarticulated thought. The action of the novel is punctuated by concerts – Nataly and Victor fell in love as they played and sang together in Mrs Burman's house. Travelling abroad, Victor and his friends take their instruments with them and play in the evening. Victor is flautist, conductor, singer. At home they break into aria – and in jocular song they say things that cannot be spoken. Nesta's godmother is Sanfredini – a great opera-singer of irregular life. Sarasate and Joachim appear briefly under the names of Duran-darte and Jachimo. All the idiosyncratic minor characters are held together in friendship by music's accord.

Music was necessary to the world of Meredith's novels from the start of his career. He struggled to render the full complexity of experience into words, he worried at language, forcing upon grammar and syntax a heightened dramatic role; at times he compressed sense so fiercely that the words on the page seem to flag and lose their meaning. He knew that his struggle with language must of its very nature leave him ultimately worsted. The 'high notes and condensings' of his comedies perfectly render the point where consciousness comes into focus; but throughout his life, and increasingly in his late novels, he was concerned with 'the sub-merged self – self in the depths'. He sought to express the action of the subconscious – and, even further in, the territory of the mind where sound and effects of motion seem to replace imagery. Beyond language lies silence – the silence of bliss or of alienation. But beyond it also lies music. Music cannot be rendered into words.

For a nineteenth-century liberal humanist, moreover, music can be used to suggest a numinous world without invoking the existence of God. That is one reason why it is so much a part of *Daniel Deronda*.

Early in his career Meredith seems to have sensed that opera, in particular, could achieve something that he was seeking in his novels: a marriage between epic action and the subtle articulation of feeling. In opera the surge of events is suspended and resolved at intervals in the intense expressiveness of aria. Meredith responded to opera's stylization of experience: the way in which its pace follows the logic of emotion rather than of time, so that there is always room to sing out the full meaning of the inner life despite the urgencies of escape or death. In the unifying of language and music Meredith recognized a poise and freedom he was seeking in his own art: 'Between realism and idealism there is no natural conflict.' Two of his early novels, *Sandra Belloni* and *Vittoria*, share the same opera-singer heroine. In the novels of the 1870s, when reason became for a time the dominant value in his work, music is less important. It tends to be used for political illustrations (in *Harry Richmond* a character compares the organ to despotism, the piano to constitutional *bourgeoisie*, and the orchestra to a republic).

But in the 1880s Meredith reached out beyond comic appraisal towards the tragic, the mysterious in human emotion. Music reasserts itself. Diana of the Crossways hears Chopin play; she and her lover, Percy Dacier, go to the opera and hear *I Puritani*. (Here the opera's title is of more significance to the novel than its music – it provides an ironic gloss on the Platonic love-affair of Diana and Dacier.) In *One of Our Conquerors* music is no longer simply a literary symbol. It is essential to the experience of life which reaches us through the novel.

By the time Meredith came to write *One of Our Conquerors*, Donizetti and Verdi were no longer the stars of the operatic horizon. Now Wagner dominated the scene. The whole movement of the novel – which alone among Meredith's work attempts to register the range of *contemporary* consciousness – seems affected by Meredith's discovery of an operatic form which is in no way absurd, which penetrates to the level of myth and symbol, and which in its use of musical speech can express the unconscious, the inner consciousness and the spoken word simultaneously. Wagner dominates the mood of the book. He is Victor's first conqueror:

that mighty German with his *Rienzi*, and *Tannhäuser*, and *Tristan and Isolda* [*sic*], had mastered him, to the displacement of his boyhood's beloved sugary *-inis* and *-antes* and *-zettis*; had clearly mastered, not beguiled, him . . . (II, viii, 212).

To Victor himself Wagner appears to be an emanation of the modern world with its gloom and turmoil and anti-rationalism: 'I held out against Wagner as long as I could.' Wagner is also closely connected to London, the metropolis, in Victor's consciousness. It seems to me to be clear that T. S. Eliot had read this novel, with its scenes of the City workers streaming across London Bridge, its constant allusions to Wagner and particularly to *Tristan and Isolde*. As the city crowds walk westward home at the end of the day, 'There is immensity, swinging motion, collision, dusky richness of colouring, to the sight; and to the mind idea. London presents it.' But reason does not permit a song of praise to London the 'Titanic work of long-tolerated pygmies' because 'the pinched are here, the dinnerless, the weedy, the gutter-growths, the forces repressing them'. And mind is 'so low down beneath material accumulations' that London cannot be celebrated as it deserves, in Song (I, v, 71–2). Victor's sense of being overwhelmed by musical experience occurred also in *Sandra Belloni* thirty years earlier. Emilia, as an Italian patriot, feels bound to be hostile to Beethoven, but finds herself overpowered by him. In a description which strikingly foreshadows E. M. Forster's account of the 'goblins' in Beethoven's Fifth Symphony, she says: 'He sees angels, cherubs, and fairies, and imps, and devils; or he hears them: they come before him from far off, in music.' And 'He seems to be the master of my soul, mocking me, making me worship him in spite of my hate. He is like a black angel.' Victor Radnor's obsession with Wagner expresses the tragic strain in his experience – at moments of personal triumph he returns exuberantly to the Italians, 'singing the great aria of the fourth act of the *Favorita*'.

Within the book's artistry the presence of Wagner symbolizes the expressive grandeur, the interpenetration of psychological, social and mythic activity to which the novel aspires. Meredith does not turn music into words as he did in *Sandra Belloni* and as writers of the period commonly did. (Vernon Lee's *Music and Its Lovers*, London, 1932, gives an account of a questionnaire she set in the early 1900s which vividly demonstrates how listeners of the period tended to pictorialize and describe music in images.) He gives us precise musical references and expects us to read the novel with the music moving in our minds, filling out the words on the page. At times the dense texture of the writing, the thronging activity of the action, the scale of the emotions and the intense introspection demanded of one as a reader has a nightmare effect like listening to a full-scale performance of *The Ring* in a room of chamber-music dimensions.

Wagner's *Tristan and Isolde* provides the basic myth of the book. Nataly thinks: 'She and Victor had drunk of a cup. The philtre was in her veins, whatever the directions of the rational mind' (I, vi, 93). How can overwhelming love find a place for itself within society? Victor's marriage to Mrs Burman was physically repugnant, demeaning. His escape with Nataly was inevitable, unregretted. But marriage is long and must live within a society. Victor wants to dominate society, Nataly longs to be independent of it. In the curious chapter near the beginning of the novel which seeks to mark out the oddities of the British through the remote sophistication of an Indian eye, Meredith quotes from 'that nationally interesting Poem, or Dramatic Satire, once famous, *The Rajah in London* (London, Limbo and Sons, 1889)'.

The doubly-wedded man and wife,
Pledged to each other and against the world
With mutual union.[3]

Victor and Nataly avoid this rejection of the world, but at the price of immense emotional strain. They cannot accept society's judgment, but they cannot live in utter isolation. Musical evenings with their friends alone can resolve the dilemma for the space of time that they last.

In the earlier version (now in the Altschul Collection, Yale University Library) the novel was entitled 'A Conqueror in Our Time'. The shift to *One of Our Conquerors* is significant. Meredith is not simply writing a satire on the times or on his hero. In the earlier version he seems to suggest that Victor's election to the status of conqueror defines what is wrong with society. But as he wrote and rewrote, his suffering intimacy with his hero increased. Victor is materialistic, superstitious, unreflective, unwise. Nataly comes to see 'his mortality in the miraculous things he did'. He does not recognize Nataly's silent tragedy. But he is also charged with emotional energy and intelligence. When in his madness he says he is a 'caged lion', the epitaph seems fitting.

This is the only one of Meredith's novels set in the City and concerned with the society he saw about him. (Its significance in Meredith's career is in many ways equivalent to *Jude the Obscure* for Hardy.) But it goes beyond social commentary and satire towards something more universal. There are other conquerors besides Victor within the book. One of them is Wagner. The other is Death. The whole book is lived in the shadow of deaths awaited and achieved. The theme is given a ritual form when Victor and his friends visit the Mausoleum at Dreux. Victor Radnor, so full of life, must thrive on the deaths of others. The 'murderous hope' of Mrs Burman's death seeps into the substance of his relationship with Nataly. Almost the finest scene in the book is that where Victor and Nataly visit the dying Mrs Burman and all dreads and delusions vanish – their obsession wizens into a quiet old woman.

The book is held – alternately cramped and stretched – on a series of obsessive parallels. In its course, four wives die, and the theme of seduction and 'fallen women' implicates almost every character in the book. The book is, ambitiously, about the state of social man – that is, fallen man. Victor's fall on London Bridge starts his journey towards self-knowledge and death.[4] It is an absurdly material representation: a City gentleman slips on a piece of peel. Victor, like the society he heads, recognizes facts, not emblems. The novel charts his journey into the 'Impalpable'.

The ageing Meredith in this novel makes his own purgatorial journey. He faced the dilemmas of his creativity: his delight in intelligence and wit, his pleasure in unravelling the web of consciousness, and yet, growing alongside these, his distrust of satire, of formulation, even of language itself. *One of Our Conquerors* was written between 1888 and 1890. It was his first work of fiction since his wife's death from cancer in September 1885. On 1 January 1886 he wrote to Morley: 'The thought often uppermost is in amazement at the importance we attach to our hold of sensation. So much grander, vaster, seems her realm of silence.' While he was at work on the book he wrote to Mrs Jessop (1 July 1889): 'My work . . . holds me to it with rigour; and I have much to say; and my time on the surface of our sphere is short.' Meredith wrote the work urgently. He was emotionally alone, ill, increasingly deaf. It is his final artistic challenge; in it he uses all 'the old lamps for lighting an abysmal darkness'. The book itself becomes an image of the obverse of consciousness. Its profundity is scarred, gloomy, at times barely decipherable. It shies away from coherence. Yet it is sometimes extremely, deliberately funny. It explores the self beyond language; even, finally, poignantly, the self beyond sound: Meredith writes out of his gathering deafness, Victor is forbidden music in his madness. The book is, perhaps, Meredith's own *Götterdämmerung*.

Notes

1 All references are to the 1st ed. and run volume, chapter, page.
2 The remarks used in *Diana* are:
   Two men (on London Bridge). 'Have you tried any of this cold stuff they sell with cream?'
   'I haven't much opinion o' that. What's it like?'
   'Well it's cheap, it's not bad: it's cooling, but it ain't refreshing.'
   'Just what I reckined it.' (Compare Memorial ed., 457.)
   Old man looking on at the cutting up of a 'family' pig: 'Ah could eat pig a solid hour.' (Compare Memorial ed., 98.)
   The second remark used in *One of Our Conquerors* is noted immediately before the old man and the pig under the same heading:
   Realistic 'This man with a lift of his little finger could convulse the Bacon Market.' (Compare 1st ed., II, vi, 152, 161. This little remark is also listed on another page as one of a series of projected 'Comediettas in Narrative', along with 'The Amazing Marriage (Gossip as Chorus)' and 'Diana (Mr N and Lord M)'.)
   This apparently trivial page of jottings establishes that Meredith was thinking about *Diana* and *One of Our Conquerors* at the same period.
   I am indebted to the Curators of Yale University Library for permission to cite the manuscript material in this essay.
3 This epigram is noted on a sheet of paper folded into one of the notebooks at Yale. The Black Notebook (the last of the series) includes several remarks used in *One of Our Conquerors* and *Lord Ormont and His Aminta*.
4 'Victor lies in his bath, thinking, after the visit to Mrs Burman. He tries to remember his Idea:
   'Only the vision was wanted. On London Bridge he had *seen* it – a great thing done to the flash of brilliant results. That was after a fall.
   'There had been a fall also of the scheme of Lakelands.
   'Come to us with no superstitious whispers of indications and significations in the fall! – But there had certainly been a moral fall, fully to the level of the physical, in the maintaining of that scheme of Lakelands, now ruined by his incomprehensible Nesta – who had saved him from falling further. His bath-water chilled' (III, xiii, 271–2).

One of Our Conquerors
and the Country of the Blue

Bernard A. Richards

The phrase 'country of the blue' occurs in a short story by Henry
James called 'The Next Time', written four years after Meredith's
One of Our Conquerors, in 1895. The country is a world of abstraction and artistic isolation inhabited by Ray Limbert during his
literary career. He is tempted to vulgarize his style to make the
money needed to support his wife and family, but he cannot do it,
and, as the narrator says, his bid for popularity merely produces
another variation of his artistic gifts, and the novel may still be
compared with the superior and distant character of the sky:

> I fidgeted to my high-perched window for a glimpse of the
> summer dawn, I became at last aware that I was staring at it
> out of eyes that had compassionately and admiringly filled.
> The eastern sky, over the London house-tops, had a
> wonderful tragic crimson. That was the colour of his
> magnificent mistake (174–5).[1]

Later, the narrator says that Limbert 'belongs to the heights – he
breathes there, he lives there' (183). Limbert moves into the
country to live, as it is cheaper. His work is nourished by springs
within, so he needs neither the society of London nor of 'goose-
green', to draw on. Once out of London, the demands of literature
as a business seem less urgent, and then drop away altogether. He is
at work on one more of what the narrator takes to be a literary gem
when he dies:

> He had merely waked up one morning again in the country of
> the blue and had stayed there with a good conscience and a
> great idea (193–4).

He lives in a world of limbo, but is not discontent to do so. Perhaps his name is a pun on this fact. The phrase has been given a wider critical currency by an article on James's attitude to art, written by R. P. Blackmur.[2] The article is unnecessarily obscure at times, and does not make sufficient allowance for the possible delusion of the narrator. Blackmur makes clear that the phrase 'country of the blue' connotes the remoteness and beauty of the visionary countries of the mind, which artists and dreamers try to reach before they die. The significance of the colour blue and its associations with the sky and imaginative distance was not new to James in 1895. He had associated the colour with aesthetic isolation as far back as *Roderick Hudson* (1875): Roderick's place of retirement in America looks towards the 'blue undulation of the horizon'.

The young heroine of *What Maisie Knew* views sophisticated and integrated ways of life as a 'prospect of statues shining in the blue and of courtesy in romantic forms' (240).

The idea of blue as a symbol of remoteness was not originated by James. William J. Lillyman has outlined its nineteenth-century history, beginning with Wordsworth, in *Otto Ludwig's 'Zwischen Himmel und Erde'* (The Hague and Paris, 1967). As far as one can see, the idea is one of the great archetypes of human thought, but it was in the nineteenth century that it gained greatest literary currency. Perhaps the first significant appearance in a novel was in Flaubert's *Madame Bovary*, published in 1856 – the same year as *Zwischen Himmel und Erde*. In pt. III, ch. vi, when Emma is beginning to get tired of Leon, she fabricates an ideal man inhabiting ethereal realms, though the process is a prelude to a fall to earth:

> Il habitait la contrée bleuâtre où les échelles de soie se
> balancent à des balcons, sous le souffle des fleurs, dans la
> clarté de la lune. Elle le sentait près d'elle, il allait venir et
> l'enlèverait tout entière dans un baiser. Ensuite elle retombait
> à plat, brisée; car ces élans d'amour vague la fatiguaient plus
> que de grandes débauches.[3]

When we read nineteenth-century novels, it is frequently necessary to develop complex habits of interpretation. At one level, we can read them as documents of morals and manners, and at another level as romances, where details of the settings and the thoughts of the characters do not seem to have a strong factual and logical connection, but do have significant poetic cohesion. This is true of

Dickens, whose novels often have a recognizable symbolic structure, as well as a more conventional structure of characterization and narrative. The symbolic structure of Dickens has only been given close attention in the twentieth century, and this has applied principally to the later novels; but even in *Dombey and Son* (1846), written ten years before *Madame Bovary*, we find characters thinking and behaving in symbolic terms. Walter Gay dreams of carrying Florence Dombey 'away to the blue shores of somewhere or other'. The novels of George Eliot and Henry James, though having any amount of apparent 'realism', are capable of being interpreted in a symbolic fashion and, what is much more significant, frequently half-invite such interpretations. George Eliot and Henry James repressed, or failed to develop, poetic modes of thought achieving expression in conventional verse forms, and these modes of thought could not but help find expression in their prose works. Meredith developed his poetic gifts, and though he expressed himself in verse he did not exclude his poetic instincts from his narrative prose works, and his novels sustain and invite a criticism in poetic terms. Barbara Hardy has submitted *Harry Richmond* (1871) to this type of approach,[4] and Bernard Brunner[5] and Joseph E. Kruppa[6] have dealt with later works. In the novels of Dickens, James and George Eliot, the 'symbolism' is less necessary to a complete understanding of the works, and we can form our views of characters and their actions by referring to page-by-page surface details. This is less the case with Meredith. As Henry James said, his action is so little grounded in what one could describe as a concrete and graspable world, and it is so difficult to evaluate characters, that we need other guides to interpretation. When coming to an understanding of Meredith's work, it is sometimes the case that reading habits nurtured by the works of Spenser and Blake are of more use than reading habits acquired in studying Richardson and Jane Austen.

One of Our Conquerors has three main characters: Victor Radnor, his mistress, Nataly, and their daughter, Nesta. Victor is attempting to win over society to his liaison with Nataly, and, though having very conservative instincts, especially as regards the emancipation of women, he does have glimmerings of half-formed and half-graspable notions for the regeneration of England and its aristocracy. These notions are his 'Idea', but their pursuit occasions a symbolic fall on London Bridge at the beginning of the novel, numerous subsequent pains at the back of the head, and an end in madness and death. His ill-directed energy and his onslaught on English society to get himself and his Bohemian family accepted are more than Nataly can stand, and it helps to drive her to the grave. In one sense, Victor is going along with 'Nature' and severing the unnatural connection with his wife, Mrs Burman; but in another sense he is violating it. The 'violation' occurs because Victor attaches more importance to his role in English society and to England's place in the Empire than to his personal and immediate relationships. He is hoping to bring his intimate life into line with his larger social plans. The setting he establishes for the scene of his intended victory over society is 'unnatural'. It is a house called Lakelands, built hastily and in secret, a red blot on Nature, 'a stately pleasure dome indeed', with the botanical and human flowers protected and nurtured under the glass of the conservatory. The very name 'Lakelands' reeks of new paint. Victor has a 'country of the blue' for himself, his family and for England, but it is a disastrous goal, as it does not take earthly realities sufficiently into account. Nesta's temperament resembles her father's. She does not have the timidity and unadventurousness of her mother, and she has her visionary country. Nesta is in the family of the disciplined and active women often found in Meredith's novels, of whom Diana of the Crossways is the most famous. Nesta is offered as the earthly counterpart of Artemis, the goddess who symbolizes the 'breath of upper air', and the spirit of strictness in the poem 'With the Huntress' (1901). Her progress in the novel is a process of reconciling idealism and the demands of Nature. She manages to use her other-worldly yearnings to live an earthly, adventurous life, not to be hampered by them. The patterns of thought I have just outlined can emerge in retrospect, when one has put down the novel, but they are very difficult to pick up in the course of reading, unless one is prepared to give symbolic or emblematic interpretations to events and scenes which have a disarming way of appearing 'realistic'. I prefer the word 'emblem' to the word 'symbol' when analysing many parts of *One of Our Conquerors*, because 'emblem' suggests delimited and specific areas of meaning which one can tag on to concrete objects or happenings, whereas 'symbol' suggests objects and events radiating multiple and mysterious meanings. There are symbolical passages in the novel, but the definiteness and localized restriction of the emblem is more common.

Ch. i begins with one of the most pregnant slips on the pavement in literature. Victor is trying to grasp ideas on the role of England and its classes. He falls and comes into discomforting contact with a member of the working class, and the episode disquiets his musings on the visionary seaman of Old England, who can be heard 'around and aloft whistling us back to the splendid strain of muscle' (8).[7] Even this early in the novel the western sky is being associated with the romantic past and future of England, and the eastern sky with the commercial past and future. The east is less inviting, as it is associated with Mammon. Victor looks east along the Thames:

> . . . along an avenue, not fabulously golden, of the deputy masts of all nations, a wintry woodland, every rag aloft curling to volume; and here the spouts and the mounds of steam, and rolls of brown smoke there, variously undulated, curved to vanish; cold blue sky ashift with the whirl and dash of a very Tartar cavalry of cloud overhead (7).

The sun is associated with money and commerce in a poem which is referred to in the novel, 'The Rajah in London'. This is one of those infuriating, non-existent literary works which is casually alluded to in Meredith's novels. This particular one is a sort of nineteenth-century *Lettres Persanes* for London. The London merchants who live in the West End and work in the City are seen as sun-worshippers. The idea is naïve, yet points to a kind of truth. The Oriental prince observes 'the march of London citizens Eastward at morn, Westward at eve', and 'attributes their practice to a survival of the Zoroastrian form of worship' (36). The fact that they so rarely see the sun makes their worship more remarkable. The sun, sky and clouds preside over London: sometimes their magnificence contemns the grime of the capital, sometimes the skies share the contamination of the earth below and sometimes the glories of the sky and the glories of the earth are related. Ch. v is called 'The London Walk Westward', and though there is not as close a correspondence of earthly activity and transcendental symbolism as in Wordsworth's 'Stepping Westward', the connection between earth and heaven is hinted at, and it is quite possible that Meredith had the poem in mind. The walk westward is from the City, home to Nataly and Nesta, on the day he is to tell them about Lakelands and his projected assault on English society. Victor hopes for a union of Nature and idealism – a union typified by the glory and optimism of the western sky over Hyde Park. It is

April and a time of promise, yet in the time-span of the novel, which is just over a year, disaster comes to Victor:

> In April, the month of piled and hurried cloud, it is a Rape of the Sabines overhead from all quarters, either one of the winds brawnily larcenous; and London, smoking royally to the open skies, builds images of a dusty epic fray for possession of the portly dames. There is immensity, swinging motion, collision, dusky richness of colouring, to the sight; and to the mind idea. London presents it. If we can allow ourselves a moment for not inquireing scrupulously . . . here is a noble harmony of heaven and the earth of the works of man, speaking a grander tongue than barren sea or wood or wilderness (39).

The skies transfigure London:

> Clouds of high colour above London City are as the light of the Goddess to lift the angry heroic head over human. They gloriously transfigure. A Murillo beggar is not more precious than sight of London in any of the streets admitting coloured cloud-scenes; the cunning of the sun's hand so speaks to us (41).

Other emblems of harmony and unification appeal to Victor as he walks westwards – the poster advertising Harlequin and Columbine, for instance. And he is fortunate in missing his wife, who is in a chemist's shop, indulging in a hypochondriac voyeurism through a mirror – away from the light of day, in a burlesque-Platonic cave of ignorance. Once near Piccadilly, presided over by the statue of Eros, he sees ahead the green and blue distances of hope and fulfilment:

> Along the street of Clubs, where a bruised fancy may see black balls raining, the narrow way between ducal mansions offers prospect of the sweep of greensward, all but touching up to the sunset to draw it to the dance (45).

This symbol of union is used frequently in the poems:

> That was the chirp of Ariel
> You heard, as overhead it flew,
> The farther going more to dwell,
> And wing our green to wed our blue.
>   ('Wind on the Lyre.')

The significance of the Park does not remain static in the novel. In a hopeful time, the Park offers tranquillity, peace and union with Nature, but it is also associated with the exclusive aristocracy, and Victor has sacrificed 'a slice of his youth' to gain a footing in 'one of these great surrounding houses' (45). The west of Wordsworth's 'Stepping Westward', on the other hand, is unequivocal:

> The dewy ground was dark and cold:
> Behind, all gloomy to behold;
> And stepping westward seemed to be
> A kind of heavenly destiny:
> I liked the greeting; 'twas a sound
> Of something without place or bound;
> And seemed to give me spiritual right
> To travel through that region bright.

The women Wordsworth meets add a touch of humanity and civilization to a scene of overpowering natural and mystical beauty, and he is helped to respond to it. In *One of Our Conquerors*, when Nesta accompanies Victor, she is almost capable of doing the same, of helping to show him the links connecting Nature and ideas, but not quite:

> she was the very daylight to his mind, whatsoever their theme of converse: for by stimulating that ready but vagrant mind to quit the leash of the powerful senses and be aethereally excursive, she gave him a new enjoyment; which led to reflections – a sounding of Nature, almost a question to her, on the verge of a doubt. Are we, in fact, harmonious with the Great Mother when we yield to the pressure of our natures for indulgence? Is she, when translated into us, solely the imperious appetite? Here was Fredi, his little Fredi – stately girl that she had grown, and grave, too, for all her fun and her sail on wings – lifting him to pleasures not followed by clamorous, and perfectly satisfactory, yet discomposingly violent, appeals to Nature (480).

The Park emblem is enigmatic. It can be used to embody the idea of the mystic union of heaven and earth; but it can also mean the idea of ultra-conservative aristocratic society, and the emblem undergoes an admonitory transformation in ch. xxxvi. It is a winter day, and it is the day when Nesta learns of her illegitimacy. Victor does not walk home, but is conveyed in Lady Grace Halley's carriage. She is an artificial drawing-room comet and a potential source of seduction for Victor. She cannot take one into 'the country of the blue'. Dreams associated with her end up on the 'bald ceiling' lit by the 'gas-bladder's tight extension upon emptiness' (422). And the Park is artificially lit too, and embodying a different family of meanings. Victor sees the possibility of a liaison with Lady Grace, and an entry into a society which will have the coldness and deadness of the winter Park:

> the campaign gathered a circling suggestive brilliancy, like the lamps about the winter park; the Society, lured with glitter, hooked by greed, composed a ravishing picture . . . (423).

In a hellish moment, Victor finds himself 'full of the grandeur of the black pit of the benighted London, with its ocean-voice of the heart at beat along the lighted outer ring' (423). Victor has a vague ideal, but not one to prove helpful and practical. It is as unrelated to the world as Nelson on his column. The statue is referred to several times, and reminds one of other passages in Meredith where statues have a stiff and unwordly existence: *Harry Richmond* in particular. Victor's progress is hard to chart. What are his ideas exactly? It is difficult to say. They occupy an uncomfortable position between Radicalism and a sympathy for a Carlylean enlightened oligarchy. They lurk behind curtains and veils. They seem to point, in Meredith's symbolic language, to a severance of heart and head, body and soul, heaven and earth. Nesta's progress is easier to chart, so is Dartrey Fenellan's: they are moving towards the state outlined by 'The Rajah in London':

> The doubly-wedded man and wife,
> Pledged to each other and against the world
> With mutual onion [*sic*]. (38)

Nesta's progress at first is to the country of the blue, which is totally abstracted from the ordinary world, and is in fact near to Ray Limbert's country and to Meredith's 'Garden of Epicurus': 'fenced from passion and mishap/A shining spot upon a shaggy map'. In so far as her dreams include men, they have the remoteness and fixity of statues. In a conversation with Nesta, the soldierly Dartrey Fenellan says, 'There's very little of the Don Amoroso in me. Women don't worship stone figures' (360). Nesta replies, 'They do: – like the sea-birds. And what do you say to me, Dartrey? I can confess it: I am one of them: I love you' (360). Her father is right in thinking that young girls demand 'definite' figures: 'no mercy is in them for the transitional' (432). Nesta's early ideals are focused at Dreux, where she encounters the monumental statue of St Louis, having been introduced to the mausoleum of the House of Orléans by her governess. Ch. xvii is a study of Nesta's reactions to the scene. The King exemplifies what she wants in a hero and a man:

> With such a King, there would be union of the old order and the new, cessation to political turmoil: Radicalism, Socialism, all the monster names of things with heads agape in these our days to gobble-up the venerable, obliterate the beautiful, leave a stoniness of floods where field and garden were, would be appeased, transfigured (179).

At this period of her life union of heaven and earth is not possible, with sex as such a disruptive force: 'there was a torment of earth and a writhing of lurid dust-clouds about it at a glimpse' (179). These early ardours are a plunge into 'mediaeval imaginativeness'. This period of her life has to be outgrown. St Louis was virginal, and, as Meredith reminds us, usurped. Nesta mistakes what is 'a message from death' as 'a lesson of life' (179). During much of the novel her own thoughts, and the opinions of other people about her, are expressed in terms of the unearthly existence of clouds, sky, birds and butterflies. Meredith is surely thinking of the association of the butterfly and the Psyche myth. Dartrey Fenellan regards Nesta as a 'blue butterfly' (388), and at a concert she is described as 'the little blue butterfly' (427). As she develops it is from a butterfly into another being of the upper air, an eaglet (455). She is associated with the swallow, and turns Dudley Sowerby's cynical philosophy of transience (adopted from Confucius) into her own symbolic language. Dudley says: 'To set one's love upon the swallow is futility.' Nesta retorts: 'May not the pleasure for us remain if we set our love upon the beauty of the swallow's flight?' (417). Her imaginative flights are bound to have their falls. Nesta's dreams are shattered first of all by the man who helped to create them – the guide to Dreux, Mr Septimus Barmby. He declares his love, and her vision of man is nothing like 'the descent of the shape celestial':

> . . . he had shivered her mediaeval forest-palace of illuminated glass, to leave her standing like a mountain hind, that sniffs

the tainted gale off the crag of her first quick leap from
hounds; her instincts alarmed, instead of rich imagination
colouring and fostering (184).

Nesta is not permanently disoriented by the experience, and an
ironic wit is her saving grace. Even so, her virgin world is disturbed, and she retires into her visionary country again, with the
image of the heroic Dartrey Fenellan growing gradually. When she
sees Dartrey in Brighton, she reads his face, and once again blue is
the impressionistic colour of perfection: 'that face of his, so clearly
lined, quick, firm, with the blue smile on it like the gleam of a
sword coming out of a sheath, did not mean hardness, she could
have vowed' (354). Nesta does win Dartrey in the end, but she has
to be brought down to earth three times more after her experience
with Septimus Barmby. Her first deflating experience is with the
young man her parents would like her to marry, Dudley Sowerby, a
stiff Tory with a distaste for metaphorical language. In ch. xxix this
is her attitude to Dudley:

> The choice her parents had made for her in Dudley, behind
> the mystery she had scent of, nipped her dream, and prepared
> her to meet, as it were, the fireside of a November day
> instead of springing up and into the dawn's blue of full
> summer with swallows on wing (348).

I have already quoted Dudley's anti-swallow maxim (417). In so
far as Dudley does inhabit the sky-world, it is as a futile rocket,
which must come down like a stick:

> Victor sighed too. He saw the earldom, which was to dazzle
> the gossips, crack on the sky in a futile rocket-bouquet (492).

When Nesta missed Dudley on a train journey, we are told that had
she seen him, 'her eagle of imagination would have reeled from the
heights' (414). He melts out of her thoughts 'like the vanishing
steam-wreath on the dip between the line and the downs' (412).
Smoke as an emblem is recurrent in the novel: a degraded and
mechanically produced cloud effect, easily dispersed. Dudley has
periodic attractiveness for Nesta, but for the most part he is too
humdrum a figure for her.

A more significant coming-to-earth for Nesta is her contact with
Judith Marsett. As in Strindberg's *The Dance of Death* (1901), the
Scriptural associations of the name are brought out: 'I did some-

thing in scripture. Judith could again' (339). Meredith's Judith is
unconventional, tortured and 'fallen'. It is through her that Nesta
gains insight into the sexual and almost animal existence lurking
beneath the veneer of society. The theme of curtained knowledge
runs through the novel. Because of Mrs Marsett, Nesta peers
behind the veil. In some ways she is horrified: she feels as if she
were 'guilty of knowing' and 'breaking out in spots' (352) before
her maiden aunts, and her new knowledge is 'crimson-lighted'
(353). But in other ways the knowledge is good and enlarges her
capacity for sympathy: 'she had a rebellious rush of sympathy for
our evil-fortuned of the world; the creatures in the battle, the
wounded, trodden, mud-stained . . .' (353). Nataly is alarmed at
Nesta's contact, and thinks that Nesta will condemn her by
associating her fate with Judith's. She underestimates Nesta's
progress. The revulsion could have been a feature of a younger
Nesta, but by this stage in the novel she is beginning to develop
the capacity of living both in the country of the mind and the world
of fact, and of attempting to reconcile the two. It is as well for
the fortunes of Dartrey Fenellan that she is developing this
capacity, as he too has fallen in her estimation by being involved
in a fight not Homeric, but burlesque-Homeric, on behalf of the
Salvation Army. Her train flight in ch. xxxiv is an attempt to
detach herself from the weight of events. It is similar to her
mother's train-ride from London to Penshurst in ch. xxv. The
train is moving, but gives the mind a context for detached reflection: 'the mind is lighted for radiation' (308). Nesta looks from the
carriage window, has music in her head, and uses elements in the
landscape for her reflective purposes:

> She passed into music, as she always did under motion of
> carriages and trains, whether in happiness or sadness: and the
> day being one that had a sky, the scenic of music swung her
> up to soar. None of her heavy burdens enchained, though she
> knew the weight of them, with those of other painful souls.
> The pipeing at her breast gave wings to large and small of the
> visible; and along the downs went stateliest of flowing dances;
> a copse lengthened to forest; a pool of cattle-water caught
> grey for flights through enchantment. Cottage-children,
> wherever seen in groups, she wreathed above with angels to
> watch them. Her mind all the while was busy upon earth,
> embracing her mother, eyeing her father. Imagination and our

ι

earthly met midway, and still she flew, until she was brought
to the ground by a shot. She struggled to rise, uplifting
Judith Marsett: a woman not so very much older than her
own teens, in the count of years, and ages older; and the
world pulling at her heels to keep her low. That unhappiest
had no one but a sisterly girl to help her: and how she clung
to the slender help! (412–13).

When she thinks of Dartrey, 'for the first time of her life she found
herself seized with her sex's shudder in the blood' (414). From this
point on Nesta's earthly imagination becomes more important.
When attempting to save her father, she walks westward with him:
'She was trying to be a student of life, with her eyes down upon
hard earth, despite of her winged young head' (430). Dartrey
recognizes and appreciates this development in her:

> Here and far there we meet a young saint vowed to service
> along by those dismal swamps: and saintly she looks; not of
> this earth. Nesta was of the blooming earth. Where do we
> meet girl or woman comparable to garden-flowers who can
> dare to touch to lift the spotted of her sex? (456).

At this stage Nesta is learning to be suspicious of heights and
abstractions. In a conversation with Dudley, she disdains 'that real
haven of refuge, with its visionary mount of superiority, offered by
Society to its elect, in the habit of ignoring the sin it fosters under
cloak' (474). This mount is a false country of retirement. Nesta and
Dartrey marry, and the marriage expresses 'a longing for the
snow-heights' (511). Now she is ready to engage in life, love and
action. She has escaped from the shadow of death, money and
society. Nataly and Victor were unable to escape and their bondage
was at once typified and instituted by Victor's wife – Mrs Burman.
It is left to the younger generation to make the escape. Victor's
energy is misdirected and dissipated. Nataly is timid, ill and not
cast in the new mould – though in many ways she is the most
attractive and life-like character in the book. Nataly does have a
vision of redemption, at least if not for her, for her daughter. Just
before the momentous journey to Penshurst, to tell Dudley of
Nesta's illegitimacy, she has a vision of what Victor promised to be,
and the vision fuses with a vision of what Dartrey can be:

> A drooping mood in her had been struck; he had a look like
> the winged lyric up in blue heavens: he raised the head of the

young flower from its contemplation of grave-mould. That was when he had much to bear: Mrs Burman present: and when the stranger in their household had begun to pity him and have a dread of her feelings. The lucent splendour of his eyes was memorable, a light above the rolling oceans of Time (307).

Nataly was 'revolutionary' in living illegally with Victor, but 'reactionary' in not being assertive enough, and continuing in the traditional role of woman as a slave and a theoretical preserver of questionable proprieties. Towards the very end of the novel Victor and Nataly encounter Mrs Burman at the point of death, and see in her face and clothes an emblem of the contradictions they have been unable to resolve, but which their daughter may resolve. They see her face 'emerge from a pale blue silk veiling; as it were, the inanimate wasted led up from the mould by morning' (487).

The whole work has a kind of poetic logic in it, but as a novel it could hardly be said to have gratified the certain known habits of association for the later Victorian public. The vaguely mystical ideas, the weighty phrases embedded in allusive passages and the distortions of syntax could be acceptable in a poem, but hardly in a novel of this length. We are less prepared to suspend disbelief in encountering a prose narrative, and ideas acceptable in a poem begin to weaken when given extended articulation in a novel. *One of Our Conquerors* makes a bid to put across many of the ideas of 'The Sage Enamoured', and though this is many ways an appalling poem the economy and nakedness of the statement has an attractiveness which is not shared by the novel:

For us the double conscience and its war,
The serving of two masters, false to both,
Until those twain, who spring the root and are
The knowledge in division, plight a troth
Of equal hands: nor longer circulate
A pious token for their current coin,
To growl at the exchange; they, mate and mate,
Fair feminine and masculine shall join
Upon an upper plane, still common mould,
Where stamped religion and reflective pace
A statelier measure, and the hoop of gold
Rounds to horizon for their soul's embrace.
Then shall those noblest of the earth and sun

Inmix unlike to waves on savage sea.
But not till Nature's laws and man's are one,
Can marriage of the man and woman be.

We must admire Meredith's courage, stubbornness and originality
in trying to do in a novel what Blake would only attempt in
Prophetic Books, but most of us are bound to be more drawn
towards half-realized neo-Platonism in poetry than in novels.

Notes

1 Quotations from Henry James are from *The Novels and Stories of Henry James*, 1921–3.
2 R. P. Blackmur, 'In the Country of the Blue', *Kenyon Review*, 1943, 595–617.
3 *Madame Bovary*, Paris, 1958, 270.
4 Barbara Hardy, ' "A way to your Hearts through Fire or Water" ': The Structure of Imagery in *Harry Richmond*', *Essays in Criticism*, 1960, x, 163–80.
5 Bernard A. Brunner, 'Meredith's Symbolism: *Lord Ormont and his Aminta*', *Nineteenth-century Fiction*, 1953, viii, 124–33.
6 Joseph E. Kruppa, 'Meredith's Late Novels: Suggestions for a Critical Approach', *Nineteenth-century Fiction*, 1964, xix, 271–86.
7 Quotations from Meredith are from *The Works of George Meredith* (The Memorial Edition), 1910.

Lord Ormont and his Aminta and The Amazing Marriage

Barbara Hardy

I want to look at these two late novels together, at the risk of doing less than justice to *Lord Ormont and his Aminta*, because they have made plain to me what I find good and bad in Meredith. Their chronological neighbourhood and their strong affinities of story and theme throw their difference in fictional quality into strong relief.

I think it is necessary to say something about the quality of Meredith's achievement. As with other very mannered artists, critics are either too totally repelled to say much of interest or too totally won over and absorbed in the mannerism to see anything wrong in it. The polarity of hostility and admiration tends to be self-perpetuating: the more rudely Meredith is excluded from the Great Tradition without much in the way of argument, the more passionately his admirers protest. The protest is very understandable. Even to read one novel properly (with the possible exception of the very accessible *Harry Richmond*) involves considerable investment of time and mental energy which naturally direct us towards justification by profits. And as with other cases of mannerism, the slow and patient reading that his obscure narrative and clotted prose demand tend to over-acclimatize us to the mannerism. This can happen with Henry James, George Moore, or Ronald Firbank, but in Meredith it is almost guaranteed by the combination of artificiality with difficulty, and in a fairly even spread throughout the novels. With James, for instance, the habituation to mannerism can happen gradually, as the novels grow more mannered and difficult, as they do, in a gradual curve, steepening towards the end. Or it can simply break off, with the late novels, so that much hostility to James is hostility to late James. But Meredith's mannerism and obscurity are present from the beginning, and though I would not want to suggest that they do not vary from novel to novel, in form and degree, there is no slow development which habituates us gradually or alienates us at certain points. Meredith criticism does tend to fall apart into all-or-nothing judgments. I think this is a pity, not because I am particularly interested in the sport of submitting literature to competitive and carefully graded examinations, but because I am interested in the imagination and values of Meredith, and believe that his admirers can afford (and need) to become tougher with their author and themselves.

Lord Ormont and his Aminta is a more readable and simple version of 'the Meredith novel' than *The Amazing Marriage*, but it is also, in my opinion, a novel which shows him at his most sentimental, and where the famous artificiality serves the interests of the sentimentality. *The Amazing Marriage* has that particularity and continuity which *Lord Ormont* lacks, and expresses and explores the same ideas and values with complexity and completeness, justifying the mannerism which postures vapidly, like Sir Willoughby Patterne, in *Lord Ormont*.

Perhaps one reason why Meredith appeals to some of us is his apparent worldliness, his refreshing difference, in candour and toughness about love, marriage, egoism, women, religion – so many of the mid-Victorian sacred cows. In worldly awareness and dislike of contemporary cant, Thackeray was, of course, before him, but Thackeray has a marvellous capacity for acknowledging the walls of convention and propriety he cannot respect, leaving them standing, effective resonators for his irony and satire. Meredith comes late enough to break down these walls, and we tend to find his sheer extension of subject and lack of moral and religious cant refreshing and exciting.

In practice I suspect that we like Meredith not because he is really less sentimental about faith and ethics and social convention than Dickens and George Eliot, but because he is sentimental about different things. His is the sentimentality of the 1890s, which still has a certain appealing, if diminishing, affinity with our own: it tends to be strongly affirmative about youth rather than babies, about sex rather than true love, about the right relationship rather than the perfect marriage, about nature rather than God, feminism rather than womanliness, discovery of identity rather than the moral change of heart. We might want to say that Meredith's beliefs are progressive, or *avant-garde* in the double sense that implies both courage and progress, but his ninetyish *avant-garde* sentimentality is still sentimentality. He can become as ludicrously ecstatic, soft and blurred on the subjects of feminism, England and co-education as Dickens could on the subjects of womanly virtue, religion and child-death. It is this sentimentality which marks Meredith at his worst, and whose triumphant absence marks him at his best. It has also, I suggest, an interesting relation to his mannerism and his obscurity. When Meredith is flaccidly and pompously directing our sympathies, his artificial style and elliptical manner can work in the interests of evasion and open invitation to the feelings. But artificianty and obscurity are still present when his values and ideas are more thoroughly and toughly analysed. There is no simple one-to-one relation.

Lord Ormont and his Aminta was published in 1894, *The Amazing Marriage* in 1895. The chronological relation was more complicated than these dates suggest, for he had been working on *The Amazing Marriage*, on and off, since finishing *The Egoist* in 1879. He was in fact writing both the last novels at once, so their twinship is as difficult to sort out as that of Esau and Jacob. Moreover, it is misleading to make too much of their similarity, convenient as it is for my purposes. It is sometimes said that novelists are always writing or trying to write (or sometimes trying not to write?) the same one novel, and a proper examination of Meredith's treatment of the amazing and unsatisfactory nature of marriage would certainly have to take in other novels too, including *Diana of the Crossways* and *The Egoist,* and also some novels not directly concerned with marriage at all, such as *The Tragic Comedians* and *One of Our Conquerors.* Amazing marriage – and few of the implications of that phrase would be irrelevant – is one of Meredith's obsessive themes, but as I am concerning myself with his last two novels, I say merely that their relationship is a fairly common one, since novelists frequently write novels in the conscious or unconscious attempt to recast or revise or rewrite the novels they have already written.

There is no simple and straightforward relation between his own broken marriage and his discussion in the novels. 'Modern Love' retold his own story with the painful eloquence and valuable reticence of poetry, and may perhaps have freed him for more impartial (or effectively disguised) contemplation of the difficulties and disadvantages of this *bourgeois* institution. In many of his novels he attacks marriage as a typically possessive and proprietorial relation, and I believe that his last novel, *The Amazing Marriage*, is the most effective mythological attack and the best novel. Perhaps it is no accident that its title comes closest to a generalized proclamation of theme, and that the framework of the novel is an argument and a struggle between a modern realistic novelist and a myth-making Dame Gossip. It has the kind of complex success that suggests that the qualities of good myth and good psychological fiction are not, after all, in opposition to each other.

The married woman was for Meredith as blatant a case of social oppression and unfair possession as the child was for Dickens or the working man for Mrs Gaskell. Let me quote a letter in which he makes this plain. He wrote it to Lady Ulrica Duncombe in April 1902:

> I give my sympathy to the stumbling human instrument of a possible progression—Have you read the Letters of Lady Sarah Lennox? Her history is instructive, you will know it. The wife of an ardent fox-hunter, she quits him for an amorous lord, and after a year retires to a penitential solitude, out of which she is drawn at last by a worthy man, to become the mother of the three Napiers. I follow her and am with her throughout. . . . By and by the world will smile on women who cut their own way out of a bad early marriage, or it will correct the present rough Marriage system. No young woman knows what she gives her hand to; she will never be wiser until boys and girls are brought up and educated together. Let me add, until English girls have wiser mothers. Such donkeys are those dames in all our classes! It is true that the upper need not to give so much instruction where knowledge is in the atmosphere—Apropos of Lady Sarah's story, an old Cornish lady told me of one ending differently. A hunting Squire of her neighbourhood had a very handsome wife, whom he valued at less than the fox's tail. One of the Vivians eyed her, admired, condoled, desired, and carried her off. Some days after, she was taken with compunction or compassion, and about midnight the forsaken squire sitting in his library heard three knocks at the window. That's Bess, he said, and let her in. She was for weeping and protesting

repentance . . . but he kissed her, taking the blame on himself, rightly, and the house was quiet. Old Lady Vivian, like many old ladies, had outgrown her notions of masculine sentiment in these matters; she said to my friend: 'What are the man's family making such a fuss about! My son only had her a fortnight!' Even young women have but a confused idea of this masculine sentiment of the complete possession, down to absorption. . . . I have tried in my time to enlighten them and humanise their males.[1]

The historical source for most of Meredith's attempts to write novels which shall 'enlighten and humanize' only make even plainer the need for enlightenment. Whatever his personal discontent, the amazing marriage was a social fact. And it is as a social fact that Meredith treats it, not attacking its permanence, its fragility, or its relation to other ties, but bringing out, in particularly plain cases of marriage between aristocrat and commoner, wealth and poverty, the acquisitive typicality of the institution. He brings this out – very noticeably in comparison with Dickens and George Eliot – not by describing the extremes of marital suffering in incompatibility, but, with increasing emphasis, in the ties and torments of reasonable, decent, complex and even compatible human beings. If we trace the subject through, especially from *The Egoist* to *The Amazing Marriage*, this kind of candour, completeness and complexity seems to grow. The squire who said, 'That's Bess', and the old lady who said, 'My son only had her a fortnight!' can usefully stay with us as models for Meredith's honest worldliness – the right kind of worldliness which is strongly opposed to cant, grandiose moralizing, and all kinds of lies, and believes like Ajax in fighting in broad daylight.

Lord Ormont and Lord Fleetwood are both aristocrats, of old family, great landed possessions and immense wealth. Their wives, Aminta and Carinthia, are commoners and very poor. In each novel it is as if Meredith wants to emphasize the psychic and sexual oppressiveness he analysed in *The Egoist* with a much clearer and fiercer attack on the institution. *The Egoist* and *Diana* were implicit attacks on *bourgeois* marriage, but their central and explicit concerns were broader. In his last novels Meredith narrows down his action and his theme. He narrowed it excessively in *Lord Ormont*, and he found the right form in *The Amazing Marriage*. In both novels he sorts out what he thinks about individual men and women getting

L*

married, getting unmarried, and finding alternatives, but the sorting out involved sentimental loss of control and distortion in the one, and very effective control in the other.

There are several ways in which both novels show an advance in identifying the subject. First, Meredith needs to show the difficulty even in a marriage of strong attachment. We never really see Diana's first marriage, but are shown its motivation, the rude assaults and assumptions surrounding a single woman: the marriage is simply written in as a hasty solution to economic need and isolation. We are told – and lengthily – that Clara has believed herself attached to Sir Willoughby Patterne, but what is dramatized is the slow and very difficult process of disentanglement. In the last two novels Meredith seems to be realizing that hard cases make bad myths: the January and May story, found in other Victorian novelists like Dickens, George Eliot and George Gissing, must not be told too allegorically or it will lack the particularity of a novel (obviously) and the typicality of the myth (perhaps a little less obviously). 'I have tried in my time to enlighten them and humanize their males': the attempt will be more eloquent if it concerns the likely ordinary case, not the terrible error of Dorothea's missionary enterprise in marrying Casaubon, or Sue's physical ill-matching with Phillotson or Connie Chatterley's bad luck with her husband's war-wound. Although Carinthia's is an amazing marriage, it is, in extravagant form, the story of recognizable affinity, passion and loss. Although there is too much ellipsis in *Lord Ormont*, we are both shown and told enough of Aminta's hero-worshipping and her aunt's mercenary and snobbish social climbing. Meredith is looking both at the social and economic reasons for marriage and the social and economic structure, even of marriages of feeling. It is, after all, self-evident that loveless and incompatible marriages are wrong, but all we can really learn from the stories of total incompatibility or abject impotence is that *bourgeois* society can make marriages, despite an absolute lack of relationship. Meredith also wants to say that *bourgeois* marriage, even based on feeling and compatibility, is a difficult and dangerous enterprise. He is letting himself in for an analysis that needs to be social and psychological. And he is making a much more fundamental criticism of the institution of marriage.

Both husbands marry 'beneath' them. Meredith's emphasis on Lord Ormont's disgust with his class and his country, and Lord Fleetwood's more intuitive version of the same feeling, excellently shifts the emphasis from the wives (both poor and both commoners) who marry high rank and great wealth. It is important not just that the women should marry out of strong feeling (though in each case there is an economic motive, most delicately handled) but that they should be seen as victims. Meredith emphasizes the purchasing-power of Ormont and Fleetwood, but he wants us to be less impressed by the actual purchase of the woman than by the power both rank and money exercise after the marriage. Aminta is deprived of social reputation, Carinthia of reputation, freedom, and security. The eventual release has great momentum, though very much more in *The Amazing Marriage*, where the relationships are much more intricate and held in suspense, and where the woman is subjected to very much greater, and very much less justified, restriction and pain. Both novels are feminist novels, and at the point of release or rescue Meredith makes this clear by forcing a large breach of convention. Lady Ormont not only leaves her 'tyrant' but goes off to live with an unconventional schoolmaster who has refused the obvious professions in favour of starting an international co-educational school. (The point is weakened when Lord Ormont dies and leaves the free lovers free to marry.) Carinthia not only leaves Fleetwood, but is willing to leave her child and to go off to the wars in Spain with her brother. (The point is weakened when this plan is frustrated and when Meredith marries her off to Owain Wythan.) He takes each action to the point of dismissing marriage as the vocation for woman, but can't quite make it.

Perhaps this is expecting too much of the liberalism of the 1890s, at least in public and moral art. But the woman is also presented in pastoral terms. As Empson would say, she is the 'swain' of Meredith's fiction. Here we find the first instance of the superiority of *The Amazing Marriage*. In *Lord Ormont* the pastoral theme is only slightly present, and made rather arch, hearty, and slightly ridiculous by associations with athletics, fresh air, and hygiene. Woman is shown as debarred from the free and healthy life, and, unable to play cricket or join in snowball fights. Aminta turns passionately to the hero-worship of a great general. Later a small girl rescues another child from drowning, helped, but from the rear, by her elder brother. Later still the declaration of love between Matey Weyburn and Brownie (Lady Ormont) is expressed and ritualized in the famous swimming scene. Last we see the free and healthy life in the progressive school in Switzerland. There is nothing wrong with these values: it was hard on girls to wear long skirts and not throw snowballs, a sea scene has great erotic potential, and there is nothing wrong with co-educational schools in healthy spots, with open windows and good food. (As is evident in the letter to Lady Ulrica, co-education was one of Meredith's designs for humanizing marriage.) But Meredith makes his pastoral small and rather ridiculous in such symbols, and, moreover, gushes over their value. I will quote some instances of his archness, his dangerous and jovial assumption of sympathy:

> Forth from the school-house door burst a dozen shouting lads, as wasps from the hole of their nest from a charge of powder. Out they poured whizzing; and the frog he leaped, and pussy ran and doubled before the hounds, and hockey-sticks waved and away went a ball. Cracks at the ball anyhow, was the game for the twenty-five minutes breather before dinner.
>
> 'French day!' said Calliani, hearing their cries.
> Then he bellowed 'Matthew! Giulio!'
> A lusty inversion of the order of the names and an Oberland jödel returned his hail. The school retreating caught up the Alpine cry in the distance. Here were lungs! Here were sprites! (xxx).

> Ah, friend Matey! And that was right and good on land; but rightness and goodness flung earth's shadow across her brilliancy here, and any stress on 'this once' withdrew her liberty to revel in it, putting an end to perfect holiday; and silence, too, might hint at fatigue. She began to think her muteness lost her the bloom of the enchantment, robbing her of her heavenly frolic lead, since friend Matey resolved to be as eminently good in salt water as on land. Was he unaware that they were boy and girl again? – she washed pure of the intervening years, new born, by blessing of the sea; worthy of him here!—that is, a swimmer worthy of him, his comrade in salt water (xxvii).

> . . . she had been privileged to cast away sex with the push from earth, as few men will believe that women, beautiful women, ever wish to do; and often and ardently during the run ahead they yearn for Nature to grant them their one short holiday truce (xxvii).

The open-air cult is understandable enough, both as an educational value and as a glance at the restricted female life – 'the thought of the difference between themselves and the boys must have been something like the tight band – call it corset – over the chest' – but its expression tends to be arch and its instances humourlessly domestic – the white ducks, 'The Jolly Cricketers', the heroine's love of long walks. It is perhaps a Surrey Nature cult which has suffered even further from week-ends and country tramps and food fads – all excellent enough in their way, but not grand enough for the real pastoral stuff.

There is nothing of the week-end pastoral about *The Amazing Marriage*. Something of the slightly ludicrous fad may cling to Carinthia's ideas about child-rearing – weaning at nine months, breathing through the nose, and sleeping in the open air. But the central symbols have a real enough ring of grandeur, with the beginning in the German mountains, with the brother and sister going out to call the dawn and walk through the forests:

> The armies of the young sunrise in mountain-lands
> neighbouring the plains, vast shadows, were marching over
> woods and meads, black against the edge of golden; and great
> heights were cut with them, and bounding waters took the
> leap in a silvery radiance to gloom; the bright and dark-
> banded valleys were like night and morning taking hands
> down the sweep of the rivers. Immense was the range of
> vision scudding the peaks and over the illimitable Eastward
> plains flat to the very East and sources of the sun (iv).

> The phantom ring of mist enclosing for miles the invariable
> low-sweeping dark spruce-fir kept her thoughts on them as
> close as the shroud. She walked fast, but scarcely felt that she was
> moving. Near midday the haunted circle widened; rocks were
> loosely folded in it, and heads of trees, whose round
> intervolving roots grasped the yellow roadside soil; the mists
> shook like a curtain, and partly opened and displayed a
> tapestry-landscape, roughly worked, of woollen crag and
> castle and suggested glen, threaded waters, very prominent
> foreground, Autumn flowers on banks; a predominant
> atmospheric greyness (v).

It is hard to make my point with quotation, impossible without. Selection can be so misleading, that I can only refer readers to each novel, and suggest that *The Amazing Marriage* establishes a real pastoral, as Wordsworth does in *The Prelude*, by three chief means: by building up, particularly, actively and variously, the landscape of the novel, especially of Germany and Wales; of creating the characters' relation with that Nature, through their sensuous and symbol-making reactions; and of extending and developing the symbols in metaphor. In *Lord Ormont* the pastoral is stagey or sentimental because Meredith has not established a Nature; it exists only in a few shorthand versions and stimuli, which will not do. In *The Amazing Marriage* we feel that Carinthia is swain, earth goddess, or whatever, because she is seen as growing with Nature, as breathing in its air, climbing its rocks, having some affinity with the austerity and grandeur which justifies the Gorgon image. In comparison, Brownie (like her name) seems a little vulgar, especially when she is watching the cricket or going for a swim. The potentially ridiculous side of Carinthia – the child-rearing fads and love of walks – is realized by the sensuous particularity which *Lord Ormont* lacks. Meredith had a real pagan feeling for Nature, but it got into one novel adequately and into the other in a tame, arch, and domesticated form. In *The Amazing Marriage* there is also the distancing effect of the two cultists, the Old Buccaneer who has taught his children how to jump with knees bent, etc., and Gower Woodseer, the pastoral and Stevensonian figure, who, as Gillian Beer[2] points out, is no less effective for being slightly ludicrous. There is no such evidence in *Lord Ormont* that there was anything ridiculous in making such a business of the open-air-life, long tramps and outdoor girls.

It is sensuously realized, but it is also poeticized. This happens in *Lord Ormont*, too: the cricket is symbolized, largely through the episode at the country inn, 'The Jolly Cricketers', where Meredith uses the inn-sign as a metaphor for spirit, health and more specialized application to the chase and rescue in the action; and the swimming metaphors, as in *Beauchamp's Career* and *Harry Richmond*, are pervasive. They are very neatly used, appearing conspicuous because having no real matrix in solidly particularized Nature, and simply and diagrammatically traced. *The Amazing Marriage* shows signs of more imaginative and less schematic image-patterns, which perhaps may have come from its longer history in Meredith's mind: its characteristic pattern is that of transfer from the literal to the metaphorical, to be found elsewhere, and particularly in *Harry Richmond*. Here, as in the earlier novel, it gives us a rich and casual texture, though the clarity remains. Thus, when Carinthia is described in terms of height, air, hardness, rock, we have seen all this in action, they are earned and substantial images, looked at one way, seen in the process of image-making, looked at in another. Meredith often shares his authorial images with his characters, and does this with the image he uses for Fleetwood, prisoner of his wishes, which he allows Henrietta to use 'independently' in a letter. The image of the Gorgon, and the mad dog, and the fire also shift in this way, and sometimes the metaphor precedes the large symbolic or even literal action.[3]

It is the integrity rather than the blurring of the symbols which I want to stress. Fleetwood is a prisoner of his will, and the image of imprisonment is a pervasive one, belonging to the pastoral treatment of marriage. As it is, in the central case and all others, it is an urban restriction, a bond and pattern imposed by civilization on Nature (a metaphor with its own good logic, by the way). In *Lord Ormont* the pastoral values are assumed; in *The Amazing Marriage* Meredith defines the pastoral nature of action and character much more profoundly – and the second novel has profundities to be defined which the first lacks. Thus, Carinthia's actual imprisonments become more important than the pastoral symbol and cut across it, so that the mean, stifling and dirty street in Whitechapel, which began as a terrible restriction for her, ends by being the city pastoralized, as at times in the London scenes of *The Prelude*, by the values of 'natural' (i.e. spontaneous, generous, uncommercial, unsnobbish, class-free) human love. But the actual pastoral movement is very important.

The rescue into freedom and love is marked by Nature imagery and felt as the return to Nature after constraint. But this is not confined to Carinthia's imprisonment and release. The criticism of society involves a complex contrast between the pastoral outsider, Carinthia, and the urban hero, Fleetwood. This is a less schematic and much more rich and complex version of the diagram of *Lord Ormont*. Lord Ormont, however, is also seen as an outsider, though what he is 'outside' is an establishment which is attacked less for its values than for giving him and his military schemes insufficient recognition and for placing England in a weak position. Neither husband-figure, it is important to see, represents the establishment in the very simple and direct way that Casaubon or Sir Clifford Chatterley represent authority, money, intellectual sterility, impotence, the old order in Church and State. The complexity of

Lord Ormont is a bit of a muddle: we are likely to sympathize with him only up to a point, and then sympathy will probably be deflected by his military values and his eventual capitulation. The complexity of Fleetwood strikes me as entirely successful.

Here it is necessary to stress the common properties, and not the differences, of the novels. In showing the husband-authority figures much more complexly, Meredith is not just making the novel more 'realistic', as we say, in the usual assumptions about complex verisimilitude, but is making a much more devastating and profound criticism of Victorian England. Lord Ormont and – very strongly – Lord Fleetwood, have something of the pastoral outsider in their make-up which reveals the destructive power of money and rank, and money – and rank-dominated relationships. The difference is that between the simple and the complex antithesis. The simple antithesis between George Eliot's Casaubon and Ladislaw, or between Lawrence's Sir Clifford Chatterley and Mellors, dramatizes and presents a conflict of values. The complex antithesis, like that between Fleetwood and Carinthia, or between Lawrence's Gerald and Birkin, refuses to mythologize by abstracting qualities and mythologizes the more effectively for showing the processes of social conditioning at work within the complete individual. So the destructive power of rank and money and all the unnatural sports of the sweet life which they command are not defined as 'that which is in opposition to Nature', far removed from the life of instinct, entirely role-determined and so on, but as 'that which can tame, corrupt and constrict even the impulsive and imaginative man'. This corruption is analysed in both novels, and it enlarges the themes of marriage and feminism, but it only gets fully, persuasively and toughly into action, language and character in *The Amazing Marriage. Lord Ormont*'s greater sentimentality, ellipsis and confusion help us to see more clearly that Meredith is doing something of great importance to all novelists – getting his ideas clearer and in the process increasing, and not diminishing, the psychological interest.

In *Lord Ormont* we have the ageing general married to the young and beautiful woman who hero-worshipped him. Betrayed by the country he has served, he is obsessed by her military weakness and by his own sense of outraged honour. He is both of, and not of, the establishment values, essentially an authority figure, deeply traditional and conventional, but driven to deny his strongest allegiances, refusing to move in respectable society, refusing to live in his family seat, refusing to have his wife presented at court. Most of these refusals make admirable plot levers, and make his motives crystal clear. But this very clarity damages the presentation of his Aminta. It is really not at all clear why she fails to see what the reader sees, possessing as she does the double advantage of long, intimate knowledge and a strong sympathy for her husband's unpopular position. Part of the obscurity may come from Meredith's reticence about the sexual history of the marriage. Aminta seems to look back to a passionate honeymoon, but it is not very clear whether a certain coolness and separateness is cause or effect of her resentment at her social position. The implications seem to be those of the January and May pattern, with some deviation. Meredith adds the sinister and fascinating touch about the possibility (but rareness and difficulty) of inflicting sexual refusal on a husband who is apparently not completely impotent, but certainly getting on. If this part of the history were clearer, Aminta might be more thoroughly placed. As it is, we are left wondering why she plays with fire with Morsfield, why she attaches such importance to living at Steignton and being presented at court, since she is carefully shown as so spirited, natural and drawn to Matey's pastoral virtues. It may be that Meredith is compressing some suggestion of change here: the second stage of her acquaintance with Matey disabuses her of some conventional notions about a gentleman's career, and she develops in 'naturalness' – if this is possible – throughout the novel. Even so, Carinthia would plainly snap her fingers at the presentation at Court, so it isn't a matter of the novel having dated. Perhaps Meredith contracted Carinthia's changes in drawing Aminta. Carinthia is shown as spontaneous, unschooled, in some ways (though less naïve than ignorant) naïve, and such qualities are important in the novel's scheme of values as well as in the motivation of her amazing marriage. She is shown, most subtly, as growing in all the externals of civilization – speech, manners, deportment – and much of this change is drawn by the language which Meredith shows very naturally and very pointedly as a growth in the accomplished knowledge and use of English. But she does not grow an inch in the disapproved 'internals' of civilization. I cannot quite accept Gillian Beer's view of Carinthia as 'uncivilized, instinctive' if she really means to imply that this is primitive and under-rational. Carinthia seems to me to acquire the analytic mode without losing anything of instinctive strength. By the time she comes to refuse her bed – 'I guard my rooms' – to

Fleetwood, she has learnt not to react instinctively and spontaneously, but to analyse, judge and defend herself by the use of her
considerable intelligence. I do not see her as a large simple nature,
but as very like Fleetwood, only on the right – that is the other –
side of civilization.

I stress this reading because it seems to me characteristic of the
novel that it avoids antithesis where *Lord Ormont* is drawn towards
it. *The Amazing Marriage* invites us to dismiss the tension we
often set up between ideological clarity and complex realism, for
in it Meredith's fundamental social insight about the possessive
marriage is inseparable from his profound rendering of the human
hearts.

Meredith shows in very great detail how painful the marriage was
for Carinthia and for Fleetwood – in his imprisonment by his
word, in her imprisonment in ignorance, in his and her love, in her
maternity coming out of rape, in his gradual realization of the
meaning of the furtive memory and its enlargement in his consciousness (this instance of Meredith's obscurity seems to be an
excellent instance of inattentiveness on the part of his readers).
He shows them both driven by outside manipulation – in the form
of the unscrupulous Henrietta and Chillon and the miserly Lord
Levellier – as well as by the corruptions within Fleetwood. Fleetwood is a brilliant instance of the *droit de seigneur* – passion, imagination, energy, courage, and generosity corrupted. His affinity with
both Carinthia and Woodseer (the name-overlap is important and
links them all with Carinthia's forests) is immensely important.
Meredith shows the terrible conditioning power of money, possession, and the roles and relations they determine, because his central
case, Fleetwood, is a creature of heart. His pride, passion and imagination are ironically betrayed by the natural man – drawn to the
beautiful Gorgon in the rocks – but betrayed more profoundly by
civilized society. He feels wildness, impulse, solitude, integrity,
courage, unconventionality, and the stroke that makes this a great
love-story is his deep and long-denied recognition that all these
things are to be found in Carinthia.

What is right as social fable and as human observation is his
inability to forget his jealous desire to buy Henrietta: he is kept
goadingly reminded of her and her husband through Carinthia, so
that what should take him away from the old love keeps it painfully
in his mind, what should free him from money-determined acts
make him insist on them. If he can't buy Henrietta, or if he hasn't

been able to buy her yet, he will keep money away from Chillon by denying it to Carinthia. I am sure Gillian Beer is right when she says that Meredith's revision was an improvement in this respect. In the original version, she tells us, there is a more elaborate and 'plausible' rendering of Fleetwood's proposal to Carinthia, which comes as a rebound impulse after he has proposed to Henrietta and been refused: 'It is with this scene dominant in our minds that we hear of his proposal to Carinthia at the ball.' She argues convincingly that the cutting of the proposal to Henrietta makes Fleetwood's motivation more and not less profound, since it shows 'that acts of impulse come not from the surface of personality but from its depths', while the first version showed the amazing marriage coming out of 'the pique of the moment rather than from some deep but imperfectly acknowledged need in his nature'.

It is this need in his nature that I want to emphasize. He needs those values expressed by and in Carinthia, Woodseer (in a more literary, doctrinaire, and comic-Meredithean or Stevensonian fashion) and in the landscape of forest and mountain, in Wales and Germany. The scenes and characters which present the pastoral have a deep appeal – not as unacknowledged as all that, even early on – to Fleetwood. He shares Woodseer's desire for solitude, freedom, hardness and grandeur, and has a contempt for what he knows and is and follows: the depths below the heights, the fouler air, money, gambling, sexual sport, fashion, culture which is bought and sold. His not very attractive contempt for his parasites and for Livia, as well as his feeling for Catholicism, must all be understood in terms of this need. The tragic aspect of the novel lies in the missed affinities. Fleetwood's case is put in reverse, for elucidation and stress: Woodseer's purity is tested and fails when he succumbs to Livia and gives her the letter that might help Carinthia, and he too gambles, and even buys new clothes out of social shame. The only one who does not succumb is Carinthia, but the hardness which is both her protection and her guarantee of integrity has to turn against Fleetwood at the end. He is right after all to see the Gorgon quality at the beginning, or to seize on it in Woodseer's vision. Their relationship is shown in fine and consistent detail. It is there in the rape, which she comes only slowly (I think) to see for what it is, just as she comes to understand the wild ride and the prize-fight; and which becomes for him the cherished sexual evidence of that charm he had first felt – the proof of the subliminal wisdom. It is revealed too in his finely defined passion for Henrietta, which combines desire, contempt, self-contempt, and a jealous desire to have her and be done with her. The sexual detail which is cloudy in *Lord Ormont* is significantly clear in *The Amazing Marriage*. Its presentation is decorous: a shameful furtive act, hardly to be mentioned, it comes in hurried glimpses and is eventually given more space in his reverie as he comes to dwell on it, from shame and new desire.

Of course, Meredith likes teasing things slowly out, and the joke here is that it is not Dame Gossip but the psychological novelist dwelling on the inner life who creates the greatest puzzle and surprise. The second sexual attempt is a different kind of teasing. We can see Meredith using a stiff and elegant dialogue, being dramatically implicit and then frankly explicit, with an eye always on character, past and present:

> 'Do you come in, my lord?'
> 'The house is yours, my lady.'
> 'I cannot feel it mine.'
> 'You are the mistress to invite or exclude.'
> 'I am ready to go in a few hours, for a small income of money, for my child and me.'
> 'Our child.'
> 'Yes.'
> 'It is our child.'
> 'It is' (xxxvii).

Meredith not only shows the use of words and refusal to use words here, but then shows Fleetwood speaking familiarly, trying to break down 'the rebuke of her grandeur of stature', trying to induce 'her to deliver her mind, that the mounting girl's feebleness in speech might reinstate him'. She forces the dialogue back into the staccato sentences, superficially like the brief, simple ones she had to speak out of 'feebleness' once, but now manipulating brevity and simplicity, as he says, 'thrusting and parrying behind masked language':

> 'Ah! You must be feeling the cold North wind here.'
> 'I do not. You may feel the cold, my lord. Will you enter the house?'
> 'Do you invite me?'
> 'The house is your own.'
> 'Will the mistress of the house honour me so far?'

'I am not the mistress of the house, my lord.'
'You refuse, Carinthia?'
'I would keep from using those words. I have no right to refuse the entry of the house to you.'
'If I come in?'
'I guard my rooms' (xxxvii).

Meredith shows the girl, who, as Henrietta patronizingly assured Chillon, learned quickly to mince her step in the dance. She chooses the weapon of brief and formal dialogue, innuendo, a stylized question and answer which forces him to make the running and, in the end, to say what he means and ask her for what she refuses. Readers with good memories may go back to the time when her brief sentences on the wedding journey made him suppose 'he would have to hear her spelling her words out next'. It does not do to see Carinthia as too instinctive and untutored. Like the heroine of James's *Washington Square*, she learns, from masters. The artificial style in this novel serves the interests of particularity, not of generalization.

Meredith creates a major feminist triumph, but it has its sadness. The fable is made possible by the brilliant analysis which the Novelist in the novel has to keep defending. He shows the importance of exhaustion and timing in the sex-war: Carinthia is in fact not unforgiving, and might have forgiven, but the last revelation of Fleetwood's attempt to seduce Henrietta comes at the wrong moment. It is no use 'coming round' or 'being converted' because, unfortunately but definitely, people come round at different stages, and Fleetwood's repentance is badly timed. Carinthia's capacity to endure is limited. What she cannot finally accept happened in the past, is only one more thing, smaller than others, but her feeling has worn out. When George Eliot's Dorothea finds that it is really love that she feels for Ladislaw, there he is waiting for her – there is a slight suggestion that it might have been too late, for George Eliot did know about these things – but the novel resolutely curves back into the conventional moral pattern. In *The Amazing Marriage* Carinthia is nearly but not totally a patient Griselda. It is a book where really creative and strongly affined people tear each other to bits, commit rape, are cold, are deeply revengeful, just give up. Something like an elective affinity is demonstrated and shown not as strong, but as fragile, as subject to change, wars, desperate men, social role, class, status and possessions. One man blows his brains out, another dies, and the fable and the psychic history reinforce each other's clarity and power. And I would say that this is why the Novelist and Dame Gossip have to struggle. Their conflict makes a good joke, and just the kind of joke Meredith loved, at once boastful and self-deprecatory. But their joint presence helps to remind us that *The Amazing Marriage* is both realistic and fabulous.

Notes

1 *Letters*, edited by C. L. Cline, iii, 1970, 1438–9.
2 '*The Amazing Marriage*: a study in Contraries', *Review of English Literature*, vii, No. 1 (January 1966).
3 For a full discussion of this kind of structure, see the chapter on *Harry Richmond* in my book, *The Appropriate Form*. The imagery in *The Amazing Marriage* works in a similar way.

Index